Christian Environmental Ethics

A Case Method Approach

ECOLOGY AND JUSTICE
AN ORBIS SERIES ON GLOBAL ECOLOGY

Advisory Board Members
Mary Evelyn Tucker
John A. Grim
Leonardo Boff
Sean McDonagh

The Orbis *Ecology and Justice* Series publishes books that seek to integrate an understanding of the Earth as an interconnected life system with concerns for just and sustainable systems that benefit the entire Earth. Books in the Series concentrate on ways to:

- reexamine the human-Earth relationship in the light of contemporary cosmological thought
- develop visions of common life marked by ecological integrity and social justice
- expand on the work of those who are developing such fields as eco-social ecology, bioregionalism, and animal rights
- promote inclusive participative strategies that enhance the struggle of the Earth's voiceless poor for justice
- deepen appreciation for and expand dialogue among religious traditions on the issue of ecology
- encourage spiritual discipline, social engagement, and the reform of religion and society toward these ends.

Viewing the present moment as a time for responsible creativity, the Series seeks authors who speak to ecojustice concerns and who bring into dialogue perspectives from the Christian community, from the world's other religions, from secular and scientific circles, and from new paradigms of thought and action.

Christian Environmental Ethics

A Case Method Approach

James B. Martin-Schramm
Robert L. Stivers

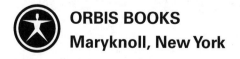

ORBIS BOOKS
Maryknoll, New York

Founded in 1970, Orbis Books endeavors to publish works that enlighten the mind, nourish the spirit, and challenge the conscience. The publishing arm of the Maryknoll Fathers and Brothers, Orbis seeks to explore the global dimensions of the Christian faith and mission, to invite dialogue with diverse cultures and religious traditions, and to serve the cause of reconciliation and peace. The books published reflect the views of their authors and do not represent the official position of the Maryknoll Society. To learn more about Maryknoll and Orbis Books, please visit our website at www.maryknoll.org.

Library of Congress Cataloging-in-Publication Data

Martin-Schramm, James B.
    Christian environmental ethics : a case method approach /
James B. Martin-Schramm, Robert L. Stivers.
      p. cm. — (Ecology and justice)
    Includes bibliographical references.
    ISBN 1-57075-499-3
    1. Human ecology—Religious aspects—Christianity—Case studies.
    2. Environmental ethics—Case studies.   3. Christian ethics—Case studies.
    I. Stivers, Robert L., 1940–   II. Title.   III. Series.
    BT695.5 .M37 2003
    241'.691--dc21

                                          200301073

For our spouses,
Lora and Karen,
with love and admiration

and

For our children,
Laura and Mark, Joel and Joshua,
with pride and hope

Contents

Acknowledgments

I would like to acknowledge the strong support of my wife, Lora Gross, and my children, Laura and Mark, in this project. Thanks go to Pacific Lutheran University for providing a sabbatical to make this project possible, and to my colleagues there who at various times have constructively criticized my work. I am grateful to the many individuals who helped me with one or another cases in this volume. Their names will remain anonymous in the spirit of protecting their privacy. I am also grateful to my colleagues in the Association for Case Teaching, especially Alice and Bob Evans, who taught me how to write and teach cases. Finally, I acknowledge the support of two very good friends, Ron Stone and Jim Martin-Schramm. Ron has been helpful in numerous ways over the years, and Jim was a joy to work with.

Robert L. Stivers
Pacific Lutheran University
Tacoma, Washington

Bob Stivers taught me Christian Ethics when I was a student at Pacific Lutheran University in the late 1970s. He has touched the lives of many students as a fine teacher, but I feel fortunate also to count him as a wise mentor and a good friend. It has been an honor and a privilege to work with Bob on this project.

Closer to home, I owe my wife, Karen, a huge debt of thanks. She read and edited every word I wrote (and re-wrote) and for that I am very grateful. Most of all, however, I give thanks for her constant love, support, and encouragement. Along with our sons, Joel and Joshua, Karen showed great patience when I left town to conduct research or spent long hours in front of the computer.

Many people assisted my research and some also read drafts of the cases and commentaries I developed. Some of these individuals are mentioned by name in the endnotes, but others can be thanked here only anonymously in order to protect their privacy. I am particularly grateful to the following colleagues at Luther College for their assistance: Dale Nimrod, Kirk Larsen, Marian Kaehler, Kevin Kraus, Harland Nelson, and Kirk Johnson. In addition, students in my Environmental Ethics and Christian Ethics courses provided very helpful feedback to drafts of cases.

Finally, I want to thank the Luther College Paideia Endowment Board for a grant that defrayed some of the expenses associated with conducting my sabbatical research. In addition, the Luther Institute in Washington, D.C., supported my research with a fellowship. These funds, together with the full-year sabbatical leave awarded by the college, made it possible for me to complete this project. I am grateful for this support and feel lucky to teach at an institution that values and enables scholarship. *Soli Deo Gloria.*

James B. Martin-Schramm
Luther College
Decorah, Iowa

Introduction

Issues in environmental ethics continue to make front-page news in the United States. In the West, raging forest fires each year rack up huge costs and ignite questions about management of the nation's forests and the wisdom of building homes near wilderness areas. In Nevada, tempers are still boiling after both houses of Congress voted to override the state's veto of the Bush Administration's plan to bury the nation's high-level nuclear waste in Yucca Mountain. Throughout the Midwest, export farmers with record plantings in genetically modified crops are keeping a close watch on overseas markets in the wake of a European Union moratorium on patents for genetically engineered foods. In Washington D.C., debates continue to swirl around a national energy plan that focuses on increasing the production of fossil fuels and gives scant attention to the development of renewable energy sources.

Despite the fact that the United States faces a host of domestic and foreign policy problems, national environmental issues like these continue to vie for the public attention they deserve. As important, but often less visible, are local and regional environmental disputes. For example, many communities around the nation continue to combat urban sprawl and the threat that mass discount retailers pose to their distinctive identities. Landowners in virtually every state chafe under constraints imposed by the Endangered Species Act and other federal regulations designed to protect and conserve natural resources. Others are challenging hazards posed by toxic chemicals and the dumping of hazardous wastes in their communities. The list of topics is almost endless.

This volume utilizes a case method approach to give particular attention to some of the current issues in environmental ethics and provides resources for engaging in Christian ethical reflection about them. The first three chapters provide foundations for moral reflection about these issues.

Chapter One examines four inter-related causes of environmental degradation in population growth, consumption patterns, production technologies, and fundamental economic and political assumptions. The chapter also identifies various attitudes toward nature and explores a spectrum of perspectives about the relationship of nature and society.

Chapter Two identifies biblical and theological resources in Christian traditions that can be brought to bear on issues in environmental ethics. While many aspects of Christianity have been utilized to justify and sanction environmental exploitation, revised interpretations and new perspectives yield a wealth of resources for moral reflection. The commentaries that accompany the cases in this volume expand upon the survey offered by this chapter. The chapter gives particular attention to an ethic of ecological justice, which seeks to unite the separate disciplines of environmental ethics and social ethics into one integrated scope of moral concern.

Chapter Three outlines the benefits of a case study approach to ethics and offers a method to engage in moral deliberation about the cases in this volume. This three-stage method requires careful analysis of a case and its primary moral problem before engaging in an assessment of the alternatives in order to make an ethical judgment about the best course of action.

The bulk of this volume consists of nine cases that raise different issues in environmental ethics. All of the cases are based on actual situations. Some names and places have been changed to protect the privacy of those involved, but the ethical problems and moral dilemmas posed by the cases are real. Each case is accompanied by a commentary that provides important background information along with normative elements in Christian traditions that are relevant to moral resolution of the issues posed. None of the commentaries, however, takes a definitive stance with regard to how the case should be resolved ethically. This is left up to the reader. The purpose of this volume is to equip readers with skills to do moral deliberation

The first case, *Rigor and Responsibility*, focuses on personal consumption issues and the stewardship of limited resources. A family in Toledo, Ohio, has inherited the land and funds necessary to build a modest lake cabin, but at least one family member has serious moral reservations about the project. Construction and maintenance of the lake cabin would consume limited energy supplies and result in further development around a scenic lake. In addition, the funds would build a second home for this family when so many are homeless. At the same time, a friend who is a contractor and in need of work has offered to build the cabin with materials recovered from other buildings. Upon completion, a busy professional couple could have a place to relax and enjoy the water sports they love with their two children. It is not clear in this case what would constitute good stewardship of resources.

Personal consumption decisions are a link to the second case, *Sustaining Dover*. Here booming sales at the Wal-Mart store in Dover, Iowa, have led the company to purchase land and make preparations for the construction of a Supercenter on the eastern edge of town. The problem is that some of the land is currently zoned as a flood plain and the company has asked the Dover City Council for permission to fill in the land and rezone it as a commercial shopping district. This crucial land use decision has prompted debates in the community about what constitutes sustainable development. Ecologically, construction in the flood plain will continue a pattern of habitat fragmentation—a major factor in the loss of biodiversity—and may increase the risk of flooding. Economically, the Supercenter will have a devastating impact on some businesses in the community and the surrounding area. Socially, many worry that the homogenous nature of the Supercenter will also erode the distinctive quality of the community of Dover. At the same time, there are counterarguments in all three of these areas that make it difficult to decide what would best serve the community of Dover in the long run.

Land use policy is also an important feature of the third case, *Market Mountain Takeover*. This case revolves around a land exchange between the U.S. Forest Service and a large timber company. When a group of young environmentalists learn that some of the few remaining parcels of old growth in the Gifford Pinchot National Forest are to be swapped for parcels of private land adjacent to the Fernow Wilderness Area, the group uses a variety of legal and illegal means to oppose the exchange. In the process, the group forms an alliance with a community that will be affected by the logging of old growth timber, but it also comes into conflict with the timber company and another environmental group that favors the land exchange. The case exposes conflicts within the environmental movement and provides an occasion to engage in moral reflection about differing strategies that can be employed to prevent environmental degradation.

In *Saving Snake River Salmon,* the focus switches from protecting old growth forests to preserving endangered species. This case focuses on the plight of endangered salmon species in a portion of the Snake River that runs through Idaho and into the southeastern corner of Washington. One of the ways to recover the endangered fish would be to remove four hydroelectric dams from this section of the river. Many environmentalists support this proposal, but most farmers and electricity consumers are adamantly opposed. Removal of the dams would reduce the availability of irrigation water and lead to higher costs for electricity and the transportation of grain that is currently shipped via barges on the river. Another option for salmon recovery focuses on the construction of a pipeline that would move young salmon around the dams, thus helping them make the long journey out to sea. Not surprisingly, an environmentalist in the case opposes this "technological fix," but a farming couple whose livelihood depends on water from the Snake River supports it. In the case commentary, moral reflection about these alternatives includes attention to historical causes of salmon decline as well as the way fundamental attitudes toward nature shape the views of key players and stakeholders.

In the fifth case, *Taking on Water,* the question is not *how* endangered species should be recovered, but rather *who* should bear the costs for their conservation? Set in the Methow Valley of Washington State, the case revolves around ranchers whose irrigation water has been significantly reduced by federal agents enforcing the Endangered Species Act (ESA). The ESA restrictions have prompted protest from ranchers who feel they have been singled out to bear a disproportionate amount of the burden associated with the conservation of endangered runs of spring chinook salmon and steelhead trout. Many blame the nine hydroelectric dams along the Columbia River for the reduced runs of these endangered species. Some ranchers believe that justice will be done only if they file a lawsuit against the federal government for taking their property without just compensation. The commentary assesses the merits of a takings case because this area of environmental policy is frequently contested and new legal developments could have significant implications for the enforcement of federal laws designed to protect species and conserve natural resources.

Hydroelectric dams provide a segue to the next case, *Sustainable Energy Futures*. Here a high school civics teacher in Houston, Texas, tries to decide how to present information to his students about President Bush's national energy plan. In this plan, renewable energy sources like hydroelectric and wind play a minor role in comparison to the emphasis placed on the exploration and production of domestic fossil fuels and the revival of nuclear power. Knowing all too well that this energy plan could have profound implications for his students in the future, the teacher struggles with whether he should take an objective stance or let his sympathies show. The commentary to the case identifies the nation's energy alternatives and provides guidelines for conducting an ethical assessment of the way the Bush plan prioritizes these options. Particular attention is given to the plan's renewed commitment to nuclear power, the proposal to open the Arctic National Wildlife Reserve to oil exploration, and the Bush administration's stance with regard to global warming.

In *Skull Valley*, the focus is on the storage and long-term disposal of high-level nuclear waste. While many know that the United States intends to bury high-level nuclear waste deep underground in Yucca Mountain, few are aware that a consortium of electric utility companies has negotiated a lease agreement with a Native American tribe in Utah to store temporarily on their reservation what could amount to the nation's current stockpile of spent nuclear fuel. In the case, a church official has to decide whether to take a public stance during final hearings before the Nuclear Regulatory Commission in Salt Lake City. She feels torn between her desire to defend the sovereignty of the tribe and her concern that they may be victims of environmental racism. The commentary addresses these concerns along with the broader question of how best to share the burden of high-level nuclear waste disposal.

The eighth case continues this focus on toxic chemicals and hazardous waste. In *Chlorine Sunset*, an environmental studies major is writing her senior paper on the chlorine chemical industry. A panel presentation during Earth Day gives her an opportunity to hear from a company spokesperson and an ardent critic of the chlorine chemical industry. Their exchange exposes a major ideological conflict about the relationship between society and nature. The critic advocates a phase-out, or sunset, on the use of these chemicals, while the industry spokesperson takes a cautiously optimistic approach. Their exchange also reveals problems related to scientific complexity and uncertainty, both of which complicate ethical reflection about the costs and benefits of organochlorines. The commentary grapples with these issues and gives particular attention to the "precautionary principle" and the important role this concept has played in recent discussions at the national and international level about toxic chemicals and hazardous waste. The commentary also utilizes the concept of ecojustice and its related norms to conduct an ethical assessment of chlorine-based chemicals.

The last case deals with genetic engineering. *Harvesting Controversy* focuses on the potential that genetically modified crops pose for increasing food production in sub-Saharan Africa—the only region in the world where hunger is on the increase. The case is set in the United States, however, and revolves around a Hunger Concerns group on a college campus that suddenly finds itself embroiled in a debate about genetically modified crops. Some members believe that these technological innovations could play a significant role in reducing hunger. Others are concerned about dangers genetically modified crops pose to human and ecological health. A crisis erupts when one member suggests that the group join a Greenpeace campaign to ban genetically modified crops around the world. The commentary provides background information about biotechnology in agriculture and assesses ethical issues posed by the case in relationship to the ecojustice norms of sustainability, sufficiency, participation, and solidarity.

The volume concludes with an appendix that contains various teaching resources for courses in environmental ethics. These resources include the description of an ecological autobiography assignment as well as several spectrum exercises that help students physically locate themselves in key debates about environmental ethics. In addition, the appendix contains instructions for examining power dynamics in cases, as well as guidelines for how students can write brief papers or make group presentations about the cases.

PART I

Foundations for Ethical Reflection

1

The Environmental Problem

Until recently the great ecological systems of the earth were a problem for human beings. Now the reverse is true. This reversal represents a revolution in the natural history of this planet. In a short period of time the human species has emerged as the dominant species in almost all ecosystems. This domination has led to the degradation of the natural environment and now threatens to return affairs to their original setting.

In the original setting humans and their evolutionary ancestors fit into ecosystems. They subsisted as hunters and gatherers at the top of food chains. They had the numbers, knowledge, and tools to cause only local damage and then they would move on and allow degraded systems to recoup. They were closely connected to nature and lived in rough harmony with it, rough because changing environmental conditions were not always conducive to easy living, and other species competed for scarce resources.

In time humans took to agriculture and developed new knowledge and more powerful tools. Population increased and new forms of social organization, usually more hierarchical and unequal, emerged. New ideas about the uniqueness of humans and their special status replaced old ideas that had connected humans to nature and encouraged respect.

Further in time humans discovered that scientific reason could be harnessed with tool making to vastly increase human power over nature. Changing ideas about economic and political relationships (notably capitalism and democracy), a shift to individualistic and materialistic attitudes, and an increased anthropocentric emphasis gave direction to this augmented power. In the space of about three hundred years the Industrial Revolution, as these changes came to be known, dramatically changed the face of the earth.

There is much to celebrate and preserve in these historical developments. The emergence of human consciousness in the evolutionary process is a momentous event. The possibility of increased freedom from starvation, poverty, disease, and death is to be prized. The arts have flourished. Humans have probed nature and discovered many of its inner workings. Individual rights have become increasingly respected. Capitalism has channeled self-interest into the production of goods and services. The list goes on. Humans have been successful in the pursuit of their material interests and their control of nature, very successful indeed.

Now this success is a problem. What humans have done well for themselves has among other things reduced habitat for animals and plants, changed climate, polluted air and water, and created a burden of toxic wastes for future generations. Another revolution, the environmental or ecological revolution, has begun and is now in conflict with traditional perceptions of success, ancient material needs and desires, and a system that has its own dynamic and momentum. What remains to be seen is whether humans can renegotiate their fit into natural ecosystems before those systems force the issue. This renegotiation will not be smooth or easy. Success is not assured. Little in the past prepares humans for the needed changes.

ENVIRONMENTAL DEGRADATION

Environmental degradation is a product of five interrelated causes: (1) too many people, (2) some of whom are consuming too much, (3) using powerful technologies that frequently damage nature's ecosystems, (4) supported by economic and political systems that permit and even encourage degradation, and (5) informed by anthropocentric attitudes toward nature.

Population

The world's human population is now over six billion and increasing at an annual rate of about 1.3 percent. Birth rates in most rich countries have declined to the point where they are in rough equilibrium with previously lowered death rates so that almost all future population increase in these countries will come from immigration. This stabilization, often referred to as the "demographic transition," was brought on largely by economic factors and was completed only after a large increase in population, the consumption of substantial resources, and the creation of considerable pollution.

Birth rates in poor countries are declining, but still exceed death rates, so that population continues to increase, in some countries in Africa at a rate of over 3 percent. While prospects for lower birth rates in some countries are not good, other countries like China and Bangladesh have made significant strides—though not without controversy. China's "one-child" policy has produced a host of human rights violations in the recent past, and Bangladesh's success at reducing fertility has not always been accompanied by other gains in social development.

The primary factor that is driving global population growth, however, is not the birth rate but rather a phenomenon described as "demographic momentum." On average, women around the world are giving birth to fewer children than they ever have before. Over the last fifty years, the fertility rate has dropped from over 6 children per woman to an average of 3.4 children today. Over this same period of time, however, the age structure in nations with high rates of population growth changed. For example, approximately 45 percent of sub-Saharan Africa is under the age of 15, and these young women and men are now entering the prime years of their reproductive lives. When this skewed age structure is combined with declining fertility rates, the result is more young couples having fewer children than their parents did. This is what demographers refer to as "demographic momentum." On the basis of this structural reality in global demographics, the United Nations projects that Earth's human population will almost certainly grow to 9 billion people by 2050 before it begins to stabilize over the course of the following century.

Looking only at the numbers, the all too obvious pollution in overcrowded cities in poor countries, and the pressures put by impoverished peoples on habitat, a popular attitude is to blame the world's ecological woes on global population growth. While there is an ounce of truth in this attitude, it misses the tons of degradation heaped on ecosystems by the activities of more affluent peoples. But the ounce of truth is this: Large and increasing numbers of people do place a burden on ecosystems. The great migration of poor people from rural areas with dense populations and little available land for subsistence farming takes a heavy toll socially and ecologically. Migrating to urban areas, poor people expand slums on land with alternative uses. Migrating to other less densely populated rural areas, desperate people move into pristine habitats and often set in motion a destructive cycle. Forests are cut down or burned. Soils are cropped until exhausted and then converted to grazing before they are taken over by more wealthy ranchers. The poor, driven by survival needs, squeezed by opportunistic ranchers, and encouraged by governments, move on to degrade still other habitats.

The social pressures on these poor people are immense. Poverty and lack of opportunities, especially for women, make bearing children attractive. Two-tiered social systems, with a few rich and many poor and held in place by custom, religion, and brute force, make little land available to the poor, increase their desperation, and force them to degrade their environments in the name of survival. Yes, expanding numbers of poor people do destroy ecosystems, but the cause is not so much population growth as it is oppressive economic and political systems.

The tendency to blame poor people is rendered even less viable by the knowledge of what is possible. Social development projects backed by appropriate environmental and population policies, adequate financing, land reform, and local control have been successful in lowering birth rates and reducing the degradation of ecosystems. Devising programs that address the needs of women and girl children is especially important. Increasing population does not necessarily have to mean increasing environmental degradation.

Consumption

Far and away the largest pressure on ecosystems comes from the consumption of people in wealthy countries. The quantities are staggering by any historical measure with the infrastructure needed to support this consumption adding additional burdens.

Many observers have commented on the extraordinary levels of current consumption in rich countries. Some celebrate it. Others are critical not only of the environmental degradation that results, but also of the injustices and

spirit-numbing effects that accompany it. The historical changes that produced these levels of consumption are complex.[1]

Rather than explore causes and the complex history of increasing levels
of material wealth, two general observations are in order. First, high levels
of consumption are critical to the functioning of modern capitalism. High
levels of demand are necessary to consume the large quantities of material
objects that the system produces. If demand slackens, producers accumulate
excess inventory and cut back purchases to reduce costs. Suppliers in turn
cut back their production and lay off workers. This is devastating to workers because they are dependent on jobs to provide the income to purchase
not only vast quantities of consumer goods, but also basic necessities. So,
however virtuous and spiritual frugality may be, it produces misery given
the shape of current economic relationships. High levels of consumption are
tied to self-interest and become very difficult to alter.

One way to avoid degrading nature is to reduce the environmental impact
of production and consumption. This will no doubt help, but less clear is
whether it will be enough. The sheer volume itself may overwhelm ecosystems even though pollution per unit of production is reduced. If this is the
case, those in rich countries face a difficult dilemma. Reduce consumption
and bring on economic depression, or press on hoping that new technology
reduces environmental degradation. Perhaps a combination of frugality and
creative stewardship will work.

Second, although numerous studies reveal that increasing levels of consumption generally do not increase personal satisfaction, consumers act as
if they do.[2] Trying to convince them otherwise elicits incredulity and accusations of elitism. Dialogue ceases and the parties retreat behind their right
to individual expression that modern culture has few resources to adjudi-
cate. Calling this apparent satisfaction spirit-numbing and excessively materialistic, caricatures of consumption as addiction, and the use of satirical
terms such as "affluenza" elicit further incredulity. And when things are
reduced to basics as they were in the terrorist attacks on New York and
Washington, the first question after the initial shock was the effect on the
economy. News stations displayed the fluctuating Dow-Jones average even
through commercials, as if to say that the health of the economy was the
heartbeat of the nation. Political leaders urged all Americans to keep demand
up. High levels of consumption are firmly in place and will be difficult to
reduce, environmental degradation notwithstanding.

Technology

Technology is a human process in which scientific knowledge is applied systematically to the practical problems of producing goods and services. While
the word "technology" frequently appears as the subject of sentences, in
reality technology does nothing. Humans do it all, and the tendency to give
technology a life of its own must be countered with the insistence that technological systems are human systems.

Indeed the essence of technology is not apparatus or artifact or even the ordered systems that put machines to work. The essence is human reason. Humans devise tools based on scientific understandings, order them with techniques, and implement them to solve problems of production. That technology seems at times to take on a life of its own only testifies to the power of modern technological processes. Technological momentum is so great today that it is arguably the number one force driving human society and environmental degradation.

Technology as a human process is remarkably ambiguous. Technologies offer: (1) increased access to multiple levels of experience, yet the dominance of narrow technical reason; (2) greater wealth, yet greater inequality; (3) more freedom, yet increased and more concentrated control and manipulation; (4) more variety, yet the cutting off of traditional choices; (5) more frequent interaction, yet the neglect of community and the increased power of impersonal bureaucracies; (6) greater potential to improve the well being of all people, yet control by small groups pursuing narrow interests; (7) greater control of nature, yet the degradation of ecosystems; (8) the promise of mastery, yet the feeling that things are out of control; and (9) unlimited power, for example, nuclear power, yet the possibility of total destruction.

A number of these ambiguities are central to understanding environmental degradation and community breakdown, especially the fifth, sixth, seventh, and eighth. The basic paradox of higher standards of living, greater choice, more leisure, and improved communications, yet greater alienation, the loss of community integrity, and the degradation of nature is particularly striking.[3] More than thirty years ago Barry Commoner was one of the first to give voice to this basic ambiguity when he pointed out that the very technologies that have improved human life and created the most economic growth were also ones that consumed huge amounts of energy and created the most pollution.[4]

Decisions about specific technologies are mostly left to the executives of the large industrial organizations that have grown up to manage them. Their decisions are made primarily on calculations of short-term economic return to their organizations, which in turn are driven by efficiency and control, the basic imperatives of technology. They give relatively less attention to persons, communities, and ecosystems as they substitute capital for people, move investments freely, and use resources. To minimize costs and increase output in the present, they discount long-term effects on nature and culture. Such a system worked tolerably well as long as output was small and most people lived simply and frugally. Today this no longer holds.

To be sure, this is an oversimplification. Nevertheless, the great productive technologies and the organizations that manage them are a significant part of the problem for the natural environment. Whether the public can balance the power that has accrued to these large organizations and redirect the technological process to other ends remains an open question and a matter of intense political conflict. The current battles over globalization are examples of this conflict.

The impacts of these technologies on ecosystems have been enormous. Take, for example, the forests of the earth. The technologies that have made the harvest of ancient forest tracts possible in a short period of time are easy to pinpoint. The chainsaw, road building equipment, draglines, and the truck revolutionized the harvest. Underlying these technologies were the skills of the large equipment operator, the expert tree faller, the accountant, the administrator, and the ideology of scientific management. Species and ecosystems have no defense against this kind of power. Evolutionary processes could not prepare other species and ecosystems for the onslaught of human reason augmented by the capacity to invent tools. Of special importance to the degradation of forest communities and ecosystems is the road building made possible by bulldozers, road graders, and other heavy equipment. Where roads go, immigrants go, forests go down, and forest dwellers go out.

Economics and Politics

The social systems that have been most successful in organizing these powerful technologies for the production of goods and services are capitalism and democracy. In a series of gradual developments beginning in the sixteenth century in Western Europe, capitalism and democracy replaced a hierarchical, feudal system based on land. Today this outcome is called modernity and has become a global phenomenon.

Capitalism is an economic system that harnesses human competitive instincts and self-interest for the social good of greater production. Decentralized free markets, private property, profit, the limited liability of corporations, patents, and the enforcement of contracts are among the mechanisms by which self-interest has been channeled into the acquisition of wealth. By any measure this system has been successful in producing massive quantities of material goods and in shifting the definition of human well being in a materialistic direction.

Democracy is a system that places sovereignty in the hands of the many and their elected representatives. As developed in Western countries, it has functioned among other things to support capitalism, to prevent accumulations of power, and to give voice to a wide range of people who had not previously participated in decisions that affected their lives. It has accomplished these tasks tolerably well, certainly better than alternative political systems.

Many celebrate capitalism and democracy often to the point of missing serious shortcomings. One shortcoming is the current incapacity of these systems to limit self-interest. If the pursuit of self-interest is one key to the success of capitalism, too much self-interest undermines this success. Take, for example, the pursuit of profit. Profits are essential to the financial health of economic enterprises. Profits play a vital role as a signaling device in the efficient allocation of resources. Profits are essential to the continuing ability of a firm to pay workers and thus to distribute income and to create the demand that produces the profits in the first place. Managers must therefore have profit as their primary motivation.

Other things being equal, profits increase as costs are reduced. Among the costs of production are the acquisition of resources, the payment of wages, and the disposal of wastes. Managers in the pursuit of profit to satisfy their own self-interest and that of stockholders therefore have an incentive to acquire resources cheaply, to reduce wages, and to pass the cost of waste removal on to the public in the form of pollution. These activities, if pursued vigorously, degrade communities and ecosystems. The competition of firms in an industry adds to these pressures. If the managers of one firm pay the full cost of resource extraction, decent wages, and all pollution costs while competitors do not, obviously they will be at a disadvantage and lose market share or be forced to reduce profits. Industry-wide agreements are one way to avoid this. Governmental regulation is another. The organization of workers in unions and the counter balancing of corporate power by non-governmental groups are still others. Industry-wide agreements are hard to come by and may be illegal, however. Governmental regulation is anathema to managers and against the ethos of free markets. Unions and non-governmental groups are difficult to organize and frequently lack financial resources. Profit is not an evil, but its aggressive pursuit may lead to destructive resource extraction, low wages, and the pollution of ecosystems.

A second shortcoming is the narrow focus of these systems on human material well-being to the neglect of spiritual well-being and the flourishing of biotic communities. These systems are so powerful in the present day, and the material objects that are their fruits so alluring, that materialism has become the dominant influence.

A third shortcoming that has contributed especially to environmental degradation is the great emphasis on economic growth. Markets work, of course, whether or not there is an increase in production. Capitalism in its modern form seems most stable in economic terms, however, when there is moderate growth. Inflation is usually low and employment levels high with moderate growth in the Gross Domestic Product (GDP). The added wealth or extra product created by growth increases the resources for solving social problems.

In the United States, growth has become the most important social goal, and the federal government has assumed responsibility for achieving it. Elected officials consider it their number one priority. Reelection frequently depends on it.

The added production and consumption produced by economic growth puts increased pressure on resource extraction. It also creates waste in abundance. The sheer volume of it all may itself overwhelm the capacity of the earth to yield resources and absorb waste, not to mention impacts on specific ecosystems.

In addition, the pursuit of economic growth in general without evaluation of the various elements that go into it leads to a bias in favor of ever-greater production and consumption no matter how it is produced. Some forms of production and consumption increase human and ecosytem well-being, for example, the planting of trees in urban environments. Others are destructive, for example, the production of toxic wastes and the consumption of products made with them and the burning of fossil fuels with the release of carbon dioxide. The present pursuit of economic growth ignores these distinctions, converting all forms of growth to the quantitative measure of money. Markets make no distinctions either. The only way to be more discriminating and to prevent degradation of the environment is to alter ways of counting what goes into the GDP, to regulate markets, or to restrict producers. Producers resist such actions and have powerful ideological and political weapons to influence outcomes.

A fourth shortcoming in the evolution of market capitalism is the aggregation of economic and political power in the large transnational corporations (TNCs) that dominate the global economy. Such aggregation is not necessary to capitalism, but under the pressure to manage costly and complex technologies this has been the direction of evolution. In some industries this aggregation results in monopolistic practices and reduced efficiency. The problem for the environment comes when this power is coupled with the pursuit of self-interest and the mobility of capital.

There is no conspiracy. The self-interest of corporate managers is the reduction in the costs of production, conversion of nature's resources into material products, the rapid passing of these products through markets, the encouragement of consumers to buy the products, and the removal of impediments to freedom of action.

That the managers of TNCs are self-interested is no surprise. Nor does it necessarily make them bad citizens. Many TNCs pay key personnel well, voluntarily undertake pollution abatement measures, and give to established charities. The problem is the social primacy of their basic interests, the incentives to pay low wages and pollute, and the overall power they have accumulated. The situation is one of unbalanced power.

The forces that might counterbalance this power are either captive or weak. In the United States the federal government played this role from roughly 1930 to 1960. Subsequent government bashing, the influence of campaign contributions, threats to move production facilities elsewhere, and the ideology of free-market capitalism largely removed the federal government, not to mention local governments, as an effective counter force. Labor unions and NGOs have relatively little power however much they are portrayed as a powerful enemy. They remain as potential countervailing powers, however, and were they to pool their strengths could serve such a role. Recent resistance by these groups at key international economic meetings is some indication that such pooling is taking place.

As for democracy, while it retains a capacity to restrain TNCs, in most developed countries it is in their service, maintained among other things by campaign contributions and a pervasive ideology. As the saying goes, "the business of America is big business."

Certain structural features of democracies also help to maintain this arrangement. The separation of powers at the heart of the U.S. Constitution was designed to prevent tyranny, but it also serves to protect entrenched interests. The fragmentation of private property arrangements makes concerted action in ecosystems such as watersheds almost impossible. Private property rights give considerable leeway for individuals to misuse the land. Water rights legislation inhibits conservation of water resources. Antiquated mining laws and grazing rights on public lands encourage misuse of the commons. Polluters must be proven guilty in legal actions instead of having to demonstrate their operations are clean before production starts or continues. Producers are seldom required to test new products for polluting side effects.

The list goes on. None of these problems, of course, is a consequence of democracy itself. They could develop under any form of government, as environmental degradation in the former Soviet bloc amply demonstrates. Democratic structures in the U.S. are not the main problem. Rather it is the disproportions of power that allow corporate interests inordinately to influence social and environmental policy.

ATTITUDES TOWARD NATURE

Some observers would end the discussion of causes at this point maintaining that ideas and values count very little in outcomes. What makes the present stress on production and consumption so strong, however, is the integration of ideas, values, and material structures. Modern capitalism, for example, is not only a way to organize production. It is also a system of ideas, and the two together have proven to be extremely powerful. The system of ideas includes a constellation of attitudes toward nature. These attitudes have been part of human culture for millennia, and have served the human species tolerably well, but today abet the degradation of nature. For humans to be in a caring relation to nature, these attitudes must change. For some this means radical change and the adoption of polar opposite attitudes. For others a synthesis of old and new attitudes is needed to care for both humans and nature.

Among the many stars in this constellation of attitudes, five warrant development. They are the attitudes of anthropocentrism, hierarchy, dualism, domination, and atomism. Their polar counterparts are biocentrism, egalitarianism, connection, cooperation, and holism.

Anthropocentric Attitudes

Anthropocentrism means human-centered and is more or less a summation of the entire constellation, since all five attitudes primarily serve human beings. That human beings, like all other species, are species-centric is no surprise. Individuals of all species concentrate on survival and reproduction and so unconsciously promote the well-being of their own kind. They are normally interested in individuals of another species only as a resource, otherwise they are indifferent. In other words, one species has only use or utilitarian value for another, and with anthropocentrism other species are counted only as they serve human interests. That they also have intrinsic value, that is value in and of themselves, is one of the changes in attitudes under current consideration.

Anthropocentric attitudes are probably genetic in origin. Since the emergence of human culture, they have also become part of cultural evolution. The genetic and the cultural reinforce each other.

Jewish and Christian traditions have contributed to anthropocentrism. The doctrine of creation in both traditions places humans at the apex of the creative process. The Book of Genesis gives dominion to human beings. With the exception of the covenant after the flood in Genesis 9 where God enters into relationship with Noah and his descendants and also independently with nature, the great covenants of the Bible are between God and humans. Judaism was forged on the anvil of conflict with Canaanite nature religions. That the Hebrews made human history, not nature, the stage of God's activity is understandable in this context. Nature becomes the backdrop for the God-human drama. Human sin in both traditions is the central problem. In the aftermath of the Reformation individual salvation emerged as a central feature of Protestantism.

Strong anthropocentric attitudes were appropriate or at least did minimal harm to ecosystems when humans wielded little power. They are inappropriate in the present context when humans have the power to exploit all ecosystems. In this new situation utilitarian attitudes lead to the devaluing of nature and consequently to exploitation. Ultimately, they undermine anthropocentrism itself, since humans are dependent on healthy ecosystems. Strong anthropocentric attitudes are also spiritually numbing because they tend to reduce human interaction with and appreciation of nature.

Biocentrism is a tempting option in this situation. Returning to nature and fitting in as an equal has a perennial appeal, for example, in romantic movements. That humans need to reduce their impact on nature and develop greater appreciation goes without saying. But to go to the opposite pole on a continuum of attitudes would not be appropriate, even if possible, for the simple reason that human beings count morally and their basic needs deserve satisfaction. Issues of human justice deserve equal consideration with environmental preservation. All species must use nature. The question for human beings today is how to use it in a way that preserves species and ecosystems and satisfies basic human material needs. Movement toward the biocentric pole is needed; how far is the pressing issue.

Hierarchical Attitudes

A hierarchical pattern of social organization and thought with a few males at the apex of the power pyramid characterizes most societies at least since the beginning of the agricultural revolution about twelve thousand years ago. It is certainly characteristic of mainline Western religious traditions where God as father or monarch rules in righteous supremacy over a great chain of being with males above females, humans above all other species, sentient species above plants, and plants above single-celled organisms. Dirt and rocks have little worth.

One reason for hierarchy is clear. It serves those who are socially powerful as a system of order. Through inheritance, competitive struggle, and sometimes even the "consent" of the dominated, individuals and groups attain positions of power, surround themselves with the trappings of authority, claim superiority for themselves, and maintain their positions with physical and ideological forms of coercion. Elite groups can usually maintain themselves as long as they do not become too oppressive, which is a constant tendency, of course. Humans need order and a benevolent hierarchy often seems to satisfy this need.

In addition, hierarchical forms take many shapes not all of which are oppressive. Intelligent and compassionate people should play leadership roles as a matter of responsibility. The exercise of political power requires decision-making and a division of labor.

Today hierarchical attitudes toward nature are clothed in the garb of scientific management. This perspective urges the use of resources to promote human well-being but in a way that conserves these resources for the future. This is an attractive perspective. Humans do need to use resources and at their own peril to refrain from destroying basic life support systems. Science and technology are critical to this endeavor. Use implies some sort of management and good management is better then bad.

In the present context, however, scientific management is also an ideology that disguises and justifies hierarchical domination. At its worst this ideology sees nature in an anthropocentric way as a resource rightly exploited by a superior human species. Managers easily lose restraint and responsibility as superiority justifies the exploitation of nature and assuages guilt. The sense of superiority is also used to justify the culture/nature hierarchy. This sense is variously stated. Humans alone are created in the image of God. They are superior because they alone possess the capacity to reason. They are the highest rung on the evolutionary ladder.

More biocentric perspectives reject superiority outright and substitute notions of equality. The capacity to experience pleasure and pain or sentience is substituted for reason as the decisive capacity. All sentient creatures are equal in basic worth. Alternatively, animals are invested with rights appropriate to their capacities, rights that humans are to respect.

From a Christian ecological perspective, claims to superiority or the tendency to rank levels of being hierarchically miss the point. When pressed on who would be first among the disciples, Jesus made clear that the last shall be first and the first last. This disdain for ranking makes way for responsibility and service as the heart of any adequate Christian ecological ethics. Essentially what is needed is an attitude of respect and care for both humans and nature, an attitude that affirms ecologically sensitive scientific knowledge and management techniques as well as the preservation of species and ecosystems.

Dualistic Attitudes

Dualism is the tendency to divide reality into polar opposites, one pole superior and the other inferior (hierarchy). The great dualisms of the Western tradition are familiar: God and world, heaven and earth, spirit-soul-mind and nature-body-matter, men and women, good and evil, winners and losers, and culture and nature.[5]

Dualistic thinking can be appropriate. It is the bedrock of some very creative efforts in philosophy, for example, those attributed to Plato. Dualisms simplify what is often a very complex reality. In times of personal and social crisis the image of a perfect realm apart secures meaning and purpose. Over against the fear of death and the vicissitudes of life the same image offers hope. Finally, this way of thinking gives light to important distinctions and differences. Males and females are not the same. Extending human ethics to nature yields mixed results, for example, in the use of rights language.

The dualistic frame of mind is also deeply troubling, especially when polar opposites are disconnected, value judgments place one pole above the other, and social custom and attitudes toward nature are formed on these judgments. The oppression of people and the degradation of nature are almost inevitable under these circumstances.

The spirit/matter dualism that informs both Western thought in general and Christianity in particular is the dualism most relevant to environmental concerns. In this dualism spirit is superior to matter as culture is to nature and is identified with males. Women and nature are further identified with matter. What emerges from the hierarchical dualism is not only the devaluing of women and nature and their consequent oppression, but an escapist mentality. The self needs liberation from the material world for life in an ideal spiritual realm in heaven, an attitude that is hardly conducive to good stewardship on earth.

Dualism also brings disconnection. This humans have done with a vengeance, sealing themselves off in air-conditioned chambers. The shopping mall becomes the place for hiking. The elaborate coffin becomes the way to avoid bodily disintegration. Nature is viewed as real estate and the spirit goes out of the land. According to Carolyn Merchant:

> [The] nature/culture dualism is a key factor in Western civilization's advance at the expense of nature. As the unifying bonds of the older hierarchical cosmos were severed, European culture increasingly set itself above and apart from all that was symbolized by nature. Similarly, in America the nature/culture dichotomy was basic to the tension between civilization and the frontier in westward expansion and helped to justify the continuing exploitation of nature's resources. Much of American literature is founded on the underlying assumption of the superiority of culture to nature. If nature and women, Indians and blacks are to be liberated from the strictures of this ideology, a

radical critique of the very categories 'nature' and 'culture,' as organizing concepts in all disciplines, must be undertaken.[6]

An end to the oppression of women and other groups thought to be different and inferior, to the degradation of nature, and to the disconnection of humans from nature is long overdue. Reconnection to nature does not mean a return to primitive living, although some may well seek to simplify their lives by living close to nature. It means being open to spirit in nature, an intention to care for nature, practices that end degradation of species and ecosystems, and a revaluing of matter. For Christians, the Hebrew idea of covenant that points to the importance of relationships is one key. In Genesis 9, to repeat an earlier reference, God is portrayed as making a covenant with both humans and other species. The sacramental tradition in Christianity is another key. However conceived, the spiritual and the material interpenetrate each other in this tradition. This also holds true for the doctrine of the incarnation where God becomes flesh, thereby also ennobling the material world.

Dominating Attitudes

Humans have manipulated nature ever since the first tool user. The gains for human well-being have been substantial, especially in the last few centuries. Disease control, better nutrition, and greater mobility are obvious examples. The gains legitimated the manipulation as long as the so-called side effects were ignored. Today the side effects can no longer be ignored. They have become main effects. The more neutral words manipulation and control are giving way to stronger words like domination and, even stronger, exploitation to emphasize what was previously ignored.

Anthropocentrism, hierarchy, and dualism merge to contribute to domination, which also has a life of its own as an attitude. From anthropocentrism comes a disregard for nature. It is a backdrop, something to be used. From hierarchy come gradations of superior and inferior, and from dualism the separation of humans from nature. The domination and exploitation of nature follows easily from each of these attitudes and from their combined effect. The desire to dominate is also rooted in anxieties about death and scarce resources.

Judaism and Christianity have added to this dominating tendency by offering a particular interpretation to Genesis 1:26–28 and other texts that speak of dominion. The correct interpretation of dominion notwithstanding, dominion has been widely interpreted as domination. Since the Industrial Revolution this interpretation has been quite common. Even the notion of stewardship has been interpreted as domination. In the United States attitudes emerged that viewed nature as uncivilized, alien, and an enemy to be conquered. The wild, uncivilized West was unfavorably compared to the more urban and civilized East. The frontier needed to be pushed back, Native Americans civilized, and the forest turned into a garden.

Such attitudes have had devastating consequences for Native Americans. Until recently the power of human technologies was insufficient for equally devastating consequences for nature. This is no longer the case as climate is altered, animal habitat is lost, species are extinguished, ozone is depleted, and streams are polluted. Ultimately, this attitude encourages a false sense of security that technology and scientific management will fix all problems.

Much more nature-friendly attitudes have recently emerged to counter domination. Some Christians have gone back to stewardship understood not as domination but as caring for and cooperating with nature. Others appeal to Genesis 2:15 that talks about "tilling and keeping," to the sabbatical for the land (Ex. 25), and to the ministry of Jesus as care and compassion.

Darwinian-based ideas of survival of the fittest, competition, and nature red in tooth and claw are yielding to new biological observations of cooperation in nature. The idea of humans as alien exploiters is yielding to one of participation and cooperation in ecosystems.

Atomistic and Individualistic Attitudes

Holistic and communal ways of thinking have traditionally characterized human societies. The modern emphasis on the individual and the division of knowledge into parts is relatively recent. In the West it is a product among other things of the scientific revolution, the emergence of a large commercial class, and the religious preoccupation with individual salvation that grew out of the Reformation.

Great advances in knowledge were made when scientists became specialists in ever-smaller areas of observation. To control a machine-like nature, scientists learned to investigate its parts and in so doing to divide and subdivide the totality of nature into specialized areas of study. They probed deeply and systematically. They simplified as much as possible into mathematical laws and principles. They tested and verified by experimenting.

Soon this atomistic, quantifiable, and empirical way of thinking came to dominate most fields of study in the academy, and the academy organized itself on the basis of distinct fields. Holistic and integrated modes of thinking receded. In the field of economics, arguably the field with the most social influence today, the focus shifted to individual consumers in competition and invested with legal and property rights. Huge gains in production and real progress in limiting the arbitrary powers of the state followed. A new middle class swelled in numbers and challenged the organic and communal ways of feudalism. The new emphasis on individual salvation turned consciousness inward to the self and outward to heaven and away from the earth. New secular modes of thought pushed the church from center to periphery.

The problem for society and the environment stems from their holistic natures. Both require integration if they are to function well. Broken up like Humpty Dumpty, they are difficult to piece together again, especially when individuals view themselves in competition on isolated paths through a hostile environment. To solve major environmental problems specialists need to integrate their specialties. To pursue the common good individuals expressing a plurality of views must come to agreement. To reintegrate fragmented ecosystems, such as watersheds, planners must pull thousands of property owners together. For these tasks more holistic, integrated, and communal attitudes are required.

In the current situation there is no moving on, no place for the individual to escape to since humans have occupied and exhausted most natural environments. The frontiers that only a century ago beckoned individuals are all gone. Individualism is a limiting way of life when the individual is divorced from social life.

In moving to more holistic, integrated, and communal attitudes, the methods of science will remain critical, however. A smothering sort of communalism is no replacement for individualism. Societies need to protect the hard-won rights of individuals. The vision is rather one of synthesis and reintegration, of individuals deeply imbued with social consciousness and toleration, and of ecosystems with humans as integrated parts.

Conclusion

While these five attitudes toward nature are not the only attitudes contributing to environmental degradation, they are the most important and demonstrate that part of the problem is the way humans think about nature. To repeat, these attitudes served humans tolerably well in times past. Current environmental difficulties are a result of what humans have done well. This realization presents a fundamental dilemma. How are humans to preserve what contributes to their well being while preserving the natural environment?

In terms of attitudes toward nature individuals and groups need to move beyond the either/or of polar opposites. Another way of viewing these attitudes is to see them on a continuum.

Continuum of Attitudes toward Nature

Developmentalist	Conservationist	Preservationist	Critical Eco-Justice
anthropocentric	←	→	biocentric
hierarchical	←	→	egalitarian
dominating	←	→	cooperating
dualistic	←	→	connected
atomistic	←	→	holistic

FOUR PERSPECTIVES

The continuum way of viewing yields further fruit. Environmental debates are informed by quite different perspectives. Ships pass in the night when those in conflict are not aware of the basic assumptions that shape their perspectives and those of others. Four perspectives stand out in environmental conflicts. While distinct, these perspectives overlap, and individuals sometimes find themselves integrating aspects of all the perspectives. These perspectives are not stereotypes but tendencies.

The attitudes toward nature and society in the preceding section are central to these perspectives. The perspectives also include competing economic and political philosophies, positive and negative evaluations of the modern technological process, and different attitudes toward materialism and spirituality.

These four perspectives are: (1) developmentalist, (2) conservationist, (3) preservationist, and (4) critical eco-justice.[7] The first three perspectives are relatively coherent and developed as modern perspectives over the last century and a half. The fourth is recent, very much in process, and finds advocates in a multiplicity of movements.

The first task is to locate these groups on the continuum of attitudes toward nature. Developmentalists generally line up on the left side of the continuum, critical eco-justice on the right, with conservationists and preservationists in the middle. To set this continuum in the context of U.S. politics and economics, those on the left of the continuum tend to be more conservative, those on the right more progressive.

Developmentalists

Developmentalists came first and their attitudes toward nature and society set the terms of the debate. They are called developmentalists because the essence of their perspective is the development of nature's resources for human well-being. In the American experience, especially in the nineteenth century, this perspective is sometimes referred to as exploitationist to highlight its characteristic attitude toward resource extraction: exploitation with little regard for environmental consequences. Today, this extreme form of the perspective is rare, although exploitation for quick profit persists.[8]

In more moderate form developmentalists seek the improvement of human well-being through the creation of durable goods and capital, not exploitation for self-serving profit. In terms of their own criteria, developmentalists have been tremendously successful, increasing the production of goods and services and in so doing transforming the shape of society and the face of nature.

As for the environmental destruction that has accompanied economic growth and resource extraction, developmentalists either claim it is overstated, describing it as an externality or side-effect, or are optimistic about technological remedies. Theirs is a faith in the abundance of resources, the efficacy of technology, the efficiency of markets, and the good will of entrepreneurs responding to competitive pressures. In their view, when markets are given to the free play of supply and demand, they will signal what is in scarce supply or threatened. Entrepreneurs and corporations will respond to these signals out of self-interest, devise and put into service new and improved technologies as need be to tap the abundant supply of resources, and thus remove or alleviate supply problems and externalities. In this way societies are kept on an upward trajectory of economic growth and increased well being.

Those problems for which there are no market solutions, for example, the enforcement of contracts, will require government intervention, but such intervention should be kept to a minimum and employ market mechanisms wherever possible. The resource extractor should have the maximum room to maneuver.

In this perspective the uneven distribution of costs and benefits that result from the free play of market forces is either temporary or the price society pays for "the rising tide that raises all boats." It is temporary, especially in poorer countries, as a step on the ladder to affluence. A short period of inequality and environmental degradation is a prelude to the affluence that will follow when the full potential of economic expansion is realized. In the long run the free play of market forces is the best way to improve human well being because it harnesses individual self-interest for the social good.

Developmentalists are unabashedly anthropocentric. Jobs and human material well being are the first priority. Humans are superior to other species and have the right to dominate nature for their own well being. Nature is distinct from culture with little or no intrinsic value, only utilitarian value for human beings. This value is measurable in terms of dollars and compared to other uses of resources similarly valued. Land and resources are factors of production and are considered as costs in the same way as labor and capital. Property rights are essential to protect the individual against encroachment from other individuals and government.

Increasingly this perspective is under critical scrutiny. Critics are skeptical about the claims made for the market system and modern technology. Side effects are seen as main effects, externalities as intrinsic to the system. Critics reject the reduction of nature to a factor of production and its quantification solely in dollar terms. They find unsatisfying the hierarchical, dominating, dualistic, atomistic, and anthropocentric attitudes at the heart of the developmentalist perspective.

Conservationists

Conservationists get their name from the movement in the late nineteenth and early twentieth centuries led in the U.S. by Gifford Pinchot to conserve resources for human use. Conservationists share with developmentalists anthropocentric ideas and values. Nature is there for human use, only this use must be wise use governed by the best science-based management practices. Conservationists emphasize scientific management and control, confident that the judicious use of technology will allow increases in the use of resources without degrading the capacity of ecosystems to continue producing.

Like the developmentalists, conservationists seek to control nature, but unlike the developmentalists to control it rationally, efficiently, and with care. Rational control presents problems, of course. Scientific understanding may be poor or in dispute, yet used as if it were objective. Ideology and political give-and-take can cloud rationality. The lure of higher income can bias objectivity.

Conservationists have less faith than developmentalists in market mechanisms and promote governmental interference in markets to ensure environmental quality. Indeed, conservationists came to prominence in opposition to "cut and run" forest practices and the abuses of corporate power in the late nineteenth century. Governmental intervention was necessary then, according to the conservationists, to avoid the degrading side effects of unregulated resource extraction and markets. The formation of the U.S. Forest Service and the subsequent assignment of vast tracts of forests in the U.S. to it for management were due to their efforts. Their emphasis on governmental intervention and management also contributed to the acceptance of government as a countervailing power to big business that culminated in the New Deal.

Conservationists are utilitarians. They believe that nature is to be used in accordance with the utilitarian principle. As articulated by Gifford Pinchot, for example, the Forest Service is to produce "the greatest good for the greatest number (of humans) over the longest period of time."

Conservationists share the assumption of abundance with the developmentalists, but do not consider abundance automatic just because market principles are followed. Abundance must be managed. Jobs and economic growth are important to conservationists, but not at the expense of healthy ecosystems. Growth must be governed by the principle of sustainability which is best calculated by scientifically trained managers.

In their stress on the good of the human community and in their regard for the future of healthy ecosystems, conservationists are less anthropocentric, dualistic, and atomistic than developmentalists and take a longer-term outlook. Healthy ecosystems and human communities should be managed for the long-term sustenance of humans, and to some minimum degree humans have to cooperate with nature in the development of resources. So while anthropocentric, conservationists exhibit some regard for the biosphere and do not separate themselves as thoroughly as developmentalists from it.

Nevertheless, hierachy, dualism, and domination lurk in notions such as scientific management. The scientific mind is seen as superior to the matter of nature's processes and assigned the task of controlling nature. Technology is the means of control. Nature is a resource with utilitarian, not necessarily intrinsic, value. The developmentalist perspective is sometimes disguised in conservationist garb, and claims for scientific management and sustainability are made to cover degrading environmental practices.

Preservationists

With preservationists comes marked difference, although at the margin with conservationists there is similarity. The essence of the preservationist perspective is the protection of ecosystems, species, and individuals of a species from degrading human practices. Preservationists thus share with many conservationists a passion for protecting the environment and sometimes even use the anthropocentric and utilitarian appeals of the conservationists to achieve their ends. Most preservationists also accept the need to give over part of nature to human resource extraction, that part being guided by best resource management practices.

Indeed, the preservationist perspective in the U.S. emerged out of the conservationist movement, and early in the twentieth century preservationists were allies of conservationists in opposition to exploitation. The event that gave birth to the preservationist movement is generally recognized to be the fight over Hetch Hetchy Dam in Yosemite National Park, a fight that ended in 1913 with a decision by Congress in favor of the dam. This battle pitted Gifford Pinchot against John Muir, who pressed for the preservation of Hetch Hetchy Valley in its pristine state. While supportive of the conservationists' introduction of scientific management in the extraction of natural resources, Muir argued with religious fervor for set-asides, such as national parks. These areas should be preserved undisturbed and never appropriated for human exploitation. They are valuable in and of themselves and deserve protection. Material abundance and utilitarian arguments do not trump the intrinsic value of these places.

John Muir was also one of the founders of the Sierra Club, which is today among the nation's most important environmental groups. Intially a wilderness venture society, today the Sierra Club is a bastion of the preservationist perspective and a group with considerable political power.

To those on the conservationist side of the continuum, preservationists push too hard for set-asides, for taking land and resources out of the economic cycle where they serve the production of weath. To those with critical eco-justice perspectives, preservationists are too timid and too supportive of the economic and political status quo, however near they may be in terms of basic perspective.

With the preservationists there is a decided shift to the right side of the continuum in terms of attitudes toward nature. Preservationists are biocentric, at least in terms of species and ecosystems. In preserves, intact and untouched ecosystems should be the norm. All species should be protected from extinction; and while humans may enjoy the preserves and admire other species, that is, consider them anthropocentrically, ecosystems, species, and individuals of a species have intrinsic value. Ecosystems come first because they are the foundation of everything else. They should be left intact to continue their biotic processes.

Some preservationists would carry this even further as a principle for relationships to all ecosystems. Biocentrism means that the needs of evolving ecosystems and species come before all but the most basic of human needs. Other preservationists would hold human needs in some sort of balance with the preservation of ecosystems and species.

As this indicates, preservationists are far less hierarchical. Humans, unique in some respects and not in others, are one species among many with no greater intrinsic value. The emergence of intelligence is an amazing and perhaps unique product of evolutionary history, but it does not make its carriers privileged or superior in a moral sense. Ethically, its main importance is to convey a sense of responsibility.

With the preservationists dualism and domination recede. Humans are part of nature and completely dependent on ecosystems. Domination yields to cooperation, dualism to connectedness and integration, not only for reasons of survival, but also for spiritual well-being.

Among preservationists the spiritual motif is quite strong. Muir was a pantheist. Many preservationists claim to encounter God in nature and see their relationship to and participation in nature in spiritual terms. This is a far cry from the scientific and managerial approach of conservationists and the economic approach of the developmentalists.

In their stress on ecosystems, species, and humans in community, preservationists are more holistic and communitarian, less individualistic and atomistic. Preservationists are strong supporters of so-called landscape, watershed, and ecosystem management approaches that have been prominent in recent environmental discussions. By management, of course, they mean something quite different from the economic management of the developmentalists and the scientific management of the conservationists. While not rejecting these forms of management, they want to expand them by looking at all elements in an ecosystem and the complex interactions that take place there. Management in this view may also mean not managing, that is, letting be. In keeping also with this emphasis on whole systems and species, preservationists play down the importance of individuals, thereby creating space for conflict with those who focus on animal rights.

Preservationists are critical of the current preoccupation with economic growth, especially forms that cause environmental degradation. Affluence is not a priority. They place little trust in markets, convinced that the market system left to itself is incapable of accounting for non-economic, non-quantifiable goods. Perservationists frequently turn to government to regulate markets and to protect ecosystems, although with less confidence than the conservationists.

Finally, preservationists do not hold modern technology in the same high esteem as developmentalists and conservationists. While not Luddites, they view the introduction of new technology and new management schemes with suspicion because of the historical role technology has played in environmental degradation.

Critical Eco-Justice

The fourth perspective on this continuum is more difficult to pin down. It is actually a group or cluster of perspectives that share in common a strong criticism of dominant social arrangements and values. In environmental conflicts this cluster has been influential in shaping ideas and values but marginal in terms of social policy, highly publicized interventions by various direct action groups notwithstanding. Carolyn Merchant's delineation of the various groups in this cluster is useful.[9]

> 1) *Deep ecologists* call for a new ecological paradigm to replace the dominant mechanistic paradigm. Opposed to reformist efforts of conservationists and preservationists, which are called "shallow ecology," deep

ecologists reverse the attitudes toward nature of the developmentalists. The crisis is so deep that only a radical transformation in thinking and being will be sufficient.

2) *Spiritual ecologists* focus on a transformation of consciousness, especially religious consciousness. Some raise up older forms of nature spirituality, such as "goddess" and Native American forms of worship, others Eastern religions, and still others neglected currents in Christianity. A movement called "creation spirituality" associated with Matthew Fox and others finds its home here.

3) *Social ecologists* stress the shortcomings of the market system and the political and economic thought of developmentalists. They also work hard to keep justice and ecology, workers and critters, together. They envision a world where basic human needs are met through an economic restructuring that is environmentally sustainable.

4) *Ecofeminists* are concerned about environmental degradation that affects bodily integrity and about women's roles in social institutions. Ecofeminists also insist that the views of developmentalists and assaults on nature and women are the result of adrocentric (male-centered), not anthropocentric, thinking. Women and nature are both victims of the same domination that stems from patriarchal ideas and institutions. Women's ways of knowing, which are closely aligned with the attitudes on the right side of the continuum, offer alternatives that will liberate both oppressed women and degraded ecosystems.

5) *Green politicians* advocate direct action or grassroots confrontation in contrast to mainline environmentalists who pursue a reformist agenda through the legislative process. Groups like Earth First and Greenpeace find the reformist agenda too timid and have used confrontational forms of involvement instead. While not so much a perspective, those in green political movements accept and are motivated by the attitudes toward nature on the right side of the continuum.

Diverse as they are, the movements and perspectives in this cluster share a criticism of current directions and attitudes. Standing as they do at the opposite end of the continuum from developmentalists, these critical perspectives exhibit little of the developmentalists' faith in the market system. Whereas developmentalists and conservationists rely on economic and scientific arguments and appeal to balancing conflicting claims, those of the critical persuasion tend to argue from ethical foundations, stressing individual and community amenity rights as opposed to property rights. Among spiritual ecologists and those of a religious bent, appeals to theology and a human spiritual connection to nature are frequent. Balancing opposing perspectives and claims is not a high priority. The term eco-justice also signifies a concern for both people and nature, although the stress on nature tends to be stronger in all but the social ecologists and ecofeminists.

As for the attitudes toward nature, those in this cluster locate themselves on the right-hand side of the continuum. They are decidedly biocentric because they see humans not as separate from but deeply embedded in and dependent on ecosystems. They assume the intrinsic value of individuals of a species, species themselves, and ecosystems. They prefer to keep the use of nature to a minimum.

Instead of domination they advocate cooperation with nature. They raise up such alternatives as appropriate technology, soft energy paths, integrated pest management, and renewable energy sources. These emphases are not anti-technological, as developmentalists claim, but pro-alternative technology. This theme of cooperation is accompanied by notions of integration and connectedness. The classic dualisms of Western thought are rejected out of hand.

Their emphasis on community, species, and ecosystems stands in contrast to the atomism and individualism at the other end of the continuum. From the science of ecology, those in the cluster borrow holistic categories. They see the individual person as part of both human communities and the larger biosphere and argue for both justice and sustainability. They talk little about economic growth as a policy goal. Sufficiency and frugality become guides for personal consumption.

Opponents lump those in this cluster with preservationists and accuse both of elitism. While it is true that many environmentalists come from more affluent sectors of society and some have been insensitive to workers, this criticism is often ideologically driven and misses the elitism of those who make the criticism. It also overlooks the fact that humans do in fact depend on healthy ecosystems whether or not environmentalists are elitist.

GUIDELINES FOR ETHICS

The question remains: What should be done by individuals in communities and ecosystems? "Should" signals ethics, and useful to doing ethics are norms to guide ethical acts directly or to inform the setting of goals.

To start gathering appropriate norms, a task that is the focus of the next chapter, the foregoing analysis of causes and perspectives is helpful. The analysis has frequently used normative language, and several norms are readily apparent. The four perspectives are themselves normative perspectives. Students of environmental ethics need to locate themselves on the continuum of perspectives or select features from each of the perspectives to arrive at their own distinct position. Included also in these perspectives are attitudes toward nature and human community. These attitudes are normative attitudes, and students should appropriate them to form their own guidelines for thought and action. A series of spectrum exercises included in the appendix to this volume helps students physically locate themselves in a range of views related to key debates in environmental ethics.

We the authors of this volume stand toward the right side of the continuum, although we draw insights from all perspectives. We think that resource use should be reduced and extraction governed by strict conservationist principles. We think noteworthy and vital ecosystems should be preserved intact.

We think that those attitudes toward nature and human community on the right side of the continuum should more and more guide social policy, but not to the exclusion of human need. Humans count. Sufficiency, not luxury, should guide our use of nature, however. Human justice should be a major consideration in environmental decisions. We do not trust in the so-called "technological fix," but do believe that science and technology are vital to sufficient production, as are the insights of economists.

We think that increased spirituality is badly needed to correct today's materialism. In environmental ethics this means finding a deep spiritual sense in nature. We believe that God is present in natural processes and can be found there by cultivating sensitivity and care. Finally, we think that ethical norms developed by humans for application in society may be extended to the natural world after allowances are made for significant differences.

Notes

1. Michael S. Northcott, *The Environment and Christian Ethics* (Cambridge: Cambridge University Press, 1996), Chapter 2.

2. Michael Argyle, *The Psychology of Happiness* (London: Methuen, 1987).

3. Ian G. Barbour, *Ethics in an Age of Technology* (San Francisco: Harper Collins Publisher, 1993), Chapter 1.

4. Barry Commoner, *The Closing Circle* (New York: Alfred A. Knopf, 1971).

5. For a scathing critique of hierarchy and dualism see Beverly W. Harrison, *Making Connections,* Carol S. Robb, editor (Boston: Beacon Press, 1985), especially pp. 25–30.

6. Carolyn Merchant, *The Death of Nature: Women, Ecology, and the Scientific Revolution* (San Francisco: Harper & Row, Publishers, 1980), pp.143f.

7. Douglas E. Booth, *Valuing Nature: The Decline and Preservation of Old-Growth Forests* (Lanham, Maryland: Rowman & Littlefield, Publishers, 1994); and Carolyn Merchant, *Radical Ecology* (New York: Routledge, Chapman & Hall, Inc., 1992).

8. Douglas E. Booth, *Valuing Nature,* p. 76. Also see Cynthia D. Moe-Lobeda, *Healing a Broken World: Globalization and God* (Minneapolis: Fortress Press, 2002), Chapters 2 and 3.

9. Carolyn Merchant, *Radical Ecology,* Chapters 4–8.

For Further Reading

Bowler, Peter J. *The Norton History of the Environmental Sciences.* New York: W.W. Norton, 1993.

Chapman, Audrey R., et al., eds. *Consumption, Population, and Sustainability: Perspectives from Science and Religion.* Washington, DC: Island Press, 2000.

Cobb, John B., Jr. *Sustaining the Common Good: A Christian Perspective on the Global Economy.* New York: The Pilgrim Press, 1994.

Cunningham, William P., and Saigo, Barbara Woodworth. *Environmental Science: A Global Concern,* Sixth Edition. New York: McGraw-Hill Higher Education, 2001.

Martin-Schramm, James B. *Population Perils and the Churches' Response* (Geneva: World Council of Churches Publications, 1997).

McKibben, Bill. *The End of Nature.* New York: Random House, Inc., 1989.

Merchant, Carolyn. *The Death of Nature: Women, Ecology, and the Scientific Revolution.* San Francisco: Harper & Row, Publishers, 1980.

———. *Radical Ecology.* New York: Routledge, Chapman & Hall, Inc., 1992.

Mies, Maria and Shiva, Vandana. *Ecofeminism.* London: Zed Books, 1993.

Moe-Lobeda, Cynthia D. *Healing a Broken World: Globalization and God.* Minneapolis: Fortress Press, 2002.

Mongillo, John F., and Zierdt-Warshaw, Linda. *Encyclopedia of Environmental Science.* Phoenix, AZ: Oryx Press, 2000.

Schneiderman, Jill S. *The Earth Around Us: Maintaining a Livable Planet.* New York: W.H. Freeman, 2000.

United Nations Environmental Program. *Global Environmental Outlook 3: Past, Present and Future Perspectives:* London: Earthscan Publication Ltd, 2002.

Wenz, Peter S. *Environmental Ethics Today.* New York: Oxford University Press, 2001.

Wilson, Edward O. *The Diversity of Life.* New York: W.W. Norton & Co., 1992.

———. *The Future of Life.* New York: Alfred A. Knopf, 2002

Websites

Environmental News Service
http://www.ens-news.com

United Nations Environmental Programme
http://www.unep.org

Worldwatch Institute
http://worldwatch.org

2

Christian Resources and the Ethic of Ecological Justice

Christians in the course of their 2000 years of history have developed a variety of traditions. Were investigators to look for *the* Christian tradition, they would not find it, although the various traditions do share common themes and some churches claim to carry the only true tradition.

Most of the traditions have developed in social and natural settings quite different from those of today. Human numbers were much lower, most people lived in rural areas, and social organizations were much simpler. Social stability, buttressed by religious traditions, mattered a lot, since disease, drought, and disruption were always threats. Subsistence ways of living were typical. Technologies were relatively unsophisticated and weak. The primary environmental problem was what nature was doing to humans, not the reverse, as is the case today. All this has changed over the past two hundred years or so.

Given the context of its development, it is not surprising that today's environmental problems receive scant attention and nature plays a secondary role in most Christian traditions. Humans are the chief concern of these traditions with nature serving mostly as a backdrop for the human drama. While Christians appreciated nature through the centuries and assumed it as the basis of all life, they did not put it at the center of their deliberations. The anthropocentric nature of Christianity has been a source of considerable criticism, some finding in it the cause of the environmental crisis.[1]

Today Christians are scrambling to piece together an environmental ethic from neglected traditions that appreciated nature. They are also proceeding indirectly by extending to nature ethical norms originally used to inform human moral problems. These ways of proceeding work tolerably well as long as those using them remember that most of the traditions and norms did not originally address current problems.

The chief problem historically for most Christian traditions has been human sin. Sin is a deep inner alienation from God, self, other humans, and nature that issues forth in specific acts that break relationships. While some acts are always alienating, for example, murder, the sin is not so much in classes of acts as it is in the breaking of relationships. Sex, for example, is not sinful in itself, but some sexual expressions cause alienation and thus are sinful. Sin continues to be the chief problem, but has only recently been related to the human-nature relationship. Today human alienation from nature looms much larger and must be a key part of any Christian environmental ethic. Humans are degrading nature in unprecedented ways, and this is sin.

While sin runs deep and is universal, it does not have to paralyze the moral life. Jesus Christ reveals in his person and work that there are resources for living with integrity in the midst of sin. Jesus identifies God as the source of these resources. God is experienced as a power that creates inner integrity or wholeness and the possibility of right relationships.

Primary to most Christian traditions is the affirmation of God's power as love, although God is also seen to have a role in the integrating powers of the universe that science studies. Love redeems humans from sin and reunites them with others without violating human freedom. Love is a free gift, never a possession, and cannot be attained by an effort of the will alone.

From another angle, sin is the refusal to accept God's gracious power of love, a refusal that leads to disintegration and a sense of brokenness or judgment. The continuing presence of love in all situations is said to be the work of the Holy Spirit.

The starting point for Christian environmental ethics is *to be* in love. This is not something the self can perform alone, however. It is something God performs in cooperation with the self, although the self is constantly tempted to think otherwise and to take charge, frequently without success. Being in love is first a matter of receiving love, letting it work in the self, and only then a matter of responding or doing in the same spirit. This is more or less the central message of most Christian traditions, although there is considerable variation in particulars. Doing has its foundation in being, in the sense of wholeness or oneness that comes from the power of God's love. Faith is a matter of relationship, of being in love first with God and then responsively with self, others, and nature.

The word "spirituality" is often used to point to the core relationship to God. God's power is experienced in a number of quite different ways, the common element to all ways being the integrated and transformed self that emerges. Most Christians readily recognize the customary religious ways of experiencing God: worship, prayer, singing, sacraments, and the preached word. God is not limited to these religious ways, but according to most traditions is free to be present in a variety of ways consistent with love.

While Christians have been standoffish for historical reasons from nature as a place where God is experienced, today this is changing. Not to be confused with nature worship, Christians are more and more experiencing and affirming the Spirit in natural settings; and properly so, for nature is Spirit-filled.[2] A walk in the deep forest or along a deserted beach, the appreciation of delicate flowers, and amazement at the complexity of the body are examples of places where the Spirit finds the self. Christians are combining the rich traditions of finding God both in human and nature spirituality.

If the foundation of all doing is the relationship of the self to God that inspires acts of love, then the beginning of environmental ethics is the appreciation of Spirit in nature. When the Spirit is present, love issues forth as sensitivity to nature. There is little hope for preserving the environment if this sensitivity is truncated, as increasingly it is as nature is traded as a commodity in markets and consumption of material goods becomes a chief end of many Americans.

Christian environmental ethics starts therefore in spirituality, but it does not end there. The human love that inspires acts of justice in society and nature also pushes the self to specific acts in particular situations. For this further push other things are needed because inspiration is not always an accurate guide for doing what is right or most helpful. The doing of good acts requires thought as well as heart, knowledge as well as inspiration. The Christian doer is sensitive to relationships in specific situations, is passionate about the facts and theories that give order to situations, and has a keen sense of the traditions that guide human actions normatively.

Sensitivity to relationships involves a strong element of intentionality. It involves a sense of the Spirit already at work in a situation, of the characters of the human actors, and of the needs of plants and animals. It is constantly in tune with feelings and the subtle changes that can make certain situations exceptional. It is aware of the self, its state of being, and its tendencies to sin, both in one's own self and in the selves of others.

Knowledge is mostly hard work. It is attaining the tools to comprehend and to practice the methods and theories of a field of study. It is acquired in a variety of social situations. Good teachers are crucial to all except the most gifted. They pass on the knowledge that has been historically useful.

Part of being knowledgeable is entering into conversation with the traditions that guide ethical action. Loving intuition needs the help of historical and current wisdom. Knowledge of where the Spirit has been and what normally leads to flourishing relationships is useful. Here rules, laws, principles, models of behavior, and so forth become important and enter into dialogue with loving intuition in order to make ethical decisions. These guides to the moral life produce norms that give direction to loving intuition and prevent an ethic of "anything goes." Christian traditions are rich in normative understandings, especially for ethical problems that recur frequently.

SOURCES OF CHRISTIAN NORMS

Christians look to a number of sources for ethical guidance. The Bible has traditionally been the first and the most important source. Gleaning ethical guidance from the Bible is not as easy as it might seem, however. The many books of the Bible were written in different periods and reflect quite different contexts and situations. The biblical writers wrote from their own locations in diverse societies and cultures. They saw and understood things differently from each other and certainly from moderns who live in a thoroughly changed world. They sometimes disagree, and what they thought was ethically acceptable in their own time, for example, slavery, has changed as culture has evolved. Compounding these differences is the availability of different interpretive schemes. Sometimes ethical conflicts result from different methods of biblical interpretation.

In spite of these complications, themes do run through the Bible, and these themes can be identified with a degree of accuracy. The biblical writers experienced the same loving God as moderns and faced many of the same problems. The Bible remains a good source of guidance and is the basic foundation for the ethic of ecological justice that guides the analysis of cases in this volume.

Theology is the second source of norms. Understandings of God's power and human sin have already been identified and are good examples of how theology guides decision-making. Understanding God as working through the power of love directs decision-makers to look for love and justice in all situations. Understanding sin as deep and universal leads the decision-maker to realistic actions that factor in the human tendency to misuse freedom.

The third source of norms is the historical traditions of the church. Christians through the centuries have devoted considerable thought to issues of nonviolence, the poor, and nature. The traditions change and sometimes yield a multiplicity of guidelines, but they also show continuity and reflect a certain amount of practical wisdom. The traditions on justice and nature are critical to this volume.

The fourth source of norms is the church in its many forms. The three previous sources all grew in church ground. The church ranges from the Church Catholic, to specific church organizations such as the Roman Catholic Church and specific Protestant denominations, to associations of churches, to the local brick and mortar church, to what in the Bible is referred to as "one or two gathered together." Likewise the ethical guidelines range from comprehensive church studies and pronouncements, to rules of organization, to community education, to the wisdom and advice of a good friend. Today churches are increasingly addressing environmental issues with many churches in the United States on record with regard to problems such as global warming, energy consumption, and habitat loss.[3]

The final source is the catchall category of other religious and ethical traditions. Christian and secular philosophical traditions in the West have had a close relationship for years, mutually informing each other. Native American traditions are rich in sensitivity to nature. Taoism is likewise rich. Buddhism holds to the interrelatedness of all beings, a helpful understanding for keeping the necessary connections to nature. Christians are free to appropriate the insights of these other traditions, to enter into dialogue with adherents of these traditions, and to join in common actions.

The development of these four sources into a comprehensive Christian environmental ethic is work that has been well done by others. One or more of the works cited at the end of this chapter would make a useful companion for readers of this volume. A method to use these sources in decision-making is available in Chapter Three. The remainder of this chapter summarizes the ethic of ecological justice that is based on these sources.

THE ETHIC OF ECOLOGICAL JUSTICE

The ethic of ecological justice is a biblical, theological, and tradition-based ethic that emphasizes four norms: sustainability, sufficiency, participation, and solidarity.[4] This ethic addresses human-caused problems that threaten both human and natural communities and considers both human and natural communities to be ethically important. The word *ecological* raises up other species and their habitats, the word *justice* points to the distinctly human realm and human relationships to the natural order.

Justice

The norm of justice used in the title of this ethical perspective is an inclusive concept. Its full meaning is given greater specificity by the four norms of sustainability, sufficiency, participation, and solidarity. Justice is, however, a norm in its own right with a distinct history in Christian ethics and Western philosophy. In Christian traditions justice is rooted in the very being of God. It is an essential part of God's community of love and calls human beings to make fairness the touchstone of social relations and relations to other species and ecosystems. Justice is not the love of Christ (*agape*). Justice involves a calculation of interests. Justice has a more impersonal quality than love because social groups are more its subject than individuals. Nevertheless, justice divorced from love easily deteriorates into a mere calculation of interests and finally into a cynical balancing of interest against interest. Without love inspiring justice, societies lack the push and pull of care and compassion to move them to higher levels of fairness. Love forces recognition of the needs of others. Love judges abuses of justice. Love lends passion to justice. Justice, in short, is love worked out in arenas where the needs of each individual are impossible to know.

The biblical basis for justice with its special sensitivity for the poor starts with God's liberation of the poor and oppressed slaves in Egypt and the establishment of a covenant, one of whose cardinal features is righteousness (Ex. 22:21–24). The biblical basis continues in the prophetic reinterpretation of the covenant. Micah summarized the law: "to do justice, and to love kindness, and to walk humbly with your God" (Mi. 6:8). Amos was adamant that God's wrath befell Israel for its unrighteousness. Important for Amos among the transgressions of Israel were injustice and the failure to care for the poor (Am. 2:6, 8:4–8, 5:11). Isaiah and Jeremiah were no different (Is. 10:1–2; Jer. 22:13–17).

In the New Testament the emphasis on justice is muted in comparison to the prophets, but the concern for the poor may be even stronger. Jesus himself was a poor man from a poor part of Israel. His mission was among the poor and directed to them (Lk. 4:16–20). He blessed the poor and spoke God's judgment on the rich (Lk. 6:20–26; Mt. 5:1–14).

The early church carried this tradition beyond the time of Jesus. Paul's concern is frequently the weak members of the community. This is his concern as he addresses a question that now seems quaint, eating meat sacrificed to idols (I Cor. 8). He affirms the new freedom in faith that is one important foundation for political freedom. Freedom is not, however, license to ignore or prosecute the weak in the pursuit of one's own consumption.

Paul is even more emphatic on equality, which with freedom is the backbone of the modern concept of justice. His statement on the ideals of freedom and equality are among the strongest in the entire biblical witness (Galatians 3:28). His commitment to freedom and equality is in no way diminished by his more conservative interpretations in actual situations where he may have felt the need to moderate his ideals for the sake of community harmony. Thus, while Paul seems to advise an inferior role for women (1 Cor. 14:34–36) and urges the slave to return to his master (Philemon), his ringing affirmation of equality in Galatians has through the ages sustained Christians concerned about justice.

In the Christian community in Jerusalem (Acts 1–5), equality was apparently put into practice and also involved sharing. In this practice these early Christians set themselves apart from the prevailing Roman culture.

For the Greeks justice meant "treating equals equally and unequals unequally." This simple statement of the norm of justice hides the complexities of determining exactly who is equal and who is not and the grounds for justifying inequality. It leads in modern interpretations of justice, however, to freedom and equality as measures of justice. It also leads to the concept of equity, which is justice in actual situations where a degree of departure from freedom and equality is permitted in the name of achieving other social goods. So, for example, most societies give mentally and physically impaired individuals extra resources and justify it the name of greater fairness. This is a departure from equal treatment, but not from equitable treatment. The problem, of course, is that self-interested individuals and groups will always ask for departures from freedom and equality and use spurious justifications. This is one reason justice needs love as its foundation and requires careful scrutiny of claims for special treatment.

In summary, justice in Christian thought is the social and ecological expression of love and means a special concern for the poor, a rough calculation of freedom and equality, and a passion for establishing equitable relationships. The ethical aims of justice in the absence of other considerations should be to relieve the worst conditions of poverty, powerlessness, exploitation, and environmental degradation and provide for an equitable distribution of burdens and costs.

Sustainability

Sustainability may be defined as the long-range supply of sufficient resources to meet basic human needs and the preservation of intact natural communities. It expresses a concern for future generations and the planet as a whole, and emphasizes that an acceptable quality of life for present generations must not jeopardize the prospects for future generations.

Sustainability is basically good stewardship and is a pressing concern today because of the human degradation of nature. It embodies an ongoing view of nature and society, a view in which ancestors and posterity are seen as sharing in present decisions. The present generation takes in trust a legacy from the past with the responsibility of passing it on in better or at least no worse condition. A concern for future generations is one aspect of love and justice. Sustainability precludes a shortsighted stress on economic growth that fundamentally harms ecological systems and any form of environmentalism that ignores human needs and costs.

There are several significant biblical and theological foundations for the norm of sustainability. The doctrine of creation affirms that God as Creator sustains God's creation. The creation is also good independently of human beings (Gen. 1). It is not simply there for human use, but possesses an autonomous status in the eyes of God. The goodness of matter is later picked up in Christian understandings of the incarnation and the sacraments.[5]

Psalm 104 is a splendid hymn of praise that celebrates God's efforts at sustainability. "When you send forth your spirit . . . you renew the face of the ground" (Psalm 104:30). Similarly, Psalm 145 rejoices in the knowledge that God gives "them their food in due season" and "satisfies the desire of every living thing" (Ps. 145:15–16). The doctrine of creation also emphasizes the special vocation of humanity to assist God in the task of sustainability. In Genesis the first creation account describes the responsibility of stewardship in terms of "dominion" (Gen. 1:28), and the second creation account refers to this task as "to till and keep it" (Gen. 2:15). In both cases the stress is on humanity's stewardship of *God's* creation. The parable of the Good Steward in Luke also exemplifies this perspective. The steward is not the owner of the house, but manages or sustains the household so that all may be fed and have enough (Lk. 12:42). The Gospels offer several other vivid metaphors of stewardship. The shepherd cares for the lost sheep. The earth is a vineyard and humanity serves as its tenant.

The covenant theme is another important biblical and theological foundation for the norm of sustainability. The Noahic covenant (Gen. 9) celebrates God's "everlasting covenant between God and every living creation of all flesh that is on the earth." The biblical writer repeats this formula several times in subsequent verses, as if to drive the point home. The text demonstrates God's concern for biodiversity and the preservation of all species (Gen. 9:16).

It is the Sinai covenant, however, that may best reveal the links between the concepts of covenant and sustainability. Whereas the prior covenants with Noah and Abraham were unilateral and unconditional declarations by God, the Sinai covenant featured the reciprocal and conditional participation of humanity in the covenant. "If you obey the commandments of the Lord your God . . . then you shall live . . ." (Dt. 30:16). Each of the Ten Commandments and all of the interpretations of these commandments in the subsequent Book of the Covenant were intended to sustain the life of the people of God in harmony with the well-being of the earth (Ex. 20–24).

At the heart of the Sinai covenant rested the twin concerns for right-eousness (justice) and stewardship of the earth. Likewise the new covenant in Christ is very much linked to these twin concerns as well as to the recip-rocal relation of human beings.

In Romans 8:18 the whole creation suffers and in 8:22 "groans in tra-vail." But suffering, according to Paul, does not lead to despair. "The cre-ation awaits in eager longing for the revealing of the children of God" (Rom. 8:19), and "in this hope we are saved" (Rom. 8:24). Suffering, as in the suf-fering of Jesus Christ on the cross, points beyond to the hope that is already partially present. Part of this hope is a return to the good stewardship of Genesis 1 and 2 before the Fall in Genesis 3.

Sufficiency

The norm of sufficiency emphasizes that all forms of life are entitled to share in the goods of creation. To share in the goods of creation in a Christian sense, however, does not mean unlimited consumption, hoarding, or an inequitable distribution of the earth's goods. Rather it is defined in terms of basic needs, sharing, and equity. It repudiates wasteful and harmful con-sumption and encourages humility, frugality, and generosity.[6]

This norm appears in the Bible in several places. As the people of God wander in the wilderness after the Exodus, God sends "enough" manna each day to sustain the community. Moses instructs the people to "gather as much of it as each of you need" (Exodus 16). The norm of sufficiency is also inte-gral to the set of laws known as the jubilee legislation. These laws fostered stewardship of the land, care for animals and the poor, and a regular redis-tribution of wealth. In particular the jubilee laws stressed the needs of the poor and wild animals to eat from fields left fallow every seven years (Ex. 23:11). All creatures were entitled to a sufficient amount of food to live.

In Christian scriptures sufficiency is linked to abundance. Jesus says: "I came that you may have life, and have it abundantly" (Jn. 10:10). Jesus rejected the notion, however, that the "good life" is to be found in the abun-dance of possessions (Lk. 12:15). Instead, the "good life" is to be found in following Christ. Such a life results not in the hoarding of material wealth, but rather in sharing it so that others may have enough. Acts 1–5 reveals that this became the model for what amounted to the first Christian com-munity in Jerusalem. They distributed their possessions "as they had need" (Acts 2:45). Paul also emphasized the relation of abundance to sufficiency: "God is able to provide you with every blessing in abundance, so that you may always have enough" (2 Cor. 9:8).

The norm of sufficiency is also supported by biblical and theological understandings of wealth, consumption, and sharing. Two general and not altogether compatible attitudes dominate biblical writings on wealth and consumption. On the one hand there is a qualified appreciation of wealth, on the other a call to freedom from possessions that sometimes borders on deep suspicion.[7] The Hebrew scriptures generally take the side of appreciating wealth, praising the rich who are just and placing a high estimate on riches gained through honest work.

Both sides are found in the teachings of Jesus. The announcement of the coming community of God carries with it a call for unparalleled righteousness, freedom from possessions, and complete trust in God. The service of God and the service of riches are incompatible (Mt. 6:24; Mk. 8:36, 9:43–48, 10:17–25; Lk. 12:15, 8:14, 11:18–23, 19:1–10). Jesus himself had no possessions and prodded his disciples into the renunciation of possessions and what later has been called "holy poverty," that is, poverty that is freely chosen as a way of life (Mt. 8:20; Mk. 1:16, 6:8f.; Lk. 9:3, 10:4).

On the other side Jesus took for granted the owning of property and was apparently supported by women of means (Lk. 8:2). He urged that possessions be used to help those in need (Lk. 6:30, 8:2f., 10:38f.). He was fond of celebrations, talking often about feasts in the community of God.

The biblical witness on consumption follows much the same pattern. The basic issue has been between self-denial and contentment with a moderate level of consumption.[8] The side of self-denial evolved into the monastic movement of later ages. The way of moderation is expressed well in I Timothy 6:6–8: "There is great gain in godliness with contentment; for we brought nothing into the world, and cannot take anything out of the world; but if you have food and clothing, with these we shall be content."

Sharing is an implication of neighbor love, hoarding a sign of selfishness and sin. Jesus repeatedly calls his disciples to give of themselves, even to the point of giving all they have to the poor. He shares bread and wine with them at the Last Supper. Paul in several letters urges Christians elsewhere to share with those in the Jerusalem community.

Sufficiency and sustainability are linked, for what the ethic of ecological justice seeks to sustain is the material and spiritual wherewithal to satisfy the basic needs of all forms of life. They are also linked through the increasing realization that present levels of human consumption, especially in affluent countries, are more than sufficient and in many respects are unsustainable. Only an ethic and practice that stresses sufficiency, frugality, and generosity will ensure a sustainable future.

Finally, the norm of sufficiency offers an excellent example of how human ethics is being extended to nature. The post-World War II stress on economic growth has been anthropocentric. Economists and politicians have been preoccupied by human sufficiency. The anthropocentric focus of most Christian traditions reinforced this preoccupation.

With increasing environmental awareness, however, this preoccupation no longer seems appropriate. And while other species are not equipped to practice frugality or simplicity, indeed to be ethical at all in a human sense, the norm of sufficiency does apply to humans in how they relate to other species. To care is to practice restraint. Humans should be frugal and share resources with plants and animals because they count in the eyes of God. All of creation is good and deserves ethical consideration. The focus on sufficiency is part of what it means to practice justice.

Participation

The norm of participation likewise stems from the affirmation of all forms of life and the call to justice. This affirmation and this call lead to the respect and inclusion of all forms of life in human decisions that affect their well-being. Voices should be heard, and, if not able to speak, which is the case for other species, then humans will have to represent their interests when those interests are at stake.[9] Participation is concerned with empowerment and seeks to remove the obstacles to participating in decisions that affect lives.

The norm of participation is also grounded in the two creation accounts in Genesis. These accounts emphasize the value of everything in God's creation and the duty of humans to recognize the interest of all by acting as good stewards. Through their emphasis on humanity's creation in the image of God, the writers of Genesis underline the value of human life and the equality of women and men.

The prophets brought sharp condemnation upon kings and the people of Israel for violating the covenant by neglecting the interests of the poor and vulnerable. They repudiated actions that disempowered people through the loss of land, corruption, theft, slavery, and militarism. The prophets spoke for those who had no voice and could no longer participate in the decisions that affected their lives (Am. 2:6–7; Is. 3:2–15; Hos. 10:12–14).

With Jesus comes a new emphasis, the kingdom or community of God (Mk. 1:14–15). While the community of God is not to be equated to any community of human beings, it nevertheless is related. It serves as a general model for human communities and is to some degree realizable, although never totally.

The community of God has its source in a different kind of power, God's power of love and justice. This power alone is capable of producing genuine and satisfying human communities and right relations to nature's communities. The community of God cannot be engineered. Technology, material consumption, and economic growth may enhance human power, but offer little help in developing participatory communities. Reliance on these powers alone can in fact make matters worse by creating divisions.

Jesus also stressed the beginning of the community of God in small things, such as seeds that grow. He gathered a community largely of the poor and needy. He gave and found support in a small inner group of disciples. In this day of complex technologies, large corporations that dominate globalization, and mammoth bureaucracies, Jesus' stress seems out of place to many. In their pell-mell rush to increase the size and complexity of social organizations and technological processes, humans are missing something, however. For effective community and participation, size counts and must be limited in order for individuals to have significant and satisfying contacts.

The concern for the poor evident in the Gospels is another support for the norm of participation. Without some semblance of justice there can be little participation in community. Extremes of wealth and poverty and disproportions of power create an envious and angry underclass without a stake in the community. Equality of worth, rough equality of power, and political freedom are prerequisites for genuine communities.

In the early church small communities flourished. The Jerusalem church, while poor, had a remarkable sense of sharing. Paul's letter to the Romans contains perhaps the most ideal statement of community ever written (Rom. 12). He also talked about the church as the body of Christ. It has many members, all of whom are united in Christ. Differences between Jew and Greek, male and female, slave and free are unimportant (Gal. 3:28). He repeatedly used the Greek word *koinonia,* rich in communal connotations, to describe the house churches he established.

All this is not to romanticize the early church. There was enough conflict to avoid sentimentalizing the notion of participation. It is difficult, the more so in industrialized societies even with their full range of communications, to achieve participatory communities. A multitude of decisions each requiring expert technical judgments and having wide-ranging consequences must be made in a timely way. Popular participation in decisions, especially when there is conflict as is in most environmental disputes, can paralyze essential processes. Expedience often results in the exclusion of certain voices and interests. Impersonal, functional ways of relating become easy and further reduce participation.

The norm of participation calls for a reversal of this trend. At minimum it means having a voice in critical decisions that affect one's life. For environmental problems it means having a say, for example, in the selection of energy and resource systems, the technologies these systems incorporate, and the distribution of benefits and burdens these systems create. All this implies free and open elections, democratic forms of government, responsible economic institutions, and a substantial dose of good will.

Finally there is the difficult problem of how to bring other species and ecosystems into human decision-making. In one sense they are already included since there is no way to exclude them. Humans are inextricably part of nature, and many human decisions have environmental consequences that automatically include other species and ecosystems. The problem is the large number of negative consequences that threaten entire species and systems and ultimately the human species, for humans are dependent on other species and functioning ecosystems. The task is to reduce and eliminate where possible these negative consequences. One reason is obviously pragmatic. Humans are fouling their own nests. Beyond this anthropocentric reason, however, it helps to see plants, animals, and their communities as having interests that humans should respect. They have a dignity of their own kind. They experience pleasure and pain. The norm of participation should be extended to include these interests and to relieve pain, in effect to give other species a voice. Humans have an obligation to speak out for other forms of life that cannot defend themselves.

Solidarity

The norm of solidarity reinforces this inclusion as well as adding an important element to the inclusion of marginalized human beings. The norm of solidarity emphasizes the kinship and interdependence of all forms of life and encourages support and assistance for those who suffer. The norm highlights the communal nature of life in contrast to individualism and encourages individuals and groups to join in common cause with those who are victims of discrimination, abuse, and oppression. Underscoring the reciprocal relationship of individual welfare and the common good, solidarity calls for the powerful to share the plight of the powerless, for the rich to listen to the poor, and for humanity to recognize its fundamental interdependence with the rest of nature. The virtues of humility, compassion, courage, and generosity are all marks of the norm of solidarity.

Both creation accounts in Genesis emphasize the profound relationality of all of God's creation. These two accounts point to the fundamental social and ecological context of existence. Humanity was created for community. This is the foundation of solidarity. While all forms of creation are unique, they are all related to each other as part of God's creation.

Understood in this context and in relation to the concept of stewardship in the Gospels, the *imago dei* tradition that has its origins in Genesis also serves as a foundation for solidarity. Creation in the image of God places humans not in a position over or apart from creation but rather in the same loving relationship of God with creation. Just as God breathes life into the world (Gen. 7), humanity is given the special responsibility as God's stewards to nurture and sustain life.

In their descriptions of Jesus' life and ministry, the Gospels provide the clearest examples of compassionate solidarity. Jesus shows solidarity with the poor and oppressed; he eats with sinners, drinks from the cup of a gentile woman, meets with outcasts, heals lepers, and consistently speaks truth to power. Recognizing that Jesus was the model of solidarity, Paul used the metaphor of the body of Christ to emphasize the continuation of this solidarity within the Christian community. Writing to the Christians in Corinth, Paul stresses that by virtue of their baptisms they are all one "in Christ." Thus if one member suffers, all suffer together; if one member is honored, all rejoice together (1 Cor. 12:26). It would be hard to find a better metaphor to describe the character of compassionate solidarity.

The norm of solidarity also finds its home in a theology of the cross. The cross is the central symbol in Christianity. It points to a God who works in the world not in terms of power *over* but power *in, with, and under*. This is revolutionary. It upsets normal ways of conceiving power. God suffers with all living things that groan in travail (Rom. 8). In the words of Jesus: "The last shall be first, and the first shall be last" (Mt. 19:30; Mk. 10:31; Lk. 13:30). The one who "was in the form of God . . . emptied himself, taking the form of a servant" (Phil. 2:6–7). The implication is clear. Christians are called to suffer with each other and the rest of the creation, to change their ways, and to enter a new life of solidarity and action to preserve and protect the entire creation.

CONCLUSION

While other norms will find their way into the commentaries on the cases in this volume, the ethic of ecological justice as outlined here is the normative perspective that informs and guides what follows. Based on the relationship of faith to a loving God and grounded in sensitivity to and appreciation of nature, this ethic is focused on current environmental challenges. It is derived from historical Christian traditions, finds its context in current social and environmental situations, and looks to the future with a sense of inclusive justice, expectation, and hope.

Notes

1. This is the so-called Lynn White, Jr., thesis. It has received considerable critical attention. See, for example: James A. Nash. *Loving Nature: Ecological Integrity and Christian Responsibility* (Nashville: Abingdon Press, 1991), Chapter 3. Steven Bouma-Prediger, *For the Beauty of the Earth: A Christian Vision for Creation Care* (Grand Rapids: Baker Book House Co., 2001), Chapter 3.

2. Sallie McFague, *Super, Natural Christians: How We Should Love Nature* (Minneapolis: Fortress Press, 1997), Chapter 2.

3. See, for example, Presbyterian Eco-Justice Task Force, *Keeping and Healing the Creation* (Louisville: Committee on Social Witness Policy, Presbyterian Church [USA], 1989); Evangelical Lutheran Church in America, *Caring for Creation: Vision, Hope, and Justice* (Chicago: Division for Church and Society, 1993).

4. James Martin-Schramm, "Toward an Ethic of EcoJustice," in Paul T. Jersild et al., eds. *Moral Issues and Christian Response* (Fort Worth: Harcourt Brace College Publishers, 1998), pp. 208–212. This ethic has antecedents in World Council of Churches discussions in the 1970s. The Fifth Assembly of the World Council of Churches in 1975 emphasized the need to create a "just, participatory, and sustainable society." A follow-up conference in 1979 entitled *Faith, Science, and the Future* gave explicit attention to the norms of sustainability, sufficiency, participation, and solidarity. See Paul Abrecht, ed., *Faith, Science, and the Future* (Geneva: World Council of Churches, 1978); and Roger L. Shinn, ed., *Faith and Science in an Unjust World* (Geneva: World Council of Churches, 1978). In 1983 the Sixth Assembly of the WCC challenged all of its member communities to strive for the integration of justice, peace, and the integrity of creation. This emphasis continued with the theme of the Seventh Assembly in 1990, *Come Holy Spirit—Renew Your Whole Creation.*

5. Sallie McFague, *Super, Natural Christians*, pp. 172ff.; and Rosemary Radford Reuther, *Gaia and God: An Ecofeminist Theology of Earth Healing* (San Francisco: HarperSanFrancisco, 1992). Chapter 9.

6. See the Commentary for the Case *Rigor and Responsibility* for a more extended discussion of sufficiency. Also, James Nash, "Toward the Revival and Reform of the Subversive Virtue: Frugality," in *The Annual of the Society of Christian Ethics* (1995).

7. Martin Hengel, *Property and Riches in the Early Church* (Philadelphia: Fortress Press, 1974), especially Chapters 2, 3, and 9.

8. Martin Hengel, *Property and Riches in the Early Church*, Chapters 7 and 8.

9. How far to extend moral considerability to other species is a controversial issue. So too is the issue of moral significance. See James Nash, *Loving Nature*, 179ff.

For Further Reading

Boff, Leonardo. *Ecology and Liberation: A New Paradigm*. Translated by John Cumming. Maryknoll: Orbis Books, 1994.

Bouma-Prediger, Steven. *For the Beauty of the Earth: A Christian Vision for Creation Care*. Grand Rapids: Baker Academic, 2001.

DeWitt, Calvin. *Caring for Creation: Responsible Stewardship of God's Handiwork*. Grand Rapids: Baker Books, 1998.

Gustafson, James. *A Sense of the Divine: The Natural Environment from a Theocentric Perspective*. Cleveland: Pilgrim Press, 1994.

Hall, Douglas John. *The Steward: A Biblical Symbol Come of Age*. New York and Grand Rapids: Friendship Press and Eerdmans Publishing Company, 1990.

———. *Imaging God: Dominion as Stewardship*. Grand Rapids: Eerdmans, 1986.

Haught, John F. *God After Darwin: A Theology of Evolution*. Boulder, CO: Westview Press, 2000.

Hessel, Dieter, ed. *Theology for Earth Community*. Maryknoll: Orbis Books, 1996.

Hessel, Dieter and Rasmussen, Larry R., eds. *Earth Habitat: Eco-Justice and the Church's Response*. Minneapolis: Fortress Press, 2001.

Hessel, Dieter and Ruether, Rosemary Radford, eds. *Christianity and Ecology: Seeking the Well-Being of Earth and Humans*. Cambridge: Harvard University Center for the Study of World Religions, 2000.

La Chance, Albert and Carroll, John E., eds. *Embracing Earth: Catholic Approaches to Ecology*. Maryknoll: Orbis Books, 1994.

McDaniel, Jay B. *Of God and Pelicans: A Theology of Reverence for Life*. Louisville: Westminster/John Knox Press, 1989.

McFague, Sallie, *Life Abundant: Rethinking Theology and Economy for a Planet in Peril*. Minneapolis: Fortress Press, 2001.

———. *Super, Natural Christians: How We Should Love Nature*. Minneapolis: Fortress Press, 1997.

———. *The Body of God*. Minneapolis: Fortress Press, 1993.

Nash, James. *Loving Nature: Ecological Integrity and Christian Responsibility*. Nashville: Abingdon Press, 1991.

Rasmussen, Larry R. *Earth Community, Earth Ethics*. Maryknoll: Orbis Books, 1996.

Ruether, Rosemary Radford. *Gaia & God: An Ecofeminist Theology for Earth Healing*. San Francisco: HarperSanFrancisco, 1992.

Rolston, Holmes, III. *Environmental Ethics: Duties to and Values in the Natural World*. Philadelphia: Temple University Press, 1988.

Santmire, H. Paul. *Nature Reborn: The Ecological and Cosmic Promise of Christian Theology*. Minneapolis: Augsburg Fortress Press, 2000.

Solle, Dorothee. *The Silent Cry: Mysticism and Resistance*. Minneapolis: Fortress Press, 2001.

3

Case Studies and Moral Deliberation

Christian ethical reflection is rooted in and motivated by Christian faith. Doing has its foundation in being. The previous chapter outlined an ethic of ecological justice that flows from being in love with God, self, others, and nature. This chapter focuses on implementing this ethic of ecological justice by putting faith into action and doing the works of love. In particular, this chapter examines the utility of the case-study approach to environmental ethics and proposes a method to engage in moral deliberation about the cases in this volume.

Case studies ground Christian ethical reflection in reality. At the heart of Christian ethics are broad injunctions expressed in simple phrases like "love your neighbor" (Mt. 22:39), "do justice" (Mic. 6:8), and "till and keep the garden" (Gen. 2:15). The problem is not identifying these norms so much as it is applying them to different situations. While many situations are similar, different details and relationships make for exceptional circumstances, conflicting norms, and moral ambiguity. Case studies are an effective tool for moral deliberation because they provide an opportunity to bring ethical resources from diverse Christian traditions to bear on specific situations with all their differences.

Pedagogically, there are several advantages to the case-study approach. Moral deliberation about specific cases tends to produce a greater degree of engaged learning than general, theoretical reflection about broad topics or issues. All of the cases in this volume are based on real situations where individuals or groups have been faced with difficult ethical choices. Readers engaged in ethical reflection about these cases have to decide how the problems should best be resolved. Theoretical discussions become concrete when a decision has to be made. There are no places to hide. The case-study approach requires a significant degree of accountability for one's ethical convictions.

Case studies promote engaged learning in other ways as well. The setting and circumstances of a case often require readers to enter foreign territory as they step into the shoes of various characters. These unfamiliar situations stimulate moral reflection in ways that familiar settings and problems do not. In addition, the use of cases in classroom settings encourages students to *apply* what they have learned in a course. In a case-study approach, learning is not measured by how much information a student has been able to store up, but rather by how well a student can use that information to do ethics. This is a more complex, and therefore more challenging task. Also, the discussion of cases can promote engaged learning as participants actively share their views with each other. Facilitated properly, discussion about cases can produce a community of moral discourse where all are engaged in ethical reflection.

Another advantage of the case-study approach is that cases provide a setting to observe relationships between individuals and communities. Communities shape moral character, establish boundaries, produce loyalties, and create frameworks of accountability. Families normally serve as the most important community in moral formation, but peer groups, fellow students, co-workers, civic groups, religious organizations, and branches of the armed services are also examples of communities that shape the values and influence the choices of individuals. Case studies provide a means to examine ways communities influence individuals faced with important moral decisions. Often these communities produce mixed loyalties in individuals, thus complicating already difficult situations. For example, in *Sustaining Dover,* it is one thing for the owner of a local business to have an opinion about a new commercial development that would produce urban sprawl, but another thing when the same merchant is elected to public office and given the responsibility to promote the welfare of the community as a whole. Duties to communities can constrain the range of an individual's choices.

Cases also provide a way to see how individuals can shape and reform the values of the communities to which they are accountable. In fact, the values and ethical standards of communities change only when they are required to do so by forces from without or individuals from within. For example, two cases in this volume feature characters faced with choices that could lead them to "swim against the tide" in order to protect old growth forests or endangered species as they call their communities to live up to the values they cherish. These case studies reveal that ethical decisions are required of *both* individuals *and* communities.

This focus on ethical decision-making leads to another advantage of case studies. Insofar as moral deliberation about cases requires an individual or group to think through and render ethical judgments, the case study method contributes to moral development. Obviously, character is shaped most significantly when the fires of experience test it, but not all lessons need to be learned the hard way. Case studies allow passions to be informed by reason and values to be clarified through judgments. Such ethical reflection can better prepare a person or a group for hard decisions that will eventually crop up in their lives.

The case-study method is flexible and can be used in a variety of ways. The cases and commentaries in this volume were written with this in mind. In some situations, the reading of a case alone will be sufficient to stimulate moral deliberation about the issues posed. This would be true in settings like Sunday morning adult forums or in academic classrooms where the discussion about a case may simply inaugurate a new unit in a course. In other situations, readers of a case can extend the depth of their moral reflection by reading the accompanying commentary. The commentaries provide background information and identify normative elements within Christian traditions that may be helpful to those who are making ethical judgments about the case. In academic settings, students might demonstrate this depth of ethical reflection in brief papers in which they wrestle with the issues and propose a resolution to the case, or in term papers that reach conclusions by drawing on the fruits of additional research. Since ethical decisions are made not only by individuals, groups of students could also be assigned to a case and asked to reach consensus about how it should best be resolved.

CASE STUDIES AND MORAL DELIBERATION: A THREE-STAGE METHOD

In these and other ways, there are several advantages to using case studies to stimulate ethical reflection. Moral deliberation is most effective, however, when it is guided or structured in a particular way. This chapter offers a method that consists of three stages: Analysis, Assessment, and Action (see Figure 1). Factors related to each of these stages are illustrated by referencing cases in this volume. In addition, the appendix to this volume includes specific guidelines for ways this three-stage method can be used in classroom settings to structure moral deliberation about cases in written assignments and group presentations.

Figure 1. Case Studies and Moral Deliberation: A Three-Stage Method

ANALYSIS

Personal Factors
Power Dynamics
Factual Information
Complicating Factors
Relationships
Ethical Issue(s)
Alternatives and Consequences

ACTION

Justification
Viability
Strategy
Reflection

ASSESSMENT

Vision and
Imagination
Moral Norms
Moral Theories
Ethical Assessment

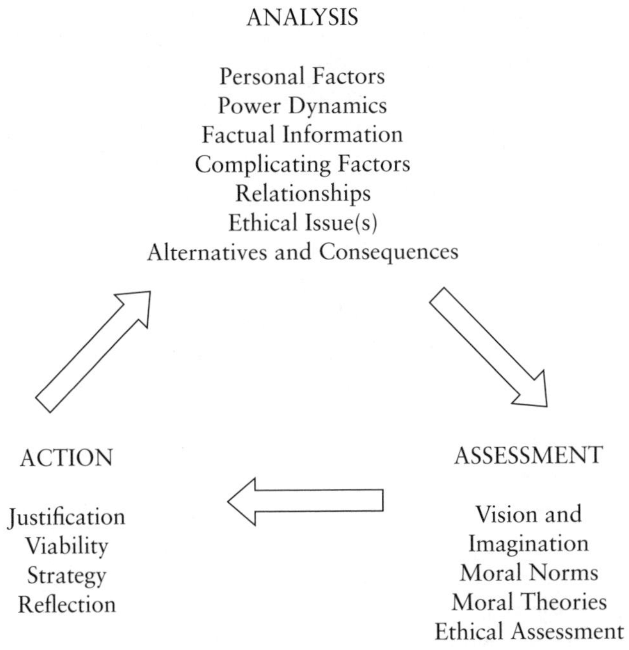

Stage I: Analysis

Good ethics depends on good information. Since ethical situations are always contextual, it is not possible to know what one ought to do until more is known about the circumstances that have produced an ethical problem. Norms like love, justice, and stewardship certainly exist to guide moral behavior, but varying circumstances often require that these principles be employed differently. In the Old Testament, the Ten Commandments are followed by a series of ethical injunctions that helped the ancient Israelites determine how these broad commandments should be interpreted in specific situations (Ex. 20:1–23:33). For example, consequences of violating the broad commandment "You shall not steal" (Ex. 20:15) are described in relationship to typical agrarian problems: "When someone causes a field or vineyard to be grazed over, or lets livestock loose to graze in someone else's field, restitution shall be made from the best in the owner's field or vineyard" (Ex. 22:5). In the New Testament, the Apostle Paul tells the church in Corinth that they are all freed from having to follow various aspects of Jewish dietary law by virtue of their justification through faith in Christ. Yet he encourages them not to eat meat offered to idols if other members of the community thought that by doing so they were engaging in the worship of false gods (1 Cor. 8:1–13). For Paul, circumstances mattered and ethics had to be adjusted accordingly. There are several factors to consider when analyzing a case that is rooted in a specific set of circumstances.

Personal Factors

A starting point is with the person doing the analysis. All knowledge is filtered through the lens of personal experience and perception. These experiences, or lack thereof, do not necessarily *determine* the stance a person will take with regard to an ethical issue, but they will *influence* to some degree a person's analysis of the situation and assessment of the moral problem. Thus, it is helpful at the outset to reflect on ways one's personal experience may affect moral deliberation about the case. For example, in *Rigor and Responsibility,* David Trapp is not sure it would be morally just to build a modest lake cabin when so many in the world have no roof over their heads. For those who have grown up with such cabins and have fond memories of them, it may be difficult to grasp David's moral anguish or even perceive that an ethical problem exists. Those who have experienced homelessness or significant poverty, however, may sympathize with David and find it hard to understand why his wife is so willing to build the cabin. Again, these different experiences in life would not necessarily determine one's view about whether the construction would reflect good stewardship of resources, but it is reasonable that these experiences could influence the way a person analyses and assesses the case.

It can also matter if a person has something at stake with regard to the issues raised in a case. Those engaged in agriculture may sympathize with

Warren Hughes and other ranchers in *Taking on Water* who have lost farm income after government agencies imposed restrictions on their use of private property in order to protect endangered species. Those who champion the welfare of all species and prize wilderness areas may be less sympathetic to the cries of unjust treatment by the ranchers, especially if they do not have anything at stake financially in the resolution of the case. Vested interests can influence the way a person analyzes and assesses a case.

Consideration of personal factors is a good first step in the analysis of a case because it is helpful to become aware of any biases that may exist at the outset. These initial biases may be justified or rejected later during the assessment and action stages, but in an effort to be objective and fair, it is important to identify these factors as best one can in order to determine whether they play a significant role in moral deliberation. Friends and communities can help individuals overcome blindness to these biases.

Power Dynamics

Another important factor to consider when analyzing a case is the distribution of power between key players or stakeholders. Ethics is largely a pointless enterprise if those engaged in moral deliberation do not have the power they need to put their values into action. In ethics, this ability to implement ethical decisions is referred to as *moral agency*. It is helpful to identify the main characters or forces of power in a case and then develop a diagram that sketches the power dynamics between them. Do some individuals or groups harbor more power than others? Are they in a position of control over others? Do factors like poverty, ignorance, or race function in ways to disempower key players or stakeholders in the case? Questions like these help to diagram the power dynamics in a case.

Groups engaged in moral reflection about a case may want to develop three-dimensional diagrams by creating "human sculptures" to probe the significance that the distribution of power has in a case (see Appendix). In classroom settings, these sculptures tap into the creativity of students and allow them to step into a case physically in order to identify with certain characters or institutions in the case. It is one thing to look at a diagram that uses names or boxes to identify forces of power and arrows to indicate the power dynamics at play. It is another thing to see a person in a supine position with the foot of another on his or her chest, or to probe the complexity of power dynamics through the positioning of various individuals or representatives of institutions in a limited space. When shared with others, these diagrams and sculptures help identify forces that empower or disempower key players or stakeholders. They can also expose whose voices are heard or not heard within the case. Sometimes they help identify key stakeholders or forces that are invisible in the case as it is presented.

Skull Valley is a case that has complicated power dynamics. The case revolves around a small Native American tribe and an agreement their leadership has signed to store spent nuclear fuel above ground on a portion of their reservation in Utah for up to forty years. This agreement with a consortium of electric utilities that produce nuclear power has to be approved by the Nuclear Regulatory Commission. In addition, the Bureau of Indian Affairs has to review the terms of the lease agreement to determine whether it is in the best interests of the tribe. Utah's political leaders are bitterly opposed to the project, but claim to be locked out of the decision-making process because treaties require the tribe to deal solely with the federal government. At the same time, the county that surrounds the reservation has signed a fairly lucrative contract with the utility consortium to provide various emergency services to the storage facility. On the reservation, the leadership of the tribe is disputed as rival factions claim to have been duly elected by the people. The lead character in the case, Deb Groenlund, feels torn. On the one hand she wants to support the sovereignty of the tribe. On the other hand, she fears this storage facility may be an egregious example of environmental racism. As the director of the Lutheran Advocacy Ministry in Utah, she is not sure if she should publicly support or oppose the project. She also wonders whether her Native American ancestry plays any role in shaping her perspective. This is a complex case where time spent diagramming or sculpting the power dynamics would be helpful.

Factual Information

Power dynamics often play a major role in disputes about facts in a case. In order to do good analysis, it is imperative that factual information be understood as completely as possible. A good first step is to examine any historical roots to the problem. In *Market Mountain Takeover,* a conflict over the logging of old growth forests is precipitated by a land swap between the U.S. Forest Service and a major logging company. Federal agencies have negotiated these land swaps in order to rectify problems associated with a "checkerboard" of land ownership that developed in the nineteenth century after the federal government gave sections of land to railroad companies to entice them to develop unsettled lands. For each section that was given to the railroads, the one adjacent was kept as federal land. While this policy may have served the best interests of the nation at the time, today this checkerboard of land ownership presents a variety of problems for the owners of private property and the government agencies charged with managing federal lands and wilderness areas. Understanding the history of this phenomenon is central to the case.

A second step in the analysis of factual information is to determine which facts are in dispute. Facts are contested in virtually all of the cases in this volume. For example, in *Skull Valley* the governor of Utah disputes findings by the Nuclear Regulatory Commission that claim the temporary storage of spent nuclear fuel within forty-five miles of Salt Lake City will not pose a significant threat to human health. Similarly, in *Harvesting Controversy,* opponents of genetically modified crops insist that these crops pose unacceptable threats to human and ecological health. In *Sustainable Energy Futures,* disputes about the extent and consequences of global warming complicate analysis of different energy paths the United States could take. In all of these cases, it is interesting to examine the relationship between disputed facts and the power dynamics at work.

A case with few facts in dispute is *Market Mountain Takeover*. Unless something changes, there is no question that parcels of old growth forest will be harvested as a part of a land swap. Here analysis needs to give attention to the way different worldviews and theoretical assumptions affect the way that characters in the case grapple with key facts. Every person uses various theories to organize factual information and knowledge. In turn, these theories and facts are perceived through broad worldviews and perspectives. Normally, people do not spend much time consciously reflecting about the theoretical framework that gives structure and meaning to their lives. Worldviews work best when they function invisibly in the background to provide coherence and structure to life. The problem comes when unexamined assumptions blind a person to other perspectives. Problems also arise when certain assumptions wind up being wrong or unproductive. Therefore, it is helpful to analyze the worldviews and broad theoretical frameworks used by key players in cases. It is also important to reflect on the way that theories and worldviews shape the *reader's* analysis of facts in a case.

Chapter Two identifies general attitudes toward nature that have played an important role in shaping the worldview of many people. The chapter also outlines four theoretical perspectives that influence the interpretation of factual information in cases dealing with environmental ethics. All four of these perspectives are at play in *Market Mountain Takeover*. The logging company reflects a *developmentalist* perspective, two different environmental groups each operate out of either a *conservationist* or a *preservationist* perspective, and the group of young tree-sitters operates from a *critical eco-justice* perspective. It is no wonder that major disagreements exist because all have very different assumptions about the relationship of humanity and nature. Good analysis of any case means giving attention to the way that different perspectives shape interpretation of the facts.

Complicating Factors

Power dynamics, theories, and worldviews are not the only things that make analysis difficult. Sometimes important information is unavailable, unfamiliar, or very complex. For example, *Chlorine Sunset* confronts readers with various problems associated with organochlorines and persistent organic pollutants. Similarly, *Harvesting Controversy* forces readers to grapple with the complicated science behind genetically modified crops. For those who lack a significant background in chemistry or genetics, it will require additional effort to understand important aspects of these cases. The same can be said for the legal issues in *Taking on Water*. In ethics, however, challenges associated with interdisciplinary work are unavoidable. It is precisely because ethical problems exist in the complexities of real life that good analysis will require grappling with unfamiliar, incomplete, or complicated information.

Relationships

Another factor that can complicate a case are relational or character dimensions that may influence the choices facing key players or stakeholders. In *Taking on Water*, Warren Hughes has a son who would love to take over the family ranch after finishing college. This appears to be one reason Warren is not keen on "selling out" to developers, even though this would be one way to deal with the reduction of irrigation water that has been the result of restrictions imposed under the Endangered Species Act. It does not appear that the case will turn on this relational dimension, but it does seem to complicate things for Warren. A similar situation exists in *Harvesting Controversy* when Karen Lindstrom has to decide whether to risk losing a friendship by voting to join a Greenpeace campaign that seeks to ban genetically modified crops. While some may see this as a complicating factor in the case, others may perceive the threat to a friendship as the primary moral problem that needs to be addressed.

Ethical Issue(s)

The fact that people differ in terms of what they perceive to be a moral problem leads to the next step in the analysis of a case: Identification of the primary ethical issue that needs to be resolved. This step is crucial, of course, because it determines the set of alternatives that will be analyzed and assessed in the next phases of moral deliberation. In some cases, there may be more than one ethical issue that needs to be resolved. Those who analyze *Harvesting Controversy* from the perspective of Karen Lindstrom may not be able to divorce their ethical assessment of genetically modified crops from the impact this view could have on Karen's friendship with Josephine Omondi, a Kenyan student and ardent advocate for genetically modified agriculture in poor, developing nations.

More often, however, legitimate distinctions can be made between what constitutes the primary ethical problem in the case and other secondary problems that may justifiably receive less attention. In *Rigor and Responsibility*, the primary ethical issue appears to be whether the construction of a lake cabin constitutes good stewardship of limited resources. A secondary ethical issue revolves around how the Trapp family will make this decision and what role the children will have in the process.

In most of the cases in this volume, the primary ethical issue centers on a choice that must be made in the near future. In *Market Mountain Takeover*, however, the ethical issue is framed more in terms of whether an action was morally justified in the past. Here the question appears to be whether the tactics employed by tree-sitters are morally justifiable in order to prevent the cutting of old growth timber. In all cases, the definition of the primary moral problem is key.

Alternatives and Consequences

Once the primary ethical issue has been identified, the last step in the analysis stage is to identify the options that exist to address this problem. Equally important is an analysis of the likely consequences associated with each option. Who will reap the benefits and bear the costs of each alternative? Alternatives that benefit a few at the expense of many, or benefit many at the expense of a few, deserve close scrutiny. Careful identification of alternatives and consideration of consequences are necessary in order to engage in ethical assessment of these options: the second stage of moral deliberation.

Sometimes the options appear to be few. For example, in *Sustaining Dover*, John Yeoman has to decide as a member of the City Council how he will vote on a landfill and rezoning request by Wal-Mart that would permit construction of a new Supercenter in an area currently zoned as a flood plain. The case and commentary describe the likely consequences of a vote in favor or against the project.

Other cases present several alternatives. In *Taking on Water*, Warren Hughes considers four courses of action he could recommend to the shareholders of the Mazama Ditch Company. They can sue the federal government, sell out to developers, invest in ditch efficiency technologies, or simply make do with less water. For reasons described in the case and commentary, however, the consequences of each option are less clear. Nevertheless, as president of the company, Warren is obligated to inform his fellow shareholders about the possible risks and rewards associated with these alternatives.

Stage II: Assessment

After the preparatory work is completed, a case is ready for ethical assessment. In this second stage of moral deliberation, each alternative and its related consequences are assessed in light of relevant moral norms. There are several factors to consider.

Ethical Vision and Moral Imagination

Just as theories shape the interpretation of facts, key stories, concepts, and ideas provide an ethical vision of the way life should be on Earth. Meta-narratives like the account in Genesis of God's rainbow covenant with Noah and all living things, or guiding principles like the concept of stewardship not only point toward an ideal, they stimulate imaginative ways to better achieve or reflect this vision. This volume extols a theocentric worldview that grounds Christian ethical vision and moral imagination in the cosmic love of God. The earth-embracing ethic rooted in this love is expressed in several aspects of diverse Christian traditions described in the preceding chapter and in the case commentaries. In this initial phase of ethical assessment, it is helpful to consider which aspects of Christian tradition shape one's view about how moral issues in a case should be resolved.

Moral Norms

These sources of ethical vision and imagination find expression in various moral norms. In ethics, norms refer to broad directives that provide guidance for a moral life. Norms help determine what one ought to do in a particular situation. In general, Christian ethical reflection has revolved around two basic moral norms: love and justice. These norms are touched on throughout this volume, particularly in the *Taking on Water* commentary. Much of this book, however, explores the ecological applicability of love and justice through their expression in an ethic of ecological justice and its four related norms: sustainability, sufficiency, participation, and solidarity.

Summarized elsewhere, these ecojustice norms help guide ethical assessment of alternatives in a case. For example, the commentary for *Sustainable Energy Futures* assesses components of President Bush's national energy plan in light of sustainability, sufficiency, participation, and solidarity. Similarly, the commentary for *Sustaining Dover* examines the relevance of these norms for assessing the social and ecological issues that surround the construction of a Wal-Mart Supercenter on a parcel of land that encroaches upon a flood plain.

On the face of it, the application of these ecojustice norms to issues in environmental ethics seems fairly straightforward. Often, however, ethical issues arise because these norms can be interpreted differently. In *Skull Valley*, Deb Groenlund wrestles with the norm of participation. On the one hand, she wants to support the tribal sovereignty of the Skull Valley Band of the Goshute Nation and their decision to host a facility for the temporary storage of spent nuclear fuel rods. On the other hand, she sympathizes with the people of Utah who feel locked out of a decision that could have a significant impact on their lives. In this case, the norm of participation cuts both ways.

In other cases, ethical issues arise because at least two of the ecojustice norms come into conflict with each other. For example, the norms of sustainability and sufficiency appear to collide in *Harvesting Controversy*. Crops that have been genetically modified to be resistant to pests and disease have the potential to boost food production significantly in poor, agrarian nations, but there are reasonable concerns about the ecological and social consequences of genetically modified crops. How should concerns about ecological sustainability be balanced with concerns about achieving sufficient food security for malnourished people? The answer to this question is not self-evident, but somehow the apparent conflict between sustainability and sufficiency needs to be reconciled.

There are also occasions when ecojustice norms come into conflict with other social norms. Economically, many subscribe to the maxim, "growth is good." Several characters in *Sustaining Dover* appeal to the norm of sustainability to challenge this normative assumption that economic growth is always beneficial. Because urban sprawl produces habitat degradation and imperils the distinctive quality of communities, a commitment to sustainability may require limits to economic growth.

Legal norms can also influence ethical assessment. It is tempting in ethics to hide behind the law. Laws often reflect the ethical viewpoint of the majority, but just because something is legal does not necessarily make it moral. The laws of the nation and the decisions of a court may be binding, but they may not be ethical. For example, it is possible in *Taking on Water* that Warren Hughes and his fellow ranchers may lose any "takings" case they file against the federal government. Those appealing to the norm of solidarity, however, may still side with the ranchers and argue that the financial burden of species conservation has fallen unfairly on a few.

Finally, ecojustice norms can come into conflict with other deeply held religious and philosophical convictions. For example, much of the religious opposition to genetic engineering is based on a concern that it violates the God-given *sanctity* of life. A smaller group of religious voices champions a limited use of genetic engineering to improve the *quality* of life, especially for human beings. Moral reflection about sustainability and sufficiency in *Harvesting Controversy* must come to terms with the way these norms may be utilized by those who wish to protect the sanctity of life or improve its quality. In all cases, ethical assessment requires careful attention to the relevance of moral norms and the way they may conflict with each other and with other norms in society.

Moral Theory

After relevant moral norms have been identified and considered, another important step is to reflect on the role moral theory plays in ethical assessment. Whereas key stories or concepts provide ethical vision, spark moral imagination, and ground moral norms, moral theories help people decide how they will use these norms imaginatively to make decisions consistent with their ethical vision. There are three types of moral theory that are relevant to the cases in this volume.

Deontology In Greek, δεί (dei) means duty or obligation. Those who take a deontological approach to ethics find themselves obligated to obey an extrinsic authority. This authority can be grounded in a sacred text like the Bible, a document like the U.S. Constitution, or in individuals like elected officials and religious leaders. Deontologists feel compelled by duty to cling to these authorities and find it difficult to sacrifice related principles to expediency. Some options are beyond the pale of ethical consideration because they would transgress an authority or violate a principle or commandment. For deontologists the means must be consistent with the ends. Consistency is one of the main advantages to a deontological approach because the source of authority is extrinsic to the person making an ethical judgment. A weakness is that principled decisions often leave little room for compromise and sometimes can be made without calculating the consequences.

In *Harvesting Controversy*, Karen Lindstrom reflects a deontological perspective when she worries that genetic engineering violates boundaries established by God as the creator of all living things. In *Skull Valley*, Deb Groenlund considers defending at all costs the principle of tribal sovereignty even though the temporary storage of spent nuclear fuel above ground on the Goshute reservation could have disastrous consequences for the tribe and millions of others nearby. In *Taking on Water*, some ranchers make principled appeals to the Fifth Article of the U.S. Constitution which states that private property shall not be taken for public use without just compensation. In all of these cases, characters feel obligated to obey certain authorities or appeal to certain fundamental principles in order to determine the ethical propriety of their options.

Teleology In Greek, τελοσ (telos) means end or goal. Those who take a teleological approach to ethics are interested in achieving an end or maximizing a goal as much as possible. People differ, however, about the goals they seek and the ends they pursue. Some may wish simply to amass wealth and power in life, while others may seek to maximize the welfare of others, including other species. Not all ends or goals are morally desirable, however. For Christians, fundamental norms like love and justice guide evaluation of these ends or goals. Nevertheless, all teleologists weigh the costs and benefits of various alternatives as they figure out how to maximize the good they seek to achieve. For teleologists, the ends can justify the means. One of the strengths of this approach to moral theory is that it takes consequences seriously. A weakness is that teleological thinking can ride roughshod over others as it makes compromises in order to maximize the good.

In the arena of public policy, assessment of costs and benefits related to particular policy options is a type of teleological reasoning commonly employed. In *Sustainable Energy Futures* there are various costs and benefits associated with the United States' energy options. In *Sustaining Dover*, elected members of the city council have to weigh the goods and harms that may befall their community if they accept or reject Wal-Mart's request to have a portion of flood plain rezoned for commercial development. In *Harvesting Controversy*, students in a campus hunger concerns group have to assess the various costs and benefits associated with genetically modified crops in developing countries. One of the problems with the cost/benefit approach, however, is that it can be difficult to predict positive or negative consequences. This is clear in *Chlorine Sunrise*. In addition, cost/benefit analysis is normally done in economic terms, but there are some things that are hard to measure financially. For example, it is hard to put a value on the identity of a community, the aesthetic beauty of a river, or the variety of services an ecosystem provides. Nevertheless, good ethics requires the consideration of specific circumstances and should include reflection about the consequences of alternatives for resolving a moral problem.

Areteology In Greek, ἀρετέ (arête) refers to excellence of moral character. Individuals or communities that take an areteological approach to ethics are primarily concerned about the way an ethical decision will reflect or affect their moral character. Actions that detract from or malform moral character should be avoided, whereas actions that reflect or build moral character should be embraced. Just as communities provide deontologists with authorities they feel obligated to obey, or conceptions of the good which teleologists feel compelled to pursue, communities also play a key role in shaping the moral character of areteologists. One of the products of this moral formation is the conscience that exists within an individual or a community. Those who employ an areteological approach to moral reasoning often appeal to their conscience as the basis for their perception of an ethical problem or as justification for the particular solution they prefer. Ends and means are evaluated in terms of how consistent they are with one's moral character and conscience. An advantage of this approach to moral theory is that life is complicated and often requires ethical decisions that have to be made quickly. In situations where authorities are unclear or there is insufficient time to calculate costs and benefits, recourse to one's conscience and moral intuition can be a very effective way to exercise ethical judgment. One of the problems, however, is that a sound conscience depends on a well-formed moral character. Many who perpetrate great evils sleep all too well at night. In addition, intuitive appeals to conscience can be very subjective. Ultimately, good ethics requires that reasons be given to justify decisions. Vague appeals to conscience can be a way to dodge this responsibility.

Issues related to moral character and conscience crop up in at least two cases in this volume. In *Rigor and Responsibility*, David Trapp's conscience is troubled by the prospect of building a lake cabin for his family when so many are homeless. In this case, it is easy to see how communities shape moral character because the pastor of David's congregation was faced with a similar decision and decided to use the resources to benefit others rather than himself and his family. As a result, David's conscience is torn. On the one hand he wants to be a rigorous disciple like his pastor. On the other hand he knows there are times when the personal consumption of resources can be morally responsible. There is no way to resolve this case without grappling with the areteological dimensions of David's troubled conscience. Similarly, as noted earlier, Karen Lindstrom is worried about the loss of a friendship in *Harvesting Controversy*. She appears to oppose genetically modified crops, but the fact that her view may hurt a friend tugs at her conscience.

Those engaged in ethical assessment of a case should reflect on the role of moral theory for at least two reasons. First, the description of key players and stakeholders in a case will indicate to some degree whether they are approaching the case primarily from a deontological, teleological, or areteological perspective. Appropriate moral resolution of the case should take this information into account. It would be inappropriate to ignore a troubled conscience or to force a principled stance on a character that appears more inclined to maximize the good. Good ethical judgments fit the circumstances.

A second reason to focus on the role of moral theory is because it shapes the view of anyone engaged in moral deliberation. In general, all people draw on one or more of these types of moral theory when they face an ethical problem. In a case-study approach to ethics, it is helpful to spend some time reflecting on which type of moral theory may be shaping ethical assessment of issues in a case and the strengths and weaknesses associated with that approach. Moral resolution of a case can prove to be difficult if the person engaged in ethical assessment is utilizing a type of moral theory different from the key decision maker in the case. This is not uncommon and that is why it is helpful to reflect on the role that moral theory plays in shaping ethical assessment.

It is not the case, however, that Christians engaged in moral deliberation can only do so exclusively as deontologists, teleologists, or areteologists. All three of these approaches to moral theory can easily be grounded in various aspects of Christian tradition. An individual can draw on all three types of moral theory to address different ethical problems. For example, in a single day, an elected official could use a teleological approach to weigh the costs and benefits of different policy options, reject a bribe to favor one of these options out of a deontological obligation to obey the law, and later rebuff the amorous advances of an aide and remain faithful to her spouse by drawing on the areteological resources of her moral character. Different circumstances create varying ethical problems that may require the use of different types of moral theory.

Ethical Assessment

The last step of the second stage of moral deliberation is to bring this reflection about moral theory into conversation with relevant moral norms in order to assess the various alternatives and consequences associated with resolving the primary moral problem. At this point, the goal is to determine which alternative is ethically preferable. This is easier to do if the various alternatives and consequences have been clearly identified during the analysis stage.

All of the commentaries that accompany the cases in this volume are designed to assist this step of ethical assessment, but they do so in various ways. The commentary for *Taking on Water* provides background information related to the four primary alternatives in the case. It also identifies general biblical and theological resources that can be utilized to assess these alternatives. For the sake of space, however, the commentary leaves applicability of the ecojustice norms to the consideration of the reader. It also contains little explicit reflection about the role of moral theory. The commentary for *Chlorine Sunset*, however, gives substantial attention to the "precautionary principle" and examines ways this deontological approach can be employed when others merely calculate the costs and benefits of products produced by the chlorine industry. A more teleological tone permeates the commentary for *Sustainable Energy Futures*. Here alternative energy paths are assessed explicitly in relationship to the four ecojustice norms and additional guidelines. In addition, strengths and weaknesses are identified for each energy alternative.

Readers will find that none of the commentaries takes a definitive stance with regard to which alternative in a case is ethically preferable. To do so would violate the pedagogical philosophy that drives the case-study approach to ethics. Ethics would be easy if it simply involved adopting the views of others. Ethical reflection is hard because it requires careful analysis and assessment in order to reach one's own moral conclusions.

Stage III: Action

Ethical reflection is also hard because ultimately it requires action. A decision about a course of action must be made in all of the cases in this volume. It is tempting to delay action through painstaking and comprehensive efforts at analysis and assessment, but ultimately a choice must be made. Choosing not to decide is after all a decision—and normally not a salutary one. At this final stage of moral deliberation there are at least four factors to consider.

Justification

Once an ethical decision has been made, and a course of action chosen, these conclusions need to be justified to others. Ethics is always a community enterprise. Reasons supporting the decision will be couched in some type of moral theory and will appeal to relevant moral norms in order to justify the ethical preference of one alternative over the others. A well-justified ethical decision will also explain why this is the best choice given the circumstances of the case. In addition, a well-crafted decision will also anticipate and respond to the most significant counter-arguments others will likely have.

Viability

As a decision is formulated, one factor to consider is whether, in fact, the decision is viable. That is, do the key players or stakeholders in the case have the power they need to put this decision into action? Is the recommended course of action unrealistic or too idealistic? If it is difficult to answer either question, the decision bears reconsideration. Good ethics gives careful attention to specific circumstances.

Strategy

Another factor that deserves consideration is whether the recommended course of action requires unique strategies in order for it to be implemented. Creative strategies for resolving the primary moral problem provide an opportunity to exercise moral imagination about a case, but they must be reasonable and justifiable.

Reflection

Finally, after reaching a decision about a case, it is important to take a step back in order to assess how one feels about the decision. The method for moral deliberation about cases that has been described in this chapter relies heavily on cognitive skills and careful moral reasoning, but ethics is not only a matter of the head, it is also a matter of the heart. Each person has a moral conscience that, when well formed, may produce nagging doubts about tentative decisions. Before rendering a final judgment and submitting it to the scrutiny of others, it is important to submit the decision to the scrutiny of one's conscience. This single step may confirm the choice and allow one to bask in the glow of a good decision. On the other hand, reflection may lead to nagging doubts and a sense of guilt that signal a need to reconsider the decision. In both situations, Christians rely on the gift of God's grace to restore and reinvigorate the moral life.

CONCLUSION

There are undoubtedly other dimensions that deserve consideration in moral deliberation about case studies. This chapter has proposed one method, but it can always be improved or revised. Ethics has always been more of an art than a science. In addition, while each stage of ethical deliberation deserves careful attention, the depth of moral deliberation about cases in this volume will vary according to the context. For example, in adult education settings, time constraints may not permit extensive discussion of power dynamics or the role of moral theory. In an academic setting, however, students writing research papers about a case may be able to utilize this method in an exhaustive way at each stage. Others writing shorter "case briefs" will have to be more selective, but through the use of this method will be better able to identify morally relevant information as they develop a position about how the case should be resolved.

There are certainly limitations to the case-study approach to ethics. By definition, cases are specific and do not always reflect broader, macro dimensions of a problem. This can be remedied by supplementing cases with other readings and lectures that provide greater context for the case. Another reality is that those who engage in ethical reflection about cases often do so on the basis of limited experience and knowledge. This problem is unavoidable, but it points to the need for a community of moral discourse that intentionally seeks a diversity of voices. Finally, there is the danger that ethical reflection about cases can be perceived through the lens of moral relativism. That is, since there is no one "right" answer represented in the commentary, one could draw the conclusion that any decision about the case is as good as any other. This false notion is normally challenged quickly, however, when reasons have to be given to justify decisions. Ultimately, ethical decisions made by individuals and communities are always accountable to the scrutiny of others. In one fashion or another, ethics is always a group enterprise.

For Further Reading

Holland, Joe, and Henriot, Peter. *Social Analysis: Linking Faith and Justice.* Maryknoll, New York: Orbis Books, 1990.

Kammer, Charles C. *Ethics and Liberation: An Introduction.* Maryknoll, NY: Orbis Books, 1988.

Lovin, Robin W. *Christian Ethics: An Essential Guide.* Nashville: Abingdon Press, 2000.

Maguire, Daniel C., and Fargnoli, A. Nicholas. *On Moral Grounds: The Art/Science of Ethics.* New York: Crossroad Press, 1991.

Stivers, Robert, et al. *Christian Ethics: A Case Method Approach.* 2nd ed. Maryknoll, New York: Orbis Books, 1994.

PART II

Cases and Commentaries

4

Rigor and Responsibility

Stewardship and the Consumption of Resources

Case

David Trapp hung up the phone and paused to reflect. He had just spoken with his good friend Al Messer. Al had offered to build the cabin. For several months David and his wife, Nancy, had considered building on the two acres of Clark Lake property left to them the year before by David's uncle. The nagging question returned to David. Now that the means were there, was it right to build?

David lived with his wife and two children on a quiet residential street on the outskirts of Toledo, Ohio. David was a lawyer with a downtown law firm that encouraged him to spend up to 15 percent of his time with clients who could not afford to pay. David always used the full allotment, considering it one way he could respond in faith to a pressing human need. David was also active in community affairs. He was vice-president of a statewide citizens' action lobby for more progressive taxation. Locally he was on the board of directors of an environmental organization, whose goal was the clean-up, preservation, and restoration of Lake Erie, and led adult education classes at his church. What troubled David the most was relating his sense of outrage at injustice to his enjoyment of good food, travel, and water sports.

Nancy Trapp was a buyer for an office furniture supplier. Her work involved increasing responsibility, and she found it difficult to leave unfinished business in the office. Recently she had been elected to a two-year term as president of the P.T.A. at the children's school. She had not foreseen the constant interruptions such a position would bring. The telephone never seemed to stop ringing, especially on the weekends when people knew they could find her at home.

Decision-making was more or less a family affair with the Trapps. David and Nancy seldom disagreed on family matters and to David's recollection never on a major one. The children, Darcy and Ben, ages ten and eight, were consulted on major decisions and their voices taken into account.

Robert L. Stivers prepared this case and commentary. The case is based on actual events. Names and places have been changed to protect the privacy of those involved.

Nathan Ferguson was the pastor of the local congregation in which the Trapps were active participants. Nathan had recently sold a piece of property he had once intended for recreational purposes. The proceeds from the sale had been donated to a church-sponsored halfway house for drug addicts in downtown Toledo. Shortly after Nathan had sold the property, he had begun to preach and teach in a low-key way on the subjects of possessions, overconsumption, and the materialism of American society. His eventual aim was to have some of his parishioners understand and consider forming a community based on the one in Jerusalem described in the opening chapters of the Book of Acts. He envisioned this community as one that was environmentally sensitive, held possessions in common, limited consumption to basic necessities, and gave liberally to programs among the poor that were based on a principle of self-reliance.

Clea Parks was David's colleague and an active participant in the church's adult education classes. What amazed David was how she could combine a concern for the poor with a way of living that allowed for occasional extravagances. Like David, Clea made full use of the firm's 15 percent allotment to work with poor clients. She was also on the board of the halfway house for drug addicts. In contrast she and her husband regularly traveled to Bermuda for tennis and golf and to Sun Valley for skiing. Last year they had flown to the Amazon for an eco-tour. This fall they were headed to the Holy Land for three weeks.

Shortly after the settlement of his uncle's will, which in addition to the two acres included enough cash to construct a modest cabin, David and Nancy had discussed the matter of building. David expressed his ambivalence. He wondered about limits to self-indulgence. His desire for the cabin seemed to be locked in a struggle with his conscience. "How can we build a second place," he asked, "when so many people are living in shelters without roofs or simply do not have a home at all? Can we in good conscience consume as heavily as we do while others are crying out for the very things we take for granted and consume almost at will? And what about the animals? Our consumption contributes to the degradation of their habitat."

He also considered the matter of energy consumption. Again directing his reflections to Nancy, he said: "Think about the energy used in construction and the going to and fro that will follow. Is this good stewardship of resources? Does it reflect our responsibility as Americans to conserve fuel? What sort of legacy are we leaving to our grandchildren, not to mention the lessons we are teaching our own children?"

He then rehearsed once again a pet theme: the excessive materialism of American society. "The Bible is quite explicit about possessions," he insisted. "Possession can easily plug our ears to the hearing of God's word. A person cannot have two masters. The rich young ruler went away empty because he was unwilling to give up his possessions. The tax collector, Zacchaeus, is commended by Jesus for his willingness to give one-half of his possessions to the poor. And Jesus himself lived without possessions, commanding his disciples to do likewise."

He paused to think about this further. "Is it possible," he asked, "to avoid the spirit-numbing nature of possessions short of self-denial? And if I'm not going to opt for self-denial, then I at least have to ask in what way my consumption helps to perpetuate a system that is getting further and further away from the simplicity of Jesus." Again he paused, adding: "I guess it all boils down to the ethics of the Sermon on the Mount that Pastor Ferguson keeps talking about. Does the rigor of the sermon's ethic represent the only valid Christian option? Is it possible to live much in excess of basic needs if this ethic is taken seriously? And if we conclude that the Sermon is not a new set of laws, what is its relevance anyway?"

Nancy's response was slow in coming both because she was sensitive to David's imaginative conscience, and because she wanted a place to separate herself from work and to teach the children the water sports she and David both enjoyed. "I can understand your commitment," she told him. "It's not a matter of guilt for you. But I just don't feel quite as strongly about those things as you do. The pressure has been getting worse lately, and I feel the need to share with you and the children in a more relaxed setting. The kids are getting older fast, and in a few years they'll be beyond the age where they'll be around to learn water sports.

"The materialism you are so concerned about," she went on to say, "has also made for creative new possibilities. It's not possessions themselves, but how we use them that makes a difference. It's the willingness to give, and we give enough what with the 15 percent of your time and the giving of more than 10 percent of our incomes to church and charity. And think about what giving up our possessions will do. Without programs to transfer our abundance to the poor, giving things up will go for naught or perhaps contribute to the loss of someone's job. That is just the way things are. Think about Al Messer."

David was not quite sure what to make of Nancy's comments. The old nagging questions kept coming back. His conscience would not let him off easily.

Then Nathan Ferguson had begun his sermons and more recently had conducted a series of six sessions in the adult education class that David led. Nathan returned time and again to the teachings of Jesus, to the Sermon on the Mount, to the rich young ruler, to Zacchaeus, to the sharing in early Christian communities, to the call of the Prophets to justice and care for the poor, and to Jesus' love for the birds of the air and fish of the sea. Nathan had not talked in a demanding or accusatory fashion, but neither had he let his parishioners off the hook. To David it seemed that Nathan's every thought had been directed straight at him.

At the office Clea hit him from the other side. At first she had merely commented on Nathan's sermons and classes. She thought Nathan was too much of a perfectionist. She appreciated his concern for the poor and the environment and how possessions can close one's ears to the Word of God. She did not, however, see how individual sacrifices produced the social change they all wanted.

She also had a contrasting view of the Sermon on the Mount. "We cannot live the Sermon," she explained. "It's impossible, and anyway wasn't intended for everyone. Ethical rigor is right for folks like Nathan, but what most of us are called to is responsibility: to the right use of possessions, to a willingness to give, and to advocacy of justice in word and deed. The choice is not between self-indulgence and self-denial. There is a third option that is living responsibly with concern for all those issues Nathan talks about and still appreciating the finer things in life."

When David told her about the lake property and Nancy's needs, Clea had begun to push him a bit harder. "Come on, David," she said half-joking, "it's all right with Jesus if you build. Jesus enjoyed life and participated in it fully. The church tradition is quite ambiguous on possessions, wealth, and nature." Another time she put it bluntly: "What right have you to force your values and views on Nancy and the children?" Lately she had been twitting him. Just the other day with a big grin on her face she called him "the monk."

Al Messer's call had jolted David and increased his sense that something had to give. Al had told David that he could build the cabin out of used lumber and had found a place where he could get insulation and double-pane window glass at reduced prices. Al had also indicated he needed the work because business had been a bit slow lately.

Nancy entered the room and guessed what was troubling David. "I know what's bothering you," she said. "If we build, those old questions about the poor, materialism, and limits to consumption will nag at you. You might not even stick to a decision to build. If we don't build, you'll feel you have let the kids and me down and miss your favorite water sports. How should we decide this?"

Commentary

Taken at face value, this case is about David and Nancy Trapp struggling to decide whether to build a vacation cabin. But at a deeper and more comprehensive level the case is addressed to all non-poor Christians; and the issue is how to live as a Christian in a materialistic world where ostentatious luxury, grinding poverty, and environmental degradation exist side by side.

This question of how to live can be given greater specificity by considering the title of the case. Should an affluent family give up what it has and follow the rigorous "holy poverty" of Jesus or is there an alternative called "responsible consumption" that stresses right use and good stewardship of material resources? Realizing that a continuum of options is possible between the "either" of rigor and the "or" of responsibility, these two options may be contrasted for the purpose of analyzing the decisions the Trapps must make.

Before addressing these two contrasting perspectives, however, there are a number of related issues that should at least be mentioned. The two most important are poverty and environmental degradation. David and Nancy's decision is not hidden in a vacuum. It stands out in a context where over a billion people are malnourished and live in miserable poverty. It stands out in a global economy in which the gap between rich and poor remains wide. It stands out in an economic system that needs high levels of consumption to stimulate growth and jobs. It stands out in a planetary system where unprecedented numbers of species are going extinct largely due to human actions, and where there is serious concern about the sustainability of natural resources and the capacity of ecosystems to absorb pollution. These issues raised by the context of the case are the very issues raised to prominence by this volume.

There are six other issues important for this case but peripheral to the main concerns. The first is family decision-making. How is this family to decide? The second stems from the Trapps' need to "get away." Would the addition of a cabin really solve the more pressing problems of overwork and overinvolvement in the community? The third is the matter of educating children. What messages do David and Nancy send Darcy and Ben by overwork and by building a second home? What sort of character are they trying to instill?

The fourth issue is raised by the inheritance. Are David and Nancy really free to give their inheritance to the poor? Although the case does not say, they probably live within the context of a larger family grouping, some of whose members might be a little upset with such unilateral action. The fifth issue is guilt. Should Christians and Americans feel a sense of guilt for their high levels of consumption? And what is the function of guilt in the Christian life? Sixth is the issue of individual action in a world of over six billion people and dominated by large social organizations. How do people like David and Nancy influence others to do justice and exercise Christianity's call for solidarity? Will individual acts of self-sacrifice make a difference?

Beyond these six issues, there are a number of issues raised by Christian traditions. How should the Bible and theology, for example, guide the Trapps' choice? What in fact do the traditions say about the issues in the case?

THE MAIN QUESTION

So how are Christians to live in a world of continuing poverty and environmental degradation? Most students react to David's dilemma with at least mild astonishment. They seem to assume that consuming goods and services in quantity is the natural thing to do and have difficulty comprehending why building is a dilemma at all. This is not surprising given the daily barrage of commercial advertising whose main purpose is to sell a way of life that encourages heavy consumption. Indeed, heavy consumption has become a way of life to many Americans, however inconsistent it is with the norms of the ethic of ecological justice.

The norm of solidarity and the overarching norm of justice make the gaps between rich and poor and the grinding poverty of so many people that goes side by side with this consumption difficult to justify. The emphasis on material things underlying this consumption is difficult to reconcile with the norm of sufficiency and biblical norms on wealth and consumption. The environmental degradation that this level of consumption causes is a serious problem for the norm of sustainability. On these grounds David and many Americans have good reason to be troubled by their consciences.

Consider first the norms of *solidarity* and *justice*. Recalling the discussions of these norms in Chapter Two, justice is rooted in the very being of God. It is an essential part of God's community of love and calls followers of Jesus Christ to make fairness the core of their social response to other persons and the rest of creation. Included in this biblical concern for justice is solidarity with the poor and now also with nature.

The biblical basis of justice and solidarity with the poor starts with God's liberation of the oppressed Hebrew slaves in Egypt and the establishment of a covenant with them (Exodus). This theme continues in the prophetic reinterpretation of the covenant. Micah summarized the law: "to do justice, and to love kindness, and to walk humbly with your God" (Mic. 6:4a, 8). Amos was adamant that God's wrath would befall Israel for its injustice and failure to care for the poor (Am. 5:21–24). Isaiah and Jeremiah were equally adamant (Is. 1:12–17, 3:13–15, 58:6–9; Jer. 22:13–17).

In the Christian Scriptures the emphasis on justice is somewhat muted in comparison to the prophets, but the concern for the poor may be even stronger. Jesus himself was a poor man from a poor part of Israel. His mission was among the poor and his message was directed to them. He blessed the poor and spoke God's judgment on the rich. On the cross he made himself one of the dispossessed. In the early Jerusalem community as recorded in Acts 1–5, the basic economic needs of all members were taken care of as the wealthier shared their possessions so none would be deprived.

Second is the norm of *sufficiency* that builds on biblical and theological understandings of wealth and consumption. Two traditions have dominated, offering two not very compatible understandings of *sufficiency*. One stresses a rigorous response to Jesus' teachings including self-denial, the giving of what one has to the poor, and a radical freedom from possessions. The other accents the right use of possessions and emphasizes responsibility and willingness to share. The first tradition may be called *rigorous discipleship* and the second *responsible consumption*. These are not meant to be polemical titles. Responsible consumption has its element of rigor and rigorous discipleship is certainly responsible. While the differences between them are significant, it is possible to accept both as valid Christian ways of living.

Parenthetically, these two traditions are also visible in the norm of *solidarity*. Historically many Christians have identified completely with the poor, even to the point of considerable self-sacrifice. Well-known modern examples such as Mother Teresa and Dorothy Day have continued this tradition. At the same time and not so spectacularly, Christians work responsibly in everyday vocations serving Christ with varying degrees of intensity and frugality.

The choice between these traditions is David's dilemma and is worthy of further exploration. The dilemma is the age-old one of the ideal and the real. On the one hand Jesus offers glimpses of the ideal in his teachings on the community of God and in his person. The community of God, he says, is already present with power, and Jesus asks his disciples to live in this power and to drop what they are doing and follow him. On the other hand, paradoxically, the community of God is still to come in its fullness. Reality is a mixture of powers; human power rightly and wrongly used and God's power of love. God's community of love stands alongside and often in contradiction to human power, and Christians must live in a world where perfect choices are seldom presented.

These two normative traditions both have biblical bases. The Hebrew Scriptures take the responsible consumption side. They praise the rich people and place a high estimate on riches gained through honest work (Gen. 13:2, 26:13, 30:43, 41:40). Alongside this praise is the obligation to care for weaker members of society (Am. 8:48; Is. 5:8–10 and 10:1–3). Nowhere do the Hebrew Scriptures praise self-imposed poverty or beggars.

The two sides are found in the teachings of Jesus. His announcement of the coming community of God carries with it a call for unparalleled freedom from possessions and complete trust in God. The service of God and service of riches are incompatible (Matt. 6:24; Mk. 8:36, 9:43–48, 10:17–25; Lk. 12:15, 8:14,18:18–23, 19:1–10). Jesus tells the rich young ruler who has kept all the laws to go sell what he has and give it to the poor (Lk. 18:18–24). Jesus himself had no possessions (Mt. 8:20; Mk. 1:16, 6:8f.; Lk. 9:3, 10:4) and prodded his disciples to go out on their missionary journeys taking nothing with them (Lk. 9:3, 10:4).

Nevertheless, Jesus took for granted the owning of property (Lk. 6:30, 10:30–37; Mt. 25:31–40). He was apparently supported by women of means (Lk. 8:2) and urged that possessions be used to help those in need (Lk. 6:30). Jesus did not ask Zacchaeus to give up all his possessions (Luke 19). He dined with hated tax collectors and was fond of celebrations, especially meals of fellowship. The examples echo the Hebrew Scriptures' stress on the right use of wealth and possessions.

This mixed mind continued in the early church. On the one side was the Jerusalem community where goods were shared in common (Acts 1–5). This seems to follow Jesus' teachings about radical freedom from possessions. The Letter of James offers little solace to the wealthy (Jas. 1:11, 2:1–7, 5:1–6). On the other side is Paul who did not address the problem of wealth, although he himself seems to have had few possessions and was self-supporting as a tent maker (Phil. 4:11–13). He did, however, stress right use, made clear his center in Christ, and called on the congregations he served to support the poor in Jerusalem. The letter to Timothy, while hard on the wealthy, leaves the door open to right use of possessions (1 Tim. 6:6–10, 6:17–19).

From these two traditions a dual ethic emerged. For the monk and the nun who surrendered his or her possessions and elected a life of chastity, holy poverty, and nonviolence, the rigor of Jesus was binding. For the great majority the rigor of Jesus became "counsels of perfection." It was deemed impossible of fulfillment and therefore binding only on those who would be perfect.

These two ways of living existed side by side with the authority of the church sanctioning both and holding them together. Implicit in this resolution of the dilemma were a troublesome hierarchy of perfection and the unbiblical notion of special merits that practicing rigor was claimed to confer. Thus, while the church held things together, it did so at the price of grading perfection and discouraging the rigor of ordinary Christians.

Protestants, following Martin Luther's dictum of the priesthood of all believers, eliminated special merit but at the price of restoring the dilemma. Monasteries and convents were closed and all believers were, according to Luther, to serve God in whatever vocation they found themselves. Where there had been two ways of life in one Church, now there was one way of life with two tendencies in many churches. Still, rigorous discipleship has continued to the present in the monastic movement within the Roman Catholic Church and in many sects that flourished in Protestantism.

One statement by Martin Luther during a "table talk" in the winter of 1542–43 catches the mind that is suspicious of wealth:

> Riches are the most insignificant things on earth, the smallest gift that God can give a person. What are they in comparison with the word of God? In fact, what are they in comparison even with physical endowments and beauty? What are they in comparison to the gifts of the mind? And yet we act as if this were not so! The matter, form, effect, and goal of riches are worthless. This is why our Lord God generally gives riches to crude asses to whom nothing else is given.

The biblical witness on consumption follows much the same twofold pattern. The basic issue was frugality versus contentment with a moderate level of consumption.

Theologically the two traditions take their cues from the paradoxical "here, but yet to come" teaching of the early church. This paradox appears in the earliest pages of the Bible. Persons are created in the image of God (Gen. 1) but with Adam and Eve fall away from God into sin (Gen. 3). It reappears again and again in the history of Israel as the Israelites wrestle with the responsibilities of the covenant and their own unrighteousness.

Jesus advises his disciples to be sheep among the wolves and to have the wisdom of the serpent and the innocence of the dove (Mt. 10:16). For Christians this paradox is preeminent in the cross and resurrection. The cross is reality at its worst and points to the depth of human sin. Sin is not some minor defect to be overcome by new techniques. Ordering force and occasionally even coercion are needed to keep sin in check.

Yet the cross is not the last word in Christianity. It is followed closely by the ever-new word of the resurrection. The resurrection points to God at work overcoming sin and death. It points as well to the possibility of "new creations" in the lives of individuals and groups and to the creative potential of love and justice. It teaches Christians that while they still live in the age of sin and death, God's love has broken in, there is hope, and their efforts in response to God's love are not in vain. Christians are invited as a result to deal with a partly open future where even small responses can make a difference.

Finally, the paradox is highlighted by Paul's sense that Christians live between the ages. They live in the old age of sin, death, injustice, and limits. Yet they are called to live according to the new age inaugurated by Jesus Christ and made present by the Holy Spirit. Insofar as they live in the old age, Christians give limited support to such things as prison systems, to less than perfect but still functioning economic and political systems, and even to wars of liberation and defense. Living in the old age involves compromises, many of which appear to be cop-outs to those who take the rigorous path.

Nevertheless, Christians are not to be serpents or to live according to the old age. They are to live in the resurrection according to the love and justice of the new age. This means pushing beyond what merely is and seeking just and sustainable societies. Living in the new age means witnessing to the ideal and may seem utopian to those who enjoy luxury and even some that follow the path of responsible consumption.

In summary, the rigorous tradition builds on Jesus' call to radical discipleship, his living without possessions frugally and simply, and his freedom from materialism. This tradition calls the disciple to a life of simplicity and sharing. It is a life of commitment to the community of God. And even if all the details are not lived perfectly, at least the disciple should aim in that direction and pray that the grace of God will provide the resources to reconcile aim and action.

As for living between the ages, the path of rigorous discipleship emphasizes the new age almost to the exclusion of the old. This exclusion comes not from failure to see the sin of the old age, but rather from the assumption that Christians are free from the old age through the power of God. Hence radical changes in ways of living come naturally, and followers make these changes with enthusiasm.

The path of rigorous discipleship is attractive. It does not bog down in the inevitable relativities and compromises of the old age. It is simple, direct, and often accompanied by communities that seem full of the Spirit. It is a valid Christian option.

Unlike the path of rigorous discipleship the path of responsible consumption does not take its main cues from the teachings of Jesus. This does not mean it is less biblical, but that it rests more heavily on the main themes of the Bible, in particular on the theological tension between the old and the new ages. Like those on the path of rigorous discipleship, Christians on this path are concerned for the poor and aware of being tied to possessions. They do not, however, take the frugality and simplicity of Jesus literally or urge the surrender of all possessions.

Reduced to basics, those who follow this tradition wrestle with what it means to live between the ages, taking both ages seriously. In contrast to the heavy stress on the new age, they point to the realities of the old age or to the ambiguity of life between the ages. The problem for them is not rigorous discipleship but how to act responsibly and to begin a process of change that will lead to greater justice and more sustainable communities. Their mood is sober, their programs moderate and reformist in nature. They also have a greater appreciation of material consumption.

This path is attractive to less ascetic Christians and to those who are deeply involved in existing structures. It is a valid Christian tradition and avoids the excesses that sometimes accompany the rigorous tradition. Most important, it accounts for the complexities of living in the world as it is.

While Christianity has been of two minds, it has been clear on one guiding norm, *sufficiency*. Sufficiency for humans is the timely supply of basic material necessities, defined as the minimum amount of food, clothing, shelter, transportation, health care, and education needed to live at some margin above mere subsistence. Sufficiency is, of course, more than a given batch of goods and services. Philosopher Martha Nussbaum has established something she calls the "flourishing life" as the goal of her development scheme. She has advanced two lists of what constitutes "the human form of life" and "good human functioning."[1] She insists it is the responsibility of political and economic institutions to ensure everyone is capable of functioning at a human level; and while her lists are exhaustive and beyond the capacity of most governments, they are a good starting place for understanding what sufficiency means.

Sufficiency for other species revolves first around the preservation and restoration of habitat for wild species. Humans do not have the capacity to oversee the survival of many species, but they can cease degrading critical habitats. Habitat loss is a major cause of species extinction. As for domestic animals that humans have taken out of wild nature, more is required. Sufficiency for them means the provision of basic material needs and proper care. This opens up a wide range of options including alternative farming techniques and even vegetarian diets.

Sufficiency must also include future generations. Sufficiency must be sustainable over long periods of time. The third norm influencing the Trapps' decision is therefore *sustainability*. The issue that sustainability raises for the Trapps is whether the forms of consumption they are contemplating degrade the environment. One small cabin on an already developed lakefront will hardly do much damage, but if their behavior were to be generalized, it certainly would. The earth can ill-afford six billion people who consume as if they were affluent North Americans.

What then are David and Nancy to do? How are they to live? If they want to live responsively to the power of God and be guided by the norms of the ethic of ecological justice, they will avoid heavy consumption, materialism, and selfish individualism. They will live sufficiently free to pursue rigorous discipleship or responsible consumption as they feel called. They will put trust where trust belongs, that is to say, in God's community, not in material possessions. What this means in practice is something that finally is a matter of conscience. Blueprints and prescriptions are not available.

GUILT

Is David driven by guilt over his own privileged place in the world—white, American, male, intelligent, and wealthy—or is guilt an inappropriate word to describe his wrestle with the ethic of ecological justice? The case does not reveal the answer. Giving David the benefit of doubt, however, it is better to see his struggle as a conscientious effort to deal with an ambiguous tradition and a changing environmental context. Christians like David may be genuinely perplexed as they try to figure out the right course because valid norms sometimes suggest quite different courses of action.

Even if David did not feel guilty, it is important to recognize that guilt is an all too common human experience and should be taken seriously. Guilt may be a warning sign of serious inner-alienation. It may be telling David that he really is living a sinful way of life and needs to change (repent).

More important for those who would categorize David as "guilt-ridden" is the possibility that they are projecting their own guilt in order to be free for a life of affluence. To dismiss David's dilemma as guilt is to miss the main point of the case.

Finally, guilt is not something that needs to paralyze action. Guilt may be genuinely experienced and may legitimately point to sin, but it is not the place to rest. Just as the resurrection follows the cross, so do forgiveness and the possibility of new life follow sin and guilt.

INDIVIDUAL ACTION

Does it really make a difference what David and Nancy decide? Does David's struggle over options available to only a select few trivialize the more important problems of world poverty and environmental degradation?

Discussions of individual action are permeated with optimistic and pessimistic extremes. The optimists insist that successful social movements are usually started and led by individuals who are deeply concerned and motivated. They urge their listeners to take the challenge and change the world. The pessimists in turn dismiss individual action as not having a chance in a world of large organizations. They urge their listeners to join movements or counsel withdrawal.

Christians are neither optimists nor pessimists. They are hopeful and realistic; hopeful because God is at work in even the darkest times, realistic because of sin. Christians act first in response to the love of God they experience spiritually and only second to achieve results. If good results follow from faithful discipleship, they should be embraced. If they do not, action is still forthcoming because of its spiritual foundation.

This simple truth does away with the debate between optimists and pessimists over individual action. The debate is misplaced. It misses the essential inspiration of Christian ethical action and substitutes reliance on human action alone.

Is David's dilemma trivial? By no means! His struggle with his conscience over appropriate levels of consumption is essential in a poverty-stricken, environmentally degraded world. It is essential for everyone, especially for those who consume heavily or could potentially consume more. Whether it is a cabin, a television set, a new computer, or a trip to the Amazon, personal consumption makes an ethical statement. It says a lot about character. So while David's specific decision will not be recorded in history books, what this generation does to relieve poverty and preserve the environment will.

Note

1. Martha Nussbaum and Jonathan Glover, *Women, Culture, and Development: A Study of Human Capabilities* (Oxford Clarendon Press, 1995), pp. 76–85. Nussbaum and Glover argue that the "human form of life" consists of: (1) mortality; (2) the human body including the needs for food, drink, for shelter, and for sexual desire; (3) the capacity for pleasure and pain; (4) cognitive capability including perceiving, imagining, and thinking; (5) early infant development; (6) practical reason; (7) affiliation with other human beings; (8) relatedness to other species and nature; (9) humor and play; (10) separateness; and (11) space to move around in. "Basic human functional capabilities" include: (1) being able to live to the end of a human life of normal length; (2) being able to have good health; (3) being able to avoid unnecessary and non-beneficial pain; (4) being able to use the senses; (5) being able to have attachments to things and persons outside ourselves; (6) being able to form a conception of the good and to engage in critical reflection about the planning of one's life; (7) being able to live for others; (8) being able to live with concern for and in relation to animals, plants, and the world of nature; (9) being able to laugh, play, and enjoy recreational activities; (10) being able to live one's own life in one's own surroundings and context.

For Further Reading

Batey, Richard. *Jesus and the Poor.* New York: Harper & Row, Publishers, 1972.

Birch, Bruce C., and Larry L. Rasmussen. *The Predicament of the Prosperous.* Philadelphia: The Westminster Press, 1978.

Cobb, John B., Jr. *Sustainability.* Maryknoll, NY: Orbis Books, 1992.

Durning, Alan Thein. *This Place on Earth: Home and the Practice of Permanence.* Seattle: Sasquatch Books, 1997.

Foster, Richard J. *Freedom of Simplicity: Finding Harmony in a Complex World.* New York: Harper Paperback Books, 1998.

Hengel, Martin. *Property and Riches in the Early Church.* Trans. John Bowden, Philadelphia: Fortress Press, 1974.

Luhrs, Janet. *The Simple Living Guide: A Sourcebook for Less Stressful, More Joyful Living.* New York: Broadway Books, 1997.

McDaniel, Jay B. *Living from the Center: Spirituality in an Age of Consumerism.* St. Louis: Chalice Press, 2000.

Nash, James A. "Toward the Revival and Reform of the Subversive Virtue: Frugality," in Audrey R. Chapman et al., eds. *Consumption, Population, and Sustainability: Perspectives from Science and Religion.* Washington, DC: Island Press, 2002.

Princen, Thomas, and Maniates, Michael, eds. *Confronting Consumption*. Cambridge, MA: MIT Press, 2002.

Rohr, Richard. *Simplicity: The Art of Living*. New York: Crossroad Press, 1995.

Shi, David. *The Simple Life: Plain Living and High Thinking in American Culture*. Athens, GA: University of Georgia Press, 2001.

Sider, Ronald. *Rich Christians in an Age of Hunger*. Dallas: Word Publishing Company, 2000.

St. James, Ronald J. *The Simplicity Reader*. New York: Smithmark Publishing Company, 1999.

Stivers, Robert L. *Hunger, Technology, and Limits to Growth*. Minneapolis: Augsburg Press, 1984. See Chapter 9.

Yount, David. *Spiritual Simplicity: Simplify Your Life and Enrich Your Soul*. London: Simon & Schuster, 1999.

Websites

Center for a New American Dream
http://www.newdream.org/

5

Sustaining Dover

*Urban Sprawl, Habitat Fragmentation,
and Sustainable Communities*

Case

I

John Yeoman was relieved to be sitting in the folding chairs instead of his customary hot seat as a City Council member. "I could get used to just being a citizen again," John thought. "It's been a long seven years." In fact, division had been growing among the 8,000 citizens of Dover for more than a decade. When he was first elected to the Council, the city was still licking its wounds financially after a failed effort to block a large developer from building Sunrise Plaza, a new retail center on the south edge of town. Concerned that the shopping center would harm the downtown business core, the city had denied the landowner's request to rezone the property. After a judge ruled in favor of the landowner, and all appeals were denied, the city of Dover was left with over $85,000 in legal fees. So John's first duty as a Council member had been to figure out where to cut thousands of dollars out of the city budget over the next few years in order to pay legal bills racked up by Council members who had preceded him.

At the start of his second term, his ward had become divided over the fate of an old, single-lane bridge that crossed the Appanoose River on the west side of town. Some had wanted to repair the bridge in order to preserve this "quaint" portion of Dover's heritage, but others had wanted to take advantage of government funds to replace the aging structure with a new, two-lane bridge. The preservationists had insisted, however, that the old bridge be restored. They had figured more prominently in city politics ever since the Dover School Board had decided to build a brand-new elementary school rather than refurbish a hundred-year-old "treasure" that was listed on the National Register of Historic Places. One year earlier the state Fire Marshall had closed the building for safety reasons.

James Martin-Schramm prepared this case and commentary. The case is based on actual events. Names and places have been changed to protect the privacy of those involved.

Now, at the end of John's second term on the Council, emotions were running high over the news that Wal-Mart intended to build a 184,000 square foot Supercenter on the eastern edge of Dover. The epitome of one-stop shopping, Supercenters vary in size, but normally include approximately 60,000 square feet in groceries, a large automotive services section, a pharmacy and a vision center, as well as dry cleaning and film processing on top of a much larger selection of household goods sold in a regular Wal-Mart store. Dwarfing all other stores in the community, including Wal-Mart's 74,000 square foot store in Sunrise Plaza, the Supercenter would be built on 31 acres of land, a third of which had up to now been designated as a flood plain (Figure 1).

Sitting in chairs reserved for the general public, John had come to attend the first of three public hearings the Dover Planning and Zoning Commission would hold over three weeks regarding Wal-Mart's request to fill in the portion of their property in the flood plain and to reclassify the land from F-1 (Flood Plain) to C-4 (Shopping Center Commercial District). After the hearings the Commission had to make a recommendation to John and the six other members of the City Council who would make the final, binding decision.

There was disagreement, however, about whether the City Council was authorized to make this decision. Last year the city's Board of Adjustment turned down a request by a local business for a "special exception" to fill in land in the same flood plain so that they could relocate their business to this

Figure 1. Map of Dover, Iowa

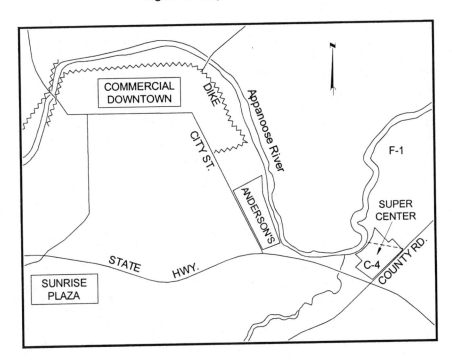

site. The business needed to relocate because they had sold their land to Wal-Mart. In rejecting the request, the Board concluded that development in the flood plain was contrary to Dover's zoning ordinance and would violate the content and purpose of the city's Comprehensive Development Plan. One of the goals of this plan is to protect and preserve flood plains as natural resources.

This decision did not bode well for Wal-Mart and its need to landfill and rezone a portion of their land for the Supercenter. Faced with almost certain rejection by the Board of Adjustment, Wal-Mart decided to request permission to fill the land from the Dover City Council. Wal-Mart adopted this strategy because an ordinance in Dover's City Code states that the dumping of approved material for landfill purposes in areas designated as F-1 flood plains is subject to the prior approval of the City Council and appropriate state agencies. After Wal-Mart submitted its request in writing to the City Council, John and other council members asked the city attorney whether the council had the legal authority to decide the matter. The city attorney assured them that they did and so a series of public meetings had now begun.

Wincing at the thought of being back in the hot seat in a few weeks, John listened as the regional representative for Wal-Mart, Max Walters, began his presentation. Dressed in casual business attire, Walters made three points in his presentation. The first was the news that the Iowa Department of Natural Resources (DNR) had just approved Wal-Mart's plan to bring fill to the site in order to raise the land to seven feet above the state's 100-year flood plain standard and one foot higher than Dover's more stringent flood plain standard. "I am sure you are as gratified as we are to receive this vote of confidence from the DNR," said Walters, holding the letter aloft. "Once the backfill process has been completed, the land will no longer be in the flood plain and our land will be at the level of other commercial establishments in the area. Like many of you, however, Wal-Mart is concerned about the water quality of the Appanoose River, which forms the western boundary of our property. As a result, we have worked with the DNR to design an eight-acre retention basin and riparian buffer zone. These two design features will filter petro-chemical and other wastes from our parking lot so that they do not enter the river. This will probably be the 'greenest' parking lot in the county! To our knowledge, every other parking lot in Dover and the city's forty miles of streets discharge their waste directly into the nearest storm sewer, and thus ultimately into the river. In addition, the retention basin and riparian buffer zone will create a small area of wetlands that will create habitat for wildlife. Our plans for the site include a prairie grass demonstration project, bat houses, and houses for songbirds. Ecologically, we want to do our part to be a good steward. Finally, whereas some developers have strenuously negotiated various tax breaks before investing in the community, Wal-Mart will pay for all improvements to our site. We will bring city water and sewer lines to our property and add a turning lane to the county road that feeds the entrance to our store at no expense to the taxpayers of Dover. In addition, we have secured federal funds to provide walking and biking trails to the store. As always, Wal-Mart will continue to be a good neighbor in the city of Dover."

Clapping heartily, Buck Sorensen, chair of the Planning and Zoning Commission, thanked Walters for his presentation and turned the podium over to Clara Laursen, Coordinator of the Appanoose River Alliance. Organized fairly recently, the Alliance is a loose coalition of environmentalists, bird watchers, anglers, hunters, and canoeists. Laursen rose to leadership in the organization when the local newspaper published the fruits of her doctoral research on water quality problems in the Appanoose River watershed. Twenty years younger than Walters and a foot shorter, she addressed the audience dressed in khakis and a t-shirt emblazoned with the logo of the Alliance.

"Members of the Commission and fellow citizens of Dover, the Appanoose River Alliance opposes Wal-Mart's request to fill in and rezone this portion of the flood plain for several reasons. The first and perhaps most important reason is that filling in flood plains destroys wildlife habitat. Habitat destruction is the single most important variable in the loss of biodiversity on our planet. Here, in Iowa, more than fifty percent of neo-tropical migrant bird species have been in decline for the last thirty years. The loss of wetlands and flood plain areas is directly related to the decline of songbirds in our backyards. We would much prefer the wetlands that nature provides to one constructed artificially and laced with toxic chemicals.

"Second, flood plains serve as natural sponges that soak up excess water in the spring after snow melts and in the summer after major storms or extended rain events. Without these flood plains, floodwaters are confined to the main channel of the river until they spill over the banks and cause considerable damage to dwellings and agricultural property—especially to communities further downstream. Flood plains are nature's way of spreading out floodwaters so that they do the least damage and provide the most benefit through the dispersion of river nutrients and the provision of wildlife habitat.

"Third, the Alliance is not convinced that Wal-Mart's retention basin and riparian buffer zone will protect the river from contamination by the road wastes collected on its 11-acre parking lot while also controlling the volume of water from its 4-acre roof. It is our understanding that the state DNR is only required by law to consider the effects of a 100-year flood upon the property in question. Left unstudied is the virtual certainty that the retention basin would fail in floodwaters that exceed the 100-year flood level. I don't think I need to remind you that the 1993 flood, which did so much damage here in Dover and throughout Iowa, did not even reach the level of a 100-year flood. When we experience another flood of this or greater size, all of the concentrated petro-chemical wastes would suddenly be flushed into the river where they could seriously degrade the quality of the water for fish and other species. We can prevent this by retaining and enforcing Dover's more stringent flood plain standards.

"Finally, given the fact that the state of Iowa has designated the Appanoose as a 'protected water area,' the city of Dover has no right to spoil the natural and scenic quality of the river by allowing a big-box retailer like Wal-Mart to construct a Supercenter right along its banks. Given these concerns, we strongly urge the Planning and Zoning Commission to reject Wal-Mart's bid to fill in the flood plain and reclassify this portion of their land from F-1 to C-4. Any decision otherwise would constitute bad land stewardship."

As the room erupted in applause, Buck Sorensen said somberly, "Thank you, Laura." Then he announced that there would be one more presentation before the floor would be opened for public comment. Coming to the microphone now was Tom Bittner, Director of Dover Citizens for Sustainable Development (DCSD). Like the Alliance, DCSD is a coalition of various groups—primarily local merchants, advocates for historical preservation, and organic farmers in the area committed to community-supported agriculture. The organization was officially founded after the failed bid to stop the development of Sunrise Plaza and had gained many new members in recent years during the bridge and school controversies. Now, in an attempt to protect their businesses while not antagonizing some of their customers, influential merchants in the organization had drafted Tom Bittner to serve as the group's public spokesperson. A recent college graduate in political science, Bittner cared passionately about sustainable development, but had little experience in local politics. Nevertheless, here he was, looking a bit uncomfortable in a shirt and tie, addressing a packed crowd.

"Ladies and gentlemen, Dover Citizens for Sustainable Development is in favor of economic growth when that development is conducted in a responsible manner and contributes to the sustainability of this community. We are not anti-growth, but the construction of a Wal-Mart Supercenter in this flood plain would be both ecologically irresponsible and economically ruinous. This community worked long and hard after the Sunrise Plaza fiasco to develop Dover's Comprehensive Development Plan. As those of you on the Commission know, that plan designates the downtown business area as a vital commercial district in Dover. In addition, the plan states that protecting the flood plain of the Appanoose River and its tributaries from 'incompatible development' will be given 'high priority.' Wal-Mart's request to build a Supercenter on the banks of the river violates both of these major features of Dover's comprehensive plan. Sprawling development in the flood plain on the eastern edge of town will destroy our downtown and it will forever end responsible farming in the flood plain. It is your responsibility, and the duty of the Council, to enforce the comprehensive plan so that these two things do not happen. As you know, just the rumor that Wal-Mart was going to build a Supercenter was enough to cause one of the three grocery stores in our town to close. Take a walk down Main Street. Count the number of empty storefronts. Yes, the downtown area survived the initial battle when Wal-Mart moved into Sunrise Plaza, but a Supercenter is too much. It will be the death-knell for local merchants. Just as important, it will be a devastating blow to the distinctive, historic character of our community. People come from far and wide to canoe in the Appanoose, to camp in our campgrounds, and to enjoy the blessings of small town life that all of us take for granted. The construction of a Wal-Mart Supercenter along the banks of our lovely river is not progress; it is yet one more denial of our heritage and an irrevocable step into the boring homogeneity of American culture! We don't have to be like everybody else. We can control the nature of economic growth in our community. We can harness the power of that economic activity to preserve this community for our children and grandchildren as well as the countryside around us. Members of the Commission, I implore you: Don't sell our community down the river. Do the right thing: Say no to Wal-Mart!"

Bittner's populist rhetoric struck a chord with many who leapt to their feet and applauded as he left the podium. Watching Bittner return to his seat like a slugger rounding third base, John found himself wondering if anyone in the room supported Wal-Mart's bid to open a Supercenter in Dover. He didn't have to wait long.

Paul Petersen was the first to speak. "Forgive me, Mr. Bittner, but you were probably in middle school when Wal-Mart first came to Dover. We had a lot of 'doom and gloom' rhetoric back then too, but take a look around. Did downtown Dover dry up and blow away? Is Wal-Mart the only game in town? Quite to the contrary. Many merchants downtown are thriving. Things are going so well that the city just spent $3 million on historic preservation and street improvements downtown. Dover has become a major retail hub in this corner of Iowa. We didn't enjoy that status before Wal-Mart came to town."

Dale Murphy, a contractor in Dover, spoke next. He noted that Dover was built in a valley carved out by the Appanoose and that the eastern edge of town was the only outlet for growth in the region. Murphy went on to point out that the city's comprehensive plan acknowledged this reality because it designated this area as a corridor for future growth. "Close that end off and the town will die. If you're not growing, you're dying," said Murphy.

Speaking next, Charlie Tieskotter commended Wal-Mart for working so closely with the DNR and warned everyone that, if the Commission or the Council ignored the DNR permit and denied Wal-Mart's legitimate request to fill in and rezone the land, the city could find itself back on the losing end of a court case.

Last, but not least, Gail Banks addressed the audience. Banks and her husband operate a modest dairy farm on the outskirts of Dover. Speaking forcefully, she said: "I'm tired of people turning their noses up at Wal-Mart. Some of you seem to be concerned only about Dover's historical heritage. I've got news for you. I'm proud of our heritage, but I'm more interested in the present and the future. Maybe some of you can afford to spend extra money on groceries and cleaning supplies, but we can't. We don't buy our clothes over the Internet from Eddie Bauer. We need the low prices that Wal-Mart gives us, and we're not alone. Take a look at their parking lot. The reason they want to build a Supercenter here is because we're all shopping a lot at their current store. They're just giving us more of what we want!"

II

Two weeks later, John Yeoman was distracted for a moment by two birds chirping and twirling through the air as he opened the door and walked into the restaurant at the C'mon Inn for a special meeting of the Dover Chamber of Commerce. Today the chamber had invited Margaret Rock, a professor from the state university and an expert on the retail industry in Iowa, to give Chamber members some sense of how a Wal-Mart Supercenter would impact Dover. Utilizing overheads and handouts jammed with data, graphs, and tables, Rock gave a clear and helpful presentation that stressed five major points. First, businesses that compete head-on with a Supercenter are most seriously hurt, in particular, grocers, pharmacists, film processors, and providers of routine automotive services. Rock's second point, however, was that some businesses would benefit from the presence of a Supercenter, especially restaurants, auto dealers, and businesses that offer high levels of expertise and support to their customers. Third, as a result of this new competition, Dover could expect a significant shift in jobs to take place. On the one hand, some jobs would be lost at businesses that cannot compete effectively with a Supercenter. Rock noted that some of these losses are very hard for the community because often they are family-owned businesses that fail. On the other hand, Wal-Mart will double its current staff of "sales associates," creating new job opportunities in the community, especially for those with experience in grocery retailing and automotive services. On top of that, there will be new wage-earning jobs created by businesses that benefit from the increased traffic near the Supercenter location. Five years later, after the economy has adjusted to this new competition, financial data from around the state indicate that Dover can expect to see a 6 percent net increase in retail sales.

Rock concluded her presentation, however, with the discouraging news that, more often than not, the original Wal-Mart store sits abandoned, while the Supercenter thrives down the road. This "dead hole" can have a devastating impact on the remaining stores in the rest of the shopping center now abandoned by Wal-Mart. John felt deflated when Rock encouraged city leaders to tackle head-on this "slash and burn" approach to retailing. He knew that was why Wal-Mart had insisted on paying for all improvements to their building site. They did not want the City Council to tie their hands in any way, especially with regard to leasing their former store to a potential competitor.

Rock's presentation was followed by responses from two members of the Chamber. John knew both of them. Karen Warren provided cheery service behind the cash register at the True-Value hardware franchise she owned together with her ailing husband in downtown Dover. Bob Ojeda was an electrical contractor whose firm had done the wiring in an addition on John's house last fall. In an effort to foster constructive conversation about the Supercenter issue, the Chamber leaders had invited both of them to share their reactions and concerns in the form of a dialogue rather than through prepared remarks.

Karen started the exchange. "As a retailer who has had to compete directly with Wal-Mart, what really rankles me is that this is not a matter of fair competition. These big-box mega stores can sell items for retail that little stores like mine can't even buy at wholesale prices. It's just not fair. For example, they're selling a Huffy bike right now for $59.99 that costs me $62.50 to buy wholesale."

"But, Karen," Bob replied, "This is just the nature of free enterprise. Businesses compete to give customers what they want. You can't blame Wal-Mart for figuring out how to skip the middleman. They buy directly from manufacturers and have the most efficient distribution system in the world. I know it seems unfair to you, but this is just how the game is played: Compete or lose. It's as simple as that."

John could almost see the steam coming out of Karen's ears as she replied. "I've got news for you, Bob. This is not a game to me. Our livelihood is on the line here. Sure, we could fold up shop and go to work at Wally World, but then what would Dover have? Dover would have lost two stakeholders in the local economy only to replace them with two wage-earners at Wal-Mart. Is the town better off with that? Where will customers go to get the service they want and the information they need?"

Bob replied, "I'm no expert or anything, but it's my understanding that every wage-earner at Wal-Mart also has the option to become a share-holder in the corporation. In fact, I know that some of their employees have made small fortunes plowing their earnings back into stock purchases. It seems to me you can be a stakeholder in this community whether you own a business or not. That's just a matter of investing yourself in the welfare of Dover. Wal-Mart is certainly doing that. Last year they donated over $17,000 to local non-profits. Now, with regard to service, apparently people value lower prices more than they do service—especially for products that they buy on a routine basis and know something about. In addition, before Wal-Mart came to Dover, you could not return merchandise for cash at most of the stores downtown; they would only give you in-store credit. Now you can return merchandise for cash at just about every store downtown."

"Well tell me this, Bob, where does Wal-Mart put its money at the end of the business day?" With ire, Karen said, "I'll tell you where it goes. It flows electronically from Dover to Wal-Mart's banks in Bentonville, Arkansas. Oh, it may spend a night or two in a bank here in Dover, but not long enough for our bankers to recycle the money in the form of loans for houses, cars, or new businesses. In contrast, the vast majority of cash held by local businesses is kept right here in the community and is invested back into the community."

"I suppose that's true, Karen, but we can't look a gift horse in the mouth. Wal-Mart only invests in communities it thinks will be successful in the future. Their decision to build a Supercenter here is a compliment to us; it's a vote of confidence in the great little city of Dover. We certainly don't want them building their Supercenter twenty miles down the road in Brandywine. Think of the tax dollars we would lose and the negative impact that would have on our economy."

"But we are going to lose our great little city, Bob. Do you really think this will be the only development in that huge flood plain? This is just the start, not the end. Soon Dover is going to look like every other town in McAmerica. We don't want that here. We have a charming community that people love to live in and come to visit precisely because it is different and not surrounded by boring strip malls and national chains. There are thousands of Wal-Marts, but there's only one Dover."

"I just don't think this has to be a case of 'either/or,'" said Bob. "Economic growth and historic identity are not inherently incompatible. Appreciation for Dover's unique heritage and picturesque qualities has never been higher. Economically, the town has never been stronger. What's not to like? A Wal-Mart Supercenter will strengthen this community; it will not weaken it. And, frankly, I wouldn't mind seeing an Applebee's or The Olive Garden move into town. Have you ever tried to order anything but a burger or pizza in this darn town?"

III

Two weeks later, John left his Goodyear dealership, ate an early dinner with his pastor, and then took a long walk along the river on the eastern edge of town before the Council meeting that evening. He knew that the vote would be close; in fact it might come down to him breaking a tie between the six other Council members. With a name like Yeoman, he was always the last one to vote.

Over and over, he rehashed the arguments in his mind. Tieskotter was probably right. If they ignored the judgment of the Iowa DNR and rejected the 3-2 recommendation of the Planning and Zoning Commission to rezone the land after it is filled, Wal-Mart would almost certainly take them to court and a judge could rule again that the City Council's decision had been "arbitrary and capricious." On the other hand, if they approved the landfill and rezoning request, the newspaper reported yesterday that property owners upstream and adjacent to the Wal-Mart site intended to sue the city for increasing the danger of flooding on their land. In addition, the plaintiffs would argue that Dover's Board of Adjustment was the appropriate body to handle the landfill request and that any decision by the City Council would violate state law. John sighed. No matter what decision they made, it looked as if the Council was going to get sued.

He still didn't understand how the DNR could approve the filling in of a flood plain. In principle it seemed to be an action that undermined the very purpose of the agency. Laursen had been helpful on that score, however, when she reminded him that the DNR does not write the laws; it merely enforces those that are on the books. The DNR's responsibility is to protect the lives and property of the people of Iowa. In this situation they had concluded that filling in this small portion of the flood plain did not produce a significantly increased risk of flooding. But the DNR's decision did not mean that Dover's hands were tied because Dover's flood plain standard of 29,000 cubic feet per second (cfs) exceeds the state's 100-year standard of 22,300 cfs. In situations like these where local standards are more stringent, the state leaves final control of flood plain areas and planning-related issues in the hands of local officials. After all, that was what had brought Wal-Mart before the City Council: They needed to have their land reclassified from F-1 to C-4. It was up to the Council to interpret the comprehensive plan and decide whether the Supercenter amounted to "incompatible development" in the flood plain. The problem, however, was that the comprehensive plan did not provide any definition of this key term. John didn't see much sense in filling in a flood plain, but he had to admit that much of Dover was built in the flood plain and had regularly flooded until the 1930s, when the Army Corps of Engineers built the dikes that now protect the town.

But John still didn't like the idea of passing even more floodwaters along to communities downstream from Dover. Just because a dike protected Dover didn't mean the city shouldn't do something about the floodwaters it could still control. Just as important, he worried about the impact that commercial development would have on wildlife that relied on the habitat offered by the flood plain. Even though John knew that the Wal-Mart land had once been home to a drive-in theater, it had been planted in either soybeans or corn for as long as he could remember. There was no doubt that the land provided habitat to some wildlife. And it was beautiful—even with Anderson's big gravel pit and road construction equipment parked here on the western bank. How should he juggle his responsibilities to others downstream with his duties to the citizens of Dover? And what about the birds? Who represented their interests? Was this good stewardship of the land?

Having reached the site, John surveyed the vast 586-acre watershed and knew why it was so appealing to developers. If Wal-Mart's bid was successful, it would probably only be the first of many. Dale Murphy was right: This was the only area within current city limits that provided the kind of space necessary for large-scale commercial development. There certainly was no other thirty-acre undeveloped parcel available to Wal-Mart elsewhere in Dover. As a businessman, he understood the benefits of economic growth, but he also had a personal stake in the matter. It was likely that he would lose a good share of his tire and auto service business to Wal-Mart. And even though he felt up to that competition, he found himself thinking about the impact the Supercenter would have on business owners like Karen Warren and her husband.

John also found himself thinking about the impact the Supercenter would have on the community of Dover and the county as a whole. He loved living here. Every year he could count on reading letters to the editor that literally glowed with praise for the beauty of the town and the kindness of its citizens. It was true that Wal-Mart's entry into Sunrise Plaza had led some local business owners to close their stores, but several years later the economy seemed strong and it appeared to John that Dover was a stable and growing community. He wasn't so sure about the other towns in the county, however. Whereas Dover had grown a bit in the last census, almost all of the other towns in the county had lost population. Citing U.S Commerce data, the newspaper had reported that farm personal incomes in the county had fallen steadily from a ten-year high of nearly $40,000 in 1990 to just over $20,000 last year. The handwriting was on the wall for the grocers in the rural areas of the county. The Supercenter's 60,000 square feet in groceries would exceed the total amount of space in grocery stores in the county outside of Dover. Given the chance to couple savings with the convenience of one-stop shopping, most of the people who patronize these rural grocery stores would probably take their business to Wal-Mart.

Finally, was Dover on the brink of losing its distinctiveness? Certainly Dover had changed a great deal since John had arrived twenty-five years ago to enroll at the college in town, but the town still seemed healthy. Fast-food chains had moved in around the same time that Wal-Mart arrived, but Sally's Kitchen was still a thriving eatery for locals and college kids downtown. Lawn chair nights still pulled a big crowd to listen to local entertainment on the steps of the County courthouse in the summer. And the annual ethnic heritage festival remained a huge draw for tourists, though it had become harder to recruit volunteers in recent years. It was true, however, that the old bridge and the hundred-year-old elementary school would probably soon fall to the wrecking ball. Like others, though, John found it ironic that one of the parties that had sold land to Wal-Mart's land developer was Dover's museum. Recognized nationally for its unique collections honoring Dover's ethnic heritage, the museum board of directors had realized that the only way they could raise the funds to expand the museum was to sell land that had been given to the museum as a bequest. How do you preserve the identity of a people or of a town? At what price?

Feeling drops of rain on his neck, John turned back towards town. Still not sure how he would vote, he continued to think as he walked—accompanied by the sounds of crickets and birds mixed with the drone of cars on the recently widened state highway.

Commentary

Ethical questions raised by this case are being debated all over the world as cities, suburbs, and towns grapple with the growth of "big-box" retailers in their communities. While the environmental aspects of the case are very important, there are also significant economic and social issues at stake. This case is not just about urban sprawl and its environmental consequences; it is also about jobs, the heritage of a town, and the quality of life in Dover. Will Dover be a *sustainable community* if Wal-Mart builds a new Supercenter there?

In order to answer this question it is necessary to understand the related and more fundamental concept of *sustainable development*. The U.N.-sponsored Brundtland Commission coined this term in 1987 to describe development that "meets the needs of the present without compromising the ability of future generations to meet their own needs."[1] Since then, people around the world have been examining various ecological, economic, and social goals that need to be integrated in order for life to flourish on Earth.

As an elected member of the City Council, John Yeoman is wrestling with ethical questions related to each of the three key dimensions of sustainable development. Environmentally, will the Supercenter development diminish habitat for migratory birds and other wildlife? Will filling in this portion of the flood plain increase the likelihood of flooding in the future? Will waste-

Figure 1. Sustainable Development

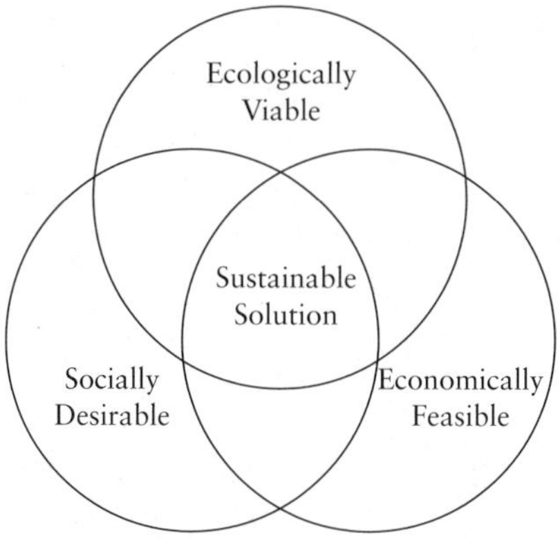

Source: F. Douglas Muschett, ed., *Principles of Sustainable Development*, St. Lucie Press, 1997, p. 56.

water run-off pose a water quality problem for the Appanoose River? The economic questions are also difficult. Will the Supercenter help or harm the merchants in Dover? Is it more important for the Dover economy to grow or for there to be a larger percentage of employer-owned stores? On the social front, is it really the case that the character of the community is at stake? When do quaint towns lose their distinctiveness and tourist appeal?

As if these problems were not enough, Dover's *Comprehensive Development Plan* requires John and the other members of the City Council to prioritize the three key dimensions of sustainable development. The comprehensive plan does a good job of identifying various social, economic, and ecological goals, but it is not clear how these competing goods should be reconciled when they conflict. The plan calls for protection of ecologically sensitive areas, but it also calls for economic growth that will benefit the citizens of Dover while preserving its downtown business core and the town's unique heritage. It is not self-evident how these goods should be ordered and thus it is difficult for John to know what position he should take on Wal-Mart's request to landfill and rezone a portion of the land for the site of the Supercenter.

Another complicating factor in the case is that it is not clear whether the City Council or the Board of Adjustment is legally charged with making the decision about Wal-Mart's request to landfill and rezone the land. The Board of Adjustment has rejected a similar proposal by another business, but the

City Council believes it is legally authorized by a city ordinance to make such decisions about filling in flood plains. Given the advice of the city attorney, it is not surprising that the council has decided to rule on Wal-Mart's request. This could prove to be unwise, however, if lawsuits are filed and the courts decide that the city has illegally impinged on the quasi-judicial role of the Board of Adjustment to make case-specific judgments about requests for special exceptions to Dover's Zoning Ordinance and its *Comprehensive Development Plan*.[2] However, no matter how this may be resolved legally, no court decision will completely resolve the various ethical issues raised by this case. Ultimately the courts may decide *who* should consider Wal-Mart's request to fill-in and rezone a portion of the flood plain, but the courts will not stipulate to either the City Council or the Board of Adjustment *what* position they should take. The ethical and policy issues will still be up to local officials like John Yeoman to decide.

In order to analyze and assess this case ethically, this commentary provides background information about urban sprawl and its consequences as well as a brief history of discount retailing and the impact that Wal-Mart stores have had on communities in Iowa. The commentary concludes with a biblical survey of the stewardship tradition and explores the relevance of the ecojustice norms to the ethical issues posed by the case.

URBAN SPRAWL:
ECONOMIC, SOCIAL, AND ECOLOGICAL CONSEQUENCES

Recent studies indicate that "big-box" discount stores represent more than 80 percent of all new retail construction in the United States.[3] The majority of these new stores are being built on the edges of communities where land is less expensive and zoning restrictions are often less stringent. Between 1960 and 1990 the amount of developed land in large urban areas of the United States grew twice as fast as the population in these cities. For example, Chicago's population increased by only 4 percent during this period of time, but the city grew in size by 46 percent. In Cleveland the population actually declined by 11 percent, but the physical size of the city grew by 33 percent.[4] At first glance this startling data may appear to exclude a town the size of Dover with a population of only 8,000 people, but some of the fastest growth is occurring beyond metropolitan areas in still-rural communities 60 to 70 miles from metropolitan areas.[5]

Low land prices and fewer zoning restrictions are only two of the factors that have contributed to the phenomenon of urban sprawl. Defined by the National Trust for Historic Preservation as "poorly planned, low-density, auto-oriented development that spreads out from the center of communities," urban sprawl is the direct or indirect result of various federal policies.[6] The most significant of these policies was the creation of the Federal Housing Administration (FHA) during the great depression of the 1930s. After millions defaulted on mortgages and the construction of new homes fell by 95 percent, the FHA changed the way that home loans were structured. Instead of a 50 percent down payment and a 10-year loan on the balance, home-buyers now had to come up with only a 10 percent down payment and could finance the rest with a 30-year mortgage. These changes put home ownership within the reach of millions of Americans and resulted in a boom in new housing construction on the edges of urban centers, especially after the Veterans Administration offered similar loan terms after World War II.[7]

At the same time, the federal government subsidized the construction of a 41,000-mile interstate highway system. Large arterial highways were built to enable workers to drive from their homes in the suburbs to their jobs in the cities. Density-efficient trolleys and buses for urban mass transit were quickly replaced by the automobile as far-flung suburbanites discovered they needed a car to get just about anywhere in their new communities. When merchants followed their customers out to the suburbs, they found that, unlike pre-war housing developments, no provision had been made for corner stores within neighborhoods. As a result, business owners studied traffic flows and built their stores along access roads to the arterial highways. As these stores clustered together, the modern strip shopping center was born.[8] It is not a coincidence that Wal-Mart wants to build its Supercenter next to the recently widened state highway that serves Dover.

Other federal and state subsidies have encouraged urban sprawl. Government funding finances the construction of regional airports, schools, water treatment plants, and other public utilities. In addition, low federal tax rates on fossil fuels encourage the use of private automobiles and the trucking of goods around the nation.[9] Not surprisingly, then, traffic is growing at a significant rate. Studies indicate that the use of motor vehicles in the United States doubled from one to two trillion miles per year between 1970 and 1990[10] and the emission of carbon dioxide, the largest contributor to global warming, doubled in the United States between 1950 and 1990.[11]

A significant amount of urban sprawl has taken place through the purchase and conversion of farmland. While rates vary from one state to another, land devoted to farming dropped 20 percent from 1.2 billion acres in 1950 to 968 million acres in 1997. More recent studies indicate that farmland is being converted to other uses at a rate of up to 2.6 million acres per year.[12] The American Farmland Trust reports that from 1982 to 1992 an average of 400,000 acres of "prime" farmland was lost per year to urban and suburban development.[13] In 1999, Iowa lost 26,000 acres of farmland to development.[14]

More than half of the nation's leading agricultural counties are within or adjacent to major metropolitan areas.[15] As housing, commercial, and industrial development take place in what formerly was farmland, property taxes increase for the remaining farmers in the area. Facing low commodity prices and stiff global competition, many farmers do the math and sell land that returns only $2,000 to $3,000 a year to a developer for a lump sum of $20,000 to $30,000 an acre. Not only do such transactions help struggling and aging farmers, they also appear to be in the financial best interests of the surrounding community. Studies indicate that "commercial and industrial property development has been shown to be the most cost effective use for land, costing a community an average of just twenty-nine cents in exchange for each dollar that is returned to the citizens in the form of wages and tax gains."[16]

While some are alarmed that U.S. agricultural acreage has declined by more than 20 percent since 1950, others point out that agricultural production has risen by 105 percent.[17] As a result of these gains in productivity, the United States is a leading global exporter of agricultural products and Americans enjoy some of the lowest food prices in the world. Defenders of urbanization thus conclude that urban growth has not adversely affected agricultural production in the United States. In addition, they cite U.S. Department of Agriculture statistics that indicate that "nearly 95 percent of the total land area of the United States remains rural—either as forest, desert, cropland, or pasture—and less than 5 percent of all land is devoted to urban uses."[18] The implication is that the nation has lots of room to grow.

Nevertheless, the development of large tracts of wetland, woodland, and prairie environments has destroyed life-sustaining wildlife habitats for many species. For example, in this case, Clara Laursen cites a recent study by the National Audubon Society which finds that "(m)ore than 50 percent of neotropical migrant [bird] species monitored in the eastern U.S. and prairie states have been in decline for the last 30 years."[19] Even though patches of green exist in residential subdivisions and around shopping plazas, these developments create habitat fragmentation that disrupts migratory corridors and breeding patterns.

Studies indicate that approximately one-half of the animals and one-third of plant species on the federal list of endangered and threatened species are dependent on wetlands.[20] More than half of the 220 million acres of wetlands found 200 years ago in the lower forty-eight states have been converted to other uses.[21] The vast majority of this conversion was done to place land into agricultural production. Since 1987, however, more wetlands have been converted to urban use than to agriculture. At the same time, it is heartening to note that only 29,000 acres of wetlands were lost per year from 1987 to 1991 in comparison with approximately 600,000 acres per year that were converted to agricultural production between 1954 and 1974. This reduction in wetlands conversion indicates that communities have begun to recognize the value of wetlands, but now need to protect them from the threat posed by urban sprawl.

In this case, John and the other council members are faced more with the protection of a portion of the Appanoose River flood plain than the conversion of a wetland. In addition to her concern about habitat degradation discussed above, Clara Laursen raised three issues with regard to development in the Appanoose flood plain. The first is that the water quality of the river might be impaired by construction of the Wal-Mart Supercenter. The second is that filling in the flood plain may lead to increased flooding elsewhere. And the third is that commercial development along the banks of the Appanoose will despoil the aesthetic quality of the river.

Turning first to the water quality issue, Wal-Mart's 31-acre site for the Supercenter in Dover is part of a 586-acre watershed that drains into the Appanoose. Eleven of these acres will be covered by asphalt to form the parking lot and the Supercenter roof will cover another four acres. In addition, Wal-Mart will lease four 1-acre parcels to other businesses on the periphery of the store, so as much as 19 acres (61 percent) of the Supercenter site will be covered with surfaces impervious to water. The following excerpt from a book recently published by the National Resources Defense Council addresses some of the concerns related to these impervious surfaces:

> It is now thoroughly documented that, as the amount of impervious cover increases in a watershed, the velocity and volume of surface runoff increases; flooding, erosion and pollutant loads in receiving waters increase; groundwater recharge and water tables decline; streambeds and flows are altered; and aquatic habitat is impaired. . . . To grasp the impact of impervious surfaces on the volume of storm water runoff, consider the effects of a one-inch rain-storm on a one-acre natural meadow: typically, much of the water from such a storm would infiltrate into the soil causing only about 218 cubic feet of runoff. . . . On a one-acre paved parking lot, however, no water could settle into the soil and the storm would cause 3,450 cubic feet of runoff, nearly 16 times that from the natural meadow. . . . Along with increased water volume come changes in composition, as contaminants, including sediment, pathogens, nutrients (such as nitrogen and phosphorous), heavy metals, pesticides, and nondegradable debris, are picked up. All told, some 67 toxic pollutants have been detected in runoff from urban areas. Another consequence is "thermal pollution": impervious surfaces, in part because of the absence of trees for shade in paved areas, can reach temperatures in excess of 120 degrees Fahrenheit and raise the temperature of water flowing over them, causing temperatures to rise in receiving waters downstream. Stream degradation begins as impervious cover in a watershed exceeds 10 percent.[22]

It would appear, however, that all of these water quality concerns are addressed in Max Walters' presentation. Wal-Mart's engineers have designed, and the Iowa DNR has approved, an 8-acre retention basin to contain any contaminated water, cool it, and filter it before releasing it gradually into the river. As an added benefit, the basin would provide a permanent 8-acre wetland where currently none exists. If Wal-Mart is the only commercial development in the watershed, then the 10 percent threshold for impervious surfaces will not be breached. John fears, however, that Wal-Mart's development might be the first of many in the watershed.

Clara Laursen also has doubts about the quality of the artificial wetland and the efficacy of the retention basin, especially during major rain or flood events. According to the U.S. Geological Survey, the 1993 flood that inundated property and caused damage to some homes in the actual town represented by the fictitious Dover only reached 18,200 cfs, less than the state's 100-year standard of 22,300 cfs, and substantially less than the community's more stringent standard of 29,000 cfs developed after a devastating flood in 1941.[23] Like many other Iowans, Laursen is not convinced that the state's current 100-year flood plain standard is stringent enough to protect the people and property of Dover as well as the water quality of the river.

Evidence that the 100-year flood plain standard may be insufficient can be found in data reported by the Federal Emergency Management Agency (FEMA). According to FEMA, property damage from flooding now totals over $1 billion a year in the United States and "[n]early 9 of every 10 presidential disaster declarations result from natural phenomena in which flooding was a major component."[24] These numbers are shocking given the fact that the United States has spent over $14 billion since the 1930s to prevent flooding on the nation's rivers. The Flood Control Acts of 1936 and 1938 authorized the construction of 260 reservoirs, 6,000 miles of levees and floodwalls, and 8,000 miles of stream channel improvements.[25] So why does the nation still suffer serious annual losses from flooding? An environmental historian reaches the following conclusion:

> The gains from flood-control works were offset by a great increase in flood plain development. But the cure [is] elementary. "*Instead of trying to keep the rivers away from man* [sic], *keep man away from the rivers.* . . . Floods are acts of God—but flood *losses* are acts of man, a payment which nature exacts in return for his occupation of her flood plain."[26]

On the basis of this argument, the construction of a Supercenter in a flood plain appears to be both ecologically and economically unwise. The complicating factor, however, is that Wal-Mart has acquired a fill permit from the DNR to raise the site above the 100-year flood plain. So, does the project constitute development in a flood plain or not? John is not sure. The DNR has found that the development will not pose significant harm to life or property in the area through flooding.

The last issue that Clara Laursen raised pertains to the scenic quality of the Appanoose River and the Protected Water Areas (PWA) program of the state of Iowa. Initiated in 1987, the purpose of the PWA is "to maintain, preserve and protect existing natural and scenic qualities of selected lakes, rivers and marshes and their adjacent land areas."[27] Some of the program's objectives seem especially relevant to the development of the Wal-Mart Supercenter site:

- Protect the existing natural and pastoral character of the area's landscape;
- Promote public health, safety and general welfare by preventing scenic and environmental damage to the area's outstanding water and associated land resources that might otherwise result from undesirable development patterns;
- Protect and enhance specific water and riparian environments in a manner which ensures continued fish and wildlife;

- Preserve natural, cultural, and scenic features which enhance recreational and educational experiences within the area.[28]

What Laursen does not mention, however, is that "protected water areas are *cooperatively* managed by people and agencies owning land along the selected lakes, rivers and/or marshes."[29] Landholders are not *required* to participate in the program; their role is strictly voluntary. Thus, John Yeoman and the other members of the City Council are not required to cooperate with the PWA, although Dover's comprehensive plan indicates that protection of flood plains is an important objective of the plan. On the private side, Max Walters could make the argument that Wal-Mart is cooperating through the creation of the 8-acre retention basin and riparian zone that will create an artificial wetland. Laursen and others, however, are still concerned that the Supercenter will spoil the scenic quality of the river since it will be built so close to the bank.

ANALYZING THE IMPACT OF A WAL-MART SUPERCENTER

Discount merchandising, of which Wal-Mart is the reigning champion, is the most recent retailing innovation that has evolved in the United States since the late nineteenth century. Prior to the Civil War much trade was conducted through itinerant peddlers. As the nation's population increased in towns and villages, customers began to shop more at new general stores and patronized peddlers less. Then, as cities emerged, general stores had to compete with stores that specialized in dry-goods, hardware, farm implements, meat products, and groceries. The general stores and specialty stores, however, soon met stiff competition from department stores, chain stores, and mail-order houses that cut costs by dealing directly with the manufacturers of goods.[30]

By the first half of the twentieth century, three giants dominated the retail sector: Sears & Roebuck, J.C. Penney, and Montgomery Ward. All three of these companies functioned as department stores, chain stores, and mail-order houses. Much of the remaining retail trade was scooped up by national variety store chains like Kresge and Woolworth as well as by regional chains around the country. Then, in 1962, K-Mart, Target, and Wal-Mart all burst upon the retail scene. Fueled by the increased purchasing power of the middle class, these three discount retailers utilized technological innovation, inexpensive locations, extended shopping hours, and weekly advertising circulars to provide low prices and a wide inventory to consumers.[31] K-Mart and Target located their stores in growing parts of metropolitan areas, but Wal-Mart (following the eccentricities of its founder, Sam Walton) decided to build its stores in small towns in Arkansas and neighboring states. By 1980, K-Mart was nipping at the heels of the retail leader, Sears & Roebuck, and Wal-Mart was not a major factor. By 1990, however, Wal-Mart had become the largest retailer in the United States.[32]

Today, Wal-Mart is the largest retailer in the *world*. Wal-Mart employs more than 1 million people worldwide at nearly 3,500 facilities in the United

States and more than 1,000 units in Mexico, Puerto Rico, Canada, Argentina, Brazil, China, Korea, Germany, and the United Kingdom. Wal-Mart estimates that more than 100 million customers per week visit a regular Wal-Mart store, a Supercenter, a Sam's Club, or a Wal-Mart Neighborhood Market. As an indication of the company's aggressive expansion plans, Wal-Mart planned to open over 300 new stores in the United States and around the world in 2002. This expansion of 40 million square feet of retail space was the largest in the company's history, and an 8 percent increase over 2001. Though new stores account for most of this space, a significant amount will be the result of expansion or relocation of existing stores.[33] This is the case in Dover where Wal-Mart intends to transform its existing store into a Supercenter and relocate it from Sunrise Plaza to the eastern edge of town.

In addition to the ecological concerns, a large share of this case focuses on the economic and social impact that a Wal-Mart Supercenter would have on the economy and community of Dover. Kenneth Stone, an economist at Iowa State University, is a nationally recognized expert on the impact of mass merchandisers on rural communities. His research has focused, in particular, on the impact of "regular" Wal-Mart stores on communities in Iowa. His first study was published in 1991 and subsequent updates have been published in 1995 and 1997.[34] Stone is also studying the impact of Wal-Mart Supercenters on communities in Iowa and will publish some of this research soon.[35]

In his 1995 study, Stone compared store sales from 1983 to 1993 in Iowa towns that had Wal-Mart stores with those that did not. During this period, Stone noted a significant shift of sales to larger towns and cities where mass merchandisers like Wal-Mart captured a substantial portion of the sales. Over the course of a decade, Stone estimates that Iowa lost 7,326 businesses in small towns and rural areas. These losses included 555 grocery stores; 298 hardware stores; 293 building supply stores; 161 variety stores; 158 women's apparel stores; 153 shoe stores; 116 drug stores; and 111 men's and boy's apparel stores.[36]

Stone's 1997 study compared retail performance in 34 Iowa towns that had Wal-Mart stores for at least ten years to retail performance in 15 towns of the same population size that did not have Wal-Mart stores.[37] The communities studied ranged in size from 5,000 to 40,000 people. The following table summarizes Stone's findings.

There are several things to note in this data, but the percentage change in total retail sales produces one of the most interesting findings. It is not surprising that towns *without* a Wal-Mart saw their sales decline by 15 percent over ten years. It is surprising, however, to see that towns *with* Wal-Mart stores saw their sales increase by 6 percent after five years, but then decline by 4 percent after ten years. Initial data from studies measuring the impact of Wal-Mart Supercenters on communities in Mississippi and Texas reveal a similar trend. In Mississippi, total sales in towns with Supercenters were up 2.2 percent after three years, but were up only 0.7 percent after five years. In Iowa, however, towns with Supercenters show a sharp 15.5 percent increase in total sales after two years. Since Wal-Mart did not open its first Supercenter in Iowa until 1998, Stone is still gathering longer range data.[38]

Total Retail Sales Selected Iowa Towns: 1985–1995	Percent Change in Sales After 5 Years		Percent Change in Sales After 10 Years	
Type of Store	Wal-Mart Towns	Non- Wal-Mart Towns	Wal-Mart Towns	Non- Wal-Wart Towns
General Merchandise Stores	+53	–14	+25	–34
Eating & Drinking Establishments	+6	–8	+5	–9
Home Furnishings	–3	–21	–1	–31
Building Materials	–17	–14	+4	–25
Specialty Stores	–5	–26	–17	–28
Apparel Stores	–11	–17	–28	–28
Total Sales	+6	–8	–4	–15

At the close of his 1997 study, Stone notes that "mid-size" towns with Wal-Mart stores have fared better economically than similar towns without Wal-Mart stores. Towns under 5,000 in population, however, have borne the brunt of the discount mass merchandisers. Some small towns in Iowa have lost up to 47 percent of their retail trade over ten years after a Wal-Mart has opened in a nearby town.[39]

So what conclusions might John Yeoman draw from this kind of data? Bob Ojeda would appear to have a point. He shudders to think what would happen to Dover if Wal-Mart was rebuffed by the City Council and decided to build its Supercenter in Brandywine. Stone's data clearly indicate that towns with Wal-Mart stores are better off economically than towns without them. While Dover is closer to the 5,000-population level than the 20,000-level that presumably represents Stone's "mid-size" category, Wal-Mart wouldn't spend millions of dollars to build a Supercenter if they thought Dover didn't have a future. Or would they? Recall that total retail sales in Wal-Mart towns have declined by 4 percent after ten years and that these sales seem to be gobbled up by retail stores in larger urban communities. Will Dover's retail sales become eroded over time just as smaller towns have crumbled in the face of competition from larger towns? Does any of this matter as far as the City Council is concerned? How far into the future should they attempt to provide for the general welfare of Dover?

Beyond the economic impact of a Supercenter on Dover, critics lift up other reasons to oppose the development of new Wal-Mart stores. Retail saturation is one concern. According to "sprawl-buster" Al Norman, the United States has more shopping centers than high schools. At the beginning of the

21st century, there are 20 square feet of retail space for every person in the United States, up from 14.7 square feet in 1986 and ten times greater than the amount per person in Britain. A sign of this excess is that there are more than 4,000 abandoned shopping malls in the United States. Wal-Mart alone has hundreds of empty buildings available for rent or lease in virtually every state in the union. Approximately 10 percent of the stores Wal-Mart owns or leases are closed around the country.[40] This, of course, is a major source of concern in Dover. What will happen when Wal-Mart moves east into the Supercenter? What will happen to the other merchants in Sunrise Plaza if Wal-Mart weighs anchor? John already knows that the company does not intend to lease the store to a potential competitor and, given the variety of goods a Supercenter offers, this will exclude many potential businesses.

Another topic touched on in the case concerns the philanthropic practices of businesses in Dover. Bob Ojeda notes that Wal-Mart donated over $17,000 to local non-profits in the previous year. As a company, Wal-Mart donated more than $190 million to various charities and other non-profit organizations during fiscal year 2000.[41] This figure, however, represents only one tenth of one percent of the corporation's total sales of $191 billion in the same year. Statistics like these lead some to conclude that Wal-Mart is not as generous as it could be. It is difficult to compile comparable philanthropic data on local businesses, but it is virtually certain that they beat Wal-Mart's record of giving.

Other issues related to Wal-Mart's business practices are not discussed in the case, but bear some mention here. One of these pertains to recent lawsuits filed against the company. For example, in the summer of 2001, six female employees filed a sexual discrimination suit against Wal-Mart. The suit claims that 72 percent of Wal-Mart's hourly sales employees are women, but only one-third of the company's managers are women. Drawing on corporate data furnished to government regulators, the plaintiffs contend that 56 percent of managers at Wal-Mart's largest competitors are women.[42] That summer, in another court, Wal-Mart paid $1 million to settle a federal lawsuit charging the corporation with violating in several states storm water drainage rules related to the Clean Water Act.[43]

On the labor front, unions are not very fond of Wal-Mart. To date, none of Wal-Mart's one million employees are members of unions. That was not the case for a brief period of time in the spring of 2000 when eleven meat-packers at the Wal-Mart Supercenter in Jackson, Texas, voted to join the United Food & Commercial Workers Union (UFCW). In response, Wal-Mart declared that it would provide only pre-packaged meats in all of its stores, thus eliminating the need for meat-packers.[44] According to the UFCW, Wal-Mart workers make an average of $3 per hour less than unionized supermarket workers, $2 per hour less than other supermarket workers, and $1 per hour less than the average retail wage earner.[45] A full-time Wal-Mart employee working 40 hours a week and earning the average pay of $7.50 per hour earns $15,000 a year, almost exactly the federal poverty rate for a family of four.[46]

Another set of issues that have plagued Wal-Mart, and frankly all other clothing merchandisers, are the frequently proven allegations that child labor has been used to manufacture garments. Bob Ortega, a journalist for the *Wall Street Journal,* chronicles this sad story in his book, *In Sam We Trust.* Fueled with information supplied by union activists, television journalists confronted Kathie Lee Gifford, whose name is featured on a line of clothing at Wal-Mart. After denying the accusations at first, Gifford became convinced by the evidence and insisted that Wal-Mart monitor its vendors to ensure that child labor not be used to manufacture her clothing line. With some reluctance the company acceded to her wishes and has made significant efforts, along with other clothing retailers, to eliminate the use of child labor in garment production.[47]

In defense of Wal-Mart, all of the concerns raised above plague virtually every large multinational corporation. Given its place as the largest retailer in the world, Wal-Mart becomes a prime target for scorn and criticism. There is no denying, however, that the company's unrivaled economic success could not have taken place without high rates of customer and employee satisfaction. As Gail Banks testifies, people around the world love to shop in Wal-Mart stores. They certainly appear to be doing some things very right. Reaffirming this view, Bob Ojeda asks, "What's not to like?" Indeed. Why shouldn't John Yeoman support construction of the Supercenter? At this point it is time to do some moral assessment of the ethical issues posed by the project.

STEWARDSHIP, SUSTAINABLE DEVELOPMENT, AND ECOJUSTICE

Several people in the case appeal to the concept of stewardship. Max Walters points to the retention basin, riparian buffer zone, and the accommodations for wildlife as evidence that Wal-Mart wants to be a good steward ecologically. Clara Laursen takes the opposite view in her presentation. For her, the destruction of wildlife habitat, the increased dangers of flooding and water pollution, and the construction of a massive store on the banks of the scenic Appanoose all add up to a clear case of bad land stewardship. John Yeoman seems to sympathize with Clara's concerns. He finds it hard to see how filling in flood plains can constitute good stewardship of the land, though he acknowledges that dikes protect Dover from floods that used to plague the town.

It is clear, however, that John is wrestling with more than just the environmental matters related to this case. As a member of the City Council, he is also concerned about the economic impact the Supercenter would have on other businesses as well as the social repercussions this project could have on the distinctive quality of Dover. Though he does not refer explicitly to the concept of stewardship when he considers these matters, it is clear that he feels an obligation as an elected public servant to make decisions that are in the best interests of the citizens of Dover, both now and in the future. John wants to be a good steward of Dover's resources.

This broader conception of stewardship is revealed through comments by some other characters in the case. Tom Bittner casts stewardship primarily in terms of preservation. He urges the Planning and Zoning Commission to preserve and protect the flood plain, local businesses, and the distinctive quality of Dover. Dale Murphy takes the opposite approach. For him good stewardship is equivalent to economic development and growth in the area. Finally, Charlie Tieskotter's comments remind John that fiscal prudence is another important dimension of good stewardship. The city can ill afford another failed lawsuit. It would also not fare well if Wal-Mart built the Supercenter in Brandywine instead.

Virtually nothing is said in the case about John's faith background, only that he had an early dinner with his pastor before the City Council meeting later that evening. The case does not say what they discussed, but it is possible that stewardship was one of the topics. If so, the pastor might have helped John trace biblical foundations for the concept of stewardship in the Old Testament and the New Testament. With this background, John would better understand how the concept of stewardship applies not only ecologically to the stewardship of land, but also to wise decisions involving everything that God has made.

In the Old Testament, interpretations of the two creation accounts can render different conceptions of stewardship. In Genesis 1:26–28, God creates human beings in God's image and blesses them saying, "be fruitful and multiply, and fill the earth and subdue it; and have dominion over the birds of the air and over every living thing that moves upon the earth." In Hebrew, the word that is translated as "subdue" *(kabash)* means literally to "put something under one's control," like a conqueror placing his foot on the throat of the vanquished. The term finds colloquial expression in the phrase, "He put the kibosh on that," which means that someone stamped out the possibility of a certain option. In this text the implication is that human beings have divine permission to control nature as they fill the earth and exercise dominion over it. This authorization to "subdue" the earth is tempered a bit, however, by two other key elements in the text. God's blessing to "be fruitful and multiply and fill the earth" is actually pronounced *first* to the birds of the air and the fish of the sea (Gen. 1:20–22). Thus, even though God wants human beings to fill the earth, it would appear that this should not come at the expense of birds and fish. They have a right to flourish too. Also, the Hebrew word translated as "dominion" *(radah)* refers to the type of rule that kings or queens exercise over their subjects. While this rule could be harsh or benevolent, it is clear from the rest of the Old Testament that God prefers rulers who care for the poor and vulnerable, maintain justice, and avoid idolatry.

Thus, the conception of stewardship that emerges from this interpretation of the first creation account in Genesis is one that views human transformation of nature as perfectly legitimate so long as it contributes to the flourishing of human beings and is not achieved through unjust means or by unduly imperiling the welfare of other living animals. It is easy to see how developmentalists are drawn to this conception of stewardship. The problem, however, is that too often stewardship as responsible dominion has been replaced with the notion that ownership sanctions rapacious domination. As modern notions of private property and increasingly powerful technologies have been joined with a permission to subdue the earth, the result has been enormous ecological and social harm. This logic of domination has sanctioned slavery, destroyed civilizations, and caused enormous ecological damage.[48] In no way, shape, or form can this sort of behavior be construed as good stewardship. God's command to have dominion over the earth is not a license to exploit it ruthlessly.

Another conception of stewardship can be located in the second creation account. In Genesis 2:4b-24 God forms the first human being *(Adam)* from the dust of the ground *(adama)*. Then God plants a garden in Eden and puts Adam in the garden with instructions to "till it and keep it." Next, concerned that Adam have a partner and not be alone, God forms out of the ground every animal of the field and every bird of the air and allows Adam to name these animals. When none of these animals proves to be a sufficient partner for Adam, God uses one of Adam's ribs to form Eve.

The conception of stewardship that can be drawn from this text is significantly different from the view in the first creation account. Whereas Genesis 1 emphasizes that human beings are created in the image of God, Genesis 2 emphasizes humanity's humble origins; God molds the first human from humus. In addition, humans share kinship with all other living creatures because they too were formed from the ground. Later, in Genesis 3, Adam is reminded that he was created from dust, and to the dust he shall return upon the event of his death. If the first creation account emphasizes humanity's independence and reign over all that God has made, the second creation account emphasizes humanity's fundamental interdependence with Earth and kinship with other forms of life. Here the vocation of human beings is not to "subdue the earth" but rather to "till and keep" God's garden. In Hebrew, the word translated as "till" *(abad)* means to bless, serve, or benefit another. The Hebrew word translated as "keep" *(shamar)* means to watch or preserve, to guard and protect. These terms render a more static and less dynamic conception of stewardship. The emphasis is more on preserving and protecting what God has made. Humans are invited to care for the earth as God "blesses *(abad)* and keeps *(shamar)*" them (Num. 6:24). Human beings are not set above other living things with permission to exercise dominion over them. Instead, God sets human beings apart to serve the needs of other forms of life through acts of service. It is easy to see how *preservationists* are drawn to this conception of stewardship in the second creation account.

The reality, of course, is that both texts are part of the book of Genesis and, thus, both texts should inform contemporary conceptions of stewardship.[49] It would appear that the ancient Hebrews realized that human beings would always be torn between the desire to preserve all that God has made and the need to use parts of God's creation in order to flourish. Stewardship is a complicated vocation.

Other texts in the Bible further illuminate the concept of stewardship. Good stewards are those who know their place and do the work of their masters

(1 Chron. 28:1), while bad stewards receive severe condemnation (Is. 22:15). In terms of duties, stewards manage substantial economic assets and sometimes also wield political responsibility (Gen. 43:16–19; 44:1–4; Mt. 20:1–16). For Jesus, the ideal steward is the one who stays on the job while the master is away and manages resources so well that each member of the household "has their food in due season" (Lk. 12:35–48). Jesus even extols the example of a dishonest or shrewd steward in one of his parables (Lk. 16:1–8). When a rich man confronted one of his stewards and charged him with squandering the master's money, the steward decided to cut deals with the master's debtors in order to ingratiate himself with them and also to recover at least some of the money that was owed to the master. When the steward presented these returns to the master, the master commended the steward for his shrewdness. At this point, Jesus laments that the children of light are less shrewd than others in society. On another occasion Jesus encourages his followers to be "wise as serpents and innocent as doves" (Mt. 10:16). From these texts it is clear that stewardship requires trustworthiness, skill, experience, and cunning. It is not just a matter of preserving what God has made but also a matter of taking some risks and using God's resources wisely.

This summary of the stewardship tradition provides a helpful background, but it does not resolve John Yeoman's dilemma. Somehow John needs to figure out what good stewardship entails in this particular situation. Somehow he has to prioritize and integrate the three key dimensions of sustainable development that were presented as interlocking but also competing spheres of moral concern at the beginning of this commentary. One resource John might use to reflect further on this case is the concept of ecojustice and its related moral norms that are described earlier in this volume. Assessment of the case through the prism of these norms might help him better discern what would amount to good stewardship. For various reasons, the norm of sustainability is particularly relevant to this case.

The ecojustice norm of sustainability expresses a concern for future generations and the planet as a whole and emphasizes that an adequate and acceptable quality of life for present generations must not jeopardize the prospects for future generations. Sustainability precludes short-sighted emphases on economic growth that fundamentally harm ecological systems, but it also excludes long-term conservation efforts that ignore basic human needs and costs. Sustainability emphasizes the importance of healthy and interdependent communities of life as the basis for the welfare of present and future generations.

It is obvious that much economic activity in countries like the United States is not sustainable ecologically in the long run. Global warming, topsoil erosion, habitat destruction, and water degradation are all harming the ecological foundation upon which economic activity takes place. It is difficult, however, for most local politicians to consider seriously their duties to future generations because the voters that elected them are the ones that call on the phone and demand that their interests be represented. This is why policy documents like Dover's *Comprehensive Development Plan* are so important: they can give politicians some cover to make difficult decisions. But ultimately politicians still have to muster the courage to use the plan to protect the future and not sacrifice it to the present. Since the protection of flood plains is a priority in Dover's plan, it is hard to see how filling in a flood plain reflects this priority. Given the high costs that are incurred each year as a result of flooding in the United States, it is clear that development in flood plain areas is wise neither economically nor ecologically. Raising land to bring it out of the flood plain simply passes the burden of floodwaters further downstream, thus violating the norm of solidarity that calls for the equitable sharing of burdens and benefits. Even though the Iowa DNR has determined that backfilling this amount of flood plain will not adversely affect the citizens of Iowa, this does not mean that citizens in other states will not be adversely affected. It is also reasonable to expect that wildlife will be impacted by this development, though it is not clear to what extent. The case does not mention any specific species that would be endangered or threatened, but it is likely that this loss of habitat would further contribute to the decline of songbirds in the area.

The norm of sustainability, however, can also be applied to the economic and social dimensions of this case. One of John's primary duties as an elected member of the City Council is to make decisions that enable Dover to flourish as a sustainable community. Economically it is clear that Dover would be better off with a Wal-Mart Supercenter than without one. If Wal-Mart closed their store in Dover and built the Supercenter in Brandywine, Dover would lose a large number of jobs and a sizeable portion of its tax revenue due to decreased sales. While it is difficult for merchants to compete with Wal-Mart, merchants in towns that do not have a Wal-Mart store fare worse than those who do. At the same time, long-range studies indicate that total sales actually decline in all towns whether they have a Wal-Mart or not because larger cities in Iowa are capturing an increasing share of total sales. This trend does not bode well for the future, but it is clear that having a Wal-Mart store in your community helps to forestall this trend.

On the social side, there are reasons to be concerned about the impact that a Supercenter could have on Dover and the rest of the county. Undoubtedly some businesses would fail, especially grocery stores and others competing head-on with Wal-Mart. Would the loss of these businesses erode the sense of community in Dover and diminish its vitality? It is true that Wal-Mart's sales revenues are not recycled as readily in communities since they are transferred electronically to Arkansas, but it is reasonable to wonder how much money is currently recycled from the local businesses that will be tipped into bankruptcy by the arrival of the Supercenter. It is likely that the cash flow and financial assets of these businesses are already weak. At the same time, John needs to consider what would happen to Dover if hundreds of Wal-Mart jobs left the community. This would significantly harm the economy of Dover and it would deal a blow to the town's self-image. While the preservationists would be delighted, others would likely be discouraged about the long-term future of Dover.

There is no denying, however, that a Wal-Mart Supercenter built on the banks of the scenic Appanoose River will impact the image of Dover. The question is whether it will deal a decisive blow to the distinctive character of the community. Since dikes protect downtown Dover from floods, commercial enterprises will only encroach upon the aesthetic beauty of the Appanoose as development takes place beyond the dikes in the watershed on the eastern edge of town. In addition, since the Supercenter would be built on land on the fringes of the community, the homogeneity of its architecture would not detract from the historic character of Dover's downtown business district. At the same time, it is likely that the Supercenter will result in another round of business failures for merchants on Main Street. Thus, tourists may arrive only to tour a downtown with quaint buildings but a growing number of empty stores. Optimists will see this as an opportunity for new ideas and investment, but pessimists will look at the decimated downtown areas in other Iowa towns and be discouraged. No matter who looks at it, however, change is going to occur in Dover. The issue is what kind of change will take place and whether it will help Dover to be a sustainable community or not.

The other ecojustice norms address additional ethical considerations in the case and deserve some brief mention. The norm of sufficiency emphasizes that all forms of life are entitled to those things that satisfy their basic needs, but it also repudiates wasteful and harmful consumption and encourages the virtues of moderation and frugality. It is clear from Gail Banks' remarks that she is looking forward to a larger variety of low prices on items at the Wal-Mart Supercenter. There is no doubt that these savings will be a significant boon to people with limited means in Dover and in the rural parts of the county. Will these low prices also encourage higher rates of consumption among wealthier people? Undoubtedly they will, but virtues are always tested by vices. Mass discounters will always appeal to greed and envy, but this is not a new phenomenon and avarice is an ancient character flaw. Ultimately, parents, religious communities, and other groups have to shape the moral character of individuals in order to cultivate virtues that can withstand the temptations posed by various vices. The formation and malformation of moral character is a complicated process that is not determined by only one factor.

Another factor to consider under the norm of sufficiency is that construction of the Supercenter in the flood plain will destroy some habitat that currently helps to provide basic needs to various animals. While the development does not apparently pose a dire threat to any particular species, it will perpetuate a pattern of habitat degradation and fragmentation that is a key factor in the loss of biodiversity.

The participation norm is relevant to several dimensions of the case, not the least of which is whether the City Council or the Board of Adjustment should be considering Wal-Mart's bid to landfill and rezone the land. Certainly some citizens of Dover believe that the City Council is usurping the authority of the Board of Adjustment to make decisions about development in the flood plain. Council members, however, believe they are legally obligated to consider Wal-Mart's request on the basis of an ordinance in Dover's City Code. This legal issue is not resolved within the timeframe of the case and so John Yeoman and the rest of the elected members of the City Council hold their public meeting to vote on Wal-Mart's request.

The participation norm also pertains to Wal-Mart's use of its considerable financial power to eliminate leverage the City Council might have wielded in order to force Wal-Mart to find a new occupant for the building that it will vacate in the Sunrise Plaza shopping center. This is disconcerting. Like small merchants, small towns find it nearly impossible to match the power of the world's largest corporation. This lack of power can be seen as well in the fact that, apart from denying the landfill and rezoning request, there appears to be little the City Council can do to prevent Wal-Mart from building the Supercenter. The city's *Comprehensive Development Plan* does not define "incompatible development" in the flood plain, and the Iowa DNR's permit to fill in the flood plain makes the issue largely moot because the land would no longer be in the flood plain. Thus, if the City Council wants to prevent the construction of the Supercenter because it constitutes "incompatible development" in a flood plain, it is likely that Wal-Mart will sue and present to a court the DNR permit that allowed them to fill in the land, thus elevating it out of the flood plain. The point is that the deck is stacked in favor of economic growth. While communities have the power to regulate where growth takes place, this power is limited; the more jaded might even say that it is largely illusory. These power dynamics may not constitute the primary moral problem in the case, but they do pose secondary issues that deserve some ethical reflection.

Finally, John grapples with the solidarity norm when he considers the impact the Supercenter will have on various merchants, especially grocers. Consumers will benefit from lower prices, increased selection, and one-stop shopping, but the costs will be borne by some merchants who simply will not be able to compete. Thus, the burdens and benefits of the Supercenter will not be shared equitably; many will enjoy the benefits, while only a few will bear the burden. This is not a new problem, however. It is inherent in the capitalist economic system. Competition leads to survival or failure in business, but the customer always benefits from increased competition so long as monopolies do not form. Given Wal-Mart's market saturation strategy, this is a real concern but not one that the Dover City Council can resolve by itself. In the end, fervent societal beliefs in the pursuit of self-interest and the value of competition make it very difficult for individuals or communities to act in solidarity with those who might be adversely affected by the construction of a Supercenter. John was elected to champion the interests of his constituents and not those of residents elsewhere. It is very difficult to take a step back to see the broader picture, and politicians who do so are normally not reelected.

Nevertheless, the case indicates that as many as three of the seven Council members may be leaning against approving Wal-Mart's request to landfill and rezone the land. Should John join them and thus form a majority? Could he justify his stance by appealing to the stewardship tradition and the eco-justice norms? Or will those same moral norms lead him to conclude that the land should be filled and rezoned so that the Supercenter can be built? How should John vote?

Notes

1. World Commission on Environment and Development, *Our Common Future* (New York: Oxford University Press, 1987), p. 8.

2. I am indebted to Jerry Freund, Kirk Johnson, Harland Nelson, Steve McCargar, and Erdman's Engineering for their assistance with various aspects of this case.

3. Kaid F. Benfield, Matthew Raimi, and Donald D. Chen, *Once There Were Greenfields: How Urban Sprawl Is Undermining America's Environment, Economy, and Social Fabric* (Natural Resources Defense Council, 1999), p. 16.

4. Donald C. Williams, *Urban Sprawl* (Santa Barbara, CA: ABC-CLIO, Inc., 2000), p. 12.

5. Benfield et al., *Once There Were Greenfields*, p. 6.

6. Definition cited in Al Norman, *Slam-Dunking Wal-Mart! How You Can Stop Superstore Sprawl in Your Hometown* (Atlantic City, NJ: Raphel Marketing, 1999), p. 17.

7. Andres Duany, Elizabeth Plater-Zyberk, and Jeff Speck, *Suburban Nation: The Rise of Sprawl and the Decline of the American Dream* (San Francisco, CA: North Point Press, 2000), pp. 7–8. Even though these loan policies helped many people afford home ownership, qualification standards still excluded many poor people—a greater percentage of whom were immigrants from other countries and black migrant workers from the South who had been displaced by the mechanization of agriculture. Their run-down homes, and often entire neighborhoods, were disqualified in a process that came to be known as "red-lining." As a result, federal mortgage policies moved people with means to the growing suburbs and left the people who were poor in depopulated urban centers. For more discussion of this topic, see Bob Ortega, *In Sam We Trust: The Untold Story of Sam Walton and How Wal-Mart Is Devouring America* (New York: Random House, 1998), pp. 112–113.

8. Duany et al., *Suburban Nation*, pp. 7–8.

9. Williams, *Urban Sprawl*, p. 6.

10. Benfield et al., *Once There Were Greenfields*, p. 30.

11. Roger Dower et al., *Frontiers of Sustainability: Environmentally Sound Agriculture, Forestry, Transportation, and Power Production* (Washington, DC: Island Press, 1997), p. 15.

12. Williams, *Urban Sprawl*, p. 13.

13. Benfield et al., *Once There Were Greenfields*, p. 64.

14. *Decorah (Iowa) Journal*, October 19, 1999, p. 1

15. Williams, *Urban Sprawl*, p. 14.

16. Ibid., pp. 19, 22–23.

17. Ibid., p. 85.

18. Ibid., p. 26. See also pp. 75–76.

19. National Audubon Society, *Population and Habitat: Making the Connection* (Washington, DC: National Audubon Society, 2001), p. 8. See also Robert A. Askins, *Restoring North American Birds* (New Haven: Yale University Press, 2000).

20. Benfield et al., *Once There Were Greenfields*, p. 70.

21. Ibid. See also Dower et al., *Frontiers of Sustainability*, pp. 67–69.

22. Kaid F. Benfield et al., *Once There Were Greenfields*, pp. 80–81.

23. Information furnished by staff at the U.S. Geological Survey office in La Crosse, Wisconsin, via a phone conversation on October 21, 2002.

24. Federal Emergency Management Agency, "Reducing Risk Through Mitigation," accessed on-line May 2, 2002: http://www.fema.gov/mit/flood.htm.

25. Adam Ward Rome, *The Bulldozer in the Countryside: Suburban Sprawl and the Rise of American Environmentalism* (New York: Cambridge University Press, 2001), p. 175.

26. Ibid., p. 179. Here Rome is quoting Peter Farb who published "Let's *Plan* the Damage Out of Floods," in *Reader's Digest*, May 1961, pp. 224–227. Italicized emphasis added by Rome.

27. Iowa Department of Natural Resources, "Protected Water Areas," accessed on-line May 2, 2002: http://www.state.ia.us/dnr/organiza/ppd/prowater.htm.

28. Ibid.

29. Ibid. Emphasis added.

30. Sandra S. Vance and Roy V. Scott, *Wal-Mart: A History of Sam Walton's Retail Phenomenon* (New York: Twayne Publishers, 1994), pp. 16–17.

31. Don Taylor and Jeanne Smalling Archer, *Up Against the Wal-Marts: How Your Business Can Prosper in the Shadow of the Retail Giants* (New York: AMA-COM, American Management Association, 1994), p. 4. See also Vance and Scott, *Wal-Mart: A History of Sam Walton's Retail Phenomenon*, pp. 24–45.

32. Ibid., p. 7.

33. Wal-Mart Stores corporate website, accessed October 16, 2001: http://www.walmartstores.com/wmstore/wmstores/Mainnews.jsp.

34. See Kenneth E. Stone, "Competing with Mass Merchandisers," *Small Business Forum*, vol. 9, no. 1 (Spring 1991); *Competing with the Retail Giants* (New York: John Wiley & Sons, 1995); and "The Status of Retail Trade in Iowa's Small Towns After Ten Years of Wal-Mart Stores," published in *Proceedings: Increasing Understanding of Public Problems and Policies-1997* (Chicago: Farm Foundation, 1997).

35. Personal communication with Stone via e-mail, September 14, 2001.

36. Stone's study is cited in Al Norman, *Slam-Dunking Wal-Mart!*, pp. 20–21.

37. Kenneth E. Stone, "The Status of Retail Trade in Iowa's Small Towns After Ten Years of Wal-Mart Stores," unpublished research, received via e-mail, September 14, 2001.

38. Stone presented these preliminary findings during a presentation sponsored by the Decorah Chamber of Commerce at the Hotel Winneshiek in Decorah, Iowa, on April 30, 2002.

39. Stone, "The Status of Retail Trade in Iowa's Small Towns After Ten Years of Wal-Mart Stores," pp. 1, 13.

40. Norman, *Slam-Dunking Wal-Mart*, pp. 24–27.

41. Wal-Mart Stores corporate website, accessed on October 16, 2001: http://www.walmartstores.com/wmstore/wmstores/Mainnews.jsp.

42. Reed Abelson, "Six Women Sue Wal-Mart, Charging Job and Promotion Bias," *New York Times* (June 20, 2001): C1.

43. Business Brief, "Wal-Mart Stores Inc.: Retailer Reaches Settlement of Clean Water Act Claims," *Wall Street Journal* (Jun 8, 2001): B4

44. Wendy Zellner and Aaron Bernstein, "Up Against the Wal-Mart," *Business Week* (March 13, 2000): 76–77.

45. Statistic cited in Bill Quinn, *How Wal-Mart Is Destroying America (and the World)* (Berkeley, CA: Ten Speed Press, 2000), p. 43.

46. Ortega, *In Sam We Trust;* cited in Norman, *Slam-Dunking Wal-Mart,* pp. 44–45.

47. Ortega, *In Sam We Trust,* pp. 318–345.

48. See Larry L. Rasmussen, *Earth Community, Earth Ethics* (Maryknoll, NY: Orbis Books, 1996).

49. For a fascinating discussion of the historical background behind these texts and their relevance for today, see Theodore Hiebert, *The Yahwist's Landscape: Nature and Religion in Early Israel* (New York: Oxford University Press, 1996).

For Further Reading

Beatley, Timothy, and Kristy Manning. *The Ecology of Place: Planning for Environment, Economy, and Community.* Washington, DC: Island Press, 1997.

Benfield, F. Kaid, Matthew Raimi, and Donald D. Chen. *Once There Were Greenfields: How Urban Sprawl Is Undermining America's Environment, Economy, and Social Fabric.* Washington, DC: Natural Resources Defense Council, 1999.

Duany, Andres, Elizabeth Plater-Zyberk, and Jeff Speck. *Suburban Nation: The Rise of Sprawl and the Decline of the American Dream.* San Francisco, CA: North Point Press, 2000.

Evangelical Lutheran Church in America. *Sufficient, Sustainable Livelihood for All: A Social Statement on Economic Life.* Chicago: Division for Church in Society, 1999.

———. *Caring for Creation: Vision, Hope, and Justice* (ELCA Social Statement). Chicago: Division for Church in Society, 1993.

Hall, Douglas John. *The Steward: A Biblical Symbol Come of Age.* Grand Rapids: Eerdmans Publishing Company, 1990.

———. *Imaging God: Dominion as Stewardship.* Grand Rapids: Eerdmans Publishing Company, 1986

Hiebert, Theodore, *The Yahwist's Landscape: Nature and Religion in Early Israel.* New York: Oxford University Press, 1996.

Norman, Al. *Slam-Dunking Wal-Mart! How You Can Stop Superstore Sprawl in Your Hometown.* Atlantic City, NJ: Raphel Marketing, 1999.

Ortega, Bob. *In Sam We Trust: The Untold Story of Sam Walton and How Wal-Mart Is Devouring America.* New York: Random House, 1998.

Rasmussen, Larry L. *Earth Community, Earth Ethics.* Maryknoll, NY: Orbis Books, 1996.

Rome, Adam Ward. *The Bulldozer in the Countryside: Suburban Sprawl and the Rise of American Environmentalism.* New York: Cambridge University Press, 2001.

Vance, Sandra S., and Roy V. Scott. *Wal-Mart: A History of Sam Walton's Retail Phenomenon.* New York: Twayne Publishers, 1994.

Williams, Donald C. *Urban Sprawl.* Santa Barbara, CA: ABC-CLIO, Inc., 2000.

Websites

American Farmland Trust
http://www.farmland.org/

Conservation Fund
http://www.conservationfund.org/

Sierra Club Campaign to Stop Sprawl
http://www.sierraclub.org/sprawl/

Smart Growth Online
http://www.smartgrowth.org

Sprawl Watch Clearinghouse
http://www.sprawlwatch.org/

Sprawl-Busters
http://www.sprawl-busters.com/

Wal-Mart Stores
http://www.walmartstores.com/

Videotapes

Understanding Urban Sprawl
1999; 47 minutes
$129 purchase; $75 rental
Films for the Humanities and Sciences
P.O. Box 2053
Princeton, NJ 08543
(800) 257-5126
http://www.films.com/

Store Wars: When Wal-Mart Comes to Town
2001; 59 minutes
$250 purchase; $85 rental
Bullfrog Films
P.O. Box 149
Oley, PA 19547
(610) 779-8226
http://www.bullfrogfilms.com/

6

Market Mountain Takeover

Land Exchanges and Protection of Old Growth Forests

Case

"I think it's just around the next bend," said Tom Matson excitedly as they twisted through still another turn in the old logging road. The pick-up strained under the weight of the plywood, tools, and other equipment in the bed. Bobby Bianchi was excited too, although her arms were heavy from turning the wheel and her body ached from bouncing over ruts and through potholes. She detected first light in the east, but still needed the dim head-lights of the old pick-up to make out that last bend. Then they were there: base camp! The takeover of Market Mountain was about to begin. They had spent a long time preparing for this moment.

Soon the others began to arrive and pile out in high spirits. The light gath-ered slowly as they started to unload and carry the materials for the tree vil-lage they intended to build in a stand of old growth about a quarter mile in from the road.

As Bobby trudged the quarter mile in for the third time, she reflected back on the phone call from Judy Sirkin that had started it all for her. A year out of college where she had studied biology and been active in campus envi-ronmental groups, Bobby Bianchi had since then worked with a social ser-vice agency doing community organizing. While in college, Bobby had done an internship with Judy Sirkin who ran a non-profit organization that scru-tinizes land exchanges between government agencies and private parties in the west. Judy had phoned because she was incensed over a land swap nego-tiated by the United States Forest Service (USFS) in the Cascade Mountains of Washington State.

"This one really irks me," Judy had said. "The Forest Service is about to wrap up an agreement to trade parcels of old growth in the Gifford Pinchot National Forest to the Saddle River Logging Company for cut-over, degraded acreage in the checkerboard[1] of the central Cascades and a few parcels of rock and ice adjacent to the Fernow Wilderness Area. Saddle River wants

---

Robert L. Stivers prepared this case and commentary. The case is based on actual events. Names and places have been changed to protect the privacy of those involved.

to expedite the agreement by getting it attached as a rider to an appropriations bill in Congress. That way they will avoid public scrutiny of the deal, appeals from groups like mine, and litigation. Saddle River's CEO claims he has only a small window of time to get the deal done and the land exchanged because he has a business to run. Once again the timber companies make out like bandits, and the public gets the shaft. And do you know what else?" she asked rhetorically. "Those guys from the Cascade Club sat in on the negotiations and signed-off on the exchange. They call themselves environmentalists but are willing to hand over what little remains of our old growth forests just to get a better view of Mt. Fernow. It's disgraceful."

Judy carried on with more details stirring up anger in Bobby too. "Enough is enough," Judy ended, "I am sick of those back room secret deals. It's time to take action. You call Tom Matson and Ann Kaufman. I'll call Marty Donaldson and Mike O'Connell down in Eugene, Oregon, and we'll get something cooking."

Bobby was not one to wince at taking action. She was committed to direct action. As a native of southwestern Washington, she had experience in the forests and with people who lived in forest communities. Getting people in logging communities to stand up to the Forest Service and the big logging companies would not be easy. These folks were reticent to start with and didn't want to alienate the powerful few who controlled their lives. The flap over the northern spotted owl over a decade ago had severely reduced the cut in the national forests of the Pacific Northwest. Loggers could not find work. Independent, local mills shut down. Logging communities were hard hit. And a lot of folks held environmentalists to blame.

Bobby had pulled out her maps to check the areas involved in the land exchange. The most objectionable part of the deal was the transfer to Saddle River Logging of two parcels of commercially valuable old growth trees near Miller, Washington. Bobby had noted that one parcel was very close to Miller and included a three-thousand-foot peak known as Market Mountain. She had wondered if the people in Miller knew that the mountain above their homes would soon be clearcut. She guessed not, and a few phone calls to friends near Miller bore her guess out.

Not only did they not know about it, but her contacts had further reported that Saddle River Logging was not very popular in Miller. Many people in Miller blamed Saddle River for several damaging mudslides that they attributed to clearcutting and poor road building in company parcels near town. Worse, Saddle River took timber from the area, but did not use local loggers or mills. They preferred to use their own crews and mills they owned miles away.

The Forest Service was not a lot more popular. Bobby's contacts had reported a lot of grumbling about the way the Forest Service had logged the Gifford Pinchot National Forest during the 1970s and 1980s. The Forest Service had offered up huge tracts of old growth trees for sale and tolerated questionable logging practices. Her contacts referred to the Gifford Pinchot as "the great sacrifice forest."

"Perhaps," Bobby had thought, "this discontent could be tapped to stop the land swap and to prevent further cutting of old growth in the Gifford Pinchot National Forest. It was worth a try, especially since the Forest Service had traded away Market Mountain. That's probably where they get their water," she thought further. "The people of Miller no doubt hunt and fish there too, and I can't imagine any of them will be happy trading their scenic view of a forested mountain for a clearcut. It sure won't help their efforts to attract tourists."

The next week she had driven up from her home in Portland, Oregon, to Miller, Washington, to find out more. It had not taken long to verify what she had been told and what she was thinking. Interviews with members of the Miller community had been depressing. Mostly old-timers without a lot of education, they recounted horror stories of over-cutting, poor logging practices, and general lack of care. "Get the cut out," everyone agreed was the only goal of the Forest Service and the logging companies. Perhaps they had been exaggerating, but even a half-truth was probably enough to get things going.

When she had told them about Market Mountain, most just shook their heads in disbelief. They seemed resigned to their fate. They were not stupid, not by any means, but they lacked the skills and perhaps the will to fight back. They had spent their lives working hard in the forest, not in protesting injustice.

Bobby had returned to Portland. By the end of the week she and Judy with the help of the others had put together a coalition of groups to fight Saddle River Logging and the USFS as well as the Cascade Club if it did not reverse itself on the exchange. Volunteers stepped forward. Tasks were eagerly accepted. Judy would monitor the agreement and get the message out in Seattle and further north. Bobby would canvas the folks in Miller and set up sessions to train townspeople in how to oppose the exchange. Mike, experienced with forest sit-ins in California, would set to work organizing the tree village. They would, all had agreed, take over Market Mountain next summer and stay there for as long as it took to win reversal. The importance of saving old growth forests and to block this trade had overridden any lingering moral qualms about breaking trespass laws. Tom Matson had agreed to work on the Saddle River Logging Company, Ann Kaufman on the USFS, and Marty Donaldson on the media.

Bobby agreed to contact members of the Salish Tribe that lived near Miller and get them on board. "Maybe the tribe would draw up a decree permitting us to occupy the land," suggested Marty. "The Salish were there first before the U.S. government stole the land. We need all the help we can get on this. Just imagine, poor-out-of-work loggers, Native Americans, and direct activists in common cause against government dinosaurs, greedy corporate types, and do-nothing, compromising environmentalists. The press will love it!"

Then the roof had fallen in. Members of the state's congressional delegation had succeeded in attaching the land exchange as a rider to an appropriations bill. One or two of those in the coalition urged them to move on to other causes, but the rest held out for the sit-in, Bobby and Judy among them. "After all," they had argued, " Saddle River Logging hasn't clearcut Market Mountain yet, and the actual exchange will not take place until next July. We could still make it tough for them."

Not much happened during the winter. Then in June as they were making final preparations for the tree village, biologists working for Saddle River had discovered endangered marbled murrelets the Forest Service had overlooked on lands that were included in the exchange. Saddle River wanted to reopen negotiations since they would not be able to log in the habitat of an endangered species. With this news their protest had taken on new life.

By late June plans for the takeover had been completed. The air was electric at their final meeting before D-Day. They had a just cause, a good plan, a good organization with willing workers, and now a fighting chance. They felt confident they could save the forest.

Near the end of that final meeting Tom Matson had stood up. He had begun slowly, then picked up passion and found words. He condemned the logging companies for seeking the quick buck and desecrating the forests. He referred to the Forest Service as the Forest Disservice, calling rangers "timber hogs" and dismissing them for being in bed with the logging companies and the politicians. He condemned "out of reach" environmentalists. "All they care about," he had said, "was improving the hiking trails for a few rich Seattleites. They don't give a hoot about the folks in Miller or the forests. We get what we deserve. Most of us Americans are so out of touch with nature we can't tell a tree from a toothpick."

He had then offered the vision of a new future where all logging would cease in the national forests, the citizens of Miller would be put to work restoring the Gifford Pinchot, and logging companies would be forced into using environmentally sustainable practices on their own lands. He ventured that this campaign was their mission and called for self-sacrifice. He ended on a spiritual note. He told about his own personal epiphany in the rainforest of the Olympic Mountains. A certain configuration in the bark of an old cedar tree seemed to come alive and tell him to save the forests. He urged them all to find spirit in nature.

Bobby was excited by Tom's words. He was certainly charismatic, she remembered thinking. She thought about her own spiritual journey and had concluded that it had hardly begun. "I feel this affinity for the forest," she said to herself, "but I find it difficult to put into words. I have always thought in philosophical terms using such concepts as animal rights, the land ethic, and sustainability. She had also wondered if it were wise to put their spirituality up front. Opponents were more than ready to identify participants in direct action with religious cults and discredit them. Better to leave spirituality to the individual. They all loved nature, but they also needed to stay on task, and right now their task was to stop this land exchange."

With that Bobby returned to her own task as porter, put down her pack, rested momentarily, and then started back for another load. By mid-morning they had completed the transfer and started construction. Mike knew what he was doing, and within a few days they had secured several platforms high up in three giant old hemlocks. The occupation began with some taking up residence on the platforms while others like Bobby fanned out to work on organization and publicity. The sense of community was intense. Someone tacked up a sign that read:

> "No monkeywrenching, tree spiking, or destruction of property."
> "Respect ALL life."
> "No drugs."
> "No alcohol."
> "Use consensus decision making."
> "Keep camp clean and stay on trails."
> "Maintain non-violence."
> "Support local communities."
> "There are no leaders."

Bobby began her work among the folks in Miller who responded as she had expected. There were a few, of course, who remained suspicious of what they called "militant activists" and "tree huggers," but most were positive. "It's about time someone around here took on Saddle River Logging and the Forest Service," they said. What at first was only moaning and groaning soon grew into full-scale criticism and action as the townspeople took things into their own hands. They visited the tree village. They brought food and joked with the sitters high up in the trees. They started to talk to each other about the threats to the town and to make plans.

Not long after the occupation had begun, members of the Salish tribe arrived and read a solemn proclamation granting permission for the activists to occupy the site. They also talked at some length with reporters about native traditions and nature. Soon after they left, two forest rangers appeared, officially serving notice that the tree village and the protesters were in violation of trespass laws. No one took them very seriously. They nosed around for a while, cautioned the sitters about safety, and joked a bit with those hanging out at base camp. Several days later the rangers appeared again, this time with a permit to occupy the site. The permit had been arranged by sympathetic townspeople.

In August Bobby drove her pick-up truck to Seattle for an open forum where Judy Sirkin was scheduled to be on the same platform with Andy Wright of the Cascade Club. It was Andy who had led the club's participation in the exchange and was now arguing for a quick renegotiation of the deal after Saddle River Logging had reopened the discussions. He was still in favor of trading Market Mountain, although on making an inspection of the site had conceded that the old growth stand was "pretty impressive."

Andy led off by defending the original exchange. He pulled out his maps and pointed to the "checkerboard" in the mid-Cascades and described the ecological fragmentation it produced and the impediments it and other human obstructions such as highways posed for wildlife transit along the north/south axis of the mountains. The land exchange would improve the habitat for wild animals and with the removal of the other obstructions give them a broader range within which to roam. In addition, Andy noted that these parcels in the mid-Cascades also contained some old growth timber that would now be protected from logging in the future. A third advantage to the deal was that swapped parcels would effectively increase the size of the Fernow Wilderness Area.

Andy went on to summarize the history of land acquisition and ownership in forested areas of the Pacific Northwest that had produced this unusual "checkerboard" configuration. He concluded that the courts would never revisit the present pattern of ownership however illegal it may have been when it was set over a hundred years ago. "The only way to get rid of the 'checkerboard' and improve habitat in the Cascades," he insisted, "is to purchase the parcels in private hands or trade." He then reviewed his many years of work on the "checkerboard" project for the local chapter of the Cascade Club, arriving finally at the exchange that included Market Mountain

"We have no formal role in negotiations that take place between the Forest Service and private parties," he claimed, "but we do have influence. We participate in public discussions with both sides, and the public looks to us as an informed and impartial observer. Congress is more apt to approve exchanges if we support them. Everyone except the radicals trusts us.

"The Cascade Club supports the disputed exchange between the USFS and Saddle River Logging because it is a net plus. You have to give up something good to get something good. We oppose the logging of old growth in principle, but will support exchanges to protect important wilderness areas. Market Mountain is on the fringe of the Gifford Pinchot National Forest, not in its heart. With this land swap the public protects old growth forests in the 'checkerboard' and a few stands adjacent to the Fernow Wilderness Area. We are ambivalent about attaching the exchange as a rider to appropriations bills. It moves things along, but removes important safeguards. The Cascade Club takes a pragmatic approach. We call it principled pragmatism. You get what you can get. You have to weigh the pluses and minuses."

With this he paused and turned to Judy Sirkin on the platform. "The opposite of our principled pragmatism is the politics of pure idealism practiced by those sitting-in at Market Mountain. I have a lot of sympathy for those with principles and passion, but I draw the line at zealotry. The activists sitting in the trees down there are zealots. They are always criticizing. They have no positive program and no tactics except takeover. They want to tear down, not build up. They simplify by focusing on Market Mountain and ignoring wilderness areas and the 'checkerboard.' They posture for the press that is gullible enough to report their simplifications and misinformation. And one more thing," he concluded, "the Cascade Club makes it a rule never to break the law."

A young man in the audience raised his hand. "What makes you tick personally, Andy?" he asked. Andy responded quickly. "I have degrees in biology and art. I am an avid bird watcher. I love the beauty of nature. I guess my perspective is based on an aesthetic appreciation of nature, but I don't feel comfortable talking about these things. It's personal. I prefer to talk in a scientific way."

Judy Sirkin then stood up to speak. She had a determined look on her face, and Bobby thought she sensed anger. "I am a forest activist," she began, "with a background in environmental studies. I am the executive director of a non-profit organization that scrutinizes these land exchanges. I am an idealist. Andy is correct; we take a principled approach. We have three bedrock principles. (1) No compromise in the national forests on the 4 percent of remaining old growth; not one more splinter is to be removed. (2) No closed-door negotiations by elitists; all meetings must be open. (3) No end-runs with riders. The full administrative process that allows for public input must be followed."

She went on to detail and criticize the exchange that included Market Mountain. She then turned to Andy and got personal: "This and other deals that Andy has brokered stink. The split between Andy and me runs deep. Sometimes it is your so-called allies that you have to watch out for. At least with President Bush you know who the enemy is. Clinton appeared to us as a friend, and a lot of environmentalists were seduced. As long as they got a place at the table, they were willing to compromise just about everything. Andy calls his perspective principled pragmatism. I say he has lost his principles. He will do anything to move his precious 'checkerboard' project along and justify it all with his precious maps. He doesn't talk to other environmental groups or local residents. Rather he appoints himself as our spokesman.

"The protest down at Miller is a beautiful thing. Twenty-one groups have formed a coalition committed to non-violent activism. They have made an unprecedented alliance with the folks in Miller. That is a remarkable feat! Yes, they have been in technical violation of the law. But what does it mean to trespass on public lands? Don't we all own it? And how does this minor infraction compare to the desecration of the Gifford Pinchot by the likes of the Forest Service and Saddle River Logging? If ever there were a case where the end justifies the mean, this is it.

"To conclude, let me also say a word about foundations. I have been moved on several occasions by deep spiritual experiences in nature. I am like Andy in that I don't talk about them very much. I am no 'woo-woo.' I prefer the language of policy, but these experiences are the core of my being. They keep me going and enhance my resolve. And from these experiences I have concluded that land and trees are not just market commodities. They have intrinsic and even spiritual value. We are ruining the land and eliminating whole ecosystems. The salmon are in deep trouble. The birds have less and less habitat. It has gotten to the point where I get physically sick when I see a clearcut. We are protesting at Market Mountain to stop this desecration. Our cause is just." With that she sat down to loud applause. Andy sat motionless.

Bobby drove back to base camp that night. She had to meet with residents of Miller and make final arrangements for a town meeting scheduled for the following week. After three attempts, Tom had persuaded Saddle River Logging to send a spokesperson. Ann Kaufman had secured a speaker from the Forest Service who knew about the exchange.

Bobby did not know how many would attend the town meeting. She had rung a lot of doorbells and put up enough posters to paper all of Market Mountain. That embarrassed her, but "what the heck," she said to herself, "it's all in a good cause."

The meeting was set for 6:30 p.m. at the Elks Hall. By 6:00 p.m. the parking lot was full. By 6:30 p.m. one hundred fifty townspeople and a few activists were there, standing room only. The townspeople were in charge and started right on time. The representative from Saddle River Logging Company defended the company's practices in the area, disclaiming any responsibility for mudslides. He said the company had entered the exchange discussions in good faith and had negotiated a fair trade, noting that the company had given up two acres for every one it received. About the rider, he said that the company merely wanted to prevent endless appeals and get on with its business.

When it came time for questions and comments, the townspeople were ready. They grilled him with sharp questions until the moderator called a halt. Bobby quietly admired him for his bravery. He left as soon as possible.

The representative from the USFS also defended the deal. He pointed to the consolidation of parcels and the scenic value of the lands they had acquired. He mentioned the difficulties of comparing the value of scenery and healthy ecosystems to the commercial value of trees. While the questions put to him were not as sharp as to the first speaker, it was clear that discontent ran high. After the meeting townspeople remained behind, talking in small groups about Market Mountain and their options.

In October the Forest Service and Saddle River Logging announced a new agreement that still included Market Mountain but removed the parcels with marbled murrelets. The state's congressional delegation attached the agreement as a rider to still another appropriations bill that passed without fanfare. It appeared the sit-in would be a failure. Winter was coming on, and it would not be much fun living up in those trees when it snowed.

They hastily called a strategy meeting at base camp. They decided to carry the protest directly to company headquarters in a Seattle skyscraper. Mustering as many as they could find—protesters, townspeople, and allies—they drove to Seattle and demonstrated in the plaza outside the skyscraper. As Bobby looked up, she could not help but think of Market Mountain. Police blocked the entrance to the building and would not allow them to enter. Tom gave another one of his fiery speeches. The company did not budge.

Two weeks later they went back, this time unannounced. They entered the building and gained access to corporate headquarters before anyone was the wiser. Office workers called police and defended their space. There was a lot of pushing, shoving, and shouting, but no one was injured. Police hauled several protestors off to jail where they were detained and soon released.

About a week later Judy Sirkin received a call from company lawyers. They wanted to talk. On the appointed day in November Judy and a few others showed up at company headquarters. The Saddle River lawyers asked, "What do you want?" Judy replied: "Market Mountain and all other old growth parcels in the Gifford Pinchot have to be stricken from the deal."

"OK," the lawyers said.

It was over. They had won!!

As Bobby returned in December to base camp for the last time to dismantle the tree village and clean up the site, she felt mixed emotions. She was elated that Saddle River had backed down, but sad that the sit-in was over. It had been a transforming experience for her. She would miss her friends. Now the woods were dark and the ground was covered with snow. Little light had gathered, even at mid-day.

The dreary light seemed to generate a series of gloomy thoughts and questions. She knew they had won, but what about the future? Were confrontational tactics the only way to get the Forest Service and logging companies to move? Were they even the best tactics? Would the Forest Service and the logging companies ever get the environmental message or would economic considerations always dominate their decisions? Would Saddle River just move on to another stand of old growth that was less well protected? And what about the deep chasm in the environmental movement; would a unified front not be more effective? As she loaded the last 2x4 into the bed of her truck, she smiled at Judy and Tom. She knew for certain where those two stood. They were ready next time around to return and save that last splinter of old growth.

Note

1. The "checkerboard" refers to the ownership configuration that resulted from federal land grants to the railroads to encourage building and settlement in the 19th century. The government made land grants of alternating one-mile square parcels transferring one to the railroad and reserving the one adjacent for public ownership. This pattern fragments the ecosystem and impedes the transit of wildlife.

Commentary

This case is based on a land exchange negotiated by the United States Forest Service (USFS) and a large forest products company. The names, places, and dates have been changed to protect the privacy of the individuals and organizations involved.

The practice whereby governmental officials trade public for private lands is well established in law but increasingly controversial.[1] While regulated, the practice has not been without abuses, including a history of what critics consider unequal exchanges and the circumvention of administrative processes that call for public input.

Land exchanges serve several purposes. Historically their most important purpose has been to eliminate private in-holdings on federal lands. In recent years they have also been negotiated to protect watersheds and other sensitive areas, to preserve the habitat of endangered species, and to consolidate both public and private holdings. The applicable laws state that land exchanges should be of equal value. Proponents of exchanges claim they are a win-win proposition. Opponents do not object to exchanges in principle, but to specific exchanges that they feel compromise important values. And there is the rub. Different groups have different values and interests, many of which cannot be quantified in terms of acres or dollars. The problem of comparing the value of scenery, intact ecosystems, and diverse habitats to the commercial value of land and trees makes the resolution of differences difficult and leaves plenty of room for ambiguity in the process of negotiation.

This case involves a complex land exchange. In the nineteenth century the federal government gave land grants to railroads to encourage them to build in the unsettled, open spaces of the west. The railroads retained some of the lands and sold others to timber companies at a nominal price. Scholars have questioned the legality of the grants themselves, subsequent sales, and further acquisitions under homesteading laws.

Congress saw fit to parcel out these lands in one-mile square blocks called sections, one granted to the railroad, the one adjacent reserved as part of federal lands. The result was a "checkerboard" of straight-line blocks along railroad right-of-ways with little relation to natural boundaries. Over time, the logging companies clearcut their sections and traded high elevation, unproductive parcels for more productive, low elevation parcels.

The "checkerboard" is pronounced in the central Cascades of Washington State where the rail lines cross the mountains, less so in the north and south Cascades where the federal government retained most ownership. The construction of Interstate 90 across the central Cascades in the 1960s further fragmented the habitat in the "checkerboard." The road also blocked the passage of animals moving along the north/south axis of the mountains. As a result, the Forest Service, encouraged by environmentalists, has been eager to cut deals to consolidate its holdings, to reduce the "checkerboard" effect, and to restore habitat.

The logging companies have also been eager to deal, obviously interested in trading cut over lands in the "checkerboard" for old or second growth forests closer to their bases of operation, even if it entails giving up more acreage than is received. Companies are also interested in expediting these exchanges. A rapidly executed trade avoids expenses associated with the retention of unproductive, cut over lands and transfers to the company forests ready to be cut for profit. It also avoids the bad publicity and delay sometimes involved in a lengthy administrative process where outside groups have an opportunity to press for less favorable terms. Thus in this case the parcel on Market Mountain was included in an exchange for lands in the "checkerboard," and the agreement was attached to a federal appropriations bill to expedite passage.

The exchange that was the basis for this case also features a conflict between environmental groups. Several groups, not just the Cascade Club in the case, were interested in consolidating the "checkerboard" and adding to wilderness areas close to the urban area around Puget Sound. Of a more pragmatic, preservationist bent and accustomed to working within the political process and arranging compromises, they were willing to trade old growth parcels in the Gifford Pinchot National Forest in the south Cascades. They participated in the negotiations leading to the agreement, had several of their own proposals included, and signed off on the agreement and publicly supported it. In opposition were groups with an idealistic, critical eco-justice perspective. They were willing to participate in an open political process, but would not accept any deal negotiated behind closed doors or that involved the compromise of old growth forests. They were and are to this day not willing to sacrifice old growth, "not one splinter," to use their words. They were well versed in direct action tactics, such as tree sitting and demonstrations at company headquarters. They were also willing to use these tactics even if it meant violation of trespass laws, which it did in the protest at corporate headquarters and in the forest until the Forest Service granted a permit. The conflict between these environmental groups remains intense. One thing for certain, the environmental movement is not monolithic.

In this case the protests led to significant alterations in the agreement between the USFS and the logging company. The total acreage in the deal was reduced, and the contested old growth parcels were retained in the national forest. It is doubtful whether the parties would have made these alterations without the pressure from the alliance of activists and townspeople. This was a remarkable alliance since most loggers are hostile to environmental groups of any kind. In the case, however, the local mill had closed, logging had all but shut down in the Gifford Pinchot National Forest, and the town was in economic transition.

The real difference in the case, however, was that the logging company had a history near the town and was perceived as distant, rapacious, and uncaring. Resentment was high and easily mobilized. The townspeople soon took initiative in the protest, provided logistical support to the tree sitters, and pressured the Forest Service, the company, the politicians, and the environmental groups involved.

THE CLASH OF PERSPECTIVES

If the townspeople were motivated by economic depression, their history with the company, and probably a sense of injustice and powerlessness, what motivated the activists? A few things stood out in interviews. The activists were young, idealistic, and with one exception came from liberal families. Teachers who had been deeply concerned about the environment were frequently mentioned as influences. Almost all tended to look at politics but not the forests in dualistic, either/or terms, for example, the evil corporations and the dinosaurs at the Forest Service versus the passionate rightness of their own cause and the vision of a protected and restored forest.

All four environmental perspectives outlined in Chapter One are represented in this case. The activists are clearly from the critical ecology perspective. Some seemed to subscribe to the insights of what Carolyn Merchant calls deep and spiritual ecology.[2] Others were silent in their basic motivation and seemed uncomfortable mixing political activism with their spirituality. Most seemed to represent Merchant's category of "political ecology." They combined outrage over what is happening in the forests and a near total rejection of corporate capitalism and established institutions with sensitivity toward nature and political activism. Many of them were members of a single, critical ecology organization, known for its direct action tactics.

At the other end of the spectrum was the logging company where the developmentalist perspective was strong. The activists and the company had little in common, not even the vocabulary to relate in a meaningful way. The company in question, after heavy criticism in the 1980s for the rapidity of its cut and the practices it used, has moved in a conservationist direction, although hardly enough for the activists to note any change. It has also been driven more by anthropocentric, economic forces than by environmental concerns. The market puts pressures on managers that opposing groups seldom recognize. As the CEO said: "We have a business to run." If he does not respond to business pressures, he will soon find himself retired and replaced by someone who will.

The activists and the company were playing a win/lose game with each other, at least on the surface. In the final resolution the company did not get all that it wanted, but it would be a mistake to say it went away empty-handed. While Market Mountain was stripped from the deal, other lands were exchanged. The protestors won a skirmish, but hardly the battle. The corporations have huge advantages in these conflicts and usually get what they want. Market Mountain was probably of little moment to them. It had become a liability in terms of bad publicity and would be impossible to clearcut. The activists won largely because they found the right combination of factors to embarrass the company and the Forest Service. They gained the moral high ground and used it well to their advantage. They will probably not get many opportunities like this, although they could well block future sales of old growth in the Cascades.

The USFS has been dominated since its inception by the conservationist perspective of Gifford Pinchot, its founder and leading philosophical influence.[3] Pinchot's mantra was "the greatest good for the greatest number (of people) over the longest period of time." In keeping with this, best science, best technology, best management, multiple-use, and sustainable yield have been the guiding principles of the Forest Service's stewardship of public lands.

Unfortunately, the science of forestry and the technologies the USFS relied on had serious environmental shortcomings that were only later identified as the science of ecology developed. The Forest Service often interpreted best management in terms of efficiency in "getting the cut out." Among multiple uses of the forests in the Pacific Northwest—logging, recreation, grazing, wildlife, and mining—logging was always the most important and tended over time to become increasingly so. Sustainability meant a constant supply of timber to keep the mills busy and to meet demand. The conservationist foundation of the Forest Service, at least in the eyes of its critics, easily merged into the developmentalist perspective of the logging companies.

In recent years the Forest Service has moved to improve its science, technology, and management and to respond to its critics. Whether this signals a basic change remains to be seen. In part it depends on the administration in Washington, DC, in part on the ground in each national forest as managers interpret basic policy. The Forest Service has ceased being a monolithic agency with a uniform ideology.

The Cascade Club in the case is in the preservationist camp, even though its local leaders are willing to give up stands of old growth in the Gifford Pinchot National Forest. They are trying to preserve habitat and restore ecosystems elsewhere and have a conflict over trade-offs. Andy Wright is well versed in the land ethic and integrated, connected ecosystems. In the heat of the conflict the activists tarred and feathered him, even though they had a number of common concerns, for example, the elimination of the "checkerboard" and the opening of the central Cascades to wildlife transit. Andy is committed to working within the political system, wielding power there, and compromising if necessary. "Principled pragmatism" describes his position quite well.

The conflict between perservationist and critical ecology perspectives in this case was intense. Each side felt a sense of betrayal. Each knew who the real opponents were, but did not let that knowledge stop it from intra-movement conflict. In part the conflict is the difference between perspectives. It is also a clash of two perennial political styles and temperaments.

Andy Wright calls the two styles the "politics of pure idealism" and the "politics of principled pragmatism." These are not precise terms, but get at the difference of style although not necessarily of temperament. The "politics of pure idealism" starts with and stresses the importance of basic principles and ideals. It takes what in ethics is known as a normative or deontological approach where in simplest form decision-makers follow rules that are based on ideals and principles. Judy says, "not one more splinter." People of this persuasion are less concerned with achieving good results or outcomes, although they want them too. Pacifism is an example of this approach. The norm of nonviolence takes precedent even in the face of unspeakable injustice.

In contrast the "politics of principled pragmatism" is more concerned with outcomes. It usually takes a consequentialist approach, seeking good results even if sometimes this means breaking the rules. Instead of "not one more splinter" those of this persuasion argue for Pinchot's utilitarian principle of the "greatest good." Instead of pacifism, they allow for justifiable violence. They are also sensitive to conflicts of "goods" or norms in actual situations.

Andy Wright thinks of himself as principled as well as pragmatic. That is to say, he tries to combine a normative with a consequentialist approach. Judy Sirkin accuses him, however, of sacrificing principle for pragmatic results.

The two approaches are frequently accompanied by different temperaments, although there is by no means a perfect correlation here. "True believers" with strong opinions and either/or attitudes find a home in the "politics of pure idealism." Practical people who like to weigh the pros and cons of an issue and are open within limits to compromise in order to achieve good results gravitate to the "politics of principled pragmatism."

The problem with "pure idealism" is what Andy calls "zealotry," with "principled pragmatism" the sacrifice of ideals. These problems arise when either approach is pursued to its extreme limit. Neither style is morally right or wrong, but the differences between them can certainly be a source of conflict.

Will environmentalists in these two camps be able to bridge their conflicting perspectives, styles, and temperaments to present a united front? That is unlikely, although they will continue to make common cause on specific issues where the main opponent is either a conservationist or a developmentalist. The politics of principle is seldom willing to compromise and the politics of pragmatism abhors "zealotry." The we/they dualism of the activists will also fuel the conflict.

Should they even try to bridge the gap? Resolving some of their differences would certainly help the movement, but they should not waste a lot of time on it. What would help is for both sides to spend more time listening to those on the ground in local communities and to stop demonizing.

Actually, the split has some advantages. The compromising work of the moderates sometimes gets a boost from having those who are of a more radical persuasion as the alternative. It makes their proposals seem more reasonable, themselves less a threat, and may well move agreements in an environmental direction. Diversity in the environmental movement promotes its health just as it does biological health in ecosystems.

At one point in the case some townspeople call the activists "radicals" and "militants." Otherwise those terms do not appear. The activists sometimes referred to themselves as "radicals," but most recognized that the label hurts effectiveness, at least in the American political context. When opponents are successful in stereotyping activists as "radical," they refocus attention on a label away from what might be legitimate criticism. This leads to easy dismissal. Following their own self-definition, the case refers to them as "activists" and their perspective as "critical" not "radical ecology."

Finally, are illegal actions ethically justifiable in such cases as this? The Cascade Club disavows illegal tactics. The activists in contrast claim that the end sometimes justifies the means. The norm should be tactics that are nonviolent and legal, but exceptions may be warranted for some actions that break the law. Philosopher Holmes Rolston puts it this way with regard to toxic pollution:

[T]oxic threats can reach a point where ethical concern demands drastic action. Greenpeace activists in Everett, Massachusetts, broke the law (trespassing and disrupting the orderly conduct of business) to plug a discharge pipe pouring toxic wastes, released from a Monsanto chemical plant into the Mystic River. . . . The toxic-threat-as-trumps rule permits and even requires participation in activist protests of this kind.[4]

The problem, of course, is that Rolston is not talking about land exchanges, but toxic chemicals. Still the principle holds. When the degradation is severe enough, illegal tactics are permissible. The question for this case is whether the degradation in the forests of the Pacific Northwest is so severe as to countenance illegal actions.

NATURE SPIRITUALITY

The expressions of nature spirituality in the case come mostly from later interviews. The individuals involved in the situation were willing to talk about their spirituality, but reluctant with one exception to make it part of their activist agenda. Several said they did not want "to muddy the water." Nearly all felt close to nature, although in varying degrees. This closeness is difficult to analyze since it involves sensibilities that rational analysis reveals only with difficulty. Art, music, poetry, and literature express this spirituality more adequately.

Several aspects of their spirituality stand out, however. First is the dualism of spirit and politics already noted. This dualism is striking because it seems to contradict the connectedness and integration they found in nature and experienced in the tree village. Perhaps the dualism can be explained as a remnant of wider cultural attitudes they too were taught. While it is orderly to think that individuals are consistent in their attitudes, this is seldom the case. Another possibility is the underdeveloped nature of their spirituality. They may have been reluctant to express what was only partly formed.

Second, most claimed that their spirituality was deeply personal. That is understandable, but they also seemed to mean individual. If probed, they would probably say that each person has his or her own unique spirituality that is beyond criticism. As with the dualism, this seems inconsistent because the tree village in the forest, the relationships to townspeople, and the protest in Seattle were communal to the core. Perhaps it can be explained as a sign of respect for the spirituality of others, or again a matter of inconsistency.

Third, none at the time of interview was connected to a church or synagogue, although one was raised Roman Catholic and another Jewish. The absence of institutional affiliation is not unusual. They seemed to find alternative religious expression in nature and in their activism. Indeed, the critical ecology perspective they represent is suspicious of, if not hostile to, both traditions and hierarchical institutions. Also in this perspective Christianity is often held responsible for the ecological crisis.

In a recent book, Robert C. Fuller claims that the 20 percent of the U.S. population with no formal religious affiliation is nonetheless deeply engaged in spiritual seeking.[5] Often disparaged by churchgoers (Judy Sirkin speaks of "woo-woo's"), Fuller finds most of these seekers remarkably mature. They are not unhealthy narcissists, facile, or superficial.

That the activists in this case are unchurched should certainly be disappointing to members of faith traditions, but not surprising. The activists have reason to be suspicious of Western religions. Many books in the Hebrew Scriptures were written in a context of conflict with the polytheistic, nature religions of their neighbors. The Hebrews made human history and the relationship to a transcendent, monotheistic God the focal point of their faith and were standoffish about nature.

Early Christianity picked up the spirit/body dualism from Greek philosophy. It separated spirit and nature, making the latter inferior to the former and carrying the suspicion of nature into the tradition.[6]

The history of these developments is, of course, more complex, but the result has been that today many Christians reject the notion of spirit in nature. This is unfortunate because such rejection cuts them off from an important source of spiritual power and neglects the more nature-centered aspects of the tradition. Specific biblical texts, the doctrine of a good creation, and understandings of the incarnation and sacraments suggest a much richer tradition on the relationships of God and humans to nature.

In mainstream Christianity nature is not identified with God as in pantheism. God is said to transcend God's creation, and there are important reasons to retain a notion of transcendence. Nor is God separated from nature as in the clockmaker god of deism and Aristotle's unmoved mover. Christianity has consistently maintained that the God who is transcendent is also immanent, that is to say, continues the work of creating, sustaining, and redeeming in both human and natural histories. This is the work of the Holy Spirit. Therefore, an understanding of spirit in nature is quite appropriate in Christianity.

For many Christians this understanding is also confirmed in experience. Efforts to reduce the experiences of spirit in nature to a psychological state of mind belie their richness and profundity. Many Christians testify they encounter a spiritual power in nature, which, when they are open to receiving it, enters and creates a sense of inner unity and transformation. All their senses are engaged and they become one with God whom they find in, with, and under material things. The encounter and the sense of inner unity pushes them out to act in society and nature in ways consistent with the power they intuitively feel. The experienced power of love invites a loving and caring response to both humans and nature. Their spirituality is the basis of their ethics. For example in the case, Judy Sirkin said that her sense of spirit in nature enhances her resolve to fight for the forests. Tom Matson described his epiphany and called for a spiritual foundation to their activism.

The great tragedy of the present moment is how much this spiritual dimension has atrophied. Today many Christians and adherents of many other religious traditions center on the human species, dualistically separate themselves from nature, look on nature as inferior, and seek to dominate matter as an object without intrinsic value. Their deep spiritual connection gets lost in the individual acquisition of "stuff." An adequate environmental ethic needs a concept of spirit in nature and deep sensuous engagement. Tom Matson is correct about foundations. They are critical to sustaining activism and personal integrity and to preserving, protecting, and restoring the integrity of creation.

THE TEMPERATE RAINFOREST

The land exchange that included Market Mountain did not take place in a vacuum, but in a context of ecosystem degradation that the activists considered a terrible wrong to both nature and to those who live in forest communities. The norms of sustainability, sufficiency, solidarity, and participation all apply to this context.

The forest products industry and the USFS, needless to say, did not consider the loss of old growth trees and the forest practices used to log them a terrible wrong. They called it sustained-yield forestry and thought of themselves within the parameters of their conservationist and developmentalist perspectives to be wisely and sustainably managing forests in the pursuit of human well-being.

The temperate rainforest of the Pacific Northwest that stretches from northern California to southern Alaska west of the Sierra/Cascade divide (known locally as the westside) is arguably the best example of a temperate rainforest on earth. Others exist, notably in Chile, New Zealand, Tasmania, and formerly in northern Europe, but the westside has the finest and most extensive stands of trees, or at least it once did. Some of the stands in especially wet and protected locations are a spiritual and sensuous delight.[7]

This rainforest is a product of gradual development since the last ice age that reached its furthest advance about 18,000 years ago. The reason why these great stands of trees are in this place is a matter of climate, terrain, and soil plus local conditions that cause variations in the size and mix of trees.

The climate is mild and wet, mild because the prevailing westerly winds bring weather systems off the cool waters of the Pacific Ocean (50–55°F). The weather systems are strongest in the winter months and bring in copious amounts of rain that are dumped on the western slopes of the mountains as clouds rise, cool, and release their moisture. In summer the storm-producing low pressure gives way to high pressure and dry weather in the forests. The combination of wet, mild winters and dry, cool summers is well suited to conifers. They are able to withstand the summer dry period better than deciduous trees that require a steady diet of moisture. In winter the conifers keep their needles and manage some photosynthesis, while the deciduous trees are dormant. The gravelly soil drains well and gives further advantage to the conifers that do not, as the saying goes, "like to get their feet wet." The generally rugged terrain creates variations in weather patterns making some areas particularly suitable to prolific growth.

To understand why the activists, indeed environmentalists of all perspectives, are concerned about the heavy cutting of the region's oldest trees, it is necessary to know something about forest succession.[8] Forests go through a cycle, although not all forests do so at the same speed or time. While there is no starting point to a cycle, it is convenient to begin with the *clearing events* that bring down a stand of ancient trees. Historically these events were fire, wind, drought, ice, mudslides, and volcanic eruptions. Today, logging has all but replaced these natural events. For several years after the clearing event certain plant species take hold (weeds, bush alders, ferns, and small conifers, especially Douglas-firs) and form a *pioneer* community that lasts ten to fifty years or so. As the conifers that do well in clearings win the competition with the pioneer species, the forest enters a stage called a *seral* community. This stage is characterized by a dense canopy, many small trees of conical shape, little undergrowth because sunlight cannot penetrate, and few dead trees or fallen logs. This stage lasts from fifty to two hundred fifty years depending on the site and gradually gives way to the last stage, the *climax* community.

The climax community, known variously as late succession, old growth, ancient, or virgin forest, is quite different from the seral community that it replaces. As losers in the competition for sunlight and nutrients die out or fall, a few large trees take over and grow to enormous size. The canopy opens here and there as even these giants fall, permitting trees and shrubs of varying age to grow in the under story. Dead, standing trees known as snags and downed logs provide habitat for animals and insects. As time goes on, the more shade-tolerant hemlocks, cedars, and spruces tend to push out the Douglas-firs that are unable to grow in the under story because they need lots of sun.

The result is a unique old growth ecosystem. Ecosystems are dynamic communities of organisms working together with their environments as integrated units.[9] The ancient forests of the westside provide a habitat that is considerably different from the habitat found in the seral communities they replace. As a result they attract a different mix of species, even though there is some overlap. This is crucial. What industrial forestry does is to eliminate not only the big trees, but also an entire ecosystem. It then replaces this ecosystem with pioneer and seral communities. Typically industrial forests are logged every fifty to one hundred years depending on the site and the market price for trees. This is not enough time for an old growth ecosystem to regenerate. With the old, big trees and the ecosystem go the species that have adapted to this community, for example, the northern spotted owl and the marbled murrelet.[10] These species become more threatened as more ancient forests are converted to lumber and replaced by pioneer and seral communities.

By the late 1980s loggers had cut 85 to 90 percent of the ancient forests in the region.[11] Some of what remained was in fragmented islands where edge effects further reduced habitat and clearcut land inhibited the passage of plants and animals from one island to the next. Little old growth remained on lands in the United States owned by the states or logging companies. Almost all old growth was on federal lands in national parks, national forests, and lands managed by the Bureau of Land Management (BLM).

FOREST POLICY

The action at Market Mountain must also be seen in the context of U.S. Forest Policy, especially during the 1980s and 1990s. The activists were responding to what they perceived as threats to remaining old growth stands and healthy forest ecosystems.

In the 1980s biologists and environmentalists became concerned about the large cut of the preceding decade and the deterioration of forest health. As the science of ecosystems and investigative techniques improved, biologists concluded that an increasing number of species were threatened with extinction. With preservationists, they focused national attention on the endangered northern spotted owl as a way to address the even bigger problem of ecosystem destruction. A period of intense political conflict followed that was dampened, but did not go away, by a new forest policy for the region under President Clinton.

Beyond preservation, intense conflict also centered on forest practices. The rate of cut in the 1970s and 1980s far exceeded previous periods, leaving what many considered an ugly patchwork of cut over lands. Clearcutting was not only ugly, but, according to critics, the practice eliminated too many "legacies" that contribute to forest health.[12]

A forest is not just a stand of individual trees but a complex web of interdependencies. Little was known about crucial elements of forest health such as soil, airflows, canopy, and the role of snags and downed logs. The Forest Service and the logging companies claimed "best science," but time and again "best science" turned out to degrade ecosystems and habitat for important species. Trees, for example, were cut to the edges of watercourses and woody debris was removed. This practice had a serious impact on stream temperatures, eliminated refuges for fish, and in many cases caused the loss of salmon spawning grounds. The decline of salmon runs in the region is partly attributable to these and other logging practices.

In addition, the Forest Service and logging companies built thousands of miles of logging roads. A significant number slid into streams during rainy seasons covering salmon spawning grounds and habitat with mud.

The list goes on: problems with replanting one species of tree (monoculture), the use of pesticides and herbicides, the reluctance to use alternative harvesting methods, and the removal of debris and increased erosion in clearcuts. Conservationists began to join preservationists and critical ecology activists in their criticism. This, they claimed, was out-and-out exploitation. A movement opposed to this exploitation even developed in the Forest Service itself.[13]

Finally, the region and the forest products industry were undergoing economic changes that added further pressures. The forest products industry by the late 1980s had lost its once dominant role in the region's economy. While logging companies were doing well financially, they significantly reduced the number they employed by 13 percent between 1980 and 1988 largely through the introduction of labor-saving techniques. A recession in the early 1980s closed inefficient mills. Increasingly production shifted to the southeastern United States due to the longer growing season there, lower transportation and labor costs (no unions), and the relative inefficiency of mills in the Pacific Northwest. In the region employment in the wood products industry dropped dramatically from the early days. Only 2 percent of jobs in Washington and 4 percent in Oregon were in the industry.[14]

Loggers perceived that further cuts would result from efforts to conserve and preserve, a perception that was strongly encouraged by forest products companies. Whole communities rose up to fight "tree huggers," who were accused of destroying a whole way of life. The numbers game became popular as opposing groups predicted the number of jobs that would be lost, the industry on the high side, environmentalists on the low side.[15]

Environmentalists seemed to think the impacts of preservation would be small and manageable. They insisted that current practices were unsustainable and that entire ecosystems and the animals that inhabited them were being destroyed. "Mass extinction" and "reduced biodiversity" they called it. They further insisted that reduced cutting, less intrusive practices, and restoration work would still provide plenty of jobs. They also pointed out that more than 25 percent of raw logs were shipped overseas with the subsequent loss of value added in finished wood products. Finally, they suggested that over-consumption, not human need, was driving demand.

To no avail. By the early 1990s the sides were drawn with most Forest Service workers and rangers, the industry, the loggers, and most elected officials on the one side, environmentalists, many scientists, and several important pieces of legislation on the other.[16] The dispute went to court, new studies supported environmentalists, voters in the region became increasingly concerned about their quality of life, and national groups took notice.

The logjam broke, so to speak, with several court decisions that all but shut down the national forests. Bill Clinton promised in his presidential campaign to intervene personally. Once elected he ordered further studies and chaired a conference in Portland, Oregon, in April 1993. The result was the eventual adoption of "modified option 9."

Option 9 applied to federal lands managed by the USFS and BLM and emerged from a process initiated by President Clinton after the forest conference. Clinton created the Forest Ecosystem Management Assessment Team (FEMAT) "to achieve a balanced and comprehensive policy that recognizes the importance of the forest and timber to the economy and jobs in this region and . . . [p]reserves our precious old growth forests."[17] Five principles guided the process: 1) the provision of new economic opportunities to meet human need; 2) the protection of the long-term health of the forests; 3) scientific soundness, ecological credibility, and legal responsibility; 4) a predictable and sustainable level of timber sales that will not degrade the environment; and 5) collaboration, not confrontation.

The President went on to say:

Your assessment should take an ecosystems approach to forest management and should particularly address maintenance and restoration of biological diversity, particularly that of the late-succession and old-growth forest ecosystems; maintenance of long-term site productivity of forest ecosystems; maintenance of sustainable levels of renewable resources, including timber, other forest products, and other facets of forest values; and maintenance of rural economies and communities.[18]

FEMAT developed a number of options that varied in four respects: (1) quantity and location of land placed in reserves, (2) activities permitted in reserves, (3) areas outside the reserves, and (4) activities allowed in areas outside the reserves. FEMAT recommended two types of reserves: "late succession" (old growth) and "riparian" (zones near watercourses). No timber harvest would be allowed in these reserves, although some thinning of maturing younger stands of trees within reserves could take place. As a matter of fact, most trees in the late-succession reserves were second growth, seral stage trees that the team hoped would mature into old growth.

FEMAT placed land outside the reserves in two categories: the "matrix" where some logging would be permitted but only with new techniques to reduce ecological impacts; and "adaptive management areas" to test "technical and social approaches to integration and achievement of desired ecological, economic, and other social objectives."[19] The intention of the latter was to allow latitude for experimentation and for cooperation between the forest managers and local communities. Both categories contained stands of old growth potentially available for harvest. While it put most old growth "off limits," FEMAT by no means called for the end of old growth logging. In the plan that emerged Market Mountain was in the matrix and thus harvestable. About 20 percent of the old growth remaining in the Gifford Pinchot National Forest was in similar fashion available.

President Clinton accepted a modified version of option 9. The new policy has reduced the cut in the national forests of the region dramatically. For several years after the adoption of the policy, forest managers put none of the remaining old growth up for sale. FEMAT gave the northern spotted owl a good chance of survival. Newer, more ecologically sound forest practices were instituted. These actions muffled the controversy. Employment losses were not as great as industry economists had predicted and partially absorbed by the booming economy in the region. Forest communities such as Miller, Washington, suffered, but not as much as those distant from major highways and urban centers. Inefficient mills, especially those dependent on a continuing supply of old growth from the national forests, shut down. Jobs in the forest were lost due to the reduced cut. Large forest products companies with their own supply of timber continued to do well, however.

Later in the 1990s the Forest Service appeared to the activists to be preparing stands of old growth in the matrix for sale. Few except the direct activists took notice, but that was a significant exception. Small groups formed to monitor timber sales, staffed on a volunteer basis by energetic and intelligent young people with a passion for preserving old growth and not afraid to hike across difficult terrain to investigate potential sales. They prepared to take action against any sale that included old growth. The tree village at Market Mountain was a product of this preparation.

Are they zealots as Andy Wright in the case claims? That they are passionate and principled there is no doubt. They are also given to strong rhetoric and the negative branding of opponents, although this is not true of all of them. They take an uncompromising, either/or stance. They are willing to act illegally. So is this zealotry? More important than labels, is it ethical?

THE FUTURE

The term "sustainable" has been commonplace in the forests of the west for years. The Forest Service early in its history made sustainable yield a cardinal principle. That has not deterred the Forest Service and logging companies from degrading the forest, either by eliminating or fragmenting old growth ecosystems or by using practices that have a deleterious effect.

In part the degradation was inadvertent. The science of forestry was relatively undeveloped, and practices thought to represent best scientific management caused harm. But this is not the whole story. The Forest Service and the logging industry have always been close. Since the inception of the national forest system, logging has been the first among equal multiple uses, especially in the Pacific Northwest. Logging in the 1970s and 1980s was hardly sustainable by any measure in spite of extensive replanting. Anthropocentric and commercial motives drove degradation.

The Forest Service and the industry have always claimed that their take from the forests was sustainable. They rightly pointed out that the replanting of trees would always mean that trees would be available for wood products. Their past use of the term "sustainability" has not been altogether clear, however. Today the term means ecological sustainability and includes the preservation of species and ecosystems. Listening to Forest Service and industry spokespersons, sustainability in contrast seems to mean a constant supply of logs for the mills. To loggers it seems to mean steady jobs. To leaders in forest communities it seems to mean a steady flow of revenues to sustain services and schools.

Among these many and confusing uses of the term, ecological sustainability is the primary concern of this volume. The focus of the other uses is found in the norms of sufficiency, participation, and solidarity. Elliott Norse provides a good definition of sustainable forestry:

> Sustainable forestry means conserving the productive basis of land by preserving the integrity of the biota and ecological processes and producing commodities without degrading other values. It means forestry based on humility and appreciation, working with the land rather than against it. It means a sustained commitment to long-term research on the basic ecological processes that maintain values of both natural and

unmanaged lands. . . . It means making no irreversible commitments that tie our hands as the world changes; more than anything sustainable forestry means maintaining our options.[20]

With this definition the following guidelines are appropriate. The Forest Service and other government agencies should preserve on public lands all remaining old growth stands that are ecologically viable. Some stands may be cut if they are heavily compromised by edge effects or isolated from other healthy stands. Such exceptions should be rare, not the rule. In the spirit of option 9 the Forest Service should allow stands of second growth to mature into old growth, especially those stands contiguous to remaining old growth stands, those that provide corridors for wildlife to transit, and those along water courses. Forest restoration should be a major undertaking of the Forest Service throughout its area of management. Preserve, protect, and restore should be its goal.

The Forest Service and private landholders should manage the remainder of the forests using practices consistent with the best science of forestry with the understanding that best science will change. Scientific criteria should come first, and only after should economic criteria govern activities.

The norm of sufficiency, as in so many environmental cases, counsels reduced consumption. Wood is a renewable resource and has excellent applications. There is no problem in cutting trees and consuming wood products as long as it is done in an ecologically sustainable way. The pressure put on the forests by the large cuts and degrading practices during the 1970s and 1980s was in part a result of heavy consumer demand.

In addition to reduced consumption are the more efficient use of resources and the recycling of waste products. With some encouragement and under market pressures, industry can be counted on to accomplish this.

Solidarity means sustainable forestry communities and jobs in the forests for those whose vocation is logging. In the case Miller, Washington, is an example of a community that became unsustainable for reasons largely beyond its control. The cut in the Gifford Pinchot National Forest dropped, the local mill closed, and jobs were lost. Tourism took up some of the slack, but not all. The activists were able to tap into resentment that had built up. While they had their own motives, the activists coming to the defense of the townspeople is an excellent example of solidarity. They joined with local folks, listened to their complaints, provided organizing skills, and let the people lead. Ignored by the Forest Service, the logging company, and environmental groups, the citizens of Miller took to the activists in an unprecedented way. Whether this alliance can be duplicated remains to be seen.

Solidarity does not mean doing things for loggers and forest communities. They must do it for themselves and they face an uphill climb to reach a sustainable future. For some it will mean continued employment in the forests in either logging or restoration work. There will always be jobs in the woods. For others it will mean giving up a way of life and moving to another location. For still others it will mean a shift in jobs. Miller is located in a place where tourism is increasing. Townspeople have tried with some success to meet this new demand.

Several strategies further the end of sustainable futures in forest communities. One is to let market forces accomplish the transition. As hard-hearted as this may sound, it is a necessary strategy. The number of loggers and mill workers needed to produce wood products to meet market demand will never be as high as in the past. Constriction of supply, the shift of production to the southeast and overseas, and labor-saving technologies will continue to mean fewer forest-product workers in the Pacific Northwest. Sooner or later workers must face this reality.

Government leaders can and should moderate the harshness of unemployment and job seeking through temporary compensation, the provision of education opportunities, assistance in job searching, and efforts to help communities capture more of the value-added in finished wood products. These strategies are basic to any understanding of solidarity. Important also, government should take steps to restrict the transfer of forest lands to other uses. Urbanization, especially suburban sprawl, gradually encroaches on forest land, reducing both habitat for animals and the number of trees available to sustain jobs.

Participation is the fourth norm in the ethic of ecological justice. The residents of Miller make it clear through their resentment and the rapidity of their response that they feel left out of decisions that affect their lives. While title to the land near the community belongs primarily to the federal government and large logging companies, their closeness to and labor in the forests no doubt give them a sense of ownership. This sense is violated as the Forest Service makes decisions for the forest and surrounding lands in Portland, Oregon, and Washington, D.C., and the logging company in Seattle. Even the environmentalists in the Cascade Club are far away. It is these distant decision-makers behind closed doors in small groups who determine their future. These same decision-makers seem to take what they want from the forests primarily to the benefit of managers and stockholders, who are even further away and more anonymous. What are left are degraded forests. The sense of violation, of being a "colonial," must be strong and alienating. This is big-time nonparticipation on a small scale.

The case presents one way to gain participation. Take it! The activists started the protest, but the townspeople eagerly picked it up and soon made themselves heard. Had they remained passive, they would have continued as parties to their own victimization.

Congress in its wisdom has enacted many laws (see Appendix A, p. 136) that include processes for public comment and recourse to the courts. In this case the logging company succeeded in persuading important members of the state's congressional delegation to circumvent public comment and objection by attaching the agreement as a rider to an appropriations bill. This too is a clear violation of the norm of participation.

Modified option 9, the policy that now sets directions for the national forests on the westside, includes provisions for Adaptive Management Areas. The designation of these areas is an effort to encourage forest managers to cooperate with local logging communities. As long as these provisions promote creative cooperation, they will contribute to increased participation. They could, however, become a cover for further exploitation of the forests as local people join the Forest Service to increase jobs and profits with little regard for ecological sustainability.

The case leaves Bobby wondering whether the Saddle River Logging Company and presumably other, large, private companies will ever be open to participation. The ethos of private property combined with the political clout of large corporations makes this unlikely anytime soon. Managers are to a degree vulnerable to public opinion, but also have resources to project the appearance of environmental concern even when little exists. Opening them to outside voices will not be easy. Direct action may remain the most effective tactic.

APPENDIX A: APPLICABLE LAWS[21]

Weeks Law, U.S.C. 485 (1911)
Authorizes the Department of Agriculture to purchase land for the production of timber. This law is often cited as authority for exchanges.

General Exchange Act, 16 U.S.C. 485 (1922)
Authorizes the Department of Agriculture to make administrative land exchanges.

Bankhead-Jones Farm Tenant Act, 7 U.S.C. 1010 (1937)
Authorizes the exchange of public land as part of land conservation and utilization projects.

Forest Service Omnibus Act, 16 U.S.C. 555a (1962)
Authorizes the exchange of lands that are being administered "under laws which contain no provision for their exchange."

National Environmental Policy Act (NEPA), 42 U.S.C.A. 4321 (1969)
Requires government analysis and disclosure of potential environmental and socioeconomic impacts of major federal actions, and public participation in the decision-making process. Provides for citizen appeal.

Endangered Species Act, 16 U.S.C.A. 1531 (1973)
Authorizes U.S. Fish and Wildlife Service to compile and update an official list of rare, threatened, and endangered species for which critical habitat is to be protected under federal law. Many land trades are prompted by the need to bring endangered species habitat into public ownership.

Federal Land Policy and Management Act (FLPMA), 43 U.S.C.A. 1710 (1976)
Requires uniform procedures and regulations for the acquisition and exchange of non-federal land. Provides for disposal of tracts of public land that will serve important public objectives. Calls for trades to be of equal value.

National Forest Management Act (FNMA), 16 U.S.C. 1600 (1976)

Requires periodic land management plans. Land exchanges inconsistent with forest plan objectives may require a forest plan amendment. Governs forest practices.

Federal Land Exchange Facilitation Act (FLEFA), 43 U.S.C. 1701 (1988)

Amended land exchange regulations to set up bargaining and negotiation process where valuations cannot be agreed upon.

Notes

1. See Appendix A, pp. 136–137, for laws that apply to exchanges and activities in the national forests.
2. Carolyn Merchant, *Radical Ecology: The Search for a Livable World* (New York: Routledge, 1992). The categories used in this analysis of the protestors come from Merchant's typology. She divides the critical (radical as she calls it) ecology perspective into five sub-perspectives: (1) Deep Ecology (Ch. 4); (2) Spiritual Ecology (Ch. 5); (3) Social Ecology (Ch. 6); (4) Green Politics (Ch. 6); and (5) Ecofeminism (Ch. 7).
3. Gifford Pinchot, "Principles of Conservation," in Peter C. List, ed. *Environmental Ethics and Forestry* (Philadelphia: Temple University Press, 2000), pp. 30–34.
4. Holmes Rolston, III, *Environmental Ethics: Duties to and Values in the Natural World* (Philadelphia: Temple University Press, 1988), p. 277.
5. Robert C. Fuller, *Spiritual But Not Religious: Understanding Unchurched America* (Oxford: Oxford University Press, 2001).
6. See Chapter Two in this volume on the Christian tradition.
7. In the Gifford Pinchot National Forest the Lewis River trail is one such location. The forests in the river valleys on the westside of the Olympic Mountains are breathtaking. The redwoods in northern California are unmatched for pure grandeur.
8. Elliott A. Norse, *Ancient Forests of the Pacific Northwest* (Washington, DC: Island Press, 1990), Ch. III.
9. Ibid., Chs. IV and V.
10. Estimates of the number of species whose primary habitat is found in old growth forests varies, but most scientists set the number at several hundred. Ibid. Ch. IV.
11. Ibid., pp. 243–252. Melanie J. Rowland, *Old Growth Forests and Timber Towns: Thinking About Tomorrow* (Seattle: University of Washington, Institute for Public Policy and Management), p. 4.
12. Kathryn A. Kohm and Jerry F. Franklin. *Creating a Forestry for the 21st Century: The Science of Ecosystem Management* (Washington, D.C.: Island Press, 1997). This is a technical volume but rich with suggestions for the new forestry. Also see Peter C. List, ed. *Environmental Ethics and Forestry*, Ch. 11.
13. Jeff DeBonis. "Inner Voice," and "Speaking Out: A Letter to the Chief of the U.S. Forest Service (1989)," in Peter C. List, ed. *Environmental Ethics and Forestry*, pp. 221–239.
14. Melanie J. Rowland, *Old Growth Forests and Timber Towns*, p. 32.
15. Ibid., pp. 39–40.
16. Because the northern spotted owl was the focus of the conflict, most casual observers thought the Endangered Species Act was the relevant piece of legislation.

This act came into play only late in the dispute after a federal judge had declared that the Interior Department had not done its scientific homework and ordered a reevaluation of the owl as an endangered species. Rather the National Forest Management Act that required the preservation of critical habitat and the National Environmental Protection Act that stipulated environmental impact statements provided the opportunity for environmental groups to go to court.

17. The Forest Ecosystems Management Assessment Team, *Excerpts from Forest Ecosystem Management: An Ecological, Economic, and Social Assessment* (United States Department of Agriculture, Forest Service et al., 1993), p. 3.

18. Ibid., p. 4.

19. Ibid., pp. 15f.

20. Elliott A. Norse, *Ancient Forests of the Pacific Northwest*, p. 255.

21. Excerpted selectively from George Draffan and Janine Blaeloch, *Commons or Commodity: The Dilemma of Federal Land Exchanges* (Seattle: The Western Land Exchange Project, PO Box 95545, Seattle, WA 98145), http://www.westlx.org. 2000, pp. 78–80.

For Further Reading

Adams, Carol, ed. *Ecofeminism and the Sacred*. Maryknoll: Orbis Books, 1992.

Aplet, Gregory H., et al., eds. *Defining Sustainable Forestry*. Washngton, D.C.: Island Press, 1993.

Callicot. J. Baird, and Nelson, Michael P., eds. *The Great Wilderness Debate*. Athens: University of Georgia Press, 1998.

Clary, David A. *Timber and the Forest Service*. Lawrence, KS: The University of Kansas Press, 1986.

DeVall, Bill, ed. *Clearcut: The Tragedy of Industrial Forestry*. San Francisco: Sierra Club Books, 1993.

George Draffin and Janine Blaeloch. *Commons or Commodity: The Dilemma of Federal Land Exchanges*. Seattle: The Western Land Exchange Project, 2000.

Jenkins, Michael B., and Smith, Emily T. *The Business of Sustainable Forestry: Strategies for an Industry in Transition*. Washington, D.C.: Island Press, 1999.

Kohm, Kathryn A., and Franklin, Jerry F., eds. *Creating a Forestry for the 21st Century: The Science of Ecosystem Management*. Washington, D.C.: Island Press, 1997.

List, Peter C., ed. *Environmental Ethics and Forestry: A Reader*. Philadelphia: Temple University Press, 2000.

Maser, Chris. *Forest Primeval: The Natural History of an Ancient Forest*. San Francisco: Sierra Club Books, 1989.

Merchant, Carolyn. *Radical Ecology: The Search for a Livable World*. New York: Routledge, 1992.

Norse, Elliott. *Ancient Forests of the Pacific Northwest*. Washington, D.C.: Island Press, 1990.

Raphael, Ray. *More Tree Talk: The People, Politics, and Economics of Timber*. Washington, D.C.: Island Press, 1993.

Robinson, Gordon. *The Forest and the Trees: A Guide to Excellent Forestry*. Washington, D.C.: Island Press, 1988.

Yaffee, Steven Lewis, *The Wisdom of the Spotted Owl: Policy Lessons for a New Century*. Washington, D.C.: Island Press, 1994.

Websites

Earthfirst
http://earthfirst.org

Greenpeace
http://www.greenpeace.org

Society of American Foresters
http://www.safnet.org

United States Forest Service
http://fs.fed.us

Western Land Exchange Project
http://www.westlx.org

7

Saving Snake River Salmon

Endangered Species and Habitat Restoration

Case

Carl Alexander sank into his recliner after a hard day cutting hay and reflected back on his reaction when he first heard the proposal. His friend Pete Nelson had stormed into the farm equipment store late last year fuming something about knocking down the dams on the Snake River. Pete calmed down after a while and explained that now in order to save remaining salmon runs environmentalists wanted to remove four dams on the Snake River between Lewiston, Idaho, and the confluence of the Snake and the Columbia Rivers in eastern Washington State.

Carl's own reaction was not as strong as Pete's, but he did feel a distinct threat. While removal of the dams would not directly affect his farming operations, except possibly to raise his already considerable energy costs, over the long haul who knew what was next. If the environmentalists won the fight over the four dams, they might go after the dams on his stretch of the Snake in Idaho, eliminating both his source of water and the power to pump it the three hundred feet up from the river to his fields. That would mean the end of his livelihood as well as those of his neighbors. The town nearby, already poor, would be wiped out.

Over time his reaction turned in a more practical direction. He knew that salmon runs on the Snake had declined 90 percent in the past thirty or forty years. He also knew that environmental laws mandated the preservation of species and that the government and environmentalists were both ready to exert pressure for enforcement. Just last year on the other side of town the federal government wanted to end all irrigation from ground water to protect the habitat of a rare snail. Fortunately a win-win solution had been found. Very few farmers had to stop irrigating, and those that did received adequate compensation. But feelings had run high on both sides, and his friend Pete had been especially vocal. If the dams on their stretch of the Snake were threatened, the place would explode.

Robert L. Stivers prepared this case and commentary. The case is based on actual events. Names and places have been changed to protect the privacy of those involved.

Following this encounter, Carl decided on a prudent course of action. Instead of joining the extremists on either side, he would seek out pragmatic solutions that gave farmers and environmentalists what they needed. Still the sense of threat to his own livelihood remained, and he was not quite sure what he should do about the dams, especially since initial efforts to find a compromise had failed.

PETE'S PERSPECTIVE

Whatever Carl thought didn't seem to make much difference to Pete, however. Shortly after the snail compromise, Pete had urged local farmers to join in opposition to dam removal. At a rally in the town hall Pete had presented a strong case. He began by reviewing the construction of the dams. "The Army Corp of Engineers," he said, "built four dams on the lower Snake: Ice Harbor, completed in 1961, Lower Monument in 1969, Little Goose in 1970, and Lower Granite in 1975. The main purpose of the dams was to make the Snake navigable for barges. Barging is the most economical way to transport grain, and if the dams are breached, transportation costs for the region's wheat farmers will increase dramatically. It takes twice as much energy to move the grain by train and four times as much by truck. And with rising fuel prices the costs will go even higher, not to mention the air pollution trucks will create. A lot of farmers will be forced out, and the world's food supply will decrease," he added.

Pete went on to note that many jobs depended on the barge traffic all the way from Lewiston, Idaho, to Portland, Oregon. "If these dams are removed, millions in wages will be lost, and workers will face unemployment," he stressed. "The recreational use of the lakes behind the dams will go as well, drying up millions of tourist dollars."

Pete really got Carl's attention when he turned to the impacts on farming. "These dams were also built to provide water for irrigation and environmentally clean hydroelectric power. Thirteen farms totaling 35,000 acres will probably go out of business either due to the elimination of their water supply or to increased pumping costs resulting from the need to lift the water higher up to the rim of the canyon." Looking directly at Carl, he added: "Those of us from around here can appreciate that. Think what would happen to your costs if they removed the dams on our stretch of the river."

Pete went on: "Energy costs will also rise as a result of knocking out the power generated by those dams. They provide 5 percent of the Northwest's power supply. Prices will have to go up to ration the reduced supply or other sources of energy will have to be substituted. Hydro is clean energy. It creates no air pollution, as does the burning of fossil fuels that are the most likely substitutes. Rising power costs, or worse, an energy shortage would hurt not only farmers like us, but also the industries that located in the Pacific Northwest because of cheap hydroelectric energy. The aluminum industry is the best example. Remember the energy crunch a few years ago? The aluminum companies laid off workers in droves."

Pete then turned to possible technical fixes. He was supportive of the hatchery program that he claimed went a long way to make up for the over fishing that he thought was the primary reason for the decline of the runs in the first place. He sided with the Army Corp of Engineers which had recently announced its preference for what it called an "adaptive management alternative." This alternative calls for technical improvements in operations and structures, such as upgraded juvenile fish facilities, additional fish transportation barges, improved turbines, and surface bypass collection structures. He thought these improvements would enhance the fish runs. He was skeptical, however, of proposals to pipe salmon downstream. "Those alternatives are not cost-effective," he asserted.

Pete concluded: "The removal of the dams will not guarantee recovery of the runs and will be expensive to boot. I think we can save the salmon, but even if we can't, the welfare of people counts more anyway. Those environmentalists who are so willing to throw out economic benefit really irk me. I urge you to join in the effort to stop the environmentalists."

THE PIPELINE PLAN

Carl thought Pete's rationale was generally sound, but over the past few months he had been working with Oliver Sanders, a former employee of the Idaho Fish and Wildlife Department. Oliver had devised a plan to build a pipeline made out of Polybutalene. The pipe would move the young salmon through the reservoirs behind the dams where there is a high level of predation and then around the dams themselves where many are killed going through the turbines or over the top of the dams. The pipe would run from the first dam below Lewiston, Lower Granite Dam, to Bonneville Dam, the last dam downstream on the Columbia River, and significantly speed the passage of the small fry.

"The fish pipeline works like this," Oliver had explained to Carl over lunch one day. "Salmon smolt traveling downstream to sea would be herded into a holding pen by sound waves transmitted by a sonic transducer. This method has been tested on the East Coast. Salmon would then be separated from other fish and sent down the pipe, through the reservoirs, and around the dams with giant pumps maintaining the water flow. In between the dams the pipe would be lowered twenty feet below the river surface. Anchors would secure the pipe to the river bottom, and foam would be wrapped around the pipe to keep it afloat.

Oliver and a few close friends had worked hard on the project. They had enlisted the support of a well-known engineering firm in the area that had done preliminary design work and made cost projections. The cost would be a fraction of what it would take to remove just one dam. The state's universities had also lent support as well as a major aqua-culture firm and Native American tribes. The next step was to test a small section with final installation to await the outcome of the tests. The big problem was the lack of funds. None of the major organizations that funded efforts to protect the salmon would touch it. Some thought it would not work; others like Pete felt that it was not cost effective.

Carl was impressed with Oliver and had joined the effort to develop the pipeline. He had spoken with state and federal officials without success, however. He was really frustrated at the stonewalling. He had concluded that public officials were too stuck in their ways or too beholden to established political power. In spite of these difficulties he still felt the plan had potential as a middle course between salmon extinction and removal of the dams.

THE FARM

Carl's sense of threat continued. It stemmed mostly from his vocation as a farmer. Carl and his wife Joanne had put a lot of work into their farm. They had been successful. After a stint in the Marine Corps including service in Vietnam, Carl had returned to the family business in the Midwest. But after eleven years during which time he had met Joanne at a dance and subsequently married her, he yearned for something different. His thoughts kept returning to boyhood memories of his grandfather's tobacco farm in North Carolina where he had spent so many agreeable summers. It took them eleven years to decide, but finally Carl and Joanne packed off to agriculture school in Kansas.

With money they had saved, they purchased 1,800 acres of sage and bunch grass desert in central Idaho along the Snake. The original owners had converted the land to agriculture a few years earlier. They had secured water rights based on the principle "first in time, first in right" that governed water allocation in the arid intermountain West. The water came from the construction of a nearby dam that was part of the system built by the Idaho Power Company to harness the Snake. The system of dams had coincidentally caused the extinction or endangerment of the last runs of salmon on the main stem of the Snake River. The original owners had used water from the dam's reservoir and cheap electricity from the dam's turbines to grow potatoes. They had a falling out in the mid-1970s and put the land up for sale. Carl and Joanne purchased the land and changed over to dairy farming. The water rights came with the farm, and Carl and Joanne thus had a secure source for irrigation, that is, as long as the dams remained intact. The conversion to dairy farming seemed less risky, especially given their inexperience.

They invested in the equipment necessary to grow hay and other crops that go into the silage to feed the cows. Starting small, they built up the herd over the years to the present 500 head. One quarter of their crops went to feed the herd, and the remainder was sold on local markets to supplement the income from the dairy operation. A reliable arrangement with a local producer of cheese had eliminated a lot of their risk. As the operation grew, they hired a manager for the dairy and concentrated on hay, barley, and lately a little corn. The division of labor had worked fairly well, although finding competent dairy managers had been a problem now and then.

The operation, while large by Midwestern standards, was about average in size for Idaho. The price for milk had been good over the years, and when it dropped to a certain level, government price supports kicked in to help avoid really lean years. Carl readily acknowledged the power of the dairy lobby and was proud of it. Good years allowed for the purchase of equipment such as harvesters and tractors. They invested gradually in an upgrade of the irrigation system. Farming had become easier as they mechanized. Still, their equipment costs were substantial, and the price they paid Idaho Power for electricity to run the irrigation pumps had recently shot up.

Carl and Joanne thought of themselves as good stewards of the land. Yes, they used lots of energy. They also used some fertilizer to supplement the manure recycled to the fields from the dairy operation. They were careful in spreading both the manure and the fertilizer to avoid run-off. For the most part they did not use pesticides, instead releasing millions of ladybugs each year as a form of integrated pest management. The only exception was those years in which huge swarms of grasshoppers moved in from the desert and threatened their entire crop. Herbicides were kept to a minimum, since rotating crops kept weeds in check. They carefully monitored the irrigation water to prevent run-off and to keep costs to a minimum.

In the early days they had hired a number of Hispanic farm laborers, mostly migrants from Mexico who worked for the summer at a rate of ten dollars per hour and then returned to Mexico and their families with the money they earned. Some were illegal aliens, but local authorities had usually ignored their presence. Carl and Joanne needed the help and had no other source of labor. In recent years the supply of farm labor had dried up due to shifting immigration laws. This forced Carl and Joanne to install mechanized pivots for irrigation. Today, they employed four farm laborers, all legal, or at least that is what they assumed. Two of them lived with their families on the farm in mobile homes Carl and Joanne had provided. They drew salaries that included health benefits. The other two lived in adequate housing on the property and were paid better than average wages. Pick-up trucks were provided for work and limited personal use.

Carl and Joanne were active in the local community. Carl was a volunteer fireman. They went regularly to the community church and participated in the life of the congregation. They were on a first name basis with most of the folks within a twenty-mile radius. Visits to stores and restaurants brought forth smiles and warm handshakes, occasionally hugs, and sometimes even neighbors fuming about dams. In spite of the hard work and the isolation of the farm, they loved both the work and their community. A lot was a stake for them if dam removal took hold.

THE ENVIRONMENTALIST

Several weeks ago one of Carl's high school classmates, Marla Rogers, had called from Washington, DC, to say she would be in Boise at a conference and would like to visit. Carl had run into her at the class reunion in the fall, and they had talked about farming and the removal of the dams on the lower Snake River. Marla called herself an environmentalist.

At the appointed time Marla pulled up outside and came in. She wanted to see the farm, so Carl showed her around while Joanne prepared supper. After supper, Marla, Joanne, and Carl turned to the matter of the dams. Marla started by noting that salmon migrating to spawn in the Columbia River watershed were a mere 5 to 10 percent of their historical number, and that 80 percent of these salmon were inferior hatchery fish. As for the various populations on the Snake River, most of the wild runs were either extinct or endangered. "Something drastic needs to be done to save what remains and build up the runs," she exclaimed.

She then ticked off the causes of the decline. "First," she said, "was the over fishing that affected all populations. The Columbia used to be famous for its many canneries. They lined the river along certain stretches. All are now gone, victims of a drastically reduced catch. There aren't enough salmon even for sport fishing. Second, loggers early on ruined salmon habitat by flushing huge numbers of logs downstream, and until recently by cutting to the edge of streams, removing woody debris, and changing the temperature of the water. Today, poorly constructed logging roads slide into water courses and cover spawning beds with silt. Third, farmers like you withdrew water from the rivers and often polluted streams with run-off from farm animals, fertilizers, pesticides, and herbicides. Fourth, miners, especially in the early days, tore up streams in search of gold and polluted them with toxic chemicals.

"Fifth came the dam builders responding to pressures for economic development. They promised cheap energy and abundant supplies of water to make the desert bloom. Dams blocked some runs completely, made it more difficult for salmon to go upstream to spawn, and took a heavy toll on juveniles heading out to sea. The irony is that farmers like yourselves, who are completely dependent on the infrastructure built by the federal government, don't even seem to know it and are among the first to criticize government intrusion into your affairs. Sixth, industries were attracted to the Pacific Northwest by cheap electricity. Workers from all over the U.S. moved to the region to enjoy the bonanza. Factories and new homes reduced both the quantity and the quality of habitat. Finally, fish hatcheries were constructed to make up for reduced habitat. Hatcheries were based on poor science from the start, cost millions of dollars with little return, and resulted in weakened runs. Worst of all, they provided the justification for the continuing loss of habitat by offering the illusion of a technological fix."

Marla summarized her case. "The causes of the decline are many, interrelated, and complex. No one cause can be isolated, and those who contribute in one way to the overall problem always blame the other guys. Add the heavy political clout of the interests exploiting salmon and their habitat, and the salmon didn't have a chance. And, of course, they had no vote in the matter."

She went on: "The decline of the salmon is encouraged by a mindset that views nature as inferior and as something to be used for human economic gain. It has no intrinsic, only utilitarian value. We call our exploitation dominion and separate ourselves so thoroughly from plants and animals that we lose all spiritual relation. And by focusing heavily on human economic good and technical solutions, we separate ourselves even further and lose sight of the whole. Ecosystems are communities of species including humans, and we need to see ourselves as part of these systems and dependent on them. This is a holistic or ecological approach in contrast to the atomistic and economic approach we have been taking." Marla concluded: "Until we change our attitudes toward nature, the salmon will continue to decline. We need · to breach the dams, drastically modify our hatchery system, prevent degrading industrial and agricultural practices, stop fishing, give more water to the salmon, and change how we think. Above all, we need to consume less. Defenders of the Snake River dams claim we will lose 5 percent of our power supply. Heck, we could easily cover that by consuming less and being more efficient."

Carl and Joanne were slow to respond. They understood the critique. They had not, however, thought very much about their relation to nature. They recognized that they depended on the dams, and that dams were part of the problem. They also knew that some of their farming practices, even as careful as they were, contributed to environmental degradation. Above all, they were keenly aware of the consequences of Marla's prescriptions. They were sure that the removal of the four dams would raise the price of electricity. Their costs could skyrocket. They were worried about the long-range precedent that could lead to the removal of dams along their own stretch of the river. Finally, they had trouble with the single-minded passion of environmentalists, government bureaucrats, and those who came to Idaho to play. They resented the way these folks waded in with an "in your face" attitude, as if they alone had the truth and the locals should get out of the way.

Carl started things off. "All that may be true, but we are pragmatists, not idealists. There is no way folks around here are going to get out of the way and let their livelihoods be destroyed, especially by outsiders. We recognize the importance of healthy ecosystems. Take the much-maligned coyote, for example. As long as they don't come in packs, coyotes help us by controlling the mice and gophers. We need them. I also understand the political pressure to preserve species and clean up the air and water. However misguided some legislation like the Endangered Species Act is, it's on the books. If its provisions kick in to preserve the salmon, we are going to be in big trouble. So I say, instead of removing the dams, let's find a way to keep the dams and preserve the salmon at the same time. Let's get something done for a change instead of constantly bickering. That's why I am for this project to pipe the salmon downstream. It's a practical solution that at least warrants taking a look at."

At this point Joanne chimed in. "I think conservation is important. God has given us dominion over the earth and we need to exercise good stewardship. But humans were created separately from the other species and alone in the image of God. We are more valuable than the salmon. Human economic good trumps environmental considerations as long as ecosystems are not destroyed. If you destroy the systems, you lose your livelihood too."

Carl then added: "There are still plenty of fish out there. Watch on the weekends the number of anglers down by the river. Who cares what kind of fish are in the river? If the salmon go extinct on the Snake to provide food for humans, what's the big deal?"

Marla shook her head indicating her disagreement and reminded Carl that Native Americans think it is a big deal to lose their most important resource. Joanne jumped in again: "I think you put that a bit strongly, Carl, but I basically agree. A lot of people in this valley are children of pioneers. They have a tie to the land, and most think of the land as a trust. But they are a fiercely independent lot and don't like the government stepping in to take charge of everything."

The mention of the government got Carl started on one of his pet peeves. "The Bureau of Land Management owns most of the land in this part of the West," he said, "and they badly mismanage it. Range fires go out of control. Water is cut off to protect snails or logging stopped to save owls. There is a constant turnover of employees. Many new employees are young and inexperienced, and not from the area. They don't know what they are doing half of the time. Yet they have a lot of control over your life and are not afraid to exercise it. Distrust of the government runs deep around here. It would be better if all the land were in private hands. When you own a piece of property, you take care of it. Those bureaucrats have no sense of caring for the land and are not invested in it. And if you think I am strong on this, you should meet my friend Pete. He would give you an earful."

The three of them talked on into the evening, and Marla left the next morning to head back to Boise and home. Late the next afternoon, Carl and Joanne sat down at the table and reviewed the conversation. Was Marla right? Should they reconsider the removal of the dams or stay the course for finding a technical solution? And what about those attitudes toward nature that Marla emphasized? How might they incorporate some of the things she said?

Commentary

Farmers in the intermountain west region of the United States and an environmentalist residing in the nation's capital are the eyes in this case for viewing a conflict over the removal of four dams on the lower Snake River. These dams provide a multiplicity of human economic goods but at substantial environmental cost. The issue of the dams and other issues this conflict raises are typical of disputes related to preserving species and ecosystems.

The first issue is that of declining salmon runs. While this case is about runs on the Snake River, the problem pertains to the entire region. Indeed, it is part of the worldwide problem of declining fish populations and mass extinction that deeply worry scientists and environmentalists.[1] Humans are almost entirely responsible for the precipitous decline of salmon runs throughout the region. Since it is hard to determine what percentage of this decline is due to the various factors, parties responsible blame other parties while covering their own guilt and avoiding remedial action.

Second, since many of the causes are related to perceptions of human economic well-being, the case raises the issue of trade-offs. How much economic well-being are Americans willing to trade for the preservation of threatened and endangered species? As long as this trade-off is viewed as a zero-sum game, conflict is inevitable.

Third is the matter of technological "fixes" to turn zero-sum into win-win games. Fish hatcheries, fish-friendly dams, and a pipeline are featured in this case as conservation measures that proponents claim will allow both the dams to remain in place and the fish to thrive. The question is not only about the workability of specific technologies, but also about reliance on new technology to mitigate damage done by old technologies. Perhaps the real problem is the technological mentality itself and levels of consumption that put heavy pressure on vulnerable ecosystems.

Fourth, farmers in the case express attitudes toward nature that are part of the overall environmental crisis. Anthropocentrism, hierarchy, and a degree of dualism are evident. So is atomism as the farmers single out economic good as the determining criterion. An understanding of dominion as domination may also be implicit in what they say. In contrast, the environmentalist Marla Rogers seems to come out of the preservationist perspective that is more biocentric, egalitarian, connected, and integrated. She obviously rejects domination as an attitude, but does not make clear how far she would go to sacrifice economic and social goods for environmental integrity. Would she advocate pulling down all the dams on the Columbia and Snake Rivers?

Fifth, the farmers express suspicion, if not hostility, toward government, even though they reap huge benefits from government subsidies. This suspicion is characteristic of the intermountain west, which today has one of the most conservative voting records on economic issues of any region in the United States. While freedom from government control has traditionally been a feature of western political ideology, until recently the voting records of states such as Montana and Idaho were not so lopsided.

This suspicion also characterizes Carl and Joanne and attaches not just to government, but also to environmentalists and tourists. They feel a sense of threat to their livelihood from outsiders and may even be a bit defensive. Given Carl and Joanne's strong sense of vocation, stewardship, and pride in their farm, this suspicion seems out of character. Writing it off as provincial is too easy.

Sixth and associated with this is the issue of sustainable farming. Carl and Joanne seem to be using fairly sound environmental practices. Nevertheless, is large-scale, heavily mechanized farming in an environmentally sensitive area really sustainable? Should humans be using scarce water resources at great expense to irrigate deserts?

Finally, and peripheral, is Carl and Joanne's employment of migrant and in some instances illegal farm workers. So little is said about it in the case that the situation is not clear.

DECLINING SALMON RUNS AND HUMAN WELL BEING

Salmon are anadromous fish.[2] They hatch in the tributaries of the Columbia and Snake, live for a while near their place of origin, and then migrate downstream to the Pacific where they adjust to salt water, feed for a number of years, and then return to spawn and die. There are a number of salmon species and they vary in important respects. Variation is also characteristic of each species and even populations of the same species in different streams. This variability has evolved because it increases fitness in changing environments, both longer-term big changes and shorter-term shifts in moisture and temperature. While salmon have been around for millions of years, their presence in such great numbers in the Columbia basin is a fairly recent phenomenon, dating from the end of the last ice age twelve to fourteen thousand years ago.

The Columbia-Snake River drainage historically was the home habitat for more salmon than any other river in the world.[3] Estimates place the number of fish entering the river system each year before Europeans arrived at between ten and sixteen million fish.[4] Today numbers have declined to between five and eight hundred thousand, or 5 percent of the original. Many populations have gone extinct, and many others are threatened or endangered.

According to fisheries biologist Jim Lichatowich, salmon are now extinct in 40 percent of the tributaries where they historically spawned.[5] In 1991 Lichatowich worked with two other biologists and concluded "that of the 214 native, naturally spawning runs of Pacific salmon, steelhead, and sea-run cutthroat trout in Oregon, Washington, Idaho, and California that were at risk, 101 were at high risk of extinction, 58 were at moderate risk, and 54 were of special concern." This decline is a disaster and a tragedy, a result of greed, exploitation, and lack of scientific knowledge. It is testimony to the rapaciousness of human beings who in their professed goal of enhancing human well-being through the control of nature actually looted it.

Lichatowich attributes the decline to the substitution of a market-driven, industrial economy for the natural economy of the Pacific Northwest. According to Lichatowich:

> Fundamentally, the salmon's decline has been the consequence of a vision based on flawed assumptions and unchallenged myths—a vision that has guided the relationship between salmon and humans for the past 150 years. We assumed we could control the biological productivity and "improve" on natural processes that we didn't even try to understand. We assumed we could have salmon without rivers. As a

direct outcome of these assumptions, we believed that human activities such as mining, logging, and fishing were unrelated to the ecological processes that produced fish. The natural limits of ecosystems seemed irrelevant because people believed they could circumvent them through technology.[6]

Included in this substitution was a change of attitudes toward nature from the biocentric attitudes of hunting-gathering Native Americans to the developmentalist attitudes of European Americans.

The substitution began almost immediately and was accomplished rapidly upon the arrival of Europeans in the region. First came the fur trappers and traders who eliminated the beaver that had co-evolved in the region with the salmon and had engineered habitat favorable to salmon fitness. The miners, whose techniques destroyed habitat directly and degraded overall water quality, soon followed the fur trappers and traders.

Loggers made an even bigger impact. They changed the temperature of water courses by cutting stream-side trees first. They used the rivers to float logs downstream to mills, often clogging the rivers for months, changing stream vegetation, and preventing passage of the migrating salmon. They used dynamite to break logjams and cleared woody debris from streams reducing important refuges. Mudslides from poorly constructed roads covered gravel beds used by spawning salmon. Today, even with improved logging practices the degradation continues.

Ranchers added to the degradation by grazing cattle and sheep alongside streams. The cattle and sheep killed streamside vegetation, trampled down stream banks, and contributed to water pollution. Ranchers and farmers, with the help of the federal government and local authorities, developed irrigation systems that reduced the flow of water needed for migration and spawning and diverted young salmon to irrigation ditches and premature deaths. Irrigation increased dramatically with the construction of the big dams in the Columbia basin beginning in the 1930s. Farmers and ranchers also eliminated wetlands to increase the land available for crops and used fertilizers, pesticides, and herbicides that ran off into streams and degraded them.

Prior to the big dam era that began in the 1930s, loggers had constructed splash dams and municipalities erected small dams to increase water storage capacity and generate power. These early dams seldom included fish ladders for the passage of the salmon. Entire runs were eliminated in a matter of a few years as salmon swam in circles in front of the dams. The Elwah River that flows out of the Olympic Mountains is a classic example. Two dams were built on the Elwah for the generation of small amounts of electricity. One of the region's finest runs of King Salmon, with some fish weighing in at over one hundred pounds, was eliminated.

The big dams built for irrigation, transportation, and hydroelectric power had an even greater impact. In the forty years between 1930 and 1970 engineers dammed nearly every stretch of the Columbia and Snake Rivers. The dams changed the face of the intermountain west and made it much more difficult for salmon to migrate. Some, for example, Grand Coulee Dam, the biggest of them all, were built without provision for the passage of fish. Grand Coulee cut off the entire basin behind it as habitat for salmon.

The main problem for migrating salmon is going downstream. Fish ladders are difficult but not impossible for salmon going upstream to negotiate. Young salmon migrate downstream to the ocean by letting the spring floods of snowmelt carry them. Reservoirs behind dams slow the flow of water and increase the time it takes to travel from spawning areas to the sea. The fingerlings are also subject to increased predation in the slack water of the reservoirs. Then, having survived that gauntlet, they must pass through turbines or go over the top of the dams. The toll is high and it is a wonder that any make it to the ocean. Dams also destroy salmon habitat. Silt covers the gravel and flooding damages the condition of spawning beds.

Jim Lichatowich summarizes the degradation of habitat:

Between 1840 and 1930 . . . the region's rivers and salmon habitat underwent significant transformation and degradation. The waves of settlers divided the watersheds among themselves according to their economic interests. The fur trappers took the beavers; the miners took the gold and gravel, the loggers took the trees and riverbanks; the ranchers took the grasslands and riparian zones; the irrigators took the water; the hydroelectric dams took the river's energy and vitality. Each group took their piece of the ecosystem with little or no regulation by the government and with little or no concern for the costs imposed on others. In the process, they pulled apart, fragmented and destroyed the salmon's home.[7]

To Lichatowich's list of groups that destroyed habitat must also be added the forces of industrialization and urbanization. While resource extraction dominated the early economy of the west, increasingly the region industrialized. With industrialization came pollution and jobs. Little was done about water pollution. Factories flushed contaminants through pipes directly into streams. Workers were attracted by the jobs and poured into the region, all needing to be fed, clothed, and housed. Critical salmon habitat gave way to roads, buildings, and suburban development.

If the fur traders, miners, loggers, farmers, industrialists, and workers destroyed and degraded habitat, it was the fishers and canners before the big dam era who turned the salmon into a commodity and decimated the runs directly, eventually eliminating even themselves. Canning as a technique for food preservation first appeared in France in the early nineteenth century.[8] At the end of the Civil War it appeared in California and soon spread throughout the west. By the 1890s canneries lined the lower Columbia River near where fishers intercepted the incoming salmon. The take peaked in 1895, and by the 1920s it was obvious that decline had set in. The catch rose and fell thereafter, but the overall direction was clear. By the 1970s the exploitation had taken its toll in spite of increasingly frantic efforts to increase numbers in state run hatcheries.

The take was enormous. Fish were caught, cleaned, packed, shipped, and consumed without regard for sustainability. What the other commercial interests did indirectly as a side-effect, the fishing industry did directly by overfishing. And they did it with little outcry and almost no restrictions.

Today with the exception of fur trappers and traders the political power of these many economic interests remains strong. As environmental awareness increased and the plight of salmon has become common knowledge, these economic interests have staunchly defended their prerogatives and made political change very difficult. Each group has rightly pointed out how other groups caused decline and wrongly exonerated itself. Politicians and managers are reluctant to take on these interests, preferring instead to pursue technological fixes that offer the possibility of sustaining salmon runs without having to get at the real causes of decline. It is to these technological fixes that the discussion now turns.

TECHNOLOGICAL FIXES

The term "technological fix" frequently appears in environmental literature. When used to criticize habitat-degrading technologies and failed efforts at remediation, it carries negative connotations. More favorably, it refers to attempts to mitigate or reverse environmental damage by developing new and better technologies. A fix is an attempt to find a win-win solution to an environmental problem that avoids the sacrifice of economic and social goods that may or may not be part of the problem. Some fixes work, some do not, and some make the problem worse. Attempts to find fixes are particularly popular in such cases as declining salmon runs where powerful political interests resist more fundamental efforts to prevent degradation, restore habitat, and protect ecosystems, especially those that are expensive and force social change. The focus on fixes frequently directs attention away from the nontechnical problems and solutions that would be effective.

Fish hatcheries and modifications to dams to make them more fish-friendly have been the two primary fixes for the problem of declining salmon runs. Neither addresses the problem of degraded habitat. The pipeline proposal in the case is an example of a modification designed to move salmon around the dams. Less well known are technologies, such as those associated with the so-called new forestry, that reduce the impact of logging and restore critical habitat.[9]

Fish culture has been around for centuries and arrived on the west coast in 1872 with the building of the first hatchery in Sacramento.[10] The concept is simple and attractive. If numbers of fish are declining, enhance numbers by employing the same agricultural principles that increased crop yields so dramatically. Improve on nature by taking control of the spawning process and protecting the small fry from predators.

So the salmon managers went to work with the support of politicians and public funding. They established a large and expensive hatchery system that had a few limited successes, but failed to stem the decline. Today 80 percent of the salmon that enter the Columbia are artificially propagated.[11] The 20 percent that are wild are a minuscule 1 percent of original wild runs!

Why has the hatchery system not arrested the decline both of wild salmon and total numbers? First, the system was not sufficiently productive to balance the numbers lost to human exploitation and inappropriate technologies. Second, at least in the early stages, managers proceeded without adequate scientific knowledge. Scientists knew little about the migration patterns of the salmon until well into the 1930s. Knowledge of salmon variability came even later as managers assumed species were genetically uniform and could be transferred between rivers. In fact populations are adapted to specific streams and once transferred are less fit. These shortcomings were compounded by inadequate knowledge about ecosystems themselves, a shortcoming that continues even today. Managers imposed without much forethought an agricultural paradigm that stressed increased production of a monoculture and used economic not ecological criteria.[12] The illusion of domination and control for human purposes is nowhere more evident.

Third, the attractive illusion of an increasing supply from hatcheries hid the need to preserve habitat and restrict over fishing. Managers overlooked the real causes of decline. Fourth, few if any streams in the basin were reserved for wild salmon. All habitats were subjected to the same degrading practices.

Have the hatcheries been a failure? Jim Lichatowich certainly thinks so, although where numbers of salmon would be today without the hatcheries is impossible to say. Decisions to restrict fishing and not to build the dams would have preserved the runs far better. In the absence of these decisions the hatcheries may have delayed but not prevented decline. One thing is certain, hatcheries are not the panacea everyone had hoped for and reliance on them to save remaining runs is not the answer.

At the same time the hatcheries were reducing wild salmon to the status of farm animals, engineers were taking measures to make the dams more fish-friendly. They installed fish ladders early on to assist salmon returning to spawn. To facilitate downstream migration, engineers have tried a number of strategies, including barging or trucking juvenile salmon around dams, putting screens over turbine intakes, and preventing the super-saturation of water below spillways. These efforts have had little effect. In September 2002 the U.S. Army Corp of Engineers decided to improve fish passage at the four dams on the lower Snake rather than removing the dams, thus continuing a failed policy.

The pipeline proposal is also a strategy for the downstream migration.[13] Its purpose is to move young salmon through the reservoirs and around the dams, dumping them below the last obstacle, Bonneville Dam. Whether it will work and be cost-effective remains to be seen. A pilot project to test feasibility and assess costs is now ready, but still awaits funding.

These examples suggest that technological fixes in the name of sustainability have a place in preventing decline. The problem is placing too much reliance on fixes when the real problem is continuing decline of habitat. Only a coordinated, integrated, and ecologically based approach to habitat preservation, restoration, and protection has much chance of success.

REMOVAL OF THE DAMS

Removing the four dams on the lower Snake River would surely slow the decline of remaining salmon populations by freeing the way for downstream migration through a difficult one-hundred-mile stretch and by increasing spawning habitat. This too would be a fix of sorts. By itself, however, it is probably not the answer. Removing the dams will do little to improve habitat conditions on the main stems of either the Columbia or the Snake Rivers and their tributaries. Nor will removal restore extinct populations. It would only be a small step toward sustainability.

The political forces arrayed against dam removal on the Snake are formidable, certainly sufficient to prevent it any time soon. There is fear of the precedent it would set for the Columbia where the economic stakes are even higher. The economy of the region is simply too dependent on Columbia River dams. Indeed, opposition to removal on the Snake is already fierce for these same economic reasons. Farmers who transport their commodities by barge lead the resistance. In order to stay competitive globally, they do not want to incur increasing costs.

Regardless of the opposition, removal makes sense if coupled with habitat restoration throughout the system. The limited economic good provided by the four dams is simply not enough to trump preservation of the salmon. Alternative modes for transporting farm commodities are more expensive, but do exist, with farmers elsewhere paying them. Little has been gained by making Lewiston, Idaho, into a seaport. The hydroelectric power that would be lost is only a small percentage of the total and could easily be covered by conservation measures, reduced consumption, and increased efficiency. Only a small number of farms are dependent on the dams for irrigation. Finally, the Rand Corporation in a recent study of dam removal concluded that it could create 15,000 new jobs, refuting claims that it would cost jobs.[14]

Dam removal on the main stem of the Columbia and maybe even on the main stem of the Snake where Carl and Joanne live would be another matter. The economic loss and the loss of electrical power would be considerable, and the threat of it enough to scare off voters in droves. Carl mentions his own anxiety and that of his friends about their livelihoods. Dam removal on the Columbia would threaten many more groups than farmers. Only the most fervent environmentalist would advocate it.

Hydroelectric power is, in addition, a relatively inexpensive and clean form of energy. While its effects on habitat are large, it produces no air or water pollution and does not add to global warming. It is a remarkable source of renewable energy. In terms of sustainability these are factors in its favor.

Given these considerations, dam removal will not happen in the foreseeable future or on a large scale in the west. This means that the region's planners must concentrate on arresting the loss of critical habitat, on restoring streams and wetlands to improve conditions for young salmon, and on making dams more fish-friendly. Technological schemes such as the pipeline warrant further exploration.

ATTITUDES TOWARD NATURE

The discussion between the environmentalist Marla and the farmers Carl and Joanne exemplify the difference between preservationists and conservationists. While their differences do not lead them to argue, they are quite pronounced. Marla clearly feels the decline of the salmon runs is a tragedy and accuses those who have damaged habitat and overfished. She advocates the removal of the four dams and efforts to restore habitat.

She then refers to a certain "mindset" that appears to be the developmentalist perspective. She calls for a holistic or ecological approach and ends with a plea for less consumption. Her values are those of a preservationist. The perspective of critical ecology may reinforce them.

Carl and Joanne object mildly. Perhaps they were only being polite to a guest and former classmate. Taking them at face value, however, outsiders may begin to understand why the farmers of the intermountain west are not so concerned about declining habitat and are deeply suspicious of government workers and environmentalists.

Carl and Joanne comprehend and acknowledge Marla's critique. They have a general understanding of ecosystems. They are well aware of the impacts of farming and dams on the salmon runs. They are willing to support proposals, such as the pipeline, which offer fixes that do not jeopardize economic goods. What they see first, however, is the conflict between their own livelihoods and the preservation of remaining runs. In this they seem like many in the intermountain west, for example, Pete Nelson in the case who is much more vocal on the conflict. Declining salmon are viewed as an "either/or" and "we/they" proposition.

In response to environmentalists who sometimes take the same view of their perceived opponents, they choose their livelihoods with Carl going so far as to say it does not make much difference what fish swim in the river. They quite frankly think the good for humans in farming outweighs the good of preserving salmon runs. Joanne expresses her view in religious terms, referring to the image of God and dominion and declaring: "We are more valuable." Carl keeps calling himself a practical man looking for a win-win solution, but in the end he says, "no big deal."

This is not the place to push the correctness of one perspective or the other. Both sides demand it. That there is a difference in attitudes toward nature with profound consequences for sustainability should be understood, however. Neither side can predict the future with any assurance. In the long range, outcomes will depend in part on technological fixes that cannot be predicted. Still, if Carl and Joanne's "stewardship" approach prevails, or worse, perspectives that are really indifferent to nature, mass extinction will continue. Reliance on technical fixes is a great gamble with the future. As with toxic substances, precaution should prevail.

ATTITUDES TOWARD GOVERNMENT

Carl, Joanne, and Pete Nelson harbor other attitudes, especially toward government bureaucrats, environmentalists, and even those who come "to play" in the state. Their attitude toward government is all the more striking because these farmers are so dependent on government-built dams and irrigation systems, not to mention other subsidies that farmers receive, such as the price supports for milk that Carl and Joanne depend on in lean years.

Suspicion of government is widespread in the intermountain west. It has hardened in recent years with states such as Idaho consistently electing politicians who advocate minimum government involvement, especially in economic life. Those outside the region often write off and reject these attitudes as provincial, but this is simplistic and too negative.

In part their attitudes are an expression of a tendency to divide social reality dualistically into opposing camps that runs across the political spectrum. This dualistic tendency has been around a long time and is deeply ingrained, probably the product of both genetic and cultural evolution. Whatever its origin, the anxious "we" locate our troubles in the enemy "they."

This tendency finds a target in the federal government because it is so ubiquitous in the region. Nowhere else in the United States does the federal government play as big a role in land use. The United States Forest Service (USFS) and the Bureau of Land Management (BLM) control so much of the land in the intermountain west that individuals feel a sense of powerlessness. Political participation in the region is high, but the sense of having no say seems even higher. People like the benefits and subsidies and consider them their due, but when public officials restrict the use of land that local people feel is their own, they resent it, no matter who owns the land. In recent years environmental restrictions have limited mining, agriculture, logging, and recreation in a major way. The possible loss of the region's dams is an even bigger threat. At the stroke of a wrecking ball these farmers could lose their livelihoods.

Freedom from restriction and the sense of ownership of both private and public land are also deeply rooted in the pioneer/cowboy legacies of the region. These legacies do not correspond to present reality, but they exert a strong hold, especially in rural areas. Ancestors moved to the region to escape restrictions and to use the seemingly infinite space to remake the desert into a garden. Individual initiative counted for a lot. They worked hard for what they were able to wrest from the dry ground, and, so the thinking goes, we are continuing their traditions, growing food to feed people. Midwesterners Carl and Joanne were not raised in this tradition, but have become a part of and now echo it. They are proud of the tradition of individual initiative, as are their neighbors. They have a strong sense of vocation. There is much in this rich tradition that is worth preserving, however much it seems anachronistic in changing social and natural environments where agriculture no longer dominates, resources no longer seem infinite, and ecosystems are in a state of decline.

The conservative economic and political attitudes of the intermountain west also reflect the current American political scene where government is under heavy attack, and the ideology of free markets predominates. Whether this ideology is appropriate in a time when resources are not as infinite as the big sky in the west is not just a matter of perspective, but also a matter of species survival. Exploitation will soon cease if ecosystems are degraded to the point where they no longer yield sufficient resources. Attitudes of sustainability and sufficiency will eventually supplant the pioneer and cowboy attitudes that underlie this ideology, but not without conflict.

SUSTAINABLE FARMING AND LABOR PRACTICES

The last two issues, Carl and Joanne's farming and labor practices, are not sufficiently developed in the case to warrant extensive comment. Their use of water from the Snake River is part of the overall problem, but the damage to salmon on their stretch of the river appears already to have been done. They are representative of the larger problems, but are not themselves deeply implicated. Their current farming practices seem to take ecological considerations into account.

Their labor practices are typical in the region. They need farm labor and hire where they can without too much concern for larger issues. They seem to have treated their workers fairly. Also, when labor becomes too scarce or expensive, they have generally made do by purchasing labor-saving equipment, thereby reducing their dependence on farm workers. These things do not exonerate them for past employment of illegal workers. Farms have always been a place for heavy exploitation and today's exploitation of migrant and undocumented workers is but a version of an ancient injustice. The norms of solidarity and participation support the elimination of this injustice.

CONCLUSION

The Roman Catholic bishops in the Columbia River watershed recently issued a pastoral letter dealing with many of the issues in this case. This pastoral takes an evenhanded approach to the conflict between human economic and social good and ecological good. It seeks to preserve both the economy of the region and the species and their habitat in the basin. At times the bishops seem overly optimistic about harmonizing these goods, but given all the pessimism, this is a welcome addition. At least they avoid the conflictual mode that stifles fruitful cooperation.

The bishops call for a spiritual, social, and ecological transformation in the region and outline four steps in this transformation. These steps include an understanding of history, an insistence on spiritual and biblical foundations, a vision for the watershed, and general steps for accomplishing this vision. In a region where economic criteria dominate, the bishops raise up ecology and justice as additional considerations. By calling attention to these neglected elements, the bishops make a genuine contribution.

With regard to the four dams on the lower Snake River, the bishops have this to say:

> The presence and health of wildlife is in many ways a sign of the health of our ecosystems, of the well-being of the people and the communities dependent on the ecosystems for their livelihood, and of our respect for God's creatures and creation. The presence and health of the salmon and other species of fish in the Columbia-Snake system, in particular, is a sign of the health of the entire region. Some urge breaching the four dams on the lower Snake River in order to improve the water environment for fish. Others advocate keeping the dams for energy and agriculture uses, and suggest other means of assuring the survival of the fish and fish-related industries. . . .
>
> We urge that serious discussions and serious scientific research continue in order to assure the presence of habitat suitable for the native fish of the region. Those discussions must always maintain a proper respect for God's creatures and a prudent consideration of the common good of the people in the area.[15]

The bishops also offer a good measure of hope:

> We see signs of hope amid the problems of the watershed. Many people live responsibly from, and work with, the gifts and goods of the Columbia and its tributaries. Many understand that their own or others' actions have caused harm. They are striving to guide human activities and shape corporate operations and community consciousness with the ethics of stewardship of creation.
>
> We see signs of hope in the scientific studies of agriculture, fishing, transportation and energy needs. Renewed hope is evident in a new consciousness among government officials and business entrepreneurs about the impact of past abuses of the rivers' environment and their expressed intention to avoid similar abuses in the future. There is hope in the various proposals for carrying out a responsible cleanup of the devastation wrought by various operations in the past.[16]

The bishops' hope is an appropriate note on which to end.

Notes

1. Edward O. Wilson, *The Diversity of Life* (New York: W.W. Norton & Company, 1992). Also see The World Watch Institute, *The World Watch Reader on Global Environmental Issues* (New York: W.W. Norton & Company, 1991), pp. 43–59.

2. Jim Lichatowich, *Salmon Without Rivers: A History of the Pacific Salmon Crisis* (Covelo, CA: Island Press, 1999), pp. 11–13.

3. Ibid., p. 180.

4. The number of returning fish varied depending on a number of factors including climate, ocean conditions, and the condition of habitat.

5. Jim Lichatowich, *Salmon Without Rivers*, p. 204.

6. Ibid., pp. 7ff.

7. Ibid., p. 78.

8. Ibid., pp. 86–96.

9. Kathryn A. Kohm and Jerry F. Franklin, eds., *Creating a Forestry for the 21st Century* (Covelo, CA: Island Press), 1997.

10. Jim Lichatowich, *Salmon Without Rivers*, pp. 123ff.

11. Ibid., p. 198. Also see T.A. Flagg et al., "The Effects of Hatcheries on Native Coho Salmon Populations in the Lower Columbia River," in H. L. Schramm, Jr., and R. G. Piper, eds., *American Fisheries Society Symposium 15* (Bethesda, MD, 1995), pp. 366–375.

12. Jim Lichatowich, *Salmon Without Rivers*, p. 117.

13. The pipeline is the brainchild of Idaho residents Delmer Boylan and Dick Woodworth. The Idaho National Engineering Laboratory, a major engineering firm, and scientists at one of the state universities have also done work on the project. The Idaho Council on Industry and the Environment, P.O. Box 255, Boise, ID 83701, issues periodic reports (e-mail: icie@micron.net).

14. As reported by the Environmental News Service, 16 September 2002. http://ens-news.com.

15. Catholic Bishops of the Region, *The Columbia River Watershed: Caring for Creation and the Common Good.* January 8, 2001, p. 14. This letter is available at the Columbia River Project, 508 2nd Avenue, Seattle, WA 98119. Also see www.columbiariver.org.

16. Ibid., pp. 4ff.

For Further Reading

Brueggeman, Walter. *The Land: Place as Gift, Promise, and Challenge in Biblical Faith.* 2nd edition. Minneapolis: Fortress Press, 2002.

Burgess, Bonnie B. *Fate of the Wild: The Endangered Species Act and the Future of Biodiversity.* Athens, GA: University of Georgia Press, 2001.

Catholic Bishops of the Region. *The Columbia River Watershed: Caring For Creation and the Common Good.* Seattle: The Columbia River Project, 2001.

Collier, Michael, et al. *Dams and Rivers: Primer on the Downstream Effects of Dams.* Diane Publishing Company, 1998.

Czech, Brian, and Krausman, Paul R. *The Endangered Species Act: History, Conservation Biology, and Public Policy.* Baltimore: The Johns Hopkins University Press, 2001.

Cone, J., and Ridlington, S. *The Northwest Salmon Crisis: A Documentary History.* Corvallis: Oregon State University Press, 1996.

Fiege, Mark. *Irrigated Eden: The Making of an Agricultural Landscape in the American West.* Seattle: University of Washington Press, 1999.

Lewis, A. *Salmon of the Pacific.* Vancouver, BC: Raincoast Books, 1994.

National Research Council. *Upstream: Salmon and Societies in the Pacific Northwest.* Washington, DC: National Academy Press, 1996.

Petersen, Keith C. *River of Life, Channel of Death: Fish and Dams on the Lower Snake.* Corvallis: Oregon State University Press, 2001.

Stouder, D.J., et al., eds. *Pacific Salmon and Their Ecosystems: Status and Future Options.* New York: Chapman and Hall, 1997.

Websites

American Rivers: Snake River Project
http://www.amrivers.org/snakeriver/default.htm

Columbia Basin Bulletin
http://www.cbbulletin.com/

Columbia River Pastoral Letter Project
http://www.columbiariver.org

East Oregonian: Endangered Dams
http://www.eastoregonian.com/dams/

Endangered Species Act of 1973
http://endangered.fws.gov.esa.html

National Marine Fisheries Service
http://www.nwr.noaa.gov/

Northwest Power Planning Council
http://www.nwcouncil.org/

NW Enernet News Service: NW Fishletter
http://www.newsdata.com/enernet/fishletter/

SalmonRecovery.gov
http://www.salmonrecovery.gov/

Save Our Wild Salmon Coalition
http://www.wildsalmon.org/

U.S. Army Corps of Engineers: Lower Snake River Juvenile Salmon Migration
Feasibility Study
http://www.nww.usace.army.mil/lsr/

8

Taking on Water

Fairness and the Cost of Species Conservation

Case

O Lord, how manifold are your works! In wisdom you have made them all; the earth is full of your creatures. Yonder is the great and wide sea with its living things too many to number, creatures both small and great. . . . All of them look to you to give them their food in due season. (Ps. 104: 24–25, 27)

I

After the congregation finished reading the psalm, Warren Hughes found it difficult to concentrate during the rest of the service. It was a beautiful May morning. The sun was shining, birds were singing, and the valley was bursting with green life. As the pastor began his sermon, Warren could hear the soothing cadence of sprinklers in the fields around the church. At this time of year almost everybody had water. Spring rains and warmer temperatures began to melt the huge snow pack in the Northern Cascades, sending waters rushing through the various creeks and tributaries that feed the Methow River. The power of this fierce, frigid water was humbling. In a sermon last year Warren's pastor had connected these raging waters to that famous passage in the book of Amos: "Let justice roll down like waters and righteousness like an ever-flowing stream" (Amos 5:24). The pastor's point was that God wants justice to be like a torrential river, clearing out wrongs in order to establish a better world.

Warren had not forgotten that metaphor and this year it seemed especially poignant. It was today's psalm, however, that had initially distracted him. He found himself thinking about the adult steelhead trout and spring chinook salmon that were beginning their 500-mile odysseys from the Pacific Ocean to spawning redds in the creeks and tributaries of the Methow. At the same time, juveniles of both species were hitching a ride on the spring

James Martin-Schramm prepared this case and commentary. The case is based on actual events. Names and places have been changed to protect the privacy of those involved.

freshet in the Methow, hoping to ride the current out to sea. The problem, of course, was that there were too few of them. Because both species spawn in freshwater but spend most of their lives in saltwater oceans, the responsibility for protecting them falls to the National Marine Fisheries Service (NMFS). Required by the Endangered Species Act (ESA) to prevent extinction and promote recovery of threatened and endangered species, NMFS added the Upper Columbia steelhead trout to the list of endangered species in 1997 and listed the Upper Columbia chinook salmon in 1999. The lives of irrigators in the Methow Valley had not been the same since.

It hurt Warren to be accused of harming these magnificent fish, but that was the conclusion the NMFS reached about three years ago. His irrigation water is supplied by the Mazama Ditch Company, which operates under a special use permit issued by the U.S. Forest Service (USFS) because the place where water is diverted out of the creek is on land in the Okanogan National Forest. The ditch supplies irrigation water to 39 company shareholders by diverting 15 cubic feet per second (cfs) out of Mazama Creek just before it reaches the Methow River. In the spring and early summer this amounts to a minor diversion of the creek's flow, but as the summer goes on and the snowmelt ends, water in the creek drops significantly. After more than a year of study and some negotiation with Warren as the president of the company, NMFS issued a biological opinion that established a 35 cfs minimum streamflow requirement for the creek. When streamflow drops below that level, NMFS concluded that diversions from Mazama Creek could jeopardize the continued existence of steelhead trout or spring chinook salmon. As a result, the USFS was obligated to stop all diversions from the creek once streamflow reached the 35 cfs threshold. After the company lost its appeal, the ditch had been shut down in early August instead of mid-October for each of the last two irrigating seasons.

Warren and his fellow ranchers were not pleased, to say the least. The NMFS streamflow requirement is substantially higher than a similar standard established by the State of Washington in 1976. In addition, the Mazama Ditch Company holds an official water claim established in 1907 indicating that the company claimed the right to divert up to 60 cfs of water from the creek, although the ditch has been diverting only 15 cfs since 1974. Thus, the shareholders thought they had legal permission to operate and had been following the rules, but now the rules had changed. When endangered species were at stake, the State of Washington no longer controlled their access to water; the federal government did.

This situation did not sit well in Okanogan County where the operations of several irrigation ditches were now constrained by ESA restrictions. As a result, the county filed a federal lawsuit last fall disputing, among other things, the right of federal agencies to usurp state control over water resources. Since the county had the financial resources to press the case, Warren and his fellow shareholders decided to join the suit as co-plaintiffs. This spring, however, the judge ruled against their motion for summary judgment finding that federal agencies like the NMFS and the USFS can condition special use permits in order to maintain minimum streamflow, especially under the powers of the Endangered Species Act.

Despite this ruling, Warren believed that Mazama Creek still provided productive habitat for steelhead and chinook even with the irrigation diversions. If the irrigators were degrading habitat and harming fish, why was the creek as or more productive than more pristine streams elsewhere in the state? Warren's opinion did not sway NMFS officials, however. Given the decline in both species, the status quo was not sufficient. It was their job to prevent further decline and increase productivity. They did tell Warren that they would consider revising the streamflow requirement if new scientific data justified it, but the Mazama Ditch Company was a small operation with no "deep pockets." Professional hydrological studies cost up to half a million dollars—far beyond the reach of the shareholders. They were stuck with the requirement.

Glancing across the aisle and down a few rows, Warren noticed Ralph Holt in his usual pew listening to the sermon. They had been neighbors for almost twenty-five years. In just the last three years, however, Ralph's black mane had turned completely gray. Along with it had come a degree of bitterness and contentiousness that Warren had seldom seen in his burly old friend. Ralph was furious about the NMFS streamflow cut off. Along with a growing number of irrigators in the valley, Ralph believed that the federal government was violating the Fifth Amendment of the U.S. Constitution by taking his water rights without just compensation. Increasingly, there was talk in the valley of filing a "takings" case against the federal government. One of the things holding some back was the cost of litigation, but now it appeared that a national legal foundation specializing in property rights cases was willing to serve as legal counsel, and another national farmer's organization had offered to pay the costs. Part of Warren was up for that battle, but he also knew the case was a long shot and that it had the potential to backfire as well. This would be another irrigation season mired in controversy.

II

Warren's wife, Valerie, had also been distracted throughout the worship service—but for a different reason. She was eager to see her daughter. After church, she and Warren were going to leave their son in charge of the ranch for the afternoon while they drove to pick up Allie at the airport in Wenatchee. Both were great kids and both were sophomores; Eric was in high school and Allie had just finished her second year at Colorado State University.

Settling in for the three-hour drive, Valerie scooted up next to her husband as he drove their old Chevy Impala. Warren said he didn't want a new car if it didn't have a bench seat, but Valerie also knew they couldn't afford one. They were not getting wealthy ranching, but their lives were rich and their family was healthy.

As they left Mazama, they joined a steady stream of cars heading south on State Route 20 (See Figure 1). The North Cascades Highway had just opened for summer travel and now visitors were streaming into the valley from Seattle and other communities on the west side of the mountains. Many of these people would just spend the day or a weekend in the Methow, but over the last decade many had bought or built vacation homes there. Soaked with rain, starved for sun, and cooped up in cities, "west-siders" craved the open space of the Methow, drank up the ever-present sun, and brought bikes, cross-country skis, or kayaks to traverse the rolling expanse of the valley and its waters.

Over time, the tourist traffic and vacation homes led to a significant shift in the valley's economy. Some ranchers sold off strips of land on the edge of their fields and others cashed out entirely. Today the largest employer in the valley does not operate a ranch or an orchard. Instead, Sun Mountain Lodge is a five-star resort with tasteful, rustic rooms, a gourmet restaurant, and an international reputation. Perched on a butte in the middle of the upper valley, the lodge has a breathtaking 360° view of the upper Methow Valley.

Valerie smiled as she thought of their own little inn. Warren humorously referred to it as a "six-pack" operation in contrast to the tasteful décor at Sun Mountain, but their twelve rooms and five cabins were normally booked every weekend during the summer and fall. Running the place was Valerie's job. Warren did the maintenance and organized horse pack trips for guests. It was a good thing they enjoyed it because, between the ranch and the inn, they were pretty tied down. Their last trip had been to Fort Collins when they dropped Allie off for college.

As they approached Winthrop, where the Chewuch River contributes its flow to the Methow, Warren noted that the national fish hatchery was still closed for construction. He wondered what changes were being made. Significant debates had raged last year over the genetic health of hatchery fish after NMFS proposed clubbing to death a particular run of hatchery salmon that was returning to spawn in the Methow and its tributaries. NMFS didn't want these hatchery fish to mate with, and thus undermine the long-term genetic survivability of, "Methow Composite Stock" salmon. Warren shook his head as he thought about that argument. After all, every salmon in the Methow Valley owes its life to one hatchery or another because a hydroelectric dam blocked the entrance to the Methow River at Pateros for fourteen years from 1915 to 1929. As far as Warren was concerned, any fish that had the wherewithal to swim past the nine dams along the Columbia River on their way from the Pacific to the Methow deserved to live—no matter where it came from. "If they can survive that, they can survive anything," thought Warren.

A few miles later, the Twisp River gave the Methow its greatest flow. Now there were irrigated fields on both sides of the highway as the valley widened. Here the ranches were bigger and some orchards were still in operation. This land was irrigated by the Methow Valley Irrigation District (MVID), which diverted water into irrigation canals from both the Twisp and the Methow

Figure 1. Map of the State of Washington and the Methow Valley

Source: Golder Associates, *Draft Report to the WRIA 48 Planning Unit and Okanogan County: Phase II-Level 1 Assessment, Data Compilation, and Technical Protocol*, March 2002, Cover.

Figure 2. Detailed Map of the Methow Valley

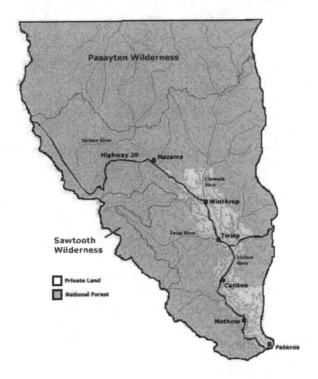

Source: http://www.methownet.com/metmap.html

rivers. By late summer, however, their diversions out of the Twisp took most of the river's flow and jeopardized steelhead and salmon. Unlike the Mazama Ditch Company, however, none of the district's operations take place on federal land. As a result, NMFS had to deal with MVID differently. Whereas Section 7 of the ESA gives federal agencies the power to curtail or stop *federal* actions that could either result in jeopardy to listed species or adversely modify their critical habitat, it does not apply to *private* actions in the same way. Section 9 of the ESA does give federal agencies the power to restrict private actions but only when it can be shown that the private action is likely to actually "take" a threatened or endangered species, not just jeopardize them. Thus, NMFS could *require* another federal agency, the U.S. Forest Service, to revise the special use permit for the Mazama Ditch Company because operation of the ditch could jeopardize listed species, but they could not impose similar conditions on MVID without evidence of an actual or imminent take. Here NMFS had to *negotiate* a solution and agreed to allow MVID to pump water out of the Methow River into the Twisp irrigation canal when diversions from the Twisp River would jeopardize protected fish. Federal and state funds would be used to pump and transfer the water. Disgusted with the unfairness of this situation, Warren said to Valerie: "It's like MVID's been pulled over for speeding, but the trooper is offering to pay the ticket for them. No one's offering to pay our ticket!"

As they wound their way down to Pateros, the road followed the river through narrow gorges. Every now and then Valerie saw some brave soul in a kayak racing through the boiling waters, but few of these river rafters live in this lower end of the valley. Unlike the northern half, there are not many new vacation homes sided in cedar and oriented to the view. Instead, most of the homes she could see were older houses and mobile homes occupied by those still eking a living from the lower Methow. Most cars she saw were at least ten years old. Fields adjacent to dwellings often served as graveyards for rusting machines and old irrigation equipment.

When they reached the southern boundary of the Methow basin in Pateros, Valerie was struck again by how the raging Methow comes to an abrupt halt as it meets the tamed and placid waters of the Columbia River. Backed up behind the Wells Dam seven miles to the south along U.S. Route 97, the waters of the Methow had now become part of the industrial river that is the Columbia. As they approached the dam, Warren said, "I know I shouldn't bite the hand that feeds us, but I wish they'd take another look at all of these dams. There may not be enough water in our creek, but that's the least of the problems these fish face. The little fry aren't strong enough to swim through these warmer slack waters, and if that doesn't wear them out the turbines either clobber them or the bigger fish eat them. Charlie Harris at NMFS so much as confessed to me that these dams are the biggest factor by far in salmon and steelhead decline, but dam removal is just not on the table. It's not fair, Valerie. With dams out of the picture, harvests down to almost nothing, and hatchery production in decline, that puts most of the burden on habitat restoration—and that puts us right in the crosshairs.

I don't mind making sacrifices for these fish, but our way of life shouldn't be sacrificed in the process." Valerie nodded her assent.

As they approached Wenatchee, the Rocky Reach Dam loomed in the distance. The huge power lines climbing up the sides of the river valley served as a visual reminder to Valerie of what is at stake. Hydroelectric power supplies virtually all the electricity consumed at a relatively low cost by the residents of Washington, including Warren and Valerie Hughes. In addition, management of the Columbia's flow along with its tributaries makes it possible to furnish large commercial orchards with the irrigation water they need to be a world leader in fruit production, especially apples. Further south, the Columbia meets the Snake River and both provide a third valuable service: agricultural commodity shipping via river barges that chug inland as far as Lewiston, Idaho, to conduct global trade. Finally, reservoirs behind each of the dams provide opportunities for recreation and expensive, scenic real estate. As Valerie took all of this in, she knew it was not likely that any of these dams would be removed in her lifetime, given their importance to the economy.

By the time they arrived at the airport in Wenatchee, however, all Warren and Valerie could think about was greeting Allie. Both beamed with joy and pride as she rushed to hug them in the small terminal. The drive home flew by as they talked non-stop about things on the ranch, life in the Methow, and Allie's studies. Warren was quiet for only a little while after Allie told them she had chosen environmental conservation as her major. Valerie stole a glance at Warren when Allie shared the news and thought he looked worried and proud at the same time.

III

"It doesn't get much better than this," thought Warren as they baled their first cutting of alfalfa in early July. Eric was throwing bales on the wagon, Warren was stacking them, and Allie was driving the tractor slowly through the 100-acre field. Later they would stack the crop in the barn to use as feed in the winter for the 90 head of cattle and the eight packhorses they kept on the ranch. In each of the last two years, however, they had barely gotten their first two cuttings. Closure of the ditch in August meant there was no water to irrigate the third crop, so Warren had to purchase hay for $7,500 to replace what they had lost. That probably didn't sound like much to most people, but it was a large expenditure for their small ranch.

Wiping his brow, Eric suggested they take a break. Since there was little chance of rain for the rest of the summer, there was no reason to hurry. Allie cut the tractor, grabbed the water jugs and cookie tin and led them over to the shade of trees along the open ditch. After they splashed some water on their faces to cool off, Warren would have been happy just to enjoy the smell of the field, the murmur of the passing water, and the company of his children—but Eric had other things on his mind. His high school near Twisp served students from all over the valley. As a result, Eric was all too familiar with the views of other irrigators in the area. Parents may not realize it, but children listen very carefully to what is said at the dinner table. Those views were exchanged in the lunchroom and on the long bus rides back and forth to school.

Leaning forward on the rock he was sitting on, Eric looked squarely at his father and asked, "What do you think of all this talk about a 'takings' case against the feds, Dad? From what I hear, some of those guys over on the Chewuch are spittin' mad. One of them is a Section 7 ditch like ours with a really tough streamflow requirement. They have been shut down entirely for the last two years while they tried to improve efficiency by lining their ditch. Then, after they spent a ton of money to put their six miles into pipe, the USFS shut them down again in May because the Chewuch dropped below the streamflow requirement. Kurt Dolan says his dad is so mad that he's threatening to take an acetylene torch and cut the lock on the headgate like those guys did down in Oregon last year. It just doesn't seem right that the feds can come in here and take our water. We have a right to this water. You showed me the claim. They can't take our property without paying us for it. That's what it says in the Constitution. We should be fighting this, Dad."

Before Warren could reply, Allie responded to her brother. "We studied the constitutional takings issue in my environmental law and policy class this spring. There's a big difference between *physical* takings and *regulatory* takings. It's one thing if the federal government wants to build an interstate through your land; then they have to exercise the public right of eminent domain, condemn the land, and reimburse the property owner at a fair market rate. In that scenario, the feds take your land and occupy it or transform it for a public purpose. That isn't our situation. There are no federal agents here. No one is occupying our land. Instead, NMFS has put a regulatory condition on the ditch's special use permit because they are required by the Endangered Species Act to prevent the extinction of steelhead and chinook. We have a right to our private property, but it's not an absolute right. Government always has the power to regulate the use of private property to promote the common good and to prevent harm to things the public values. In these situations, the Supreme Court has ruled consistently that a regulatory taking can occur only when the regulations cause the landowner to lose all or almost all of the economic value of the property. I don't see how we can make a case for that. We still get two of our three cuttings of alfalfa. Now, that ditch over on the Chewuch might be able to make a stronger case, but their land still has a lot of economic value. An awful lot of people are looking to buy land in this valley."

Eric shot back. "So you'd like to see these ranches carved up into little five-acre ranchettes for hobby farmers and city slickers who just want to get away from it all? What about our way of life, Allie? NMFS is standing up for the fish, but who is standing up for us? Ultimately, this isn't about our land; it's about our water. NMFS says they're not taking away our water right, but they sure as heck are taking away our water. What's the point of having a water right if you can't use it? They are *physically* taking our water. Once August hits, we won't have it and they will. It seems pretty cut and dried to me. I think we ought to get on board and sue NMFS for taking our property without paying us for it. What have we got to lose?"

Finally Warren spoke up. "Actually, Eric, we do have something to lose. Sure, it would be nice to be paid for the value of that third cutting of alfalfa, and the guys in the Chewuch have a much bigger stake riding on this, but any irrigators who sue the feds will have to prove first of all that they have a valid water right. That's easier said than done. It's true that our claim dates back to 1907, but that piece of paper does not guarantee our right to that amount of water today. Back in the homesteading days farmers staked a claim to a certain amount of water, filed a notice with the county, and then just had to put the water to beneficial use for irrigation, the watering of live-stock, and use in the home. But here's the catch. If you want to ensure that you have the right to use water under your claim, then you have to show that the water claim was "perfected" by proving that the water was actually put to beneficial use before 1932. In addition, if there is any five-year period of time when the water or some of it was not used, then you lose your right to use that water or whatever portion was not in continuous use. Now, we certainly know that this land has been continually irrigated for the last 50 years because Grandpa bought this ranch back in the early fifties, but we would have to do a lot of research to prove that the previous owners actually put the claimed water to beneficial use before 1932 and continually irrigated the ranch. If you can't establish that proof, then you lose your share of the water right. That's a pretty big risk. Of course, it's not a big risk if you already know for certain that your land meets the usage requirements. And there's no risk at all if you don't rock the boat and just lay low."

Warren paused for a moment and then continued. "On the other hand, Eric, last year a judge in the Federal Claims Court issued a decision along the lines of the argument you just made. When NMFS shut down water diversions for an irrigation district in California, the court ruled that NMFS had the authority to do that under the ESA, but they also ruled that NMFS could not take the water to protect endangered species without paying for it. That's one of the main reasons that legal foundation has been lining up irrigators in the Methow for a lawsuit. They think they have a pretty good shot at establishing a takings claim. It's not a perfect parallel, however. The irrigation district in California had a contract that obligated the state to furnish them with their water. Nobody in the valley is in that situation, so I'm not sure what to think."

When Warren finished talking, Eric and Allie didn't know what to say. Neither of them knew about these important distinctions and recent developments in the law. Both looked at their father with a renewed sense of respect and appreciation. Warren was a kind and humble man, but he was no fool. It wasn't a coincidence that he was president of the ditch company.

IV

Despite Warren's elected position, there was nothing he could do when the Forest Service closed the ditch's headgate on August 7. A few days later Dick Ellingson drove over from his ranch. They were virtually neighbors. Only Ralph Holt's land lay between them.

"How ya doin,' Warren?"

"Been better, Dick. Ralph is seething mad about the shut-off. He's been bending my ear but good the last few days. It's the principle of the thing that really makes him angry. He's made some adjustments to live with less water, but he can't get past the feeling that he's getting ripped off. He keeps saying, 'They shouldn't be able to get away with this' and 'You ought to be doing something about it. We didn't make you president for nothing.'"

Dick nodded his head in sympathy. "You're in a tight spot, Warren. I'm glad I'm not in your shoes."

"So what's up, Dick? You need a hand with something?"

"Well, I don't quite know how to say this, Warren, but Sarah and I are thinking pretty hard about calling it quits. Heck, it's a tough go even when we do have water all summer—you know that. We're not getting any younger, either. And we don't have a strong back around like Eric. Anyway, there's this developer over in Seattle that's been talking to us about a planned development on our 125 acres. They figure to put in 25 homes and would like to have more land if they could. In fact, last week he called and asked me if you and Ralph would ever consider selling and getting out of ranching. All together that would give them nearly 400 acres to work with, and your land has a better view up-valley toward the Cascades. I told him, though, that I doubted either one of you would be interested."

Dick's news took Warren by surprise, but he tried not to show it. Ever rational, Warren avoided the sense of loss he was feeling and posed some pragmatic questions. "How would this development influence the build-out cap, Dick? Doesn't that '76 water management plan limit each of the seven sub-basins in the valley to under 300 new homes? If we all went in together, wouldn't this chew up a big chunk of the future growth that is allowable in the upper Methow? I think a whole lot of people might be pretty upset if we scooped up most of the market before others had a chance to cash in. Plus, if we pull our water out of the ditch for the development, that might affect the viability of the whole ditch. Have you thought about that?"

"I know, Warren. Those are all good questions. But the Planning Unit is working on another basin plan and its current draft looks kindly on planned developments. Apparently it would also let us build new homes above the current cap because the water would come from about half of the irrigation water we've been diverting in the past, although we'd have to provide evidence of continuous, beneficial use of our water right and get it converted to year-round use. The unit has to submit its plan to the state next year, but if all goes well we'd have the green light for the development fairly soon.

The developer wants us to sign a sale agreement contingent on the approval of the new basin plan. I guess Sarah and I are just about ready to do that. It's serious money, Warren. They're offering to pay us $40,000 for each five-acre parcel. That's a million bucks. Sarah and I could retire a few years earlier than we had planned and enjoy life a bit more. It's been pretty stressful around here lately."

Not knowing what else to say, Dick limped back to his truck and said, "Anyway, I just thought you should know. Drop on over if you and Valerie want to talk about it any more." Then, looking over his glasses, Dick said, "I haven't worked up enough guts yet to bring it up with Ralph." Warren snorted at that last comment and flashed a grin at his old friend. They shook calloused hands and then Dick drove back over to his ranch.

V

The Mazama Ditch Company always held its fall meeting on the third Wednesday in October. Normally the ditch would have just closed, all the hay would be put up in the barns, and the fall colors would already be past their peak. But this was the third year in a row that the ditch had been shut down nearly three months early. It was going to be a tough meeting. Ralph told Warren last week that he was going to make a motion that their ditch company join others who are filing a "takings" lawsuit against the federal government. At the same time, Dick had confided in Warren that he and Sarah had signed the tentative sale agreement with the developer in Seattle. At home, Valerie thought things were manageable. They had found the money to replace the third cutting of alfalfa and were watering livestock from their domestic well. They could get by, she said.

Warren stared at his notepad. He always gave a short speech at these meetings. None would be more important than the one he would give tomorrow. Like it or not, Warren was a leader. His opinion mattered. People respected him. Some would be swayed by his views. Others would think twice before they acted. What should he say to them?

Bundled up against the chilly breeze, Warren was sitting on a boulder where Mazama Creek flows into the Methow River. It was an interesting scene. The creek water just seemed to disappear as it hit the riverbed. The Methow was dry as a bone. It always got this way by mid-October. The Methow River is a "dropped reach," which means it flows *under* the riverbed at certain points. Thus, the creek's flow did still contribute to the Methow, but it had to percolate down to reach the river.

Warren thought back to the day they brought Allie home from school in May. The psalm had made him think about the salmon and steelhead out in the ocean. By now the spring chinook had to have found a spawning site in the creek, because there was no way they were going to get past this dry stretch of the Methow. Likewise, some steelhead were just hanging out in the stream, getting bigger and hoping to survive the harsh winter ahead for their run to sea next spring. These were amazing fish; somehow they knew the Methow would dry up and they planned their lives accordingly.

Warren also found himself thinking again about that text in Amos, "Let justice roll down like waters. . . ." Certainly NMFS had taken actions to bring justice to fish that could not defend themselves. At the same time, at this very moment, water was spilling over dams on the Columbia generating electricity, but still posing huge barriers to these fish. It was true that electricity rates had gone up because they were managing the dams a little differently in order to improve fish survivability, but everyone shared that cost through higher electricity bills. It didn't seem like many had been forced to make additional sacrifices like some of the irrigators in the Methow.

Warren also agreed with Ralph, at least in principle. If the government is going to take your property, they have a legal obligation to pay for it. If the benefit of species conservation is going to accrue to the public, then the costs should be borne by the many, not a few. To Ralph and others it was a simple matter of justice. Warren knew, however, that it was not that simple. A takings case was an up-hill battle at best, and even if they won, some ranchers might still lose their water if they could not prove their land had been continuously irrigated over the years.

Warren also thought about Dick and the new vacation homes that might spring up on his land. Should he and Valerie think about cashing out too? Would that be so bad? More than half of their income comes from the services they provide to "west-siders" who love the valley too. Nobody would miss the livestock they raise. Their production is just a tiny portion of the cattle industry in the state. Plus, the land is probably better suited to residential use than agriculture because it would certainly be less water-intensive. Instead of mounting some heroic fight against the feds, Warren considered encouraging members of the ditch company to think about selling their land and water to developers. Wouldn't it be a win/win situation for all involved? West-siders would have the land they want, ranchers would have more money than they have seen in a long time, and there would be a lot more water for fish in Mazama Creek and the Methow River. But then Warren thought about his son. Eric had already expressed interest in taking over the ranch after he finished college. He loved this way of life.

A third alternative was for the shareholders to make improvements to their earthen ditch in order to make it more efficient and less leaky. This would be expensive, however, and it was not clear how much more water it would buy them in August when the creek's flow dropped off considerably. Up to that point there was little reason to be more efficient since there was plenty of water in the creek from all the snowmelt and the amount of their diversion was relatively small. Warren knew most of his colleagues were not eager to make this kind of an investment in ditch efficiency. No one in the Mazama Ditch Company had very deep pockets.

The last alternative was for the shareholders to "bite the bullet" and figure out how to continue ranching with less water under the new ESA restrictions. Warren knew this was not what many of the shareholders wanted to hear, but landowners all over the country have the use of their private property constrained by governmental regulations designed to protect the public and to promote the common good. Warren could argue that the restrictions posed by governmental regulations are a price that has to be paid in order to live in a civil society. It is simply not possible economically for government to reimburse landowners every time a regulation reduces the value of their property. That's one of the reasons why a *regulatory* takings case would be out of the question. They would have to show that the ESA regulations denied them virtually all economic use of their property, and they could not make that case. Instead, Warren could appeal to his fellow shareholders to see the loss of their third cuttings of alfalfa as an ethical and patriotic sacrifice they are making to protect endangered species. Warren knew, however, that some would not abide this appeal since they were not convinced their sacrifice was necessary. Nor did some think it was fair that they should bear a disproportionate share of the burden associated with protecting endangered species.

With a sigh, Warren got up and started to walk back to the ranch. Somehow he had to figure out what he would say tomorrow at the meeting. He was the president of the ditch company, after all.

List of Acronyms

CFS	Cubic Feet Per Second
DOE	Washington State Department of Ecology
DWR	California State Department of Water Resources
ESA	Endangered Species Act
MVID	Methow Valley Irrigation District
NMFS	National Marine Fisheries Service
PU	Methow Basin Planning Unit
USFS	U.S. Forest Service
USFWS	U.S. Fish and Wildlife Service

Commentary

[The Takings Clause] was designed to bar Government from forcing some people alone to bear public burdens which, in all fairness and justice, should be borne by the public as a whole.

Armstrong v. United States, 364 U.S. 40, 49 (1960)[1]

Government could hardly go on if to some extent values incident to property could not be diminished without paying for every such change in the general law.

Pennsylvania Coal Co. v. Mahon, 260 U.S. 393, 413 (1922)[2]

These two quotes from rulings issued by the U.S. Supreme Court frame the legal debate about the constitutional takings issue in *Taking on Water*. Do the restrictions imposed on the operation of the Mazama Ditch Company amount to an unconstitutional taking of the shareholders' water claim, or are the financial implications of this regulation under the Endangered Species Act (ESA) a fair price they must pay in order to live in a democratic society ruled by the force of law?[3] This question will be examined thoroughly later in the commentary. For now it is important to realize ethically that this question can be posed more broadly: How should costs associated with a moral and public good like the preservation of endangered species be distributed fairly?

One of the problems, of course, is that it is not always clear what amounts to "fairness and justice." Normally justice is understood in relationship to the principle of *equality*. In this context, a fair distribution of a burden or a benefit results in all parties getting an equal share. Thus, if justice is synonymous with equality, all U.S. citizens should bear an equal amount of the burden associated with preventing extinction and promoting recovery of endangered species. There are practical problems with this approach, not the least of which is the limited resources of the government's purse, but one thing is clear from the *Armstrong* decision: It would violate the principle of equality to force "some people alone to bear public burdens."

It is not the case, however, that the Mazama Ditch Company, or ranchers and irrigators as a whole, are being singled out to bear the costs of protecting steelhead trout and spring chinook salmon. For example, the case notes that electricity costs have risen for ratepayers in the region as the Bonneville Power Administration devotes less water to hydroelectric power generation and more water for fish habitat and migration. In addition, state and federal taxpayers have assisted individual ranchers as well as ditch companies caught in the pincers of ESA restrictions by paying a large percentage of the costs associated with building new fish screens, lining ditches, drilling wells, or pumping water from alternative sources. Thus, when seen through the prism of justice as equality, it is hard to argue that irrigators have had to bear the burden of species conservation alone.

But this is not Warren's argument. He thinks a disproportionate amount of the burden is being placed on the shoulders of irrigators, and that this is unjust. Here Warren appeals to the conception of justice as *merit* or *just dessert*. Sometimes it is more just not to give everyone an equal share, but rather to distribute burdens on the basis of who bears greater responsibility for the problem. In other words, to each their due. Warren thinks the cost of species conservation is falling disproportionately on people like irrigators because most of the efforts to recover species are focused primarily on habitat restoration. He thinks the nine dams along the Columbia River do greater damage to steelhead trout and spring chinook salmon than the amount of habitat degradation attributable to the operation of the Mazama Ditch.[4] To Warren it is unfair that options related to removing some of these dams have been taken off the table for political reasons. Thus, Warren appears willing to bear some of the burden of species conservation, but he does not want to be the only one making a sacrifice and he thinks others should do much more. Irrigators like Ralph Holt believe justice will not be done until the federal government compensates them for the water they have taken to protect endangered species.

These differing conceptions of justice are just one of the factors that complicate this case. Another factor is that Warren does not have the luxury of only assessing this case personally. As the elected president of the Mazama Ditch Company, the other shareholders are looking to him for leadership. Warren's colleagues expect him to help them decide what their next course of action should be. Some shareholders could even decide to sue him as president of the company for not delivering the irrigation water to which their share says they are entitled. It is not likely that a court would find Warren liable for restrictions imposed by federal authorities, but it is clear that Warren's role brings with it professional obligations that do not burden others. As Dick Ellingson admits, Warren is in a "tight spot."

So what should Warren do? What advice should he give to his colleagues at the upcoming meeting of shareholders? This commentary provides various resources for answering these questions. Since this casebook seeks to bring Christian theological reflection to bear on issues in environmental ethics, the commentary begins with a brief discussion of Jewish and Christian traditions relevant to aspects of *Taking on Water*. From there, the commentary provides background information about the Methow Valley and the Endangered Species Act before it turns to examine each of the alternatives Warren considers at the end of the case. A significant portion of the commentary is devoted to assessing the merits of a takings case by the Mazama Ditch Company since debates about unconstitutional takings are among the most rancorous disputes in environmental policy and law.

BIBLICAL AND THEOLOGICAL RESOURCES

This case revolves around the fundamental importance of water, the welfare of species, the use of property, and the role of law to protect the common good. Christians can draw on various aspects of their tradition as they grapple with ethical issues related to these topics.

Water and Its Divine Significance

There is much that can be said here, but four biblical observations will suffice. The first is that water is so fundamental to life that both creation accounts in the book of Genesis simply assume its existence. In the first account, God's *ruah* (breath/spirit) sweeps over the face of the waters prior to God's separation of light from darkness on the first day of creation (Gen. 1:2b). Then, prior to God's creative acts in the second account, "a stream would rise from the earth and water the whole face of the ground . . ." (Gen. 2:6). The point is that God does not have to create water because it is already there; water is fundamentally a part of divine reality. Living in arid lands, the ancient

Hebrews were keenly aware of the relationship of water to the divine.

Secondly, the biblical writers emphasize that God provides water for the flourishing of all creation, not just human life. It is clear from the first creation account that the waters of Earth are to be a place where species thrive:

> And God said, "Let the waters bring forth swarms of living creatures, and let birds fly above the earth across the dome of the sky." So God created the great sea monsters and every living creature that moves, of every kind, with which the waters swarm, and every winged bird of every kind. And God saw that it was good. God blessed them, saying, "Be fruitful and multiply and fill the waters in the seas, and let birds multiply on the earth." (Gen. 1:20–23)

It is interesting to note that this blessing to "be fruitful and multiply" is given first to the fish of the sea and the birds of the air *before* it is given to human beings. The psalms reiterate this theme that God waters creation so all forms of life may flourish. The psalmist writes: "You visit the earth and water it, you greatly enrich it; the river of God is full of water . . ." (Ps. 65:9). Psalm 104 emphasizes that fish in the ocean and creatures on land all look to God to "give them their food in due season" (Ps. 104:28). God provides water to be a blessing to all forms of life.

Third, God uses water as a means for personal, social, and planetary transformation. For example, God uses water in the sacrament of baptism as a means of *personal* transformation to bring new members into the body of Christ. God uses water as a means of *social* transformation by parting the waters during the Exodus so the Hebrews might escape slavery in Egypt. And God uses water as a means of *planetary* transformation to water the trees of life in this life and the next. In Genesis, water flows from Eden to nourish "every tree that is pleasant to the sight and good for food, the tree of life also in the midst of the garden, and the tree of the knowledge of good and evil" (Gen. 2:5–10). At the end of the Bible, in the book of Revelation, the river of life waters the trees of life in the New Jerusalem whose twelve kinds of fruit will bring healing to the nations (Rev. 22:1–2). From the perspective of the biblical writers, God uses water to transform every aspect of life.

Finally, provision for the thirst of the poor and defenseless is a fundamental measure of one's faithfulness to God. In Isaiah 3, God takes bread and water away from those who exploit the poor (Is. 3:1, 13–15). Later in Isaiah, God not only offers immediate relief of thirst, God plants and waters a garden to provide long-term support for all who are thirsty and hungry (Is. 41:17–19). Jesus reflects this tradition of the prophets in Matthew 25. When the condemned ask Jesus, "When was it that we saw you hungry or thirsty?" Jesus replies: "Truly I tell you, just as you did not do it to one of the least of these, you did not do it to me" (Mt. 25:41–46). The distribution of water is always a matter of justice.

God's Covenant with All Species

The biocentric scope of God's moral concern is best seen in the "rainbow" covenant God makes with Noah, his descendants, and "every living creature" (Gen. 9:8–17).[5] Admittedly, the story is morally ambiguous since it depicts a wrathful God so infuriated by human sinfulness that he drowns all life on the planet except for the faithful Noah, his family, and a remnant of every species. In addition, God tells Noah and his sons that "[t]he fear and dread of you shall rest on every animal of the earth, and on every bird of the air, on everything that creeps on the ground, and on all the fish of the sea; into your hand they are delivered" (Gen. 9:2). Nevertheless, God makes a unilateral promise to all living creatures that "never again shall all flesh be cut off by the waters of a flood, and never again shall there be a flood to destroy the earth" (Gen. 9:11b). In an interesting move, God assures Noah that God will remember to keep this covenant each time God sees a rainbow among the clouds (Gen. 9:16). Apparently God had a tendency to forget things!

Today some refer to this Noachic or Rainbow Covenant as the first endangered species act. As one reviews the various lists of creatures that were protected in the ark, it is clear that their utility to human beings was not the overriding value. Representatives of all species were to be saved, even "every creeping thing" and "unclean animals" (Gen. 6:20; 7:2). After the flood, when God tells Noah and his family to open the doors of the ark, God expresses hope that these species will once again "be fruitful and multiply" and "abound on the earth" (Gen. 8:17). While it is true that no fish are listed among the various species Noah brings into the safety of the ark, it would be ludicrous to exempt the welfare of fish species from the broad scope of God's moral concern. In the event of a flood, presumably fish can take care of themselves. The point of the covenant is to emphasize God's unbreakable bond with every creature God has made. God desires that all forms of life have the opportunity to flourish. Another important lesson to be drawn from the story of Noah's ark is that "we are all in this boat together"; the welfare of human beings and other forms of life all depend on God's grace. Moreover, as creatures of the same God, human beings share a fundamental kinship and interdependence with all other species.

Land, Property, and the Common Good

Even a cursory review of Scripture reveals that human ownership of property is limited and should be directed toward preserving the common good.[6] While the ownership of property is assumed throughout the Bible, it is clear that God is regarded as the ultimate owner of all that exists. The psalmist writes, "The Earth is the Lord's, and all that is in it" (Ps. 24:1). Other psalms indicate the rest of creation knows and actively celebrates this truth, which human beings easily forget (Pss. 19; 104). Within this context, it is clear that nature's value is grounded theocentrically, not anthropocentrically. That is, nature has value because God thinks it is "good, very good" (Gen. 1:31), not only because it has some utility or monetary value to human beings. Thus, the use of creation should benefit all species, not only one. Through springs, streams, and plants, God seeks to provide for all by "giving them their food in due season" (Ps. 104:27). Land use decisions that profit human beings but jeopardize the existence of other species violate God's desire that all species live and flourish.

In general, human ownership of land should be guided by the concept of stewardship.[7] Like the servant in Jesus' parable, human beings are charged with caring for God's household (oikos) until Christ's return (Lk. 21:33–44). Christ should also serve as the model of dominion that human beings are given in Genesis 1. Rather than lord our power over the earth in order to dominate it, appropriate Christian ethical care for the land means using the various forms of power at our disposal to serve the land and make sacrifices for the welfare of its creatures. It is true that the concept of stewardship seems to imply that God is detached from and disinterested in the welfare of creation, and that human beings could be viewed as both the measure and the measurers, of all things, but these are pitfalls that can be avoided with a fuller reading of the rest of Scripture. Stewardship is not a license to do as we please with the land, but rather to do what pleases God.

Beyond the general ethic of stewardship, human ownership of property is further constrained by various laws and regulations that seek to protect the fertility of the land as well as the welfare of wild animals and those who are poor and vulnerable. In the Jubilee legislation in the book of Leviticus, landowners are required to let their land lay fallow every seven years (Lev. 25:1–7). Since this fallow year would vary among property owners, wild animals and poor people would always be able to glean something to eat from fields. In addition, corners of fields were not to be harvested each year so that those cut off from the fertility of the land would have a chance to eat (Lev. 19:9; Dt. 23: 24–25). Although these and other restrictions limited the property rights of landowners and reduced their capacity for financial gain, they were imposed in order to protect the land, wild animals, and the most vulnerable members of society: the poor, the orphan, the widow, and the sojourner.

These regulations on land use were not only a way to protect the vulnerable; they were also a constructive way to demonstrate love for one's neighbor. The command to love one's neighbors runs throughout both testaments of Scripture. Jesus says all of the commandments can be summed up in the command to love God and to love our neighbor as we love ourselves (Mt. 22:37–40). The righteous person does no wrong to his or her neighbor (Ps. 15:3). In addition, Jesus makes it clear in the Parable of the Good Samaritan that our neighbors are not only those who live nearby, but include anyone whom we can help or harm through our actions or the lack thereof (Lk. 10:25–37). This means land use decisions need to be evaluated not only on how they benefit the landowner, but also on how they affect others. At the same time, love of neighbor requires all people be treated fairly, including landowners. Justice is a necessary dimension of neighbor love. It is not fair for some to bear burdens that all should share. Neighbor love holds together these twin concerns for the common good and the welfare of individuals within it. In addition, in Romans 13, Paul indicates that God establishes the forces of government to promote justice and protect the common good. Thus, neighbor love requires that all work together for the common good. This is proving to be a challenge in the Methow Valley.

THE METHOW VALLEY AND THE ENDANGERED SPECIES ACT

This case takes place in a beautiful section of north central Washington State. The Methow (pronounced Met'-how) Valley derives its name from the Methow River whose headwaters begin near the 9,000-foot crest of the Cascade Range and then flow south approximately 80 miles to Pateros where the Methow contributes its flow to the Columbia River. The river drains a 1,805 square mile catchment and is part of a closed hydraulic system. Besides groundwater resources, annual precipitation is the only source of water in the basin, with the vast majority arriving in the form of snow in the mountainous region of the upper valley. As a result, river flows vary according to the size of the annual snowpack and the change of temperature.[8] According to data gathered through the 2000 U.S. Census, less than 6,000 people currently live in the Methow Valley. Private lands constitute only 9 percent of the landholdings.[9] All other land is managed by state and federal agencies, with the U.S. Forest Service (USFS) managing approximately 80 percent of all land in the basin.

Anthropologists believe the first human inhabitants of the valley arrived 8,000 to 10,000 years ago. According to an early 19th century explorer, the people living in the valley at that time referred to themselves as the "Smeethowe." Members of the Yakama tribe believe their Methow relatives named themselves after the "land of plenty" that gave them "a place to have a good time." Early pioneers learned that "Methow" was the Indian word for "sunflower," a plant that grows readily in the valley and was a mainstay of the Indian diet.[10] For the long winters, however, the Methow Indians relied heavily on the plentiful supply of salmon and deer.[11] In this way, the tribe lived in a sustainable relationship with the river and the resources of the land for thousands of years.

This way of life was brought to a rapid end in the mid- to late 1800s when foreign explorers and settlers "discovered" the valley. Not long after the Methow Indians came into contact with these people, members of the tribe began to die from a mysterious disease that caused great suffering. Like other tribes, eventually one-third to one-half of the Methows died of smallpox and other contagious diseases to which they had no immunity.[12] In 1871, the U.S. Congress declared that Indian tribes would no longer be regarded as independent nations. In the same year, President Ulysses S. Grant established the Colville Reservation in eastern Washington and proclaimed it to be the new home for various tribes, including the Methow.[13] Ironically, after the tribe had been forced to abandon its land, another presidential executive order set aside the Methow Valley as part of a different reservation for four other tribes. This new reservation was short-lived, however, when miners discovered precious minerals in the upper valley. In 1886 President Grover Cleveland abolished the new reservation and opened the Methow Valley to mining claims and pioneer settlement.[14] By the turn of the century, the resources of the valley were being mined and logged extensively. Though some Methows migrated back to the Twisp area from the Colville Reservation in the summer months, the land had lost its original stewards.

Under the Homestead Act of 1862, settlers in the valley could claim up to 160 acres if they proved they had lived on the land for five years, made improvements to it, and paid a $15 filing fee. One of the improvements these homesteaders pursued was the irrigation of their dry fields. Between 1900 and 1910, twenty different irrigation ditches were carved out of the rock and gravel that forms much of the soil in the Methow Valley. Most of these ditches are still in use today. Sturdy horses pulling heavy logs gouged out the initial channels, then farmers banded together and used picks, shovels, and a few explosives to finish the work. Property owners who worked on the project received shares in the ditch company. With the exception of the Methow Valley Irrigation District, none of these ditches were built with any public assistance other than the land acquired through the Homestead Act. By the 1930s, irrigation provided profits for many ranchers and orchardists in the valley. The orchard sector fell away after 1968, however, when a 50° below zero cold snap killed most of the apple trees.[15] Since then, ranchers have utilized most of the water in these ditches to irrigate pastures and crops like alfalfa used for livestock feed.

As the case indicates, life in the Methow Valley changed dramatically for irrigators in the late 1990s when the National Marine Fisheries Service (NMFS) added the Upper Columbia steelhead trout and the Upper Columbia spring chinook salmon to the list of endangered species. In addition, the U.S. Fish and Wildlife Service (USFWS) listed the bull trout as endangered during this period of time. Suddenly ditches that had operated with little governmental intervention for virtually a century found themselves constrained by new federal standards designed to protect and recover these endangered species.

All ditches have not shared this impact equally, however. Ditches that operate exclusively on private land have borne a smaller share of the burden than those that originate on or cross over federal lands. This is because the Endangered Species Act imposes greater obligations on the federal government and the impacts of federal agency decisions than it does on private landowners. Section 7 of the ESA requires that federal agencies consult with either the USFWS or the NMFS to determine whether any action by the agency may jeopardize the continued existence of a threatened or endangered fish species or adversely affect its critical habitat. The product of this consultation is a biological opinion issued by either the USFWS or the NMFS that determines whether or not the agency action will jeopardize the listed species or adversely modify its habitat. If the opinion finds neither is likely to occur, the action can proceed. If, however, the action does pose jeopardy to the species or adversely affects its habitat, then "reasonable and prudent alternatives" must be included in the biological opinion, which may or may not allow the action to take place in some revised fashion.[16]

In this case, the U.S. Forest Service was required to consult with NMFS because the water diversions they authorize via the special use permit to the Mazama Ditch Company could potentially jeopardize the continued existence of listed species or adversely modify their critical habitat in Mazama Creek. The biological opinion that was the product of this consultation concluded that operation of the Mazama Ditch under the special use permit could result in a "take" of the protected species.[17] Thus, in order for the USFS and the Mazama Ditch Company to avoid prosecution under the ESA, NMFS set forth as one of the "reasonable and prudent alternatives" in the biological opinion a mandate that the Mazama Ditch Company cease diversions once the streamflow in the creek dropped below 35 cfs. Similar restrictions have been imposed on several other "Section 7" ditches in the valley. Eric refers to one of these, the Skyline Ditch, on the Chewuch River.

The economic consequences of ESA restrictions on Section 7 ditches vary around the valley. Members of the ditch represented by the fictitious Mazama Ditch Company have had to purchase hay that they could have grown by irrigating their third crop of alfalfa. This impact is modest compared to costs the Skyline Ditch has experienced over the last two years as they spent over $2 million encasing their six-mile ditch in pipe. Skyline made these improvements to increase efficiency after the USFS reduced by two-thirds the amount of water they could divert from the Chewuch River and NMFS established a new streamflow requirement to protect listed species. The only reason Skyline has been able to make these expensive improvements is because the majority shareholder in the ditch association is a wealthy individual. There are other factors that further complicate the Skyline situation, but it serves as one of the most dramatic examples of the economic consequences of ESA restrictions in the Methow Valley.

Given these financial impacts, it is not surprising that many irrigators like Ralph Holt want to sue the federal government for taking their property without just compensation. This commentary turns now to assess the basis for a "takings" case by the Mazama Ditch Company along with the other alternatives Warren is considering.

ASSESSING THE VIABILITY OF A FEDERAL TAKINGS CASE

The "Takings Clause" is found at the end of the Fifth Amendment to the Bill of Rights in the U.S. Constitution: "[N]or shall private property be taken for public use, without just compensation."[18] For most of U.S. history the clause has been applied only to situations where government entities physically occupied or appropriated private property for some public use, but did not compensate the owner. For example, a "physical takings" would occur if a highway was built on a portion of private property without just compensation. In 1922, however, the Supreme Court ruled in *Pennsylvania Coal Co. v. Mahon* that governmental restrictions on the use of private property could also amount to a taking that would require just compensation.[19] This decision opened the door to "regulatory takings" lawsuits that have increased in number over the last thirty years as new environmental laws like the Endangered Species Act and the Clean Water Act impose land-use restrictions on property owners. Since then, the Supreme Court and other state and federal courts have on a case-by-case basis honed the procedures, principles, and criteria they use to determine whether a regulatory or physical taking has occurred. The Mazama Ditch Company could file either a regulatory or a physical takings case against the federal government, but it cannot do both. The rest of this section assesses the viability of both approaches.

Preliminary "Ripeness" Factors

Shareholders of the Mazama Ditch Company would have to file their takings case in a federal court since the ESA restrictions that have allegedly resulted in a taking were imposed by two federal agencies, NMFS and USFS. Claims for $10,000 or less can be heard in U.S. District Court, but it is likely that the company's case would exceed this limit and thus it would have to be filed in the U.S. Court of Federal Claims in Washington, D.C. Established by Congress to hear all cases demanding financial restitution by the U.S. government, the court consists of 16 active judges who are appointed for 15-year terms. According to a definitive source on takings law, "[t]he court considers itself a people's court—an equalizer between citizens and big government."[20]

Before the Court of Federal Claims will hear a case, however, several factors are considered to determine whether a case is "ripe" for decision. The first has to do with the six-year statute of limitations Congress has established for takings claims against the federal government. Takings cases must be filed no later than six years after the taking was alleged to have first occurred. When *Taking on Water* concludes with Warren's reflections, it appears that a little over three years have passed since the ESA restrictions were first enforced. Thus, if the ditch company wants to be compensated for the taking of water that began at this time, it would appear that the company has a little less than three years to file a takings case.

The second, and perhaps most important, hurdle for shareholders is they must be able to prove to the court that they hold a vested property interest in the water they claim the federal government has taken.[21] As Warren points out in the case, the company holds a water claim that dates to 1907, but this is no guarantee that the company has a valid right to the amount of water under the claim as of today. The Mazama Ditch Company would have to prove that the claim was "perfected" no less than fifteen years after the State of Washington enacted its Water Code in 1917. That is, the company would have to prove that the original shareholders had "perfected" their water claim by putting the water to full "beneficial use" before 1932. Beneficial use was defined originally by the State of Washington as the irrigation of fields, watering of livestock, and the use of water for domestic purposes. In 1994, the Court of Federal Claims rejected a regulatory takings case filed by ranchers in Nevada because they had failed to "perfect" their water right under state law.[22]

In addition, the shareholders in the Mazama Ditch Company would have to demonstrate that the water has continuously been put to beneficial use since 1932. If at any point some of the water has not been put to beneficial use for a period of five years or more, the property owner *relinquishes* the portion of the claim not being used. If none of the water was used for a period of five years or more, the entire claim to the water is deemed *abandoned* and thus relinquished. Finally, the State of Washington has crop *efficiency* requirements for the beneficial use of irrigation water. If irrigation ditches are too inefficient or irrigators are too profligate in their application of the water, the amount of water that is valid under a water claim could be reduced.[23]

Determining all of this could prove difficult because under current law the only way to clearly establish the validity and extent of a water right is to hold a general adjudication of the water rights on a stream before a superior court in the State of Washington. General adjudications have been few and far between in Washington. In addition, they can take years and are extremely expensive. The General Stream Adjudication on the Yakima River started in 1977 and still goes on today, twenty-five years later. No adjudications have occurred on the Methow or the Chewuch. So there is no certainty about the validity and extent of anyone holding claims on these rivers. In addition, if adjudication is initiated, shareholders risk losing all or a part of the water they currently enjoy through the relinquishment, abandonment, and efficiency policies of the State of Washington. This is no small risk as far as Warren is concerned.

A third hurdle facing the shareholders of the Mazama Ditch Company is whether they can demonstrate to the Federal Claims Court that they have exhausted all avenues of appeal.[24] It would appear from the information supplied in the case that the company could satisfy this requirement. After the biological opinion was issued, the company filed an appeal that was rejected. With the terms of the NMFS opinion final, the company joined Okanogan County in filing a federal lawsuit that challenged the authority of federal agencies to regulate water resources controlled by the State of Washington. Like the appeal, the company lost this lawsuit as well when a federal judge ruled NMFS and USFS acted within their powers and under the authority of the Endangered Species Act. It is not clear from the case whether the plaintiffs believe there are grounds to appeal the judge's decision, but if they do, and the appeal is rejected, then it appears all avenues of appeal will have been exhausted.

Water Rights and Property

Another factor that must be considered before assessing the viability of a regulatory or physical takings case is the degree to which state and federal courts have viewed water rights as private property. On the one hand, most courts have held that water rights qualify as property deserving some measure of constitutional protection in takings cases. On the other hand, courts have viewed the property interest in water rights as "distinct from, and less powerful than, private interests in *real* property" like land.[25]

There are at least three reasons courts have not accorded water rights a significant degree of protection under the Takings Clause. The first is because most state constitutions establish that water belongs ultimately to the state, not private persons. Thus, while individuals possess water rights that are a form of property, these rights are usufructuary property interests in a public good. Second, these water rights are specifically limited to beneficial uses. If the water is not put to a use that benefits the public, the water right can be revoked or conditioned. Third, water rights have received less protection under the Takings Clause because the public has a major interest in the allocation of limited water resources, especially in arid Western states. These water resources make life possible not only for human beings but also for many other creatures, especially aquatic species. Thus, in order to protect human communities and endangered species, federal and state laws sanction regulation of existing water rights.[26]

Courts have used these three principles either individually or collectively to reject nearly all takings claims based on the regulation of water supplies by forces of government. As recently as 1999, "no court [had] yet declared governmental action undertaken pursuant to the Endangered Species Act to effect an unconstitutional taking of private property."[27] This is the main reason Warren views a takings case as "an uphill battle at best."

The Regulatory Takings Approach

Since the shareholders of the Mazama Ditch Company have incurred financial losses stemming from ESA restrictions imposed on their special use permit, it appears at first glance that a regulatory takings claim would be the appropriate course of action to take.

In 1978, the U.S. Supreme Court handed down a decision in *Penn Central Transportation Co. v. New York City* that identified three factors the court considered in order to determine whether a regulatory taking had occurred. These factors have been further refined in subsequent cases, but they remain central today. These factors are:

> The *economic impact* of the regulation on the claimant and, particularly, the extent to which the regulation has interfered with distinct *investment-backed expectations* are, of course, relevant considerations. . . . So, too, is the *character of the governmental action.*[28]

One of the things left unclear in the *Penn Central* decision was how large the economic impact would have to be in order to produce a regulatory taking. Since then, "courts have generally held that it is only the elimination of *all* (or nearly all) beneficial use of property that is a taking."[29] The Mazama Ditch Company would not appear to have a very strong case for a regulatory taking on the basis of this criterion. For each of the last three irrigating seasons, the shareholders have received approximately two-thirds of the beneficial use of the water to which their water claim says they are entitled. They have not lost all, or nearly all, beneficial use of the water. Furthermore, their landholdings still retain significant value and could be put to economic uses other than agriculture. The Skyline Ditch would be able to make a better case under this *economic impact* criterion.

At first glance, the *investment-backed expectations* criterion appears to be less relevant with regard to a regulatory takings case filed by the Mazama Ditch Company. Courts have used this criterion to deny regulatory takings claims when investors should have had a reasonable expectation that their economic activity could have been constrained or curtailed by government regulation. Since virtually all shareholders in the Mazama Ditch Company acquired their shares prior to passage of the Endangered Species Act in 1973, this criterion would appear to be moot in relationship to them. Federal attorneys, however, could argue that the shareholders should have known that their water rights could be curtailed when water levels were too low based on prior allocation doctrine. Under that argument, the shareholders would not have a reasonable expectation that the water would always be there for them to use. It is not clear under the investment-backed expectations criterion whether shareholders should have anticipated restrictions related to eventual ESA regulations or whether they should have realized that their access to water could have been curtailed by government for other reasons. This would have to be settled in court.

The best chances for a regulatory takings claim by the Mazama Ditch Company may rest on the third criterion, *the character of the government action*. The Supreme Court has clarified this criterion in three subsequent decisions. In 1980, the Court ruled in *Agins v. City of Tiburon* that a government restriction or regulation might produce a taking "if the ordinance does not substantially advance legitimate state interests" or "denies an owner economically viable use of his land."[30] If either of these two tests are met by the government action, then the government action is likely to be considered a taking. In 1987, the Court ruled in *Nollan v. California Coastal Commission* that an "essential nexus" must exist between the regulation and the legitimate interests of the state. Finally, in 1994, the Court ruled in *Dolan v. City of Tigard* that there must be a "rough proportionality" between the impact of the regulation and the projected impact of the development.[31]

It would appear that the ESA restrictions imposed on the Mazama Ditch Company's special use permit do advance legitimate state interests, namely, the protection of threatened and endangered species and their critical habitats. In addition, an "essential nexus" exists between the ESA restrictions and the federal government's efforts to protect the critical habitat of steelhead trout and spring chinook salmon. The shareholders, however, may choose to seize on the *Dolan* emphasis on "rough proportionality" in order to make their case for a regulatory taking. They may wish to argue that the impact of the ESA restrictions causes more harm to the shareholders than the good the restrictions achieve for protected species. In addition, the company could argue that the dams along the Columbia River have a greater impact on fish than small-scale irrigation ditches in the Methow Valley, but irrigators have borne a disproportionate share of the burden associated with protecting and recovering listed species. However, given the fact that no court in the nation has ever awarded a regulatory taking based on restrictions imposed by the Endangered Species Act, a regulatory takings victory appears to be unlikely. The only remaining alternative for the company is to file a physical takings case.

The Physical Takings Approach

As noted earlier, the Takings Clause has been interpreted throughout most of the history of the United States to preclude the physical appropriation or occupation of private property by government without just compensation. The physical occupation of property by government is easy to recognize when a highway is carved through a portion of a farm, or an army base is erected on a parcel of land. With the increase of various forms of governmental regulation, however, a new issue has emerged: Can governmental restrictions or regulations produce a *physical* taking of private property?

In 1982, the Supreme Court ruled in *Loretto v. Manhattan Teleprompter* that "the government can require submission to regulation, but where the regulation results in a permanent physical occupation, the government must pay."[32] In 1991, the 2nd Federal Circuit Court clarified in *Hendler v. United States* that "permanent does not mean forever, or anything like it."[33] If government occupies or appropriates property only for a certain period of time, the physical invasion is nevertheless complete and permanent for that fixed period. In 1992, the Supreme Court ruled in *Lucas v. South Carolina Coastal Council* that, when a property owner suffers a physical invasion of his or her property, "no matter how minute the intrusion, and no matter how weighty the public purpose behind it, we have required compensation."[34]

The question in *Taking on Water* is whether the ESA restrictions imposed on the special use permit issued to the Mazama Ditch Company amount to a physical taking of private property. As Warren notes in the case, a recent decision by the U.S. Court of Federal Claims suggests that a physical takings case by the company might be viable. In 2001, one of the sixteen judges in the Court of Federal Claims issued a decision in favor of the Tulare Lake Basin Water District in California, which claimed the federal government took away their contractually conferred water right through restrictions imposed under the Endangered Species Act. When this book went to press, the federal government had not indicated whether it intended to appeal this decision. If it does, the first course of appeal will be made to the Federal Circuit Court, and the last course of appeal will be to the Supreme Court.

Given the precedent this decision may set, it is important to better understand the details of the *Tulare Lake* case and the way it is similar and dissimilar to the situation faced by the Mazama Ditch Company. In *Tulare Lake,* the plaintiffs had contracts with the California Department of Water Resources (DWR) to receive an allotment of water. This water was diverted out of the Feather and Sacramento Rivers, both of which provide habitat for winter-run chinook salmon listed under the ESA. After the DWR initiated consultation with NMFS and USFS under Section 7 of the ESA, these agencies issued biological opinions finding that continued diversions would jeopardize the listed salmon. While NMFS and USFS did include "reasonable and prudent alternatives" that allowed water diversions to continue, they also reduced the amount available to the water-users. The plaintiffs then filed suit in the Court of Federal Claims charging that the reduction in available water was an unconstitutional taking of private property.[35]

In his decision, Judge Wiese ruled the plaintiffs had a property right to an amount of water stipulated in a contract and that the federal government's restriction of that right constituted a physical taking of private property. Judge Wiese writes:

> Case law reveals that the distinction between a physical invasion and governmental activity that merely impairs the use of that property turns on whether the intrusion is "so immediate and direct as to subtract from the owner's full enjoyment of the property and to limit his exploitation of it." *United States v. Causby,* U.S. 256, 265 (1946). . . .
>
> In the context of water rights, a mere restriction on use—the hallmark of a regulatory action—completely eviscerates the right itself since plaintiffs' sole entitlement is to the use of the water. . . . Unlike other species of property where use restrictions may limit some, but not all of the incidents of ownership, the denial of a right to the use of water accomplishes a complete extinction of all value. . . . To the extent, then, that the federal government, by preventing plaintiffs from using the water to which they would otherwise have been entitled, have rendered the usufructuary right to that water valueless, they have thus effected a physical taking.[36]

This decision does not dispute the legal authority of federal agencies to enforce the Endangered Species Act by restricting the use of water rights, but it does indicate that "the [federal] trump card can no longer be played for free."[37] If the federal government wants to restrict water rights in order to protect listed species, the federal government must compensate the owners of the water right. This precedent-setting decision has major implications if it withstands any subsequent appeals.

There are at least two significant ways the *Tulare Lake* case differs from the Mazama Ditch Company's situation. The first is that the judge determined the plaintiffs in *Tulare Lake* had valid water rights that entitled them to the exclusive use of their allotted amounts of water. Furthermore, the court found these water rights were grounded in a contract between the plaintiffs and the California Department of Water Resources. The Mazama Ditch Company possesses only a water claim, which provides less certainty about the validity and extent of the property right in water. In addition, the company does not have a contract with any state or federal agency for the delivery of the water. The company does operate under a special use permit issued by the USFS, but a federal judge in the U.S. District Court, Eastern District, ruled the USFS could revise the conditions of the special use permit in order to comply with ESA restrictions. Revision of these restrictions does not constitute a breach of contract.

So, where does this leave Warren and the other shareholders of the Mazama Ditch Company? They may have a reasonable chance of winning a physical takings case, but before they could file the case, it appears they would have to convert their water claim into perfected water rights for the share-holders. This will take a substantial amount of time and significant expense, but it also poses significant risks for landowners who may lose the amount of the water they receive or see it reduced after the State of Washington utilizes the relinquishment, abandonment, and efficiency standards. On a more positive note, it certainly helps that two national organizations are willing to pay the bills and provide the company with expert legal counsel for a physical takings case. The Pacific Legal Foundation submitted *amicus curiae* (friend of the court) briefs on behalf of the plaintiffs in the *Tulare Lake* case, and it is likely they would play a role in any takings case filed by the firm.

ASSESSING OTHER ALTERNATIVES

While a takings case receives the most attention in *Taking on Water,* Warren does mull over other alternatives at the end of the case. These alternatives can be summarized in three phrases: The shareholders can "sell out," "get efficient," or "bite the bullet."

Sell Out. Dick Ellingson presents this option to Warren, but presumably all shareholders in the Mazama Ditch Company could decide to sell some or all of their land to developers of residential and vacation properties. There are literally millions of people on the west and wet side of the Cascades, and many crave the sun and open spaces. Currently, 28 percent of all residential properties in the Methow Valley are vacation homes and cabins.[38]

Yet there are limits to growth in the valley. In 1976, the State of Washington adopted into law the Water Resources Management Program for the Methow River Basin, which established minimum streamflow requirements for the various rivers and tributaries in the basin and limited future withdrawals of surface waters to a maximum of 2.0 cubic feet per second (cfs) in each of the valley's seven sub-basins.[39] Since ground water is in significant continuity with surface water in the basin, this 2 cfs limit produced a cap on the number of new wells that could be drilled, and thus the number of new homes that could be built in the valley. Some of the sub-basins in the valley have already reached their legal limit, which means that additional homes cannot be constructed there. Warren, Dick, and other shareholders in the Mazama Ditch Company live in a sub-basin that has not reached its "build-out" cap; 289 new homes could still be constructed in their sub-basin, but after that no additional homes could be built without revision of the 1976 Methow Basin Plan.[40]

In 1998, the Washington State legislature passed into law the Watershed Management Act. Among other things, this law made it possible for citizens to play a larger role in shaping the plan that manages their local watershed. The Methow Basin Planning Unit (PU) was formed in 1998 and comprises 27 members, including officials from relevant state agencies, representatives of local governments, and citizens representing different interest groups. The purpose of the PU is to focus "on areas of particular importance to local citizens, assess water resources and needs, and recommend management strategies."[41] Ultimately, the PU will develop a new watershed management plan, which, if approved by the State's Department of Ecology, would replace and revise the constraints imposed under the 1976 basin plan. This is the "Planning Unit" that Dick Ellingson refers to in his conversation with Warren.

One of the things the PU has been studying is the wisdom of promoting more "planned developments" in the valley. These developments would make a more efficient use of water because property owners could draw only 700 gallons a day from a group well instead of the 5,000 gallons per day which is currently permitted for standard domestic wells. In the case, irrigators like Dick Ellingson could sell all or a portion of their land to a developer along with all or some of their irrigation water. It takes 2.3 acre-feet of water either to irrigate one acre of land over a 155-day irrigation season or to supply a 700 gallon per day well for year-round use. Thus, if land were sold in five-acre parcels, irrigators would have to sell the rights of one acre of irrigated land for each five-acre parcel that is developed. In order to do so, however, ranchers would have to perfect their share of the company's water claim into a state-issued water right for year-round use. This is a lengthy process that bears risks that have already been noted. Apparently Dick Ellingson is not afraid of these risks.

Even if irrigators like Dick are able to convert their share of the water claim into a year-round water right, there is still no guarantee that the PU will adopt a friendly policy toward planned developments. In the past, environmental groups have protested vigorously and blocked successfully major developments in the Upper Methow Valley, including the development of a large ski resort. Due to their pressure, the 1976 Basin Plan includes a prohibition against group wells.[42] In order to sanction the use of group wells for planned developments, the PU would have to withstand new pressure from environmental groups that would likely remain opposed to such developments because they would increase population growth in the valley. In addition, the PU has to persuade the State Department of Ecology (DOE) that the conversion of irrigation water for year-round residential use does not jeopardize streamflow requirements in the Methow River and its tributaries. If DOE officials are not persuaded, they can veto the new plan before local governments can adopt it into law. Finally, even if both of these obstacles can be overcome, the soonest a new watershed management plan for the Methow basin could be approved is 2008. This means that developers and irrigators who want to sell out like Dick Ellingson would have to live with uncertainty for several years.

Another problem related to using irrigation water for planned residential developments is that, at some point, the reduced flow of water will undermine the viability of the ditch. Property owners at the end of the five-mile Mazama Ditch would gradually see their amount of available water decline and eventually vanish as the ditch's water claim is reduced by the State to reflect conversions of the claim into various individual property rights. Furthermore, since the water claim belongs to all ditch shareholders, irrigators wishing to convert their share to a perfected water right would have to receive permission to do so by a majority of the shareholders in an official vote. One can only imagine how controversial such requests would be and the kind of enmity it could provoke. While it may be possible for a few shareholders to convert their shares and not affect the viability of the ditch, at some point either all would have to "sell out" or none. Given the current limits of the 1976 basin plan, and the draft status of the PU's current plan, it appears there are several risks associated with selling out to developers. Individuals, of course, could still choose to sell their ranches to others, but at this point it is not likely the land could be further sub-divided to permit more residential development—at least not to the extent developers have in mind.

Get Efficient

A second alternative that receives little attention in the case is the degree to which the Mazama Ditch Company could use water more efficiently, especially later in the irrigation season when the streamflow requirement leads to a shutdown in ditch operations. The entire length of their five-mile earthen ditch is unlined. This is not unusual in the Methow Valley. Prior to the restrictions imposed under the Endangered Species Act, virtually all ditches in the valley were simply carved out of the rock and soil. Normal operations require a period of time to "prime" these ditches. That is, the initial diversions of water flow down the ditch until the ground underneath the ditch becomes so saturated that water no longer leaks as readily into the ground, but rather travels further down the ditch to the places where it will be applied as irrigation water for fields. Lining the ditch with a relatively inexpensive but thick layer of polyethylene plastic would prevent the leakage of water into the ground, but it still exposes water in the ditch to evaporation. The most efficient means of transporting irrigation water from the point of diversion to the point of application is via pipe. The drawback to this method is the expense. It cost the Skyline Ditch Company approximately $400,000 per mile to encase their six-mile ditch in pipe.

The actual company represented by the fictitious Mazama Ditch Company has ruled out encasing their ditch in pipe because it would be too expensive.

In addition, lining the ditch would not make much of a difference because the ditch is fully primed in August when the streamflow requirement causes the ditch to shut down. Lining the ditch might buy the shareholders another week of water, but it would not be enough to fully irrigate the third crop of alfalfa. Thus, this efficiency option does not appear to be very viable for Warren and his colleagues.

Viewed more broadly, the lining and piping of other ditches in the valley has produced unfortunate and unforeseen consequences in the valley. Some landowners living near ditches that have recently been lined or encased in pipe have seen the water level in their wells drop significantly, and in some cases, drop below the level of the pumps. Other property owners living along the shores of small lakes in the valley have seen the level of the lakes drop significantly—to the point that docks no longer reach the shoreline and oxygen levels in the lakes imperil fish survival.[43] While the Methow Valley is in the midst of a significant drought, it appears that lake and well levels have declined because much of the water that leaked through earthen irrigation ditches actually recharged groundwater storage in gradient areas below the ditch. As a result, some property owners are faced with drilling deeper wells and declining property values. This is another, indirect cost related to the conservation of endangered species.

Another consequence of lining or piping irrigation ditches is that water no longer leaks back into the Methow River and its tributaries, and thus no longer contributes to the streamflow of these waters and the critical habitat for listed species. This factor became a source of bitter debate when NMFS was developing its biological opinion for the creek represented in the case by the fictional Mazama Creek. Ultimately, the NMFS biological opinion gave little credence to a 1992 study conducted by the U.S. Fish and Wildlife Service which concluded that, "Irrigation, at least at current levels in the Methow River basin, may be more beneficial than detrimental to salmonid habitat because of its positive influence on groundwater."[44] Many ranchers bitterly disagreed with the NMFS conclusion and still believe that, because of the unique hydrology and geology of the Methow River basin, irrigated ranches live in a symbiotic relationship with fish in the basin's rivers and streams. NMFS remains unconvinced, however. Its studies indicate that the dewatering of streams and rivers at the point of diversion poses more harm to the habitat of listed species in those areas than the unquantifiable benefit that may result from irrigation water flowing back underground into the basin's rivers and streams. In any case, for financial and philosophical reasons it is not likely that the Mazama Ditch Company will vote to invest in the lining or piping of their ditch.

Bite the Bullet

This leaves Warren with one last option. He can try to persuade his fellow shareholders that they should "bite the bullet" and figure out how to continue ranching with less water in the future. Certainly all of them have had to make adjustments for each of the last three irrigation seasons, and all of them are still engaged in ranching. Somehow they have absorbed the financial loss of their last cutting of alfalfa. If they have managed to remain afloat thus far, they can probably cope in the future.

One option that is not discussed in the case is that shareholders could apply to the Washington State Department of Ecology for permission to drill "deep wells" on their property. These wells would tap into aquifers that are in less immediate continuity with surface waters in the basin and could only be used to replace irrigation water after the streamflow requirement shuts down the ditch. The problem is that shareholders would still have to go through the process of converting their share of the water claim into a perfected water right. In addition to the risks associated with this process, each landowner would have to finance the $35,000 it would cost to drill the well, or spend considerable time and intellectual energy filling out complex federal and state grant applications that could pay all or most of the costs.[45] If shareholders were willing to take the risks, and could arrange the financing, this is one way they could continue ranching with little loss of water under the ESA restrictions.

Ranchers like Ralph Holt might be willing to take the risks associated with perfecting their water right, but would rather go the route of filing a takings case than drilling a deep well. For Ralph it is the principle of the thing that makes him mad. He doesn't think it is fair that the federal government can take water to which he is legally entitled and give it to endangered fish without compensating him for it. Somehow Warren will have to speak to this issue when he addresses the company shareholders. As the case notes, Warren could appeal to the ethical and patriotic sensibilities of his colleagues, but many are not convinced their sacrifices are necessary. Nor do many think that their sacrifices will be effective when it comes to protecting endangered species and their habitats. They think it is unfair that a disproportionate share of the costs associated with the conservation of steelhead trout and spring chinook salmon fall on their shoulders. Rather than "bite the bullet," they would rather fight their battle in the courts.

CONCLUDING THOUGHTS

One thing painfully evident in this case is that the State of Washington did not consider the biological needs of fish when the process for establishing water rights was initiated over a hundred years ago. This, of course, is not a problem that is unique to the State of Washington. All over the United States water resources have been allocated in ways that have discounted or rendered invisible the needs of fish. With the passage of the Endangered Species Act, laws governing water resources will have to be reformulated in order to reflect the value the public has now placed on the protection and recovery of endangered species. Viewed more broadly, this change in law is only one of many changes that will be necessary as a mechanistic worldview that sanctions the exploitation of the world's resources is gradually replaced by an ecological worldview that recognizes the value and interdependence of all living creatures and their habitats.

Still, there are costs associated with extending the scope of ethics and law to protect and recover endangered species. This case asks how these costs should be shared fairly. This question about how burdens should be shared is grounded in the ecojustice norm of solidarity. While Christians often extol the virtue of self-sacrifice, this presumes one's sacrifice is freely chosen out of love for the neighbor. In light of human sinfulness, however, Christians have also realized that the force of law is often required to compel people to make sacrifices for others that they fail to make out of love. Within the context of law, though, Christians have also sided with those who argue that justice is not served when some are forced to bear a burden alone that should be shared by the many. The question in *Taking on Water* is whether the Mazama Ditch Company is being placed in the position of bearing a disproportionate share of the burden associated with the protection and recovery of endangered species. If the company filed and won a physical takings case, would justice be done? Or would justice be better served if another alternative were chosen? If you were Warren, which alternative would you choose? How would you justify your decision in relationship to the biblical and theological resources discussed in this commentary as well as the ecojustice norms of sustainability, sufficiency, participation, and solidarity described elsewhere in this volume?

Notes

1. Robert Meltz et al., *The Takings Issue: Constitutional Limits on Land Use Control and Environmental Regulation* (Washington, DC: Island Press, 1999), p. 103.

2. Ibid., p. 104.

3. The public seems to be divided on this question. In a recent survey, 61 percent agreed that "landowners should not have the right to use their property in ways that endanger a species," but 57 percent also agreed "landowners prevented from developing their property because of endangered species laws should be paid for any lost income by the public." See Brian Czech and Paul R. Krausman, *The Endangered Species Act: History, Conservation Biology, and Public Policy* (Baltimore: Johns Hopkins University Press, 2001), pp. 140–141.

4. For more information about dams and their impact on endangered fish species in the Pacific Northwest, see the commentary for another case in this volume, "Saving Snake River Salmon."

5. I draw heavily here from an interpretation of this text by James A. Nash in *Loving Nature: Ecological Integrity and Christian Responsibility* (Nashville: Abingdon Press, 1991), pp. 100–102.

6. For a helpful discussion of biblical texts related to the "takings" debate, see Ann Alexander et al., *This Land is Your Land, This Land is God's Land: Takings Legislation Versus the Judeo-Christian Land Ethic* (Wynnewood, PA: Evangelical Environmentalist Network, 1997).

7. For more extended discussions of the concept of stewardship, see the commentaries for two other cases in this volume, "Sustaining Dover" and "Harvesting Controversy."

8. Golder Associates, *Draft Report to the WRIA 48 Planning Unit and Okanogan County: Phase II-Level 1 Assessment, Data Compilation, and Technical Protocol,* March 2002, Sections 3-4. Accessed on-line May 23, 2002 at: http://methow_planning_unit.golder.com/home.htm.

9. Ibid., Section 9-2.

10. Sally Portman, *The Smiling Country: A History of the Methow Valley,* 2nd ed. (Winthrop, WA: Sun Mountain Resorts, 2002), p. 371.

11. Ibid., pp. 27–28.

12. Ibid., p. 37.

13. Ibid., p. 33.

14. Doug Devin, *Mazama: The Past 100 Years* (Seattle: Peanut Butter Publishing, 1997), p. 46.

15. Portman, *The Smiling Country,* pp. 263–280.

16. *Endangered Species Act,* U.S.C. §1536, accessed on-line at the U.S. Fish and Wildlife Service website on June 18, 2002 at: http://endangered.fws.gov/esa.html.

17. "The term 'take' means to harass, harm, pursue, hunt, shoot, wound, kill, trap, capture, or collect, or to attempt to engage in any such conduct." See *Endangered Species Act,* U.S.C. §1533, accessed on-line at the U.S. Fish and Wildlife Service website on June 18, 2002 at: http://endangered.fws.gov/esa.html.

18. *The Bill of Rights, U.S. Constitution.* Accessed on-line at the U.S. Library of Congress website on June 19, 2002 at: http://memory.loc.gov/const/bor.html.

19. Meltz et al., *The Takings Issue: Constitutional Limits on Land Use Control and Environmental Regulation,* pp. 14–15.

20. Ibid., p. 43.

21. Ibid., p. 569. More specifically, the shareholders need to demonstrate that they held a vested property interest *as of the date of the alleged taking.* While a valid claim is a valid water right, the validity of the Mazama Ditch Company's water rights may be in jeopardy if there is not enough historical evidence to show that the water right was perfected (put to beneficial use) before 1932 and that there was no five-year period of time thereafter when the water was not put to beneficial use.

22. Ibid., 88., 468–469. The case was *Fallini v. United States,* 31 Fed. Cl. 53 (1994).

23. I am indebted to Peter Dykstra, a water rights attorney at the Mentor Law Group in Seattle, and Robert Turner, a senior policy advisor at the National Marine Fisheries Service in Lacey, Washington, for my understanding of how water claims can be converted into perfected water rights.

24. Meltz et al., *The Takings Issue: Constitutional Limits on Land Use Control and Environmental Regulation,* p. 46.

25. Ibid., p. 458. Italics in the original.

26. Ibid., pp. 459–463.

27. Ibid., 467.

28. *Penn Central,* 438 U.S. at 136–137. Cited in Meltz et al., *The Takings Issue: Constitutional Limits on Land Use Control and Environmental Regulation,* pp. 130, 132. Italics in Meltz.

29. Meltz et al., *The Takings Issue,* p. 132. Italics in Meltz.

30. *Agins v. City of Tiburon,* 447 U.S. 255, 260 (1980). Cited in Meltz et al., *The Takings Issue,* p. 137.

31. Meltz et al., *The Takings Issue,* pp. 136–137; 143–144.

32. Ibid., p. 121.

33. *Hendler v. United States,* 952 F.2d 1364, 1376 (Fed. Cir. 1991). Cited in Meltz et al., *The Takings Issue,* p. 125.

34. Cited in Judge Wiese's decision in *Tulare Lake Basin Water Storage District et al. v. United States*, No. 98-101L (Cl. Ct., 2001), p. 9.

35. I am indebted to Peter Dykstra at Mentor Law in Seattle for the background to this case and the legal analysis he offers in "Water for Fish: Recent Interplay Between Western Water Rights and the Endangered Species Act," *Environmental & Land Use Law Newsletter*, Vol. 28, No. 2, July 2001, pp. 1–5.

36. *Tulare Lake Basin Water Storage District et al. v. United States*, No. 98-101L (Cl. Ct., 2001), pp. 9–10. This decision was filed April 30, 2001, and is available on-line via the U.S. Court of Federal Claims website at: http://www.uscfc.uscourts.gov/2001.htm.

37. Peter Dykstra, "Water for Fish: Recent Interplay Between Western Water Rights and the Endangered Species Act," p. 4. With the liability issue settled in favor of the plaintiff, what still remains to be decided are the amount and nature of the compensation owed by the federal government. When this book went to press these issues had not yet been resolved.

38. Golder Associates, *Draft Report to the WRIA 48 Planning Unit and Okanogan County*, Section 9-2-5-2.

39. Ibid., Section 1–1.

40. I am indebted to Dick Ewing for his analysis of development options that exist for the shareholders of the Mazama Ditch Company. Ewing is a member of the Methow Basin Planning Unit, which is legally charged with the task of developing a new watershed management plan for the Methow Valley.

41. Golder Associates, *Draft Report to the WRIA 48 Planning Unit and Okanogan County*, Section 2-2.

42. See Devin, *Mazama: The Past 100 Years*, pp. 117–151. See also Portman, *The Smiling Country*, pp. 227–242.

43. K. C. Mehaffey, "Has fixing leaks harmed lakes?" *The Wenatchee World*, May 28, 2002, pp. A1, A6. See also Carol Stull and John Hanron, "Salmon recovery efforts killing Twin Lakes, group claims," *Methow Valley News*, May 22, 2002, accessed on-line June 27, 2002 at: http://www.methowvalleynews.com/es_52_02salmon.htm.

44. James W. Mullan et al., *Production and Habitat of Salmonids in Mid-Columbia River Tributary Streams* (Washington, DC: US Fish and Wildlife Service, 1992), Monograph I, p. vii.

45. I am indebted to Steve Devin, a rancher in the Upper Methow, for my understanding of this issue.

For Further Reading

Bates, Sarah F., Getches, David H., MacDonnell, Lawrence J., and Wilkinson, Charles F. *Searching Out the Headwaters: Change and Rediscovery in Western Water Policy*. Washington, DC: Island Press, 1993.

Brueggemann, Walter. *The Land: Place as Gift, Promise, and Challenge in Biblical Faith*. 2nd ed. Minneapolis: Fortress Press, 2002.

Burgess, Bonnie B. *Fate of the Wild: The Endangered Species Act and the Future of Biodiversity*. Athens, GA: University of Georgia Press, 2001.

Czech, Brian, and Krausman, Paul R. *The Endangered Species Act: History, Conservation Biology, and Public Policy*. Baltimore, MD: The Johns Hopkins University Press, 2001.

Devin, Doug. *Mazama: The Past 100 Years*. Seattle: Peanut Butter Pubiishing, 1997.

Green, Blaine I. "The Endangered Species Act and Fifth Amendment Takings: Constitutional Limits of Species Protection. *Yale Journal on Regulation.* Vol. 15, 1998, pp. 329–385.

Lichatowich, Jim. *Salmon Without Rivers: A History of the Pacific Salmon Crisis.* Washington, DC: Island Press, 1999.

Meltz, Robert, Merriam, Dwight H., and Frank, Richard M. *The Takings Issue: Constitutional Limits on Land Use Control and Environmental Regulation.* Washington, DC: Island Press, 1999.

Nash, James A. *Loving Nature: Ecological Integrity and Christian Responsibility.* Nashville: Abingdon Press, 1991.

Portman, Sally. *The Smiling Country: A History of the Methow Valley,* 2nd ed. Winthrop, WA: Sun Mountain Resorts, Inc, 2002.

Sagoff, Mark. "Muddle or Muddle Through? Takings Jurisprudence Meets the Endangered Species Act." *William and Mary Law Review.* Vol. 38, March 1997, pp. 825–993.

Shogren, Jason F., and Tschirhart, John, eds. *Protecting Endangered Species in the United States: Biological Needs, Political Realities, Economic Choices.* New York: Cambridge University Press, 2001.

Shogren, Jason F. *Private Property and the Endangered Species Act: Saving Habitats, Protecting Homes.* Austin, TX: University of Texas Press, 1998.

Stanford Environmental Law Society. *The Endangered Species Act: A Stanford Environmental Law Society Handbook.* Stanford, CA: Stanford University Press, 2001.

Websites

Center for Environmental Law and Policy
http://www.celp.org/

Columbia River Pastoral Letter Project
http://www.columbiariver.org

Endangered Species Act of 1973
http://endangered.fws.gov/esa.html

Methow Basin Planning Unit
http://methow_planning_unit.golder.com/home.htm

National Marine Fisheries Service
http://www.nmfs.noaa.gov/

Pacific Legal Foundation
http://www.pacificlegal.org/

Sun Mountain Lodge
http://www.sunmountainlodge.com/

U.S. Court of Federal Claims
http://www.uscfc.uscourts.gov/

U.S. Fish and Wildlife Service: Threatened and Endangered Animals and Plants
http://endangered.fws.gov/wildlife.html

Washington Environmental Council
http://www.wecprotects.org/

Washington State Department of Ecology, Methow Watershed
http://www.ecy.wa.gov/programs/eap/wrias/48.html

Videotapes

A Last Wild Salmon
1997; 50 minutes; ASIN: B00005ML6E
$24.99 Purchase
Watervisions
479 Shanon Way
Tsawwassen, Delta
Vancouver, BC, Canada, V4M 2W6
(604) 943-2332
http://www.watervisions.com/WSALMON.HTM

9

Sustainable Energy Futures

Economic and Ecological Ramifications of U.S. Energy Policy

Case

Ron Blanchard put down the weekly newsmagazine and the article on President Bush's energy plan he had been reading. The reporter had reviewed the particulars of the plan and the debate that it had triggered. Ron wondered if it were possible to come up with a coherent energy strategy for the United States, given the deep conflicts of interest and differing assumptions involved.

Ron thought about the high school civics class he taught in Houston, Texas. Perhaps the president's energy plan and the congressional debate about it might be the focus he needed for this year's class. After all, it was his students' futures that were at stake. But what would he teach, and how could he be even-handed when he had his own distinct ideas and the debate was so divisive? His recent move from Seattle to Houston to be near his family had brought home to him how differently regions of the country look at energy supply and demand.

President Bush's plan also brought to mind his visit to northern Alaska ten years before. The Church and Society Committee of his church had asked Ron to attend the annual clan gathering of the Gwich'in people. The Gwich'in had requested support in their efforts to block oil exploration and production on the so-called 1002 lands in the Arctic National Wildlife Refuge (ANWR) to the north of the Gwich'in reservation across the Brooks Mountain Range.

Ron remembered fondly the weeklong gathering in the Arctic mid-summer night. Not only did the natural beauty of the place impress him, but he had also learned quite a bit about Gwich'in culture and the concern of this Native American group for the environment. The Gwich'in were worried in particular about the damage that could be done to the fragile Arctic tundra

---

Robert L. Stivers prepared this case and commentary. The case is based on actual events. The names and places have been changed to protect the privacy of those involved.

where the porcupine caribou spent most of the summer raising their young and fattening on the rich vegetation. The caribou needed the sustenance provided by the north slope of the Brooks Range to survive the bitter winters in the taiga forest on Gwich'in lands to the south. Gwich'in subsistence living depended on a healthy and sustainable herd. The caribou were their main source of food. A deep bond had also developed between the Gwich'in and the herd over the centuries. The caribou were integral to Gwich'in culture, religion, and identity. Were the porcupine caribou herd to decline, the culture, already under assault from more powerful western ways, might decline further. Thoughtful Gwich'in saw oil production as a grave peril both to themselves and to the herd.

Congress designated the 1002 lands in 1980 as a special area in ANWR to be set aside for environmental value and petroleum production. To open the lands for production requires a further act of Congress. Repeated efforts to open the 1002 lands have failed. Now the Bush plan, prepared by a task force under the leadership of vice president Dick Cheney, proposed still another opening to meet the increasing demand of consumers and to reduce dependence on foreign sources. Estimates vary, but most experts think that were it the sole source, the 1002 lands could yield only enough oil to meet the total U.S. demand for oil for a period of six to twelve months.

Opening ANWR to oil production was only a small part of the Bush plan, so small in fact that some observers speculated that it was included as a gift to loyal Alaskans or to draw attention away from other elements in the plan that served special interests. To be sure about the plan and the specific proposal on ANWR, Ron went to the website of the U.S. Department of Energy. At first glance the plan seemed to have merit. Up front it recommended steps to mitigate the effects of high energy costs on low-income consumers. There was an entire chapter devoted to the environment. The recommendations to increase the supply of fossil fuels contained phrases, such as, "in an environmentally sound manner" and "consistent with good environmental practice." Ron was not sure what these phrases meant, and the plan did not spell them out, but it was clear that at least the appearance of good environmental practice was a concern.

There was also a chapter on energy conservation, but careful reading made it clear that by conservation Bush did not mean reduced consumption. Conservation would be accomplished by new technologies driven by the financial need to reduce energy costs. Recommendations on standards for electrical appliances were weak and qualified by such phrases as "technologically feasible" and "economically justified." As for raising the fuel economy of motor vehicles (Corporate Average Fuel Economy or CAFE standards), the plan called for only a "review" and qualified any raising of standards with the term "without negatively impacting the U.S. automobile industry." In a subsequent vote on the issue, Senators rejected raising standards altogether under pressure from the oil and auto industries and their workers.

Finally, the plan advocated tax-credits for renewable energy. That was good, thought Ron, but he had heard Dick Cheney on the evening news dismiss reliance on both renewables and conservation as insufficient to meet the nation's need for an increased supply of energy to meet rising demand. Cheney was much more concerned about sustaining the economy than the environment.

In fact the heart of the Bush plan is increased energy production, chiefly from fossil fuels (oil, natural gas, and coal) and nuclear fission. This is to be accomplished by government grants and tax-credits to industry, relaxation of regulations, a renewed commitment to nuclear, and quicker permitting, processes. Ron had read that fuel industry representatives had been the key consultants and had offered most of the recommendations to increase supply. He could not be sure, however, since the Bush administration refused to share key elements of the process with the public or Congress. How the administration arrived at its recommendations would apparently remain a secret. Ron also read that a number of top government posts related to energy had been filled with appointees from industry. Environmentalists had all but been closed out of the process it appeared. To Ron it seemed that corporate America would certainly be the big winner.

As for nuclear energy, Ron was not as confident as Bush and Cheney, who seem to assume that design innovations have made nuclear fission safer. But what about costs, disposal of wastes, and the fears of ordinary people? Fears about attacks on nuclear installations had increased enormously since the terrorist actions of September 11, 2001. The plan seemed to minimize these factors.

Most disturbing was the failure to mention global warming. After careful study a few years back, Ron had concluded that scientists predicting warming were making the best case. The case was not ironclad, but both theory and accumulating evidence strongly indicated a link between the burning of fossil fuels and warming. That link is carbon dioxide, an inevitable by-product of fossil fuel consumption. While CO_2 is found only in small amounts in the atmosphere, there is clear evidence of increasing levels. Scientists think that CO_2 produces a "greenhouse effect," acting like a blanket and trapping heat reflecting from the earth to space. Studies of ice cores from glaciers indicate an historical correlation between increasing CO_2 levels and warming. Most efforts to model climate point in the same direction. Recent evidence seems to confirm the relation. Worldwide temperatures have risen at least one degree Fahrenheit in recent years.

On the other side, critics of global warming claim that the relation has not been substantiated. It remains in the realm of theory. Computer programs, they say, are still inadequate to model something as complex as climate. Empirical evidence of warming, they add, is a result of natural fluctuations and unrelated to energy consumption. Ron concluded that the Bush energy plan assumed that these objections were all valid, a conclusion reinforced by Bush's rejection of the Kyoto Treaty to reduce levels of CO_2 emissions worldwide.

When he had finished reading, Ron turned off his computer and returned to his desk. There is a wide gulf, he thought, between what the Bush plan recommends and what environmentalists have been calling sustainable energy futures. Not only do they differ in particulars, such as production in ANWR, but their basic assumptions are also far apart. Bush is confident that the marketplace, technical virtuosity, increased efficiency, and the deregulation of industry will both increase economic growth and solve energy and environmental problems. Environmentalists are skeptical, quick to point out the shortcomings of these assumptions and the past environmental degradation they have encouraged.

The points of difference do not stop there, but involve a host of other considerations. Ron ticked them off. Bush thinks the problem is providing an increased supply of energy. Environmentalists claim we are consuming too much and in a way that degrades ecosystems. They advocate reduced demand and a shift to renewable sources of energy. Bush wants to drill in ANWR and resuscitate nuclear fission; environmentalists adamantly oppose both. Bush insists that oil exploration in ANWR will not cause substantial ecological damage; environmentalists see any damage as too much. Bush dismisses global warming; environmentalists and most scientists think that consumption of fossil fuels even at present levels will have disastrous future impacts. Bush thinks that economic expansion and high material standards of living are the essence of the American way of life. Environmentalists reject this vision as excessively materialistic and raise up neglected spiritual dimensions. Finally, Bush has great confidence in corporate America and reduced regulation, but environmentalists see the degradation of the environment from past industrial practices and a need for continued regulation. Given these differences, Ron wondered if there could even be a dialogue, much less a coherent energy strategy the public would accept.

Ron called his long-time friend and energy company executive, Glen Stone. As Ron expected, Glen was enthusiastic about the Bush plan. Not only would his company do well, but Glen also thought the strategy would reduce U.S. dependence on foreign sources, a big consideration given the instabilities in most major oil-producing countries. He argued that alternative sources of energy are still too expensive and would not be sufficient to meet the expanding demand of the American people. He went on to say that jobs depend on a vigorous economy. A recession brought on by increased energy prices or, worse, shortages would hurt a lot of folks.

As for ANWR, Glen talked at length about the new technologies already in use that would minimize any damage. "We really have improved our production methods," he said, "and will leave only a temporary and small footprint on the land." He concluded by pointing out that production in ANWR had the support of other native groups in Alaska, in particular the Inupiat who live on the north slope of the Brooks Range. The Gwich'in, he claimed, were pretty much alone in their opposition.

Glen's enthusiasm notwithstanding, Ron felt the need to listen not only to oil company executives and the Gwich'in, but also to his own Christian faith. Ron stood up and pulled from the shelf behind his chair a copy of the energy policy statement of the Presbyterian Church that had helped him ten years ago in his visit with the Gwich'in. Occasioned by the energy problems of the 1970s and now somewhat dated, the policy nonetheless remained relevant. Just to be careful he also pulled from the same shelf a recent, more general Presbyterian environmental policy statement, "Restoring Creation for Ecology and Justice." Together, he reasoned, these statements would provide basic guidelines for assessing the Bush plan and the need to drill in ANWR. He would have to be careful in his class, however, with how he presented theological foundations. It would not be appropriate for him to overstep boundaries in a state-supported institution.

The Presbyterian energy policy was based on what was called an "ethic of ecological justice" that sought to combine concerns for both humans and the environment. Four norms were central to this ethic: (1) justice, meaning fairness or equity with a special concern for poor human beings; (2) sustainability, that is, the long-range capacity of energy systems to supply basic human needs at a reasonable cost to the environment; (3) sufficiency, meaning the provision of basic needs, not poverty or luxury; and (4) participation, having a voice in decisions that affect one's life. The more general environmental policy statement used the same norms and added a fifth, solidarity, to bring in the aspect of community.

These four general norms were then given greater specificity by an additional twelve guidelines that included efficiency, adequacy, renewability, appropriateness, risk, cost (both monetary and environmental), flexibility, and aesthetics. The energy policy then applied both general and more specific guidelines to the then current energy situation, which, Ron concluded, had not changed that much over the intervening twenty years.

The policy called among other things for an accelerated transition from fossil fuels to renewable sources, such as solar. It considered conservation a high priority and safeguards to protect humans and the environment essential. It shifted the burden of proof to those who would override environmental safeguards on behalf of human economic sufficiency. It called for efforts to protect the poor from rising energy prices and for increased investment in mass transportation and more efficient motor vehicles. Finally, it recommended the phasing out of power from nuclear fission because of unresolved political issues, ecological damage, and potential risks to human life.

So how was he to put all this together in a unit for his class? Should he merely lay the Bush plan out and let the students react? Should he present the differing assumptions of Bush and his environmental critics? Should he use the ethic of ecological justice as the basis for study? Should he remain neutral or try to move the students in the direction of his own developing environmental consciousness? As for oil production in ANWR, where should he stand?

Commentary

Two primary visions of the future vie with each other to control the direction of U.S. energy policy. Developmentalists such as President Bush and Vice President Cheney advocate increasing the supply of energy and would assign large corporations the primary task of finding new sources and generating power. They assume technological innovations and market mechanisms will overcome resource limits and pollution problems. Willing to entertain a few conservation measures and endure limited environmental regulation, they advocate a minimum of government intervention in markets. Their vision of the future is economic. In this vision economic growth will provide ample wealth for every person as long as the nation stays the course of market capitalism.

In contrast, a new vision of a sustainable energy future with broad support in the environmental community has emerged. Its proponents see government and the corporate sector cooperating to provide sufficient energy supplies while protecting the environment. They recommend dispersed and less intrusive technologies and a shift to renewable energy sources. They value frugality and a more equitable distribution of income, wealth, and power. They are more ecocentric as opposed to anthropocentric and focus on environmental limits to continued economic expansion.

These two visions are generating increasing political conflict. Ron Blanchard in the case weighs these two visions in order to come up with a course unit on energy as the nation struggles to find a coherent energy policy. The need for such a policy became evident in the 1970s with an oil embargo and declining domestic reserves of oil. The need has grown due to political instability in major oil-producing regions, to expanding demand, and to increasing awareness of environmental degradation.

The problems confronting the nation are numerous, interrelated, and urgent. First are the problems clustered around the question of sustainability. On the one hand many forms of energy used today threaten ecological sustainability. The burning of fossil fuels (oil, natural gas, and coal) contribute to global warming. Coal-fired utility plants emit sulfur dioxide and nitric oxides that precipitate out as acid rain degrading lakes and streams. Cars emit a number of air pollutants and create photochemical smog. The pumping of oil and gas and the strip mining of coal do damage to ecosystems that provide critical habitat for species. In addition, fossil fuels are not renewable and will eventually become more scarce and expensive.

Likewise, dams built to generate renewable and inexpensive electric power from the water cycle degrade critical habitat. Nuclear energy, while long-lasting, presents mammoth problems of waste storage and safety including the threat of terrorist attack.

On the other hand are fuels that are not as damaging to the environment, but threaten the economic expansion that President Bush holds so dear. Solar sources and solar derivatives such as wind and hydro, are renewable and thus long-lasting, but may not provide enough power to meet high levels of demand. Many renewable forms remain expensive and for several the necessary infrastructure is not in place or even planned. The burning of hydrogen, the most abundant atom, to power motor vehicles shows promise, but is expensive to separate from oxygen in water molecules. Again, no infrastructure is in place. Nuclear fusion offers an almost unlimited source of energy, but costs may be astronomical and scientists have not yet and may never solve the problem of containing the fusion reaction.

Clustered around sufficiency, the second of the norms in the ethic of ecological justice, are concerns about meeting basic energy needs at a reasonable cost to society and ecosystems. What constitutes basic energy need is itself controversial. The Bush administration's energy plan, predicated on the developmentalist vision, assumes high and expanding levels of consumption and is designed primarily to fuel expanding demand. Sufficiency means success in this endeavor.

To those who advocate a sustainable energy future, these levels of consumption are far too high and should be reduced and kept down. Sufficiency to them means meeting genuinely basic needs, not inflated wants. While unable to come up with a number, they are certain that it is far less than present levels of consumption. The problem, as they see it, is high and increasing demand.

To reduce levels of consumption they recommend conservation measures. Conservation is a vague term, but in the context of energy discussions it generally means increased efficiency, less waste, and reduced demand. Efficiency means more energy output for less input and is usually attained by increasing the amount of heat from a given source or shifting to more efficient sources.[1] Less waste means matching energy source to end use and the reduction of pollutants and heat loss. Reduced demand means less consumption and greater frugality.

Conservation measures have become increasingly important since the oil embargo of the 1970s exposed U.S. dependence on foreign sources. U.S. oil reserves are declining. The Persian Gulf region and the states of the former Soviet Union have the largest petroleum reserves.[2] Instabilities in both regions have increased U.S. vulnerability. Conservation is a primary way to reduce this vulnerability. Since the terrorist attacks on September 11, 2001, energy conservation has become a matter of national security.

Clustered around the third norm, participation, are three important questions. First, how are energy decisions to be made? The National Energy Policy Development Group (NEPD) led by Vice President Cheney apparently put the administration's energy plan together primarily from recommendations suggested by representatives from the energy industry.[3] Who actually participated remains a mystery because the administration refuses to tell the public. The need for congressional approval and involvement has added a measure of popular participation, but still the process seems to have been limited. However limited the process was, future deliberations should be more transparent and offer opportunities for those affected to have a voice.

The second question has to do with the nature of the technologies used to produce energy. Complex, technically sophisticated, and centralized technologies, for example, nuclear ones, do not permit much participation. In contrast decentralized forms like solar do.

The third question involves jobs. For better or worse participation in the economy means having a job. Energy policies and systems should increase meaningful employment. Labor-saving technologies may not necessarily be the best for a sufficient and sustainable energy future.

The final norm in the ethic of ecological justice is solidarity and has to do primarily with questions of distribution and bearing the burden of increased energy costs. The distribution of income and wealth in the U.S. is increasingly unequal.[4] As energy costs rise, the poor will bear a heavier burden. They already bear the heavier burden of disease and premature death from pollution, because energy facilities and toxic waste dumps are seldom located in wealthy neighborhoods.[5] They also lose out on political power that is generally correlated to levels of income and wealth.

To sum up, energy choices are social choices with serious ecological ramifications. The mix of energy sources and levels of consumption Americans elect today will shape society and impact the environment for years to come. These choices are critical.

GUIDELINES FOR ENERGY DECISIONS

The four norms in the ethic of ecological justice set the general direction. The case offers further guidelines based on these norms and the current energy situation.[6] These guidelines serve as an evaluative tool to assess energy policies and various energy alternatives, such as trade-offs between coal, nuclear, and solar options. Given the number and variety of guidelines, decision-makers should not expect a perfect fit. Some guidelines will suggest one direction or option, others different directions and options. Many decisions will be close calls with pluses and minuses nearly equal. For the purposes of this commentary, the following guidelines deserve attention:

1) *Equity* concerns the impact of policy decisions on various sectors of society with special concern for the poor and vulnerable. Burdens and benefits should be assessed and distributed so that no group gains or loses disproportionately.

2) *Efficiency* is the capability of an energy policy or alternative to provide power with the input of fewer resources. It also means frugality in consumption and a decrease in pollution. New technologies are essential to satisfying this guideline.

3) *Adequacy* addresses the complex problem of supply. Policies and energy alternatives should be sufficient to meet basic energy needs. The meeting of basic needs takes priority until they are satisfied, then gives way to other guidelines, especially frugality and conservation.

4) *Renewability* refers to the capacity of an energy option to replenish its source. Reliance on renewable sources should take priority.

5) *Appropriateness* refers to the tailoring of energy systems to (a) the satisfaction of basic needs, (b) human capacities, (c) end uses, (d) local demand, (e) employment levels, and (f) the health of ecological systes. Energy decisions should lead to a variety of scales and levels of technical complexity.

6) *Risk* concerns the potential of an energy policy or alternative to harm human health, social institutions, and ecological systems. Low-risk options are preferable.

7) *Peace* points to the potential of an energy policy to decrease the prospects of armed conflict. While international cooperation is essential to a sustainable energy future, energy dependence should be avoided to prevent disruption of supplies.

8) *Cost* refers to monetary costs as well as other social and environmental costs. All costs should be included in the prices consumers pay for energy.

9) *Employment* concerns the impact of a policy or alternative on employment levels, skills, and the meaningfulness of work. Policies and systems should stimulate the creation of jobs and new skills.

10) *Flexibility* points to the capacity of policies and options to be changed or reversed. High flexibility is preferable, and systems subject to sudden disruption should be avoided.

11) *Participation and timely decision-making* refer to the processes used to set energy policies and choose alternatives. Processes should allow for those affected to have a voice without leading to endless procrastination.

12) *Aesthetics* points to beauty as one aspect of a flourishing life. Policies and alternatives that scar the landscape should be avoided.

ASSESSING MAJOR ENERGY OPTIONS

The energy alternatives available to energy policy-makers are too numerous to consider in detail. Below is a list of the major alternatives, notes on each, and a summary assessment:

1) *Conservation* or energy efficiency, while technically not a source of energy, is an alternative that avoids the increased use of other sources.
    a. Forms: more efficient consumption of energy, for example, weatherization and energy-saving industrial techniques; more efficient production and distribution of energy; consumption restraints, for example, higher efficiency standards for appliances and motor vehicles.
    b. Strengths: the costs and risk are low; encourages sufficiency and appropriateness; flexibility is high; easily reversed.
    c. Weaknesses: constraints on consumption could reduce employment; potential is limited in the long range.
    d. Assessment: this option offers savings without a significant change in the quality of life. Conservation should be a top social priority and vigorously promoted by incentive programs and public and private investment.

2) *Solar* energy was the principal form of energy for centuries and now offers promise as a sustainable and appropriate fuel.
    a. Forms: thermal applications, such as the heating and cooling of buildings; biomass, such as the burning of wood and alcohol from food grain; solar electric, such as power towers, photovoltaics, wind, ocean thermal, and hydroelectric power.
    b. Strengths: renewable and low risk; a variety of scales sets a standard for appropriateness; efficiency, as measured by fitting energy source to end use, and flexibility are high.
    c. Weaknesses: many forms are not yet cost-competitive, although this is improving; infrastructure is lacking; storage of energy is a problem; large tracts of land are needed for power towers; hydroelectric impacts species and ecosystems.
    d. Assessment: along with conservation, solar energy should be a priority for research and development and for public and private investment. Costs of most solar forms are becoming more competitive as technical innovation and economies of scale reduce the price relative to other sources. Wind offers perhaps the most potential and is already cost-competitive. Hydroelectric is inexpensive and does not cause air pollution, but these benefits need to be measured against the costs it imposes on species and ecosystems.

3) *Oil and natural gas* while flexible, suffer from a fatal flaw as energy sources for the future. They are not renewable and supplies will become increasingly scarce.
    a. Forms: oil, gasoline, various kinds of natural gas, oil shale, tar sands.
    b. Strengths: flexibility; infrastructure in place; variety of end uses and scales; easily understood; low cost; gas is relatively clean burning; abundant if shale and tar sand resources are exploited.
    c. Weaknesses: nonrenewable; cost will rise as oil becomes more scarce; air and water pollution; CO_2 by-product causes global warming; dependency; geopolitical distribution is poor.
    d. Assessment: Nonrenewability and contribution to global warming are the greatest weaknesses. Although exploitation of shale and tar sands would extend the supply of oil, to exploit these sources in Canada and the U.S. would be expensive, cause ecological damage, and be aesthetically disastrous. Efforts should be increased to reduce consumption of these very flexible fuels.

4) *Nuclear* is the most controversial and least understood of the alternatives.
    a. Forms: conventional reactors (fission); breeder reactor (fission); fusion.
    b. Strengths: Supplies would be long-lasting with the breeder reactor and fusion; safety record is good; does not contribute to global warming; no air pollution.
    c. Weaknesses: the possibility of major accidents and radioactive contamination; long-term storage of radioactive wastes; vulnerability to terrorist attack; nuclear weapons proliferation; breeder reactor

and fusion not developed and may never be developed; high cost; inappropriate in terms of scale, centralization, technical complexity, and participation; political sensitivity.

d.   Assessment: the dilemmas posed by a major commitment to nuclear energy remain formidable. On the one hand, the provision of basic needs, the availability of long-lasting supplies, and the problems with the burning of coal make this energy system difficult to rule out. On the other hand are the factors that make this alternative incongruent with the ethic of ecological justice. Among these are the risks, real and perceived; the cost of making it reasonably safe and environmentally sound; the effects on future social institutions and values; the tying up of large amounts of capital; the threat of terrorist attack; and the constant threat of nuclear weapons proliferation.

5)   *Coal* remains the chief source of energy to generate electrical power. Its attractiveness increases as nuclear costs rise and perceived dangers increase.

a.   Forms: the direct combustion of coal; synthetic fuels.

b.   Strengths: coal is in plentiful supply in the industrialized nations; costs are competitive; can be used in a number of appropriate scale burnings.

c.   Weaknesses: the risk associated with the burning of coal, including mine accidents, black lung disease, air and water pollution, acid rain, land degradation with strip mining, global warming, and respiratory ailments; low on aesthetics; transportation is costly and cumbersome; resources are scarce in poor countries.

d.   Assessment: coal and nuclear energy are often mentioned as the major fuels for a transition to sustainable futures. Neither is very attractive, although the provision of basic needs may dictate reliance on one or the other. Coal is a "messy" fuel even as millions are spent on cleaner power plants.

6)   *Hydrogen* will probably be the primary source of fuel for motor vehicles in the long term. Development has begun, but technological improvements and mass production are well in the future.[7]

a.   Forms: using solar, wind, or other renewable sources of energy, hydrogen is separated from oxygen in water, then recombined in a fuel cell to produce electricity, the by-product being steam. Also hydrogen can be produced from the reformation of natural gas.

b.   Strengths: pollution free, long-lasting, and a plentiful source.

c.   Weaknesses: large quantities of energy are needed to separate hydrogen from oxygen; highly flammable; no infrastructure in place; not yet cost-competitive; current technologies require use of platinum, which is a rare metal; only in initial stages of development.

d.   Assessment: Hydrogen as the primary source of fuel for motor vehicles is decades off, although the technology is developed enough to make prospects good. Since hydrogen is the most abundant element, supply will be no problem.

THE CONTEXT OF THE BUSH ADMINISTRATION'S ENERGY PLAN

Before assessing the Bush administration's energy plan using the four norms in the ethic of ecological justice and the twelve guidelines, it is important to recognize the context in which the plan was developed. The U.S. business community is a critical constituency for Republicans, if not necessarily in terms of raw votes, certainly in terms of money and public relations. This constituency, while hardly of one mind, is generally conservative in the sense of protecting the prerogatives of management and promoting commercial interests. Matters of economy, especially economic growth and low rates of inflation, are central objectives.

The business community is dominated by developmentalist and to a lesser degree conservationist perspectives. While there are differences in this community on the matter of government regulation, generally this community is *laissez faire* except when it comes to government purchases and subsidies. The environment is of secondary concern, although this is changing with increased environmental awareness. Environmental degradation is not considered a major problem because new technologies are assumed to be available to solve pollution problems or limited resource availability.

That the Bush administration favors increasing energy supplies and handing the job to large corporations is not surprising. It is a logical outcome of a perspective sincerely believed and a desire to serve an important constituency. In terms of the norms of the ethic of ecological justice and the twelve guidelines, the Bush plan correlates the norms of sufficiency and solidarity, claiming that sufficiency means high levels of consumption and economic growth. The administration translates the concern for the poor into policy through high levels of employment that are thought to be the only way to relieve poverty. In the words of former President John F. Kennedy: "A rising tide raises all boats."

From the guidelines the administration stresses efficiency as productivity, adequacy of supply, lower monetary costs to industry, high employment, and timely decision-making. These are all reasonable emphases in the economic climate of the past century.

Whether appeals in the plan to environmental soundness and consistency with good environmental practice are mere window dressing is difficult to judge. Probably not, given the assumptions of the perspective. Also, while the environmental record of the Bush administration has been spotty, it does not advocate wholesale abandonment of major environmental safeguards.[8] Finally, the appearance of being anti-environmental is not politically wise in a time of increasing awareness. It is therefore safe to assume that the administration has at least minimal concern for environmental preservation, particularly forms that do not require economic sacrifice.

Many Americans share the administration's perspective. Many more understand the dynamics of unemployment and vote their pocketbooks first. Far fewer have a working knowledge of environmental complexities and the capacity to assess the threat of environmental degradation.

Appreciation of the context and the concerns that dominate the plan does not mean acceptance, however. To those of preservationist and critical eco-justice perspectives and even to some conservationists the plan is fatally flawed. In terms of the four general norms these critics note the lack of participation of critical groups in the development of the plan and question the premise that economic growth raises all boats. In fact during the past decades the boats of the wealthy have risen much faster, and many others have been by-passed by economic expansion. These critics also think the plan with its assumption of ever increasing consumption is unsustainable on environmental grounds.

In this case Ron Blanchard summarizes the essential information and assumptions of the Bush energy plan. Detailed recommendations are to be found in the eighth chapter of the plan itself.[9] The House of Representatives has passed the plan, the Senate has passed a different version, and the issue is still in doubt. The Senate did, however, reject drilling for oil in the Arctic National Wildlife Refuge. It appears that the essentials of the Bush plan will pass Congress with the exception of drilling in the wildlife refuge.

ASSESSING THE BUSH ADMINISTRATION'S ENERGY PLAN

The Bush administration's energy plan has several strengths. With regard to the twelve guidelines the plan is strong on *efficiency* in terms of energy use, if not in terms of reduced consumption. If *adequacy* of supply is defined as the meeting of expanding energy wants, the plan is good for the short term and provides some incentives for shifting to more sustainable sources. The plan supports tax credits for the research and development of *renewable* energy sources, even though it does not place much short-term reliance on these sources.

The plan considers the critical *risk* factor to be the threat to economic growth and current standards of living. It provides for both, assuming again that human ingenuity will bring forth the necessary new technologies to avoid environmental constraints.

Under the administration's plan, other things being equal, *employment* levels should remain high. The planners correctly assume that jobs in today's economy are directly related to economic growth. Were energy shortages to appear, unemployment would probably rise with attendant political consequences.

The plan calls for a multiplicity of approaches and thus factors in some *flexibility*. Decisions for fossil fuels, nuclear, and hydro have environmental consequences, however. The plan opts for timely *decision-making* by reducing regulation, facilitating permits for new infrastructure, and opening up federal lands that were previously off-limits.

The effects of the administration's plan on *national security* and prospects for reducing *armed conflict* are impossible to predict. Certainly having ANWR on-line will not do much for energy independence. Still, the plan could reduce dependence somewhat by increasing U.S. production.

Whether the plan will deliver on these positive elements is also difficult to assess, as so much depends on the development of new technologies and on the private sector serving the public good. The Bush administration is highly optimistic on these counts, and, as a consequence, is willing to keep running what amounts to a radical experiment on the environment.

Negatively, critics of the plan point to several shortcomings. The plan starts with the status quo of free market capitalism and extends its sway by giving the business sector a large measure of freedom to pursue its interests. This system, while productive, has seldom by itself produced an *equitable distribution* of income and wealth. Channeling public funds to corporations will not change this. The sole hope for the poor is in high employment levels. The equitable distribution of costs and benefits seems of little moment to the administration.

While the plan stresses increased economic *efficiency*, it says little about the efficient workings of ecosystems or about reduced consumption of energy. Insofar as excessive consumption drives environmental degradation, the plan heads in the wrong direction.

Adequacy of supply is a matter for the short term in the plan. Defining adequacy in terms of basic needs is nowhere to be found. Unlimited economic expansion is the real concern.

The administration's plan nods in the direction of *renewable sources,* but little more. An economy based on renewable sources is not part of the plan's vision, and those pursuing this path are little more than virtuous, according to Vice President Cheney. To environmentalists the government has a role in pushing the nation in the direction of sustainable energy paths. The plan only nudges.

The plan relies on large corporations and large-scale, complex technologies, such as nuclear power. It ignores any notion of *appropriate technology.*

Risk has mostly an economic meaning in the plan. Risks to the environment and costs to animals and people are assumed away with technological fixes. Global warming is dismissed and so are the high levels of risk associated with a commitment to nuclear energy. While environmental compatibility is a strong theme, nowhere is it spelled out. The planners assume the use of fossil fuel, nuclear, and hydroelectric sources is compatible with environmental protection. So much is glossed over that stated commitments to environmental protection become suspect.

How the plan promotes energy *security,* reduced dependence on outside sources, and peace is a mystery. Even if domestic production of oil and gas is stimulated, high levels of fossil fuel consumption will continue. Domestic production will simply not be adequate for such consumption.

The monetary *cost* of meeting ever-increasing demand will be stupendous. Scientists, engineers, and managers will demand their due, and the consumer will pay. Global warming, degraded ecosystems, and the mass extinction of species are not counted as costs.

Reliance on fossil fuels, nuclear energy, and hydroelectric power is lacking in *flexibility.* Environmentalists are calling for a much greater commitment to a wide range of very flexible renewable sources, most of which are easily altered if problems arise.

The closed process that resulted in the plan and the handing over of most energy decisions to the private sector, the reduction of regulations, and the speeding up of energy decisions do not lend themselves to increased *participation*.

Aesthetics are not a factor in the plan. How the strip mining of coal, the location of oil production facilities in pristine wilderness, and more power plants are aesthetic is difficult to fathom.

All these criticisms come, of course, from an environmental perspective that is rejected by the administration. The current situation is, however, forcing choices between basic perspectives, assumptions about the future, and basic ways of living. The choices made today will have a far-reaching effect.

NUCLEAR POWER, ANWR, AND GLOBAL WARMING

Three specific problems warrant further analysis: (1) the renewed commitment to nuclear energy, (2) the exploration for oil in ANWR, and (3) the administration's dismissal of global warming. The renewed commitment to nuclear energy is highly risky, even if, as the administration claims, technological advances have made an already safe technology even safer.[10] Certainly nuclear technologies can never be fail-safe, and problems with weapons proliferation, long-term waste storage, and terrorism cannot be avoided. The problem with weapons proliferation remains real. The threat of terror attack has increased significantly since September 11, 2001. The development of a deep geological repository at the Yucca Mountain site in Nevada is better in terms of safety than current on-site storage at power plants. There are, however, lingering questions about the geological stability of Yucca Mountain and the vociferous objections of Nevadans about the selection of their state. With few exceptions (see the Skull Valley Case in this volume) no one wants his or her home and the homes of generations to come to be converted into a dump, especially for the thousands of years it will take for radioactive waste to decay.

The administration recommends that the federal government ease the way for nuclear power and build the repository. President Bush has moved vigorously to overrule Nevadans and did so with the support of Congress, few of whose members are from Nevada. Environmentalists remain in opposition, partly so to keep in place what has become an impediment to the expansion of nuclear power. Actually, environmentalists have given a mixed reception to nuclear energy over the years, some in spite of its risks seeing it as preferable to available alternatives such as coal and hydroelectric. Other environmentalists deny the trade-off between these equally risky alternatives and maintain that conservation, reduced consumption, and renewable energy sources offer better options.

The second problem is the administration's proposal to open ANWR to oil exploration and exploitation.[11] Ron Blanchard in the case seems most concerned about this one provision because of previous exposure to the Gwich'in people, the Native American group that lives immediately south of ANWR. In 2002 the House of Representatives approved opening ANWR to oil production, but the Senate rejected it. So for now it remains closed. This is the sort of proposal, however, that can be rejected dozens of times and still remain alive. The decision not to open is always reversible, while approval is needed only once and represents an irreversible decision once drilling begins. As a result, the proposal keeps coming back every few years pushed by the oil industry and Alaskans for economic reasons.

At first glance opening ANWR does not seem to do much to increase supplies. The oil would be pumped out in short order and could easily be compensated for by conservation measures. It offers a measure of independence, but hardly enough to insure security.

Ron Blanchard suspects it figures so prominently because it is symbolic of the overall economy/environment trade-off that is central to energy decisions today. He suspects it is a lightening rod to attract attention from the many other controversial features of the administration's plan. Losing the battle for ANWR would be of little moment to the administration or the oil industry, give environmentalists a sense of battle victory in a lost war, and facilitate "compromise" on more essential elements, such as increasing supply and giving the oil companies what they want.

The environmental impacts of exploration and drilling in ANWR are not known, but the U.S. Geological Survey thinks several animal species could be harmed.[12] The industry and their environmental critics so exaggerate their cases that discerning truth from ideology and propaganda is very difficult. Skepticism is recommended. The fact of the matter is, however, that drilling is proposed for one of the most critical habitats in ANWR, which in turn is one of the last pristine areas on earth. Scientists are unsure of impacts. Past experience with oil production on the North Slope of the Brooks Mountain Range in Alaska is mixed, and ANWR is sufficiently unlike other areas to make comparisons difficult. Whatever else, the plan is highly risky especially for the relatively little oil available. It hardly seems worth it.

Native Americans in Alaska generally support drilling, but there are important exceptions within and between tribes. The Inupiat on the North Slope support it and stand to gain considerably. The Gwich'in who live south of the range stand to lose the most and strenuously oppose drilling. Their source of subsistence and the basis of their culture is the porcupine caribou herd that winters on Gwich'in land and then in May treks through the Brooks Range to the 1002 lands on the North Slope where females calve and the herd fattens on the rich Arctic tundra. Drilling is proposed for the herd's richest summer habitat. The Gwich'in fear both for the herd and for the integrity of their own culture that is already under assault from globalizing forces. For now the matter is closed, but expect it to resurface anytime.

The third problem is global warming. The administration devotes all of five paragraphs to global warming in its plan and does not include the terms "global warming" or "greenhouse gases" in its glossary.[13] President Bush has admitted that humans are the primary cause of global warming, but has dismissed it as a major problem without offering any explanation.

The temperature of the earth's atmosphere has fluctuated over its history, and scientists have ways of measuring these fluctuations by investigating ice cores and fossil records. What these investigations reveal are alternating cycles of warming and cooling over long periods and smaller episodes of fluctuation within these longer cycles. Warming and cooling are thus natural elements of a dynamic atmosphere, and differentiating human-induced warming from natural fluctuation presents a problem.

Some scientists think the longer-term fluctuations are random. Others relate them to variations in the sun's cycles, the moon's orbit, or the earth's orbit. Some of the fluctuations appear to be caused by catastrophic events.[14]

Were it not for the so-called "greenhouse" gases (water vapor, carbon dioxide, methane, and others), the earth's atmosphere would be about 33°C cooler. Scientists have known about the warming effect of these gases for over a century. The theory is well established and appears to be verified by the evidence. These gases absorb infrared rays (heat) from the sun, but they reflect much harmful solar radiation back into space. By trapping heat, these gases serve as a blanket and keep the earth warmer than it would be otherwise. While carbon dioxide is only a small fraction of the gases in the atmosphere, periods of warming coincide historically with elevated levels. Carbon dioxide is the chief culprit, accounting for 60 percent of added gases.[15]

Since measurements began in 1959 on the top of Mauna Loa in Hawaii, levels of carbon dioxide have increased about 15 percent. Average temperatures have risen in the twentieth century by 0.6°C or 1°F. The 1990s was the warmest decade in the past one thousand years. The oceans have warmed, apparently absorbing some of the heat that would have warmed the atmosphere even more. There is a notable loss of ice in both polar regions with a 42 percent decline in the thickness of Arctic ice. Sea levels are rising.[16]

All this is circumstantial evidence, of course, but it points consistently in the same direction. In addition, most models of climate change point strongly in the direction of further overall warming, although the details vary from model to model.

The main source of added carbon dioxide is the burning of fossil fuels—oil, natural gas, and coal. The United States is the leading source of CO_2 emissions. Most scientists now think the evidence is conclusive: Global warming in the past century is largely caused by human beings. According to the Intergovernmental Panel on Climate Change (IPCC), a United Nations designated body of two thousand scientists: "There is new and stronger evidence that most of the warming observed over the past 50 years is attributable to human activities."[17]

Unless unprecedented action takes place, temperatures will warm significantly in coming decades. Ice will melt, sea levels will rise, and low-lying coastal areas will be inundated. Storms will increase in their intensity. Biodiversity will decrease even further. Infectious diseases will increase. Many regions will experience increased drought, and weather patterns will change in unforeseen ways. The IPCC concludes in its Third Assessment Report: "We are courting climate catastrophe unless our burning of fossil fuels and release of CO_2 is sharply reduced."

The Kyoto Treaty has recently emerged from international negotiations to stabilize and reduce the release of greenhouse gases. The Bush administration has dismissed this treaty. In a separate action it has recommended the "grandfathering-in" of the worst polluting coal-fired power plants. Its energy plan calls for an increase in supply of fossil fuels to meet energy demand. The administration's position is clear. Global warming either does not exist or will be solved by new technology and market capitalism. Reduced levels of economic growth due to shortages are a far more serious problem.[18]

The administration may be correct. It would seem based on sound science, considerations of sustainability, and the precautionary principle, however, that a more prudential course is in order. Conservation combined with research and development on renewable sources of energy would seem to be the preferred direction.

CONCLUSION

Ron Blanchard will have a difficult time explaining the complexities of U.S. energy policy to his students. Even if he had a year, the task would be difficult. Comprehension requires basic knowledge of economics, politics, the natural sciences, and ethics. The depth and breadth of knowledge required are unfortunate because today's energy choices will be an important factor in determining tomorrow's society and the future of the global environment. Energy choices are that critical.

Notes

1. Amory Lovins of the Rocky Mountain Institute in Colorado has been the most persuasive advocate of conservation. He has estimated that raising the average fuel efficiency of cars and small trucks by one mile per gallon would save 295,000 barrels of oil a day. His two most widely read books are *Non-Nuclear Futures: The Case for an Ethical Energy Strategy* (Cambridge, MA: Ballinger Publishing, 1975), and *Soft Energy Futures: Toward a Durable Peace* (Cambridge, MA: Ballinger Publishing Company, 1977).

2. William P. Cunningham and Barbara Woodworth Saigo, *Environmental Science*, 6th edition (New York: McGraw-Hill Corporation, 2001), p. 481.

3. *Newsweek Magazine*, May 14, 2001, pp. 20ff.

4. Douglas A. Hicks, *Inequality and Christian Ethics* (Cambridge: Cambridge University Press, 2000), see Chapter 4 especially.

5. See the case "Skull Valley" and the accompanying commentary in this volume.

6. United Presbyterian Church in the U.S.A. and the Presbyterian Church in the U.S., *The Power to Speak Truth to Power*, A Public Policy Statement with Background Analysis, 1981.

7. Seth Dunn, "Decarbonizing the Energy Economy," in The Worldwatch Institute, *State of the World 2001* (New York: W.W. Norton & Company), pp. 84, 96 ff.; The Sierra Club, *Sierra*, July/August 2002, vol. 87, no. 4, p. 32.

8. Danielle Nierenburg, "U.S. Environmental Policy: Where Is It Headed?" *World Watch*, vol. 14, no. 4, July/August, 2001.

9. Department of Energy, *Reliable, Affordable, and Environmentally Sound Energy for America's Future*, Department of Energy website: http://www.energy.gov/.

10. William P. Cunningham and Barbara Woodworth Saigo, *Environmental Science,* pp. 485–491.

11. Robert L. Stivers, "Oil and the Caribou People," in Robert L. Stivers et al. *Christian Ethics: A Case Method Approach*, second edition (Maryknoll: Orbis Books, 1994), pp. 144–164.

12. Sam Howe Verhovek, "Drilling Could Hurt Wildlife, Federal Study of Arctic Says," *The New York Times,* March 30, 2002.

13. Robert U. Ayres. "How Economists Have Misjudged Global Warming." *World Watch,* September/October 2001, vol. 14, no. 5, p. 14.

14. William P. Cunningham and Barbara Woodworth Saigo, *Environmental Science,* p. 385. United Nations Environmental Program (UNEP), *Global Environmental Outlook 3* (London: Earthscan Publications Ltd., 2002), pp. 214f.

15. UNEP, *Global Environmental Outlook 3,* p. 214.

16. Ibid., p. 214.

17. Ibid., p. 152. Also see IPCC (2001), *Climate Change 2001: The Scientific Basis. The Contribution Working Group I to the Third Assessment Report* (Cambridge, Cambridge University Press).

18. Robert U. Ayres, "How Economists Have Misjudged Global Warming."

For Further Reading

Berger, John L. *Charging Ahead: The Business of Renewable Energy and What It Means for America.* New York: Henry Holt & Co., 1997.

Berinstein, Paula. *Alternative Energy: Facts, Statistics, and Issues.* Westport, CT: Onyx Press, 2001.

Cathran, Helen. *Energy Alternatives: Opposing Viewpoints.* San Diego: Greenhaven Press, 2002.

Flavin, Christopher, and Lenssen, Nicholas K. *Power Surge: Guide to the Coming Energy Revolution.* New York: W.W. Norton, 1994.

Geller, Howard. *Energy Revolution: Policies for a Sustainable Future.* Washington, DC: Island Press, 2003.

Gelbspan, Ross. *The Heat Is On: The High Stakes Battle over the Earth's Threatened Environment.* Reading, MA: Addison-Wesley Publishing Co., 1997.

Hostetter, Martha. *Energy Policy.* New York: H.W. Wilson, 2002.

Johansson, Thomas B. *Renewable Energy: Sources of Fuels and Electricity.* Washington, DC: Island Press, 1993.

Lovins, Amory. *Non-Nuclear Futures: The Case for an Ethical Energy Strategy.* Cambridge, MA: Ballinger Publishing, 1975.

———. *Soft Energy Paths: Toward a Durable Peace.* Cambridge, MA: Ballinger Publishing, 1977.

Orr, Robert Bent Lloyd. *Energy: Science, Policy and the Pursuit of Sustainability.* Washington, DC: Island Press, 2003.

Websites

American Petroleum Institute
http://www.api.org

American Wind Energy Association
http://www.awea.org/

Center for Renewable Energy and Sustainable Technology
http://www.crest.org/index.html

Gwich'in Steering Committee
http://www.alaska.net/~gwichin

National Energy Policy: Bush Administration
http://www.whitehouse.gov/energy/

National Resources Defense Council
http://www.nrdc.org

10

Skull Valley

*Nuclear Waste, Environmental Racism,
and Tribal Sovereignty*

Case

I

Deb Groenlund leaned back in her desk chair. She had been Director of the Lutheran Advocacy Ministry in Utah for only six months. Like the other state directors, Deb focused on issues like welfare, health care, and education. Now she was confronted with an issue unlike any other she had ever faced. Suddenly her office felt very small. "I've gotta get out of here," she thought.

Driving west, past the Temple, Deb navigated the streets of Salt Lake City until she reached the entrance to Interstate 80. She was heading for the center of the controversy, the Skull Valley Goshute Indian Reservation (Figure 1). On May 20, 1997, the Skull Valley band of the Goshutes signed a lease agreement with Private Fuel Storage (PFS), a consortium of eight electric power utilities that own and operate thirty-three nuclear power plants around the United States (Figure 2). In the lease, the Goshutes agreed to store temporarily on their reservation what could amount to the nation's entire current stockpile of commercially produced, spent nuclear fuel. After the Bureau of Indian Affairs (BIA) reviewed the lease and deemed it in the best interests of the tribe, the Nuclear Regulatory Commission (NRC) began its multi-year review of the license application. Several years later, it now looked as if the NRC might render a final decision within the next year. Another round of public hearings was scheduled to begin next week. Deb had asked her advisory council whether she should offer any comments or take a stand about the project at the hearings. They had left that decision in her hands.

Passing the airport on the western edge of Salt Lake City, Deb zipped past a coal train heading east on rails parallel to the interstate, the same rails that

---

James Martin-Schramm prepared this case and commentary. The case is based on actual events. Names and places have been changed to protect the privacy of those involved.

Figure 1. Regional Location of Skull Valley Indian Reservation in Utah

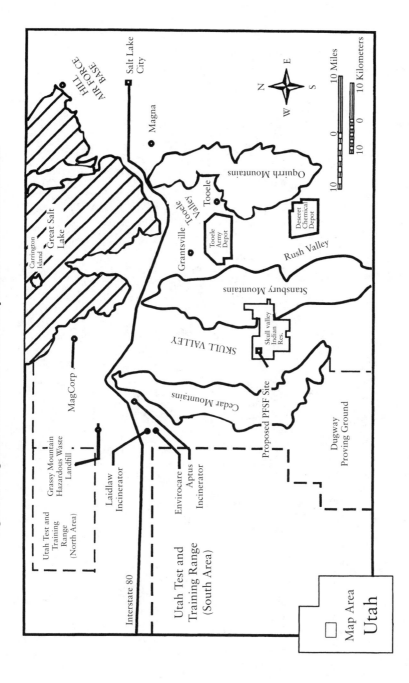

Source: U.S. Nuclear Regulatory Commission, Office of Nuclear Material Safety and Safeguards et al., *Final Environmental Impact Statement for the Construction and Operation of an Independent Spent Fuel Storage Installation on the Reservation of the Skull Valley Band of Goshute Indians and the Related Transportation Facility in Tooele County, Utah,* NUREG-1714, Vol. 1, December 2001, Section 1, p. 2.

Figure 2. Locations of PFS Reactors in the United States

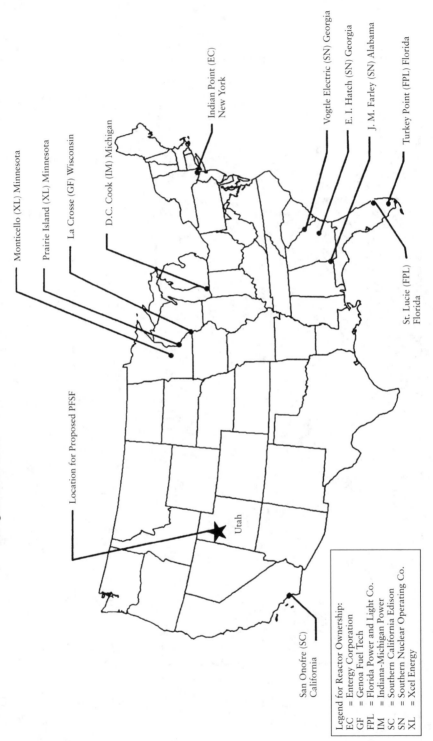

Monticello (XL) Minnesota

Prairie Island (XL) Minnesota

La Crosse (GF) Wisconsin

D.C. Cook (IM) Michigan

Indian Point (EC)
New York

Vogtle Electric (SN) Georgia

E. I. Hatch (SN) Georgia

J. M. Farley (SN) Alabama

Turkey Point (FPL) Florida

St. Lucie (FPL)
Florida

Location for Proposed PFSF

Utah

San Onofre (SC)
California

Legend for Reactor Ownership:
EC = Entergy Corporation
GF = Genoa Fuel Tech
FPL = Florida Power and Light Co.
IM = Indiana-Michigan Power
SC = Southern California Edison
SN = Southern Nuclear Operating Co.
XL = Xcel Energy

Source: U.S. Nuclear Regulatory Commission, Office of Nuclear Material Safety and Safeguards et al., *Final Environmental Impact Statement for the Construction and Operation of an Independent Spent Fuel Storage Installation on the Reservation of the Skull Valley Band of Goshute Indians and the Related Transportation Facility in Tooele County, Utah*, NUREG-1714, Vol. 1, December 2001, Section 1, p. 4.

would carry the spent nuclear fuel rods toward the reservation. About 30 miles from the city, she passed the exit for Tooele and found herself thinking about the threats to human health that lay south down *that* road. Just to the west of town sits the Tooele Army Depot, one of the largest U.S. weapons depots in the world. Further south of Tooele sits the controversial Deseret Chemical Depot—home to nearly 50 percent of the nation's aging stockpile of chemical weapons. In an effort to destroy these decaying weapons before they pose a threat to human health in the region, the military is working around the clock to incinerate over a million rockets, missiles, and mortars packed with sarin, mustard gas, and other deadly agents.

Now, approximately 40 miles from Salt Lake City, Deb exited I-80 and drove south toward the reservation. On her left rose the picturesque mountains of the Stansbury Range. To her right, the Cedar Mountains hugged the skyline in the west. Between these two mountain ranges lay the stark, desolate beauty of Skull Valley.

It was not long before Deb passed a sign for Iosepa, a former settlement founded by a group of Hawaiians that had converted to Mormonism in 1875 and then migrated to live in the Zion that was Salt Lake City. When leprosy invaded their community in 1896, however, the group never recovered. Ostracized by their fellow Mormons, the community slowly began to die. The few survivors returned to Hawaii in 1917, leaving behind a graveyard with 79 plots.

"Graves may be all that remains of the Goshutes soon," thought Deb. At one point, anthropologists think that there may have been as many as 10,000 Goshutes roaming the Great Basin between Nevada's Ruby Mountains and Utah's Wasatch Range. After the first settlers arrived in 1847, the Goshute population dropped to less than 1,000, besieged by hunger and sickness. Driven to desperation, some of the Goshute warriors started to attack stagecoaches, thus igniting the Goshute War of 1863. After the war, Abraham Lincoln signed a peace treaty with the 650 survivors and herded them onto lands that eventually became two separate Goshute reservations; one in Skull Valley and the other in the Deep Creek Mountains along the border between Utah and Nevada. Over 140 years later, the Skull Valley Band had dwindled to just over one hundred members, with only thirty living on the reservation. The treaty had certainly not ensured the welfare of the seventh generation of Goshutes. Utah, however, was thriving—recently serving as host to the 2002 Winter Olympics.

About twenty miles down the road, one lone sign marked the northern boundary of the reservation. A few moments later Deb pulled over, got out of her car, and gazed out across Skull Valley toward the Cedar Mountains in the west. "This is it. This is where the storage facility would be built," she thought (Figure 3). Up to 4,000 casks, each storing 10 metric tons of spent nuclear fuel with a radioactive half-life of 10,000 years would be stored above ground for up to forty years. The massive 16-foot tall concrete and steel casks would be stored upright on pads of reinforced concrete three feet thick spanning nearly 100 acres. Some of these casks were already being stored in other states on property outside reactors, but utilities were running out of space and would soon have to shut down some reactors if they no longer had room to store the spent nuclear fuel on-site. Deb knew that was precisely what some environmentalist groups wanted. "It's one way to bring an end to nuclear power," thought Deb, "but you've still got to do something with the existing nuclear waste."

As she understood it, the casks would be stored temporarily in Skull Valley for no longer than forty years until the Department of Energy (DOE) opened a permanent disposal site, presumably Yucca Mountain in Nevada. Of course that was supposed to happen in 1998. Wrapped in scientific and political controversy, now it looked as if the soonest Yucca Mountain would open was 2010. Like many other Utahans, Deb worried that this "temporary" site in Skull Valley would become a permanent repository by default. Both the Goshutes and the PFS insisted, however, that the DOE and the NRC would never let that happen because it would violate federal law.

Suddenly a noise broke Deb's concentration and she wheeled around to see a steer crossing the road to graze on the western side of the open range that was Skull Valley. He seemed oblivious to her presence. As she got back into her car, Deb noticed the vapor trail of a fighter jet cruising at a high altitude somewhere over the Wendover bombing range on the western side of the Cedar Mountains.

Driving south again, in a few minutes Deb approached the only commercial establishment on the reservation, the Pony Express—a convenience store and gas station. Parking next to a battered Ford Pinto, bells on a string jangled Deb's arrival as she entered the store. The clerk glanced over her shoulder and nodded her greeting. Deb nodded back and began to peruse the sparse shelves. Grabbing a Coke and a bag of corn nuts, Deb brought her items to the counter and presented them to the clerk. Even though Deb was likely one of only two or three customers that day, the clerk wasn't chatty—though she was pleasant enough. In short order, Deb handed over two dollar bills, the clerk made change, and the transaction was completed. Halfway out the door, though, Deb stopped.

"Excuse me. Would you mind if I visited with you for a bit," asked Deb?

The clerk initially wavered, but then shrugged her assent. There was only one chair, so both of them stood, facing each other across the counter.

"So, you folks have some big stuff going on out here these days," said Deb.

"Not much, really," replied the clerk. "We're still in the middle of nowhere. It just seems like a few more folks come driving in to have a look around."

Extending her hand, Deb said, "I'm sorry, my name is Deb. Deb Groenlund. I'm from Salt Lake City."

"I'm Mary, Mary Moon." Her skin felt cool and dry in Deb's hand.

"Do you live on the reservation, Mary?"

"Uh-huh, I live here with my aunt." Mary looked to be in her late twenties.

"What do you think of the nuclear waste proposal," asked Deb?

There was a pause before Mary replied. "Oh, I'll believe it when I see it. I have my doubts it'll happen. The politicians are certainly doing everything they can to stop it."

Figure 3. Artist's Rendering of PFS Storage Facility on Skull Valley Goshute Reservation

Source: Private Fuel Storage, Response to Questions about the Operation of the Private Fuel Storage Facility: A Report to Citizens of Utah, February 2001. Used with permission.

"So you favor the project," asked Deb?

Another pause. "Yeah, I guess I do. I signed the resolution supporting it back in '97. 'Course, I also signed the resolution electing new officers a few months ago," said Mary.

"Are members of the band changing their minds about the project," asked Deb?

"Oh, a few are," said Mary warily, "but some are just fed up with the leadership."

"Why is that," asked Deb?

Eyes narrowing, Mary asked, "'You some kind of reporter or something?'" Deb shook her head.

"Good."

"So why are they fed up with the leadership?" asked Deb again.

"Oh, because the money we're already getting from PFS isn't being distributed to everybody, and they refuse to tell us how much we will get once they start storing the stuff here."

"But you still support turning your reservation into a storage site for high-level nuclear waste?" asked Deb.

Deb's question produced an awkward moment of silence. Finally, Mary leveled her gaze on Deb and replied, "You know, that's really none of your business. This is our reservation. Sovereign land. You folks in Salt Lake haven't done a thing for us for over a hundred years. We've got to look after ourselves. We've got to survive."

Ashamed, Deb said, "I'm sorry, Mary. You're right. We certainly have done little to help your tribe." Then, after a brief pause, Deb asked, "But aren't there any other ways to promote economic development on the reservation?"

"Like what," replied Mary? "We looked into selling bottled water from the mountain springs on the reservation, but who's gonna buy water that might be laced with toxic chemicals from the chemical weapons incinerator? We also looked into vegetable farming like the Iosepa did, but people still remember how the army killed thousands of sheep with nerve gas back in the sixties. Do you really think people will want to eat anything that comes out of our soil? We've tried to get others to build facilities out here, but we haven't had much luck. Oh, we had a company testing rocket engines for a while, but they pulled out in a huff last year when we raised the rent. Like most other tribes we even looked into a casino, but that won't work because Utah is full of Mormons who won't gamble. I suppose we could graze more head of cattle, but that's not enough to support the families that are out here, let alone the whole band."

"I see," replied Deb softly. She looked down, shifting her weight to the other leg. Finally, uneasily, she asked the question that subconsciously had driven her out to the reservation. "What do you think about those who say that you are the victims of environmental racism; that once again white people are taking advantage of Indians?"

Mary's eyes flashed with anger. "You know, I think it's racist to deny us the right to develop our reservation in the way we choose. Somehow we have to live up to some ideal you white people have for us as Indians, but you can do whatever you want to the earth. We didn't build the Deseret Chemical Depot. We didn't build Dugway. We don't own the hazardous waste land-fills to the north and west of us. You people do. But you have the nerve to come in here and challenge our decision. Who do you people think you are? Talk about injustice!"

This conversation was over.

II

Chastised and depressed, Deb turned her car back towards the north, back towards the interstate. There was no point going any further south since the road dead-ended into the Dugway Proving Ground. There the U.S. Army conducts tests to combat biological and chemical weapons like anthrax, nerve gas, and bubonic plague. No one is allowed to enter Dugway without a security clearance. Signs warn trespassers that they may be stopped with deadly force.

When Deb reached the Interstate and turned east toward Salt Lake, she turned on her car radio. Between the static, Deb quickly realized that she was picking up the noon talk show, "Utah Live." Since the NRC was resuming its public hearings next week, Bob Marshall, the host of the show, had devoted yet another day to the nuclear waste storage controversy. Setting her cruise control to 75 mph, Deb settled in to listen to the rest of the hour-long program. The first thing she heard clearly was the end of some remarks by Lawrence Eagleton, a special assistant to Governor Leavitt.

". . . The bottom line is that the citizens of Utah do not want to become the nation's nuclear waste dump. We decided a long time ago that we didn't want to build nuclear reactors in Utah. Ninety percent of the spent nuclear fuel in this nation is stored east of the Wasatch Range, and that's precisely where it should stay. We haven't produced it, so we shouldn't have to store it. It's a simple matter of fairness."

"I'm sorry to break in here, Bob," interjected Ron Gaard, a senior spokesman for Private Fuel Storage. "But is it fair for Utah to draw power off the national grid and refuse to acknowledge that twenty percent of that power comes from nuclear power plants? We live in the *United* States of America. Should Utah enjoy the benefits without sharing some of the burdens of our great nation?"

Eagleton shot back his reply. "I've got news for you, Mr. Gaard. Utah is already paying a heavy price for the nation's development of nuclear energy. Thousands of our citizens have died from cancers caused by radioactive fall-out from the testing of nuclear weapons. The families of these 'downwinders' are still suffering. We've paid our dues. Why should Utah shoulder the entire burden of storing the nation's high-level nuclear waste? Why not allow the burden to be more widely distributed as it is now? As I understand it, casks of spent nuclear fuel are now being stored at more than a dozen locations in several states around the nation. Why bring all of it here? If it's so safe, why not leave it there?"

"Those are fair and reasonable questions," replied Gaard. "Recall that when the federal government encouraged utilities to generate electrical power with nuclear energy, the original plan was to reprocess and recycle the spent fuel. President Carter brought a halt to this plan with an executive order aimed at curbing the proliferation of weapons-grade plutonium. As a result, the federal government provided a legal guarantee in 1982 that they would take responsibility for the permanent disposal of spent nuclear fuel. For both of these reasons, utility companies did not build large storage facilities into their plant designs. Now, after the federal government has failed to make good on its promises, these materials are piling up at our plants. For various reasons, for many utilities, it is simply not possible to store much more of this waste on-site. Without more storage capacity, these plants will have to shut down. By 2010, 70 of the nation's 103 reactor units will have run out of space in storage pools. Faced with this need for storage off-site, several utility companies concluded that it would be much more cost-effective, and safer from a security perspective, to store these materials in one place. In addition, by storing these materials temporarily on the Skull Valley Goshute Reservation, the waste would be much closer to its ultimate destination, Yucca Mountain. This temporary storage facility would then free up space back at the reactor sites and the burden of nuclear waste storage would continue to be shared around the nation."

"Mr. Eagleton, does the state have other concerns?" asked Bob Marshall.

"Indeed we do, Bob. We have several concerns about the potential impact this facility could have on the safety and well-being of the citizens of Utah. For starters, each and every one of those 4,000 casks of spent nuclear fuel will travel by rail past a large share of the population of our state. They plan on shipping 5 casks on 40 trains every year for twenty years. That's almost one train per week for two decades! And *when*, not *if*, one of these 'mobile Chernobyls' derails and some of this high-level nuclear waste is spilled, we have no idea how many lives may be lost. What we do know is that it will cost over $300 billion to clean up the mess. Moreover, if the train derails near I-80, it could also bring traffic to a halt indefinitely on one of the most important routes for commerce in the nation. These risks are simply unacceptable."

"And they are also unrealistic," replied Ron Gaard. "The NRC calculates the probability of a worst-case accident over the course of the whole life of the project to be less than one in a *billion*. There are now more than 2.5 million shipments of radioactive material per year in the United States by highway, railroad, and air. While most of these involve the transport of low-level nuclear waste, not one person has ever been harmed by any release of radioactivity from these shipments. In the handful of accidents that have involved the transportation of spent nuclear fuel rods, each transportation cask remained completely sealed. The NRC regulates very tightly the design of these casks and the conditions for their transfer. We face greater risks every day from the transportation of gasoline, liquefied natural gas, and other toxic chemicals on our rails and highways."

"I suppose I would be more sanguine about the transportation risks if I lived in Minnesota like you do, Mr. Gaard," offered Eagleton in his rejoinder. "We also find unacceptable how vulnerable these casks would be to threats from the air and the ground. The Goshute reservation lies between Hill Air Force Base in the east and two bombing ranges to the west. I shudder to think what might happen if one of those planes crashed into the complex, or if ordnance they were transporting accidentally fell on the storage facility."

"As you know, Mr. Eagleton, the NRC addressed both of these concerns in its Safety Evaluation Report and found both concerns to be unwarranted. In fact, it found the likelihood of a plane crash to be less than one in a million. Moreover, actual tests and computer simulations both confirm that the security of the casks would not be breached in the highly unlikely event of either of these calamities. The NRC has dealt with both of these concerns and has taken them off the table."

"Well, after the September 11 terrorist attacks, we think the NRC should put them back on the table," replied Eagleton. "Who among us could have imagined that horrible day? God only knows how much hell a terrorist could wreak given the opportunity to target our nation's entire stockpile of spent nuclear fuel rods."

Ron Gaard replied, "I am confident that the NRC will take all steps necessary to ensure the safety of the project. In fact, the Atomic Safety and Licensing Board decided recently to gather additional seismic data in Skull Valley and they are also revisiting the terrorist and fighter jet issue. The citizens of Utah can rest assured that the NRC will not approve this project unless it is confident that it can be operated in a safe manner. In the history of the U.S. commercial power industry, there has never been a radiation-related fatality or injury to workers or to the public. That is largely due to the NRC. I can think of no other regulatory body with a better track record when it comes to public safety."

Shifting gears, Bob Marshall raised a different set of issues. "Mr. Eagleton, you don't think the democratic process has been followed in this whole affair, do you?"

"That is true, Bob. The state of Utah has largely found itself locked out of the decision-making regarding this unprecedented project. Do you think it is right that 60 to 70 adult members of the tribe can make a decision that imperils the welfare of the nearly two million citizens of Utah? Shrewdly, or callously, Private Fuel Storage has protected itself from public scrutiny by hiding behind the skirt of Goshute tribal sovereignty. They are simply using this tribe to get rid of nuclear waste. The state of Utah, on the other hand, has great respect for the Goshute people and wants to work with them, and other tribes, to promote economic development on their lands that benefits all of the people of Utah."

"Mr. Eagleton, you know as well as I do that your last remark has been an empty promise. You held out the hope for economic development assistance in a bill that was passed through the legislature last year, but the $2 million budget for this particular line was left unfunded. Instead, you sought

$1.6 million to wage a political and legal battle that would bog this project down in the courts. The Goshute people should speak for themselves on this point, but in my opinion they have received nothing from the state of Utah except grief. Is it any wonder that they have turned to us to improve their lives in the future? Now, with regard to avoiding public scrutiny, Mr. Eagleton, you also know full well that the 1,200-page license application we submitted to the NRC is a public document. In addition, you know that the state has been invited by the NRC to participate in every step of an extensive review process that is now ending its fifth year. Every step of this process has been subject to full public scrutiny."

"Is that so? Is that how you would characterize your 'arrangement' with Tooele County?" replied Eagleton. "Did you not work behind the scenes with the county commissioners to basically buy their support for the project? How much hush money are you paying to Tooele County, Mr. Gaard?"

"I resent both the tone and the substance of these allegations, Mr. Eagleton. The democratically elected commissioners of Tooele County sought the best interests of their citizens when they signed an agreement to provide important services to the PFS storage facility. Since the facility will be built on the Goshute reservation, the county will not receive any property taxes from the operation even though they are obligated under a memorandum of understanding between the tribe and the county to provide emergency and other services when necessary. In order to compensate the county for these services, and in lieu of taxes, the parties agreed to a range of payments based on a per cask mitigation fee and the length of time these casks remain in storage. In addition, prior to the opening of the storage facility, PFS agreed to pay a $5,000 monthly fee to compensate the county for administrative expenses related to the planning and licensing process. In return for both fees, the commissioners agreed not to impose any new taxes or otherwise oppose the project and pledged to assist PFS in obtaining the necessary easements, rights-of-way, waivers, and permits related to the project."

As Bob Marshall stepped in to start wrapping up the show, Deb found herself thinking about whether the state was talking out of both sides of its mouth when it came to the storage of nuclear waste. After all, a private company, Envirocare, was currently processing 97 percent of the nation's low-level nuclear waste at a facility just to the north and west of the Goshute reservation in Tooele County. And now Envirocare was requesting permission from the state to dispose of even higher levels of this waste at their facility. At the same time, news reports indicated that Envirocare had recently contributed large sums of money to Governor Leavitt's campaign coffers. Deb did not take it as a good sign that the legislature had ordered state regulators to give prompt attention to the company's request.

III

Back in her office, Deb reread her notes from the files in front of her. As the Director of the Lutheran Advocacy Ministry in Utah, it was her job "to advocate for just, sound and compassionate public policies based upon the officially adopted social justice policy positions of the Evangelical Lutheran Church in America (ELCA)."

After careful review of the social statements, messages, and social policy resolutions officially approved by the ELCA, Deb found some direction with regard to the issues of nuclear waste disposal and environmental racism. The ELCA's 1993 social statement on environmental issues, *Caring for Creation*, contained two passages that were relevant in a general way:

- "As congregations and other expressions of this church, we will model the principle of participation. We will welcome the interaction of differing views and experiences in our discussion of environmental issues such as: Nuclear and toxic waste dumps; logging in ancient growth forests; . . ."
- "We will examine how environmental damage is influenced by racism, sexism, and classism, and how the environmental crisis in turn exacerbates racial, gender, and class discrimination."

The ELCA's 1993 social statement on racism, however, contained several passages that seemed quite pertinent to the PFS/Goshute project. Deb reviewed the text she had highlighted in *Freed in Christ: Race, Ethnicity, and Culture:*

- "A wall of hostility stands intact. Captive on one side of the wall, people with access to opportunities and institutions are largely unaware of their own cultural biases or the worth of other cultures. On the other side of the wall, people scarred by slavery and other forms of degradation and suffering have seen their cultures ridiculed and reviled, or destroyed."
- "Racism—a mix of power, privilege, and prejudice—is sin, a violation of God's intention for humanity. . . . Racism infects and affects everyone, with an impact that varies according to race, ethnicity, or culture, and other factors such as gender or economic situation."
- "When we rebuild walls of hostility and live behind them—blaming others for the problem and looking to them for solutions—we ignore the role we ourselves play in the problem and also in the solution. When we confront racism and move toward fairness and justice in society, all of us benefit. . . . We expect our leadership to name the sin of racism and lead us in our repentance of it."
- "So, the Church must cry out for justice, and thereby resist the cynicism fueled by visions that failed and dreams that died. The Church must insist on justice, and thereby refuse to blame victimized people for their situations. The Church must insist on justice, and thereby assure participation of all people. The Church that pursues justice will face and address difficult, social, political, and economic problems such as: . . . [H]ow race and ethnicity figure in political decisions on immigration, crime, and environmental pollution."
- "The Church that confesses Christ in public demonstrates its commitment through involvement in public life—globally and locally, nationally and in neighborhoods. Through public events such as elections or town meetings, through public bodies such as legislatures or volunteer groups, church members help to forge political will and consensus."

On the subject of tribal sovereignty, Deb had dug up some important language buried in a resolution that was passed by a two-thirds vote at the ELCA's biennial Church-Wide Assembly in 1991. The resolution designated 1992 as a "year of remembrance, repentance, and renewal" throughout the church with regard to Native Americans. In a section subtitled "Solidarity and Advocacy for Native Americans," the resolution affirmed "the commitment of the Evangelical Lutheran Church in America to support the sovereignty of Native American tribes, to speak out for just treatment of Native Americans, and to promote harmony, reconciliation and mutual understanding within and among our communities."

As she thought about the situation, Deb found herself evaluating four options. She could join the leadership of the state of Utah and take a public stand against the project either on the basis of the threat it poses to the health and safety of present and future generations of Utahans or as an egregious example of environmental racism and injustice. Alternatively, she could take a stand defending the tribal sovereignty of the Goshutes as well as their own ability to determine whether they are the victims of environmental racism or injustice. The third option would be not to take a stand at all, but rather to state publicly that the ELCA is concerned about both environmental racism as well as tribal sovereignty, and to encourage more opportunities like these hearings where all viewpoints can be heard before any final decision is reached. The fourth option would simply be not to speak at the hearings since members of the ELCA constitute a tiny minority in Utah.

"What should I do?" Deb wondered. The hearings begin next week.

LIST OF ACRONYMS

BIA	Bureau of Indian Affairs
BLM	Bureau of Land Management
DOE	Department of Energy
DOI	Department of the Interior
ELCA	Evangelical Lutheran Church in America
EPA	Environmental Protection Agency
FEIS	Final Environmental Impact Statement
GAO	General Accounting Office
MRS	Monitored Retrieval Storage Facility
NCWA	North Cedar Mountains Wilderness Area
NIMBY	Not In My Back Yard (Syndrome)
NRC	Nuclear Regulatory Commission
NSP	Northern States Power Company
PFS	Private Fuel Storage
PFSF	Proposed Fuel Storage Facility
SNF	Spent Nuclear Fuel
STB	Surface Transportation Board

Commentary

Before turning to assess ethical issues this case poses, some background information is necessary.

In 1982 Congress passed the Nuclear Waste Policy Act, which required the Department of Energy (DOE) to start taking spent nuclear fuel (SNF) from utilities by January 31, 1998. The Act also directed the DOE to begin studying sites for the underground geological repository where this spent nuclear fuel would be stored permanently. In 1987, responding to constituents who were concerned that nuclear waste might be stored permanently in their state, Congress amended the Nuclear Waste Policy Act to require the DOE to focus on developing Yucca Mountain in Nevada as the site for the permanent repository. In addition, Congress amended the Act to create the Office of the Nuclear Waste Negotiator to find a volunteer host community for a monitored retrievable storage facility (MRS) that would store the waste on an interim basis until a permanent facility could be built.[1]

The Skull Valley Band of the Goshute Indians was one of seventeen Native American tribes that expressed interest when the Office of the Nuclear Waste Negotiator invited communities around the United States to consider becoming a host for an MRS facility.[2] In 1992 the federal agency awarded the band a $100,000 grant to do a preliminary study. Upon completion of that study, the tribe's executive committee concluded that it was in the best interests of the tribe to pursue the matter further. Shortly thereafter, the federal agency awarded the tribe a $200,000 grant to study the possibility in greater detail. These funds were used primarily to tour nuclear storage facilities in the United States, France, Sweden, England, and Japan. The tribe also used grant funds to visit with environmental groups like Greenpeace that oppose interim nuclear waste storage facilities.[3]

Upon conclusion of the second phase of the study process, the General Council of the Skull Valley Band met to receive a report from the leadership. The General Council consists of the adult members of the tribe, those age 18 and older. A majority agreed at this meeting that the tribe should offer their reservation as an interim storage site and authorized the leadership to submit a formal proposal. At approximately the same time, the Mescalero Apaches also expressed serious interest in serving as a host community. In January of 1995, however, Congress eliminated funding for the Office of the Nuclear Waste Negotiator—again in response to constituent concerns that nuclear waste might be stored in their states.[4]

Cut off now from a federal contract, yet still convinced that temporary nuclear waste storage was in their best interests, both the Goshutes and the Mescaleros decided to pursue a relationship directly with the utility companies. Negotiations with the Mescaleros are described later in this commentary. Over the course of six months in 1996–97, the Goshutes negotiated a lease agreement with Private Fuel Storage (PFS), a consortium of eight utility companies that own and operate 33 nuclear reactors around the United States.[5] The following utilities are members of the consortium: Genoa Fuel Tech, American Electric Power, Southern California Edison, Southern Nuclear Company, First Energy, Entergy, Florida Power and Light, and Xcel Energy—formerly Northern States Power headquartered in Minneapolis.[6]

In December 1996, more than two-thirds of the tribe's General Council signed a resolution authorizing the tribe's executive committee to sign the lease agreement with PFS. Representatives of the Bureau of Indian Affairs (BIA) also attended this meeting. The BIA began review of the terms of the lease agreement in December and approved the final version of the revised and amended lease agreement on May 23, 1997.[7]

The Nuclear Regulatory Commission (NRC) began its licensing review of the PFS/Goshute proposal in June of 1997. The staff of the NRC reviews technical aspects of the proposal. In September 2000, NRC staff issued a 391-page *Safety Evaluation Report* concluding that the facility would meet all federal safety standards during "normal, unusual, and accident conditions."[8] In December 2001, NRC staff published a 1,500-page *Final Environmental Impact Statement* (FEIS) about the PFS/Goshute proposal with the following recommendation:

> The environmental review staffs of the NRC, BIA, BLM [Bureau of Land Management], and STB [U.S. Surface Transportation Board] have concluded that (1) measures required by Federal and State permitting authorities other than the Cooperating Agencies, and (2) mitigation measures that are proposed in this FEIS to be required would eliminate or ameliorate any potential adverse environmental impacts associated with the proposed action specified by PFS in its NRC license application, BLM right-of-way application(s), and STB rail line application. In addition, upon completion of the project and before termination of the NRC license and the BIA lease, the closure and decommissioning of the facility would make the project area available for other uses by the Skull Valley Band.
>
> The NRC staff and the Cooperating Agencies have concluded that the overall benefits of the proposed PFS [(f)acility] outweigh the disadvantages and costs, based upon consideration of
> * the need for an alternative to at-reactor SNF storage that provides a consolidated, and for some reactor licensees, economical storage capacity for SNF from U.S. power generating reactors;
> * the minimal radiological impacts and risks from transporting, transferring, and storing the proposed quantities of SNF canisters and casks;
> * the economic benefits that would accrue to the Skull Valley Band during the life of the project; and
> * the absence of significant conflicts with existing resource management plans or land use plans within Skull Valley.[9]

This favorable recommendation paved the way for final approval until the Atomic Safety and Licensing Board, an independent judicial arm of the

NRC, decided in mid-2002 to conduct further review of threats to the PFS facility posed by earthquakes, terrorist attacks, and the crash of fighter jets conducting military exercises in the area. With regard to the latter, the Board issued a ruling in March 2003 concluding, "there is enough likelihood of an F-16 crash into the proposed facility that such an accident must be deemed credible."[10] As a result, the facility cannot be licensed until this safety concern is resolved. At this point, the Board's ruling leaves PFS with three alternatives. First, they can try to persuade the U.S. Air Force to reduce the number, and/or alter the pattern, of F-16 flights over Skull Valley. Second, they can present evidence to the Board that the facility's storage casks would sufficiently withstand the crash of an F-16 fighter jet. Third, PFS can also appeal the Board's ruling to the five commissioners of the NRC.[11]

When this book went to press in Summer 2003, PFS had not determined how it would respond to the ruling, but it is virtually certain that PFS will either appeal or attempt to resolve the safety concerns that have been raised by the Atomic Safety and Licensing Board. At some point in the future, the Nuclear Regulatory Commission will still have to make a decision about whether to license the PFS/Goshute MRS facility. When this decision is finally made, it will resolve the legal status of the project, but it will not necessarily resolve the ethical issues raised by this case. Some of these issues will now be addressed in relationship to two of the ecojustice norms introduced earlier in this volume. The norms of sustainability and sufficiency are relevant to aspects of this case, but the major issues revolve around the norms of participation and solidarity.

PARTICIPATION

The ecojustice norm of participation emphasizes that the interests of all forms of life are important and must be heard and respected in decisions that affect their lives. The norm is concerned with empowerment and seeks to remove all obstacles to participation constructed by various social, economic, and political forces and institutions. The norm places an importance on open debate and dialogue and seeks to hear the voices or perspectives of all concerned.

At least four issues revolve around the norm of participation. The two most important issues involve claims of tribal sovereignty and evidence of conflict within the tribe. Other issues are related to the agreement Tooele County negotiated with Private Fuel Storage and to actions the state of Utah has taken to oppose the project.

Tribal Sovereignty

The Skull Valley Goshutes are one of 554 Indian nations within the boundaries of the United States. The Goshutes trace their claim to tribal sovereignty back to the peace treaty they signed with Abraham Lincoln in 1863 and the executive orders that Woodrow Wilson signed forty years later establishing their reservation.[12] Article IV of the U.S. Constitution deems treaties ratified by Congress to be "the supreme law of the land."[13]

Like other tribes, the Goshutes had to give up vast swaths of land and other concessions in order to gain the right of self-governance on tribal home-lands and reservations. Many of these tribes saw even these precious land-holdings slip from their grasp when Congress opened up tribal lands to sale in an effort to make individual Indians private landholders. Over a fifty-year period beginning in 1880, more than 90 million acres of Indian land were sold to people who were not Indians. Today, the lands of these native peoples consist of only 56 million acres on 314 reservations and amount to approximately 2 percent of the nation's landmass.[14]

Nevertheless, in 1830 the Supreme Court established the right of Indian tribes to be free from control by the states in which they are located. When the state of Georgia declared Cherokee laws to be null and void, the court declared that the Cherokee nation is "a distinct political society, separated from others, capable of managing its own affairs and governing itself." At the same time, however, the Supreme Court also defined Indian tribes as "domestic, dependent nations." This term is still the subject of much dispute today.[15]

Decisions by Congress over the last two decades have renewed tensions between states and Indian nations. When Congress amended the Clean Water Act, they gave Indian tribes the same authority as states to set water pollution standards. Thus, when the Isleta Pueblo decided to act on this new authority, they forced the city of Albuquerque to spend $300 million to clean up the Rio Grande before the river enters the tribe's reservation. In 1988, when Congress approved gambling on Indian reservations, that decision ignited a whole new set of tensions between states and native peoples. Today, approximately one third of all tribes now operate some form of gambling and take in more than $6 billion a year. Several states fought the development of these casinos for social and economic reasons, but lost in court because these states permit gambling in some form.[16]

Over the course of these legal battles, an important distinction has emerged in federal law: "Where a state prohibits a particular activity under its laws, then the state may prohibit that activity on tribal lands as well; but where the state only regulates how that activity is conducted, then the tribe—and not the state—has power to regulate the activity on reservation lands."[17] If this distinction were applied to the Goshute proposal to store high-level nuclear waste on its reservation, it would appear that the state of Utah would have little ground on which to stand. This is because the state of Utah has granted a permit to a private corporation, Envirocare, to landfill and otherwise dispose of 97 percent of the nation's low-level nuclear waste.[18] In addition, the state is considering a proposal from Envirocare to dispose of higher levels of nuclear waste. If the analogy with gambling holds, the courts may not make a distinction between high and low levels of nuclear waste, just as they have chosen not to make a distinction between bingo parlors and major casinos.

Regardless, it is important to recognize that the Goshutes' tribal sovereignty is still subject to the power of the Nuclear Regulatory Commission. Whether the NRC approves or denies the PFS/Goshute lease agreement, the mere fact that it will make such a pivotal decision indicates how qualified and limited are Goshute appeals to tribal sovereignty. The question whether the Goshutes are *misusing* their tribal sovereignty to store high-level nuclear waste will be examined later in the commentary.

Tribal Conflict

It is clear from Mary's conversation with Deb Groenlund that not everyone in the tribe is of like mind. In fact, ever since 1996 when the tribe's General Council gave its approval to the PFS lease agreement, several members of the tribe have either opposed the plan or filed lawsuits against the Bureau of Indian Affairs for endorsing the plan.[19] On the one hand, this is evidence of a significant amount of disagreement within the Skull Valley band. On the other hand, it indicates that a democratic process appears to be operating. Few major policy decisions at any level of government lack serious and substantial opposition. It should come as no surprise that the Goshutes are not fully united about the nuclear waste storage plan.

A separate issue is raised by Mary's comment that current tribal revenues are not being distributed equally. In a May 2000 interview with *Outside* magazine, the chairman of the Skull Valley band describes supporters of the PFS project as "shareholders" and explains that they receive "dividends" for their support. Those who have not signed General Council resolutions supporting the project complain that they receive nothing or very little in comparison to other members of the band that support the project. The chairman, however, denies that this is the case. In fact, when members of the tribe filed a lawsuit in U.S. District Court in the summer of 1999 claiming that the chairman of the tribe was bribing members to gain their support for the PFS project and his leadership of the tribe, the court dismissed the suit. A similar lawsuit against the Bureau of Indian Affairs was dismissed without prejudice.[20] Thus, it is not clear that funds are currently being mishandled. The staff of the NRC, however, make it clear in an appendix to the FEIS that "it is the choice of the members and their leadership to decide how the funds are used and distributed."[21] Thus, legally, it appears that the leadership is not required to distribute proceeds from the PFS lease agreement equally to all members of the tribe.

Another issue revolves around disputes about the official leadership of the tribe. In September 2001, 38 adult members signed a resolution electing new members to the tribe's executive committee. These members claim that their votes constitute a majority of the adult members of the tribe. It is not clear, however, how many adults constitute the tribe's General Council.[22] Members of the Skull Valley band live in various communities in Utah as well as in other western states. Regardless, the existing tribal leadership deemed the September election illegitimate, held its own meeting of the General Council in October, and claimed to retain the support of the majority of the tribe. Representatives of the BIA attended this second election. A few days after the second vote, the BIA indicated that it supported the existing leadership in a letter to the Nuclear Regulatory Commission. This action has prompted dissident members of the tribe to file a lawsuit against the BIA protesting their decision to recognize the existing leadership. Other lawsuits have been filed as both factions attempt to control the financial assets of the tribe.[23]

According to the Director of the Utah Division of Indian Affairs, this leadership dispute is complicated by the fact that the Skull Valley Band of Goshutes is not like other Utah tribes. Several decades ago, the tribe chose to retain a traditional form of government and thus is not governed by terms of the 1934 Indian Reorganization Pact. As a result, the tribe has no charter and no constitution. This means that election rules and other governance procedures are easily altered.[24]

So who does represent the tribe? To what extent does this conflict within the tribe matter ethically? Clearly, tribal governance procedures differ significantly from the democratic processes of communities in the United States. How should the norm of participation be applied to tribal governance and conflicts? What weight should be given to the fact that federal agencies and federal courts continue to recognize the existing leadership of the tribe?

Tooele County

In the case, Utah's spokesperson Lawrence Eagleton views with disdain the agreement Tooele (pronounced Tw-illa) County negotiated with PFS. It is true that the county's three commissioners worked behind the scenes to negotiate the agreement with PFS, but they claim that they did not violate the public trust because only matters involving the expenditure of county funds need to be discussed in public meetings of the commissioners. Moreover, the commissioners note that the agreement was approved at a scheduled public meeting. Both of these facts are accurate, but it is also the case that one of the county commissioners was not re-elected in the fall of 2000. Instead, the citizens of Tooele County elected a retired postmaster and former school board member who officially opposes the PFS/Goshute project and was the first to call the attention of the public to the agreement the county had quietly negotiated with PFS.

To date, however, the citizens of Tooele County have not been overly concerned about the dangers posed by hazardous and toxic waste, even though a survey of at least one community in the county reveals higher rates of cancer, respiratory disease, birth defects, and other health problems.[25] To some extent this is because the huge county operates the West Desert Hazardous Industry Area, which employs over 900 people and produces over $2 million a year in mitigation fees from firms like Envirocare and the U.S. chemical weapons incinerator complex. These fees, like those that may be paid by PFS in the future, have built a $20 million county hospital and have reduced the property taxes the county levies on its landholders. Revenue projections for the PFS agreement range from a minimum of $90 million to more than $200 million over the possible 40-year lifetime of the project.[26]

So, is PFS simply buying the support of the county through its agreement to pay substantial mitigation fees in the future and a modest "preoperational" fee in the present? Certainly Lawrence Eagleton views the agreement in this light. In fact, the situation is a bit more complex. To some extent the county has PFS "over a barrel." In order for PFS to get a license from the NRC, it has to demonstrate that the storage facility will be covered by various government services including law enforcement, fire safety, and emergency response. Because PFS could not provide these services by itself, it had to enlist the support of the county. Faced with future expenses but no means to levy taxes to support these services, the county commissioners negotiated the fees described above. In return, the county commissioners agreed to support the project publicly. It is this aspect that leads Eagleton to refer to the monthly $5,000 preoperational fee as "hush money." If county officials publicly oppose the PFS/Goshute plan, PFS may exercise its right to withdraw the agreement. Nothing, however, prevents current county commissioners from exercising their conscience, and the citizens of Tooele County can always elect new commissioners who might vote to rescind the agreement. Despite Eagleton's concerns, Tooele County is not a pawn of PFS and, in many respects, "holds the cards" to PFS getting a license from the NRC.[27]

State of Utah

Unlike the commissioners of Tooele County, the governor of Utah, Michael Leavitt, has declared that high-level nuclear waste will be brought to Utah "over my dead body." After the county signed its agreement with PFS, the Governor seized the county road that leads to the reservation from Interstate 80 and made it a state highway. Shortly thereafter a sign was erected prohibiting the transport of high-level nuclear waste. During the 2000 session of the Utah state legislature, the Governor introduced and supported various bills aimed at stopping the PFS/Goshute storage facility. As Ron Gaard states correctly in the case, one of these bills funneled a large amount of money to lawyers working to oppose the project and left unfunded a promise to assist the Goshutes and other tribes with economic development. More importantly bills were passed that prohibited the shipment of high-level nuclear waste into Utah, barred Tooele County from providing services to the storage facility, levied $150 billion in up-front fees on PFS, and imposed a $10,000 per day fine on any person or organization that provides services to the PFS/Goshute project. Both PFS and the Goshutes have challenged these laws in U.S. District Court, arguing that they violate constitutional protections of interstate commerce, ignore the Goshute right to tribal sovereignty, and usurp federal authority over the regulation of radioactive materials.[28]

In the NRC review process, the state of Utah has been one of the officially recognized parties in the process from the outset. As a result, the state has presented its concerns about the PFS/Goshute project directly to the NRC staff and the Atomic Safety and Licensing Board.

Another officially recognized party, the Southern Utah Wilderness Alliance, persuaded the NRC to examine more closely the environmental impact of the thirty-two mile rail spur that would transport the casks of spent nuclear fuel to the Skull Valley Goshute Indian Reservation from a transfer point near Interstate 80. In its current design, the rail spur would cross a two-mile patch of a proposed North Cedar Mountains Wilderness Area (NCWA). In the past, Governor Leavitt consistently opposed the establishment of this and other wilderness areas in Utah, but now he apparently supports the NCWA even while the state is engaged in a bitter federal lawsuit with environmental groups about what parts of Utah are truly roadless, and thus worthy of a wilderness designation.[29]

Given this range of activity in the PFS/Goshute controversy, it is difficult to support Lawrence Eagleton's claim in the case that the state of Utah has been "locked out" of the decision-making process. While the state may not find itself in an ideal role, the interests of the citizens of Utah are being represented in the decisions that affect their welfare in the present and the future.

SOLIDARITY

The ecojustice norm of solidarity emphasizes the kinship and interdependence of all forms of life and encourages support and assistance for those who suffer. The norm highlights the fundamental communal nature of life in contrast to individualism and encourages individuals and groups to join together in common cause and stand with those who are the victims of discrimination, abuse, and oppression. Underscoring the reciprocal relationship of individual welfare and the common good, solidarity calls for the powerful to share the plight of the powerless, for the rich to listen to the poor, and for humanity to recognize its fundamental interdependence with the rest of nature. Insofar as solidarity leads to the equitable sharing of burdens, the norm manifests the demand for distributive justice.

There are two key ethical issues in this case related to the norm of solidarity. The first is whether the PFS proposal to store spent nuclear fuel temporarily on the Skull Valley Goshute Indian Reservation is an example of environmental racism and environmental injustice. The second key issue is how the burden of storing this waste and disposing of it permanently should be shared fairly among the citizens of the United States.

Environmental Racism and Environmental Justice

The term *environmental racism* was coined in 1982 by Benjamin Chavez, the future director of the National Association for the Advancement of Colored People, while protesting the dumping of highly toxic polychlorinated biphenyls (PCBs) in Warren County, North Carolina. Evidence of environmental racism can be found in the disproportionate number of waste facilities and polluting industries located in communities of people of color. Evidence of environmental racism can also be found in the way environmental laws have been enforced, or not enforced, in white communities and communities of people of color. Environmental racism pertains not only to actions that have a racist *intent*, but also to actions that have a racist *impact*. It occurs when people of color are either targeted or bear a disproportionate level of the burden created by the disposal of toxic wastes or the pollution produced by industry. *Environmental justice* broadens the scope of this concern to include people of any race, class, or income level.[30]

A 1987 report by the United Church of Christ put environmental racism in the national spotlight. The study noted that "[t]he proportion of minority members in communities with commercial hazardous waste facilities is double that of communities without such facilities. Where two or more such facilities are found, the proportion of minority members is nearly triple that in otherwise comparable communities."[31] In 1992, the *National Law Journal* published a similar study exposing "a racial divide" in the way the Environmental Protection Agency (EPA) implemented Superfund laws related to the cleanup of toxic wastes.[32]

After other studies by government agencies and non-governmental organizations substantiated additional cases of environmental injustice and environmental racism, President Clinton signed an executive order in February 1994 establishing environmental justice as a national priority. At the heart of this executive order is the following requirement:

> Each Federal agency shall conduct its programs, policies, and activities that substantially affect human health or the environment, in a manner that ensures that such programs, policies, and activities do not have the effect of excluding persons (including populations) from participation in, denying persons (including populations) the benefits of, or subjecting persons (including populations) to discrimination under, such programs, policies, and activities, because of their race, color, or national origin.[33]

In addition, the order also explicitly states that "[e]ach Federal agency responsibility set forth under this order shall apply equally to Native American programs."[34]

Both of these aspects of the executive order have significant implications for the case. The Bureau of Indian Affairs (BIA) in the Department of the Interior reviews contracts related to the lease of Indian trust lands. As such, it is required under the executive order to conduct an environmental justice review of projects that may adversely impact Native American tribes. Unlike the BIA, the Energy Reauthorization Act of 1974 created the Nuclear Regulatory Commission as an *independent* federal agency. Although independent agencies, such as the NRC, are only *requested* to comply with the executive order, NRC staff worked together with staff from the BIA and other cooperating federal agencies to conduct an environmental justice review of the PFS/Goshute project. This environmental justice review featured "an analysis of the human health and environmental impacts on low-income and minority populations" resulting from activities related to the PFS/Goshute MRS facility.[35] Following NRC policy, the staff focused their impact assessment primarily within a four-mile radius around the Skull Valley Indian reservation, though a fifty-mile radius was utilized to examine the impact local transportation routes to the facility could have on low-income and minority populations. Their findings were published in December 2001 as a part of the project's *Final Environmental Impact Statement:*

> Examination of the various environmental pathways by which low-income and minority populations could be disproportionately affected reveals no disproportionate high and adverse impacts from construction or normal operations. There are also no credible accident scenarios by which such impacts could take place. Thus, the cumulative effect of the proposed PFSF [Proposed Fuel Storage Facility] and other activities on environmental justice concerns through direct environmental pathways is small. When considering past, present, and foreseeable future actions, the impacts from the proposed PFSF would add little to the indirect and cumulative impacts and are considered to be small.[36]

Despite this official finding with regard to environmental injustice, there are good reasons to suspect that the PFS/Gosgute project constitutes a case of environmental racism. In many respects, storage of spent nuclear fuel rods on the reservation of a Native American tribe could be viewed as the completion of a painful circle of death and exploitation. The vast majority of the mining and milling of uranium in the United States since 1950 has taken place on or adjacent to Indian reservations.[37] Approximately 25 percent of the 15,000 workers employed in these activities were members of various tribes, especially Navajos. A large number of these workers were eventually diagnosed with diseases and other health problems caused by their exposure to radiation.[38] In addition, Native Americans not directly engaged in uranium extraction and processing have been exposed to dangers posed by groundwater contamination, radon exposure, and pollution of the air via tailings dust. Studies indicate that Indians living near uranium mines face the same health risks as those engaged in mining.[39]

Native Americans have also suffered from the production of nuclear weapons. The testing of nuclear bombs produced fallout on native lands in Nevada, Utah, and other western states. In New Mexico, the dumping of liquid and solid waste from the Los Alamos laboratory from 1944 to 1952 left radioactive sediment on the sacred lands of the San Ildefonso Pueblo. In Washington, the Hanford nuclear reservation released more than 440 gallons of irradiated water upstream from the Yakama Reservation between 1945 and 1989.[40]

In Minnesota, the Prairie Island Mdewankanton Sioux have had to combat the dangers posed by the nuclear power industry. In 1973 and 1974, Northern States Power Company (now Xcel and leader of the PFS consortium) completed the construction of two nuclear reactors within a few hundred yards of the Prairie Island Indian Reservation. Grace Thorpe, a Native American activist and opponent of nuclear power, offers the following account of the ensuing problems:

The facility was on the site of an ancient Indian village and burial mound dating back at least two thousand years. On October 2, 1979, a twenty-seven-minute release of radiation from the plants forced evacuation of the facility, but the tribe was not notified until several days later. By 1989 radioactive tritium was detected in the drinking water, forcing the Mdewankanton to dig an eight-hundred-foot-deep well and construct a water tower, completed in 1993. Prairie Island residents are (now) exposed to six times the cancer risk deemed acceptable by the Minnesota Department of Health.[41]

The story does not end there, however. After Congress removed funding for the Office of the Nuclear Waste Negotiator in 1995, a consortium of 33 electric utilities headed by Northern States Power (NSP) approached the state of Minnesota and proposed that the legislature approve the construction of a monitored retrievable storage facility (MRS) for spent nuclear fuel on land adjacent to the NSP reactor facility at Prairie Island. The utilities did not expect the Mdewankanton Sioux to oppose the plan since the tribe, like the Skull Valley Goshutes, had applied for and received a $100,000 Phase One grant to explore the possibility of establishing a MRS facility on the reservation. The tribe, however, apparently never seriously considered approving such a facility. Grace Thorpe explains the motives of the tribe:

> The intent was to use the government's money to prove that neither an MRS nor a nuclear power plant should be located at Prairie Island. One study showed that the cancer risk would be twenty-three times greater than the stated standard. At the time of the NSP initiative, a survey showed that 91.6 percent of the tribe opposed the construction of the MRS. The tribe fought the NSP proposal before the legislature and won. They subsequently declared the Prairie Island Reservation a Nuclear Free Zone.[42]

Rebuffed in Minnesota, NSP focused its energies on an agreement with the Mescalero Apaches in New Mexico. Like the PFS agreement with the Goshutes, the terms of the lease with the Mescaleros called for the tribe to store up to forty thousand metric tons of spent nuclear fuel for no longer than forty years on their reservation. In return, the tribe could expect to receive as much as $250 million. When the leaders of the tribe brought the project to a vote on January 31, 1995, they were surprised when a majority voted to *reject* the proposal by a vote of 490 to 362. Two months later, however, members of the tribe mustered the signatures to bring the proposal up for a second vote and this time the measure was *approved* by a vote of 593 to 372. Despite this apparent vote of support, the proposal has not moved forward and appears to be "dead in the water" because the NRC discovered a seismic fault under the location of the proposed facility. The Mescaleros have taken this setback in stride, however, because they own and operate several lucrative business ventures including a major casino, a five-star ski resort, and a large timber operation. The Mescaleros can survive without the MRS facility.[43]

The financial situation of the Goshutes, however, is much more dire. The case accurately describes several failed efforts to promote economic development on the Skull Valley reservation. The chairman of the tribe describes the PFS/Goshute proposal as a matter of ensuring the tribe's "survival."[44] Nevertheless, Native American activists like Grace Thorpe dismiss Goshute appeals to tribal sovereignty to support a MRS facility on the Skull Valley reservation. Thorpe writes:

> Allowing utilities to build MRS facilities on our lands . . . is not an expression of sovereignty. Those supporting such sites are selling our sovereignty. The utilities are using our names and our trust lands to bypass environmental regulations. The issue is not sovereignty. The issue is Mother Earth's preservation and survival. The issue is environmental racism.[45]

It would be false, however, to give the impression that all Native Americans share Thorpe's views. In fact, several tribes refuse to take a stand on the issue and affirm the sovereignty of tribes to make decisions with which they may disagree. In addition, it is dangerous to divide Native Americans into "good" traditionalists and "bad" assimilationists. Mary Moon resents being forced into one of these camps and refuses to live up to some romantic ideal of Indians living in harmony with the land.

In the case, it appears that Deb Groenlund shares Grace Thorpe's views about tribal sovereignty and environmental racism, at least until her unsettling conversation with Mary Moon. What should Deb do? Clearly some Indians believe this is a misuse of tribal sovereignty, but a majority of the Skull Valley Goshutes thinks that locating a MRS on their reservation would be an appropriate use of sovereignty. Would it be paternalistic or imperialistic for Deb to publicly oppose the wishes of the tribe? Is this a case of environmental racism or not? The Goshutes, after all, have voted to approve this project; it is not being forced upon them. Or is it? Deb could argue that the Goshutes are being forced to approve this use of their reservation because they are in the circumstances of financial duress. What other alternatives do the Skull Valley Goshutes really have?

Sharing the Burden of Nuclear Waste Disposal

Currently, 103 commercial nuclear reactors produce 20 percent of the nation's electricity and serve approximately 50 million people.[46] Over 90 percent of these reactors are located east of Utah at 66 locations in 31 states.[47] By 2001, these commercial reactors had produced approximately 36,500 metric tons of spent nuclear fuel (SNF).[48] By 2046, the Nuclear Regulatory Commission projects that these reactors will have produced

105,414 metric tons of SNF.[49] In addition to the challenges posed by the disposal of commercially produced high-level nuclear waste, the federal government must also find a permanent repository for a large amount of defense-related SNF and other high-level nuclear waste produced by nuclear-powered submarines and aircraft carriers.[50]

As was noted earlier, the federal government is legally obligated to store all high-level nuclear waste and spent nuclear fuel in a permanent underground repository. Until the federal government opens such a facility, however, the generators and owners of this waste have the responsibility to both provide and pay for the interim storage of it.[51] To date, 21 reactor units have run out of room to store spent nuclear fuel in cooling ponds. Many of these utilities have received approval from the NRC to store the fuel in casks above ground, normally on the grounds of the reactor facility. By 2010, 74 reactor units will have run out of storage space in their cooling ponds. Some of these reactors will also have run out of storage space above ground, which may require the utilities to cease reactor operations even before 2010. These are the driving factors behind the PFS/Goshute storage proposal.[52]

To date, the federal government has spent $7 billion studying the scientific feasibility of establishing a permanent repository for high-level nuclear waste and spent nuclear fuel at Yucca Mountain in Nevada.[53] This project has been mired in scientific and political controversy since 1987 when Congress mandated that the Department of Energy focus solely on the Yucca Mountain location.[54] In December 2001, the General Accounting Office (GAO) issued a report about the status of the project. The nonpartisan, investigative arm of Congress concluded that the Department of Energy is "not ready to make a site recommendation" because 293 scientific and technical issues remain unresolved. As a result, the report encouraged the Bush administration to postpone any decision to build a permanent repository at Yucca Mountain.[55]

Ignoring the GAO's advice, President Bush decided early in 2002 to accept the Department of Energy's recommendation that a permanent geological repository for high-level nuclear waste be established at Yucca Mountain. Shortly afterwards, the governor of Nevada vetoed the President's decision under rules established in the 1982 Nuclear Waste Policy Act. Under the same rules, the U.S. House of Representatives and the U.S. Senate voted by large margins to override Nevada's veto in the summer of 2002. These votes in Congress cleared the way for the Department of Energy to request a license from the Nuclear Regulatory Commission to operate a permanent repository at Yucca Mountain. Like the PFS/Skull Valley proposal, this licensing review process is currently estimated to take at least five years. Legal battles will also likely delay the construction and opening of the facility. As a result, it is not likely that Yucca Mountain would be operational until at least 2010.

If and when Yucca Mountain does open, the facility is designed to store a total of 77,000 tons of spent nuclear fuel and high-level nuclear waste.[56] Storage of commercially produced spent nuclear fuel is limited, however, to

63,000 tons. The remaining space in the facility is reserved for the storage of defense-related nuclear waste.[57]

In debates about the PFS/Goshute proposal, the state of Utah has strongly expressed its concern that Yucca Mountain cannot accommodate the total amount of commercially produced SNF that the Nuclear Regulatory Commission projects will be produced by 2046. If the Yucca limit of 63,000 is subtracted from the NRC projection of 105,414, the remainder is 42,414 metric tons of SNF for which there is no permanent home. The state does not believe it is coincidental that this figure is virtually identical to the amount of SNF that PFS wants to store on an interim basis for up to 40 years on the Skull Valley Goshute Indian Reservation. Given the uncertainty about Yucca Mountain, the state fears that the "temporary" storage facility in Skull Valley will become permanent because the waste will have no other place to go.[58]

In response, PFS has sought to reassure the citizens of Utah that the Department of Energy and the Nuclear Regulatory Commission would not allow the Skull Valley MRS to be converted to a permanent repository. This would be a violation of law because Congress has mandated that permanent disposal must take place deep underground in a geologic repository.[59] In addition, if the Department of Energy did not take possession of the spent nuclear fuel at the end of the forty-year lease, the utilities that own the fuel would still have a legal and financial obligation to take back the fuel and find another interim storage facility.[60] Nothing, however, prohibits PFS from entering into new negotiations with the Skull Valley Goshutes after the initial lease expires if both parties are interested in drafting a new lease arrangement. Any new lease would still have to be approved by the NRC, however.

From this overview, it is clear that the storage and ultimate disposal of high-level nuclear waste is a major public policy issue on the verge of becoming a national crisis. From California to New York, people all around the nation are saying, "Not in my backyard!" This NIMBY syndrome is behind the decision of Congress to focus solely on Yucca Mountain as a permanent repository. The NIMBY syndrome also fuels political and legal battles around the nation aimed at rejecting pleas by utilities to increase the amount of spent nuclear fuel that can be stored on a temporary basis in casks above ground. It is hard to blame the nuclear power utilities for this problem. It is the federal government that has not lived up to its promise to open a site for the permanent disposal of this waste. In fairness to the federal government, however, the Atomic Energy Agency did have a plan for dealing with spent nuclear fuel, but they could not have predicted that President Carter would eliminate the reprocessing of the fuel.[61] Finally, all citizens of the United States must shoulder some of the blame for failing to muster the political will to deal with this problem in an effective way. In many respects, U.S. citizens driven by the NIMBY syndrome have helped to drop this issue in the laps of the Goshutes. After all, no other community in the nation has stepped forward to store high-level nuclear waste on either an interim or a permanent basis. Over 50 million people in the nation enjoy the benefits of nuclear power, but refuse to accept the burdens associated with its waste.

As Deb acknowledges in the case, many see this waste bottleneck as the most effective way to bring to an end the nuclear energy industry in the United States. When utilities run out of places to store spent nuclear fuel on an interim basis, federal law requires them to shut down the reactors. Over time, this means that people of the United States will have to find other ways to either produce or conserve 20 percent of the nation's current energy supply. Investments in renewable energy production, energy-efficient technologies, and changes in patterns of consumption could go a long way to meet this challenge, but none of these measures resolve the issue of nuclear waste.

Even if nuclear waste is not produced in the future, the United States is still faced with the challenge of storing temporarily or disposing of permanently the high-level nuclear waste that has been produced to date. This raises the question of whether it would be better to store existing stockpiles at over seventy locations around the country or to consolidate these stockpiles in one place. In the case, Ron Gaard contends that it would be more cost-effective and easier to provide a high level of security if spent nuclear fuel was all stored in one place. The state of Utah, however, argues that if it is safe to store spent nuclear fuel where it is now, then it should remain where it is—presumably in perpetuity.

There lies the rub. The radioactivity of spent nuclear fuel has a half-life of at least 10,000 years. Is it morally responsible to store thousands of steel and concrete casks containing this waste above ground at dozens of locations around the nation for thousands of years? Is it safer to entomb such highly radioactive waste in a geological repository deep under ground? Like it or not, and absent any new alternative strategies, disposal underground still appears to be the best option. But Yucca Mountain is not open, and it is not clear it will open any time soon. If the NRC awards a license for the PFS/Goshute interim storage facility, this could give the nation forty more years to figure out how to dispose of the waste permanently. At the same time, once the waste has been transferred to an Indian reservation, it is possible that the nation would forget that a long-term disposal problem still exists.

So, who should bear the burden (and reap the benefits) from storing the nation's high-level nuclear waste, either on an interim or a permanent basis? On the face, it seems clear that those who benefit the most from nuclear energy should also shoulder most of the waste burden. But how realistic is it to expect that millions of people in 31 states will abandon the NIMBY syndrome in order to muster the courage and political will to address this problem in a responsible manner? Isn't it more likely that they will still try to externalize the costs by dumping the problem on others? Are there any signs of hope on this front? Are there viable options on the table? It would not appear that there are.

That leaves the PFS/Goshute interim storage plan. The Goshutes are no less intelligent than other people in the United States, and together with other people in Tooele County, they have shouldered more than their fair share of the nation's toxic and hazardous waste. Whereas most U.S. residents live a middle-class lifestyle or better, virtually all Goshutes on the reservation live below the poverty line. In addition, while most people in the United States are members of the white, dominant culture, the Goshutes are members of a tribe that now constitutes a tiny fraction of its former glory. If the NRC approves the project, some members of the tribe would qualify for jobs constructing and operating the $3.1 billion facility. Once operational, revenues from the lease agreement would provide private healthcare for tribal members on the reservation who now have to travel over 200 miles to the closest office of the Indian Health Services. In addition, PFS revenues would be utilized to build a religious and cultural center on the reservation to help the band preserve their disappearing heritage. Funds would also be available to encourage members of the band to return to the reservation through subsidized housing construction and other infrastructure improvements.[62] Finally, it is rumored that the PFS lease agreement would make members of the band instant millionaires.

Deb needs to weigh these factors when she considers her stance on this issue. Are members of the dominant culture taking advantage of the Goshutes by tempting them to accept the nation's current stockpile of commercially produced, spent nuclear fuel? Or are the Goshutes shrewdly taking advantage of the failure of members of the dominant culture to face an environmental problem of their own creation? If the NRC approves the forty-year lease agreement, the Goshutes have good reason to believe that it will be safe to operate the facility for the length of the contract. At the conclusion of the lease agreement, the Goshutes should be much better off financially and will not necessarily have to sign another lease agreement. Nor is it guaranteed that the NRC would approve a new lease agreement, in which case the utilities would have to take back the fuel they had stored temporarily on the Skull Valley reservation.

Examining the proposal from these financial and health perspectives, it is clear that there may be significant benefits for the Skull Valley Goshutes. But what about cultural concerns? Would the tribe be selling its soul to accept the waste? Is the storage facility an insult or betrayal of "Mother Earth"? Is Grace Thorpe right that the Goshutes are threatening the foundations of their very culture through this "misuse" of tribal sovereignty? Certainly Mary Moon gives a powerful response to these questions in her impassioned response to Deb's questions. How is it that Christians do not lose sleep over the invention and use of nuclear energy, but they expect Native Americans to maintain a principled opposition to storing nuclear waste on religious terms? Is it possible for Indian cultures to embrace the costs and benefits of certain technologies just as other cultures have done around the world? Is it the case that Christians put Indians on a pedestal and insist that they live up to some environmental ideal?

In the end, it is clear that those who have produced the waste should bear the burden of dealing with it. This moral responsibility seems to be escaping many today. Is it completely out of the question, therefore, to see the limited good (and harm) this project could do for the Skull Valley Goshutes? Is it beyond the pale of ethical respectability to support the Goshutes in their proposal to store temporarily most of the spent nuclear fuel produced in the United States? Or is this, truly, one of the most egregious cases of environmental racism to date?

What position, if any, should Deb take during this last round of hearings conducted by the NRC?

Notes

1. Private Fuel Storage website, December 17, 2001: http://www.privatefuelstorage.com.

2. Grace Thorpe, "Our Homes Are Not Dumps: Creating Nuclear-Free Zones," in *Defending Mother Earth: Native American Perspectives on Environmental Justice*, Jace Weaver, ed. (Maryknoll, NY: Orbis Books, 1996), p. 51.

3. Skull Valley Goshutes website, December 17, 2001: http://skullvalley-goshutes.org. Also, see interview transcripts of Leon Bear, chairman of the Skull Valley Goshutes, at the KUED-7 online companion website for a documentary about the Skull Valley controversy: http://www.kued.org/skullvalley/documentary/ interviews/ bear.html

4. See KUED interview with Leon Bear, http://www.kued.org/skullvalley/documentary/interviews/bear.html. See also Bear's comments in an article by Kevin Fedorko, "In the Valley of the Shadow," *Outside*, May 2000, vol. 25, no. 5, p. 124.

5. Skull Valley Goshutes website, December 17, 2001: http://skullvalley-goshutes.org.

6. Private Fuel Storage website, July 17, 2002: http://www.privatefuelstorage.com/ project/partners-pfs.html.

7. Private Fuel Storage, *Response to Questions about the Operation of the Private Fuel Storage Facility: A Report to Citizens of Utah*, February 2001, p. 6.

8. Jim Woolf, "Federal Report Calls N-Storage Site Safe," *The Salt Lake Tribune*, October 7, 2000. Accessed on-line at http://www.sltrib.com. All subsequent references to articles in *The Salt Lake Tribune* have been accessed at this website.

9. U.S. Nuclear Regulatory Commission, Office of Nuclear Material Safety and Safeguards et al., *Final Environmental Impact Statement for the Construction and Operation of an Independent Spent Fuel Storage Installation on the Reservation of the Skull Valley Band of Goshute Indians and the Related Transportation Facility in Tooele County, Utah*, NUREG-1714, Vol. 1, December 2001, p. iv.

10. Donna Kemp Spangler, "Goshute repository is denied a license," *Deseret News*, March 11, 2003. See also Associated Press, "U.S. Withholds Approval for Nuclear Waste Storage on Indian Reservation, *The New York Times*, accessed on-line March 11, 2003, at www.nytimes/com/2003/03/11/politics/11UTAH.html; and Environmental News Service, "F-16's Shoot Down Skull Valley Fuel Storage," accessed on-line March 12, 2003 at http://ens-news.com/ens/mar2003/2003-03-11-02.asp. It is likely that the Board was influenced by the fact that on October 25, 2002, two F-16 fighter jets collided and crashed while on a routine training mission over the Utah Test and Training Range. This is the largest missile and bomb testing range in the United States and it is located within twenty miles of the Skull Valley reservation. Every year over 5,000 flights and bombing missions are conducted over the range. See Judy Fahys, "N-Waste: Jet Crash a Risk?," *The Salt Lake Tribune*, April 11, 2002; see also, "Pilot error blamed for October crash of 2 F-16Cs jets," *Deseret News*, February 3, 2003.

11. U.S. Nuclear Regulatory Commission, "NRC Board Issues Decision on Private Fuel Storage Application," *NRC News*, No. 03-028, March 10, 2003.

12. Timothy Egan, "New Prosperity Brings New Conflict to Indian Country," *The New York Times*, Sunday, March 8, 1998. Accessed on-line December 7, 2001 via *The New York Times* premium archive: http://query.nytimes.com/search/advanced.

13. *The Constitution of the United States*, Article IV. Accessed July 17, 2002, at the U.S. Library of Congress website: http://memory.loc.gov/const/const.html.

14. Timothy Eagan, "New Prosperity Brings New Conflict to Indian Country."

15. Ibid.

16. Ibid.

17. Office of Studies, Evangelical Lutheran Church in America, *Gambling: A Study for Congregations*, 1998, Session Six, "Gambling on American Indian Reservations," accessed on-line December 10, 2001, at http://www.elca.org/dcs/session6.html.

18. Judy Fahys, "N-Waste Disposal Plan Wins Support, *The Salt Lake Tribune*, November 15, 2001.

19. Kevin Fedorko, "In the Valley of the Shadow," *Outside*, May 2000, vol. 25, no. 5, p. 119. Copies of legal correspondence furnished by Anne Sward Hansen, December 5, 2001.

20. Kevin Fedorko, "In the Valley of the Shadow," pp. 166–67. See also Jerry Johnstone, "Goshutes players in new game," *Deseret News*, September 28, 2001. Accessed on-line at http://deseretnews.com/dn. All subsequent references to articles in the *Deseret News* have been accessed at this website.

21. U.S. Nuclear Regulatory Commission, Office of Nuclear Material Safety and Safeguards et al., *Final Environmental Impact Statement for the Construction and Operation of an Independent Spent Fuel Storage Installation on the Reservation of the Skull Valley Band of Goshute Indians and the Related Transportation Facility in Tooele County, Utah*, NUREG-1714, Vol. 2, December 2001, Appendix G, p. G-244.

22. John Parkyn, chairman of the Board of Private Fuel Storage, claims that "slightly over half" of the tribe's 126 members are adults and members of the General Council. Personal e-mail communication with John Parkyn on January 17, 2003.

23. See Anonymous, "Goshutes Appear to Elect Anti-Nuke Officer Slate, *The Salt Lake Tribune*, September 23, 2001; Jerry Johnstone, "Goshutes feuding: Vote ends in 'draw,'" *Deseret News*, September 24, 2001; Angie Welling, "Goshutes Sue 3 Utah Banks," *Deseret News*, October 23, 2001; Jerry Johnstone, "BIA names tribal chairman," *Deseret News*, October 27, 2001.

24. Jerry Johnstone, "Goshutes players in new game," *Deseret News*, September 28, 2001.

25. See Chip Ward, *The Grantsville Community's Health: A Citizen Survey* (Salt Lake City: HEAL West Desert Healthy Alliance, 1996). Jason Groenewold, Director of Families Against Incinerator Risk, also provided me with helpful information about toxic waste and the PFS/Goshute proposal.

26. Personal conversation with Gene White in Tooele, Utah, December 3, 2001. Draft copy of the terms of agreement between PFS and Tooele County furnished by Bruce Whitehead, President of W.S. Adamson and Associates, Inc., the public relations firm for PFS. See also KUED interviews with Gene White, Gary Griffith, and Terryl Hunsaker: http://www.kued.org/ skullvalley/documentary/interviews.html.

27. Ibid.

28. See Jerry Spangler, "Leavitt faces defining battle," *Deseret News*, August 8, 2000, A1, 4; Donna Kemp Spangler, "Utilities, Goshutes Challenge Utah Laws,"

Deseret News, December 13, 2001; Judy Fahys, "Utilities, Tribe Sue to Overturn N-Waste Rules," *The Salt Lake Tribune*, December 14, 2001.

29. Judy Fahys, "Feds Want More Data on N-Waste Rail Spur," *The Salt Lake Tribune*, December 5, 2001.

30. J. Timmons Roberts and Melissa M. Toffolon-Weiss, *Chronicles from the Environmental Justice Frontline* (New York: Cambridge University Press, 2001), pp. 9–11.

31. Cited in the introduction to *Faces of Environmental Racism: Confronting Issues of Global Justice*, 2nd ed., Laura Westra and Bill E. Lawson, eds. (New York: Rowman & Littlefield, 2001), pp. xvii–xviii.

32. Ibid., p. 5.

33. President William J. Clinton, Executive Order 12898, *Federal Actions to Address Environmental Justice in Minority Populations and Low-Income Populations*, section 2–2. Accessed on-line December 20, 2001at http://www.epa.gov/civil-rights/docs/eo12898.html.

34. Ibid., section 6–606.

35. U.S. Nuclear Regulatory Commission, Office of Nuclear Material Safety and Safeguards, et al., *Final Environmental Impact Statement for the Construction and Operation of an Independent Spent Fuel Storage Installation on the Reservation of the Skull Valley Band of Goshute Indians and the Related Transportation Facility in Tooele County, Utah*, p. 6–21.

36. Ibid., p. 6–39.

37. Jace Weaver, introduction to chapter by Grace Thorpe, "Our Homes Are Not Dumps: Creating Nuclear-Free Zones," in *Defending Mother Earth: Native American Perspectives on Environmental Justice*, p. 47.

38. Grace Thorpe, "Our Homes Are Not Dumps: Creating Nuclear-Free Zones," p. 50.

39. Ibid., p. 50.

40. Jace Weaver, introduction to Grace Thorpe, "Our Homes Are Not Dumps," p. 49.

41. Grace Thorpe, "Our Homes Are Not Dumps," p. 50.

42. Ibid., p. 52.

43. Ibid..

44. Leon Bear, "The State of the Skull Valley Band of the Goshute Indian Tribe," *The Salt Lake Tribune*, January 28, 2001. See also Kevin Fedorko, "In the Valley of the Shadow," p. 169.

45. Grace Thorpe, "Our Homes Are Not Dumps," p. 54.

46. James A. Lake et al., "Next-Generation Nuclear Power," *Scientific American*, vol. 286, no. 1, January 2002, p. 73. Globally, 438 nuclear power plants produce 16 percent of the world's electricity.

47. Private Fuel Storage website, December 17, 2001: http://www.privatefuel-storage.com. See also, NO! The Coalition Opposed to High Level Nuclear Waste, *White Paper regarding Opposition to the High-level Nuclear Waste Facility Proposed by Private Fuel Storage on the Skull Valley Band of Goshute Indian Reservation in Skull Valley, Utah*, November 28, 2000, p. 3.

48. Private Fuel Storage, *Research regarding DEQ Information on Private Fuel Storage (PFS)*, p. 5.

49. Nuclear Regulatory Commission, *Draft Environmental Impact Statement for a Geological Repository for the Disposal of Spent Nuclear Fuel and High-Level Radioactive Waste in Yucca Mountain, Nye County, Nevada*, vol. I—Impact Analyses, July 1999, p. 1–23. Cited in NO! white paper, p. 8.

50. Private Fuel Storage, *Response to Questions about the Operation of the Private Fuel Storage Facility*, p. 12.

51. Private Fuel Storage, *Research regarding DEQ Information on Private Fuel Storage (PFS)*, p. 3.

52. Ibid., p. 2.

53. Editorial, "Is Nuclear Power Ready?" *Scientific American*, vol. 286, no. 1, January 2002, p. 6.

54. Anonymous, "Nuclear Waste: Current Situation," *Congressional Quarterly*, vol. 11, no. 22, June 8, 2001, pp. 496–98.

55. Josef Hebert, "GAO: Indefinitely Delay Yucca N-Waste Decision," *The Salt Lake Tribune*, December 1, 2001.

56. Editorial, "Is Nuclear Power Ready?" *Scientific American*, vol. 286, no. 1, January 2002, p. 6.

57. NO! white paper, p. 8.

58. Ibid.

59. Private Fuel Storage, *Research regarding DEQ Information on Private Fuel Storage*, p. 1.

60. Private Fuel Storage, *Response to Questions about the Operation of the Private Fuel Storage Facility*, p. 12.

61. President Carter's executive order was rescinded during the Reagan administration. Thus, there are no legal barriers to reprocessing spent nuclear fuel in the United States. The primary obstacles to pursuing this option are renewed concerns about the proliferation of weapons-grade plutonium and the fact that reprocessing is expensive. Economically, it is less expensive to mine uranium and fabricate new fuel rods than it is to reprocess spent nuclear fuel. Information furnished by John Parkyn, chairman of the Board of Private Fuel Storage, in a private conversation on January 17, 2003.

62. See KUED interview with Leon Bear, http://www.kued.org/skullvalley/documentary/interviews/bear; see also Jerry D. and Donna Kemp Spangler, "Toxic Utah: Goshutes divided over N-storage," *Deseret News*, February 14, 2001.

For Further Reading

Bryant, Bunyan, ed. *Environmental Justice: Issues, Policies, and Solutions*. Washington, DC: Island Press, 1995.

Bullard, Robert, ed. *Unequal Protection: Environmental Justice and Communities of Color*. San Francisco: Sierra Club, 1994

Camacho, David, ed. *Environmental Injustices: Political Struggles, Race, Class, and the Environment*. Durham, NC: Duke University Press, 1998.

Clayton, Eva M. "One Step Forward, Two Steps Back: Environmental Justice Remains Elusive in Many of Our Communities." *Church and Society*, vol. 86, July–August 1996, 104–111.

Evangelical Lutheran Church in America. *Sufficient, Sustainable Livelihood for All: A Social Statement on Economic Life*. Chicago: Division for Church in Society, 1999.

———. *Caring for Creation: Vision, Hope, and Justice* (ELCA Social Statement). Chicago: Division for Church in Society, 1993.

———. *Freed in Christ: Race, Ethnicity, and Culture* (ELCA Social Statement). Chicago: Division for Church in Society, 1993.

Faber, Daniel. *The Struggle for Ecological Democracy: Environmental Justice Movements in the United States*. New York: Guilford Press, 1998.

Fedorko, Kevin. "In the Valley of the Shadow." *Outside*, May 2000, vol. 25, no. 5, 114–128.

Foreman, Christopher. *The Promise and Peril of Environmental Justice.* Washington, DC: The Brookings Institution Press, 1998.

Lester, James P. *Environmental Justice in the United States: Myths and Realities.* Boulder, CO: Westview Press, 2001.

Manning, Marable. "Environmental Justice: The Power of Making Connections," in *Theology for Earth Community*, Dieter Hessel, ed. Maryknoll, NY: Orbis Books, 155–64.

Massingale, Bryan. "An Ethical Reflection upon 'Environmental Racism:' In the Life of Catholic Social Teaching," in *The Challenge of Global Stewardship*, Drew Christiansen, ed. Notre Dame, IN: University of Notre Dame Press, 1997, 234–250.

Newton, David E. *Environmental Justice: A Reference Handbook.* Santa Barbara, CA: ABC-CLIO, 1996.

Roberts, J. Timmons, and Melissa M. Toffolon-Weiss. *Chronicles from the Environmental Justice Frontline.* New York: Cambridge University Press, 2001.

Weaver, Jace, ed. *Defending Mother Earth: Native American Perspectives on Environmental Justice.* Maryknoll, NY: Orbis Books, 1996.

Webb, Benjamin S., ed. *Fugitive Faith: Conversations on Spiritual, Environmental, and Community Renewal.* Maryknoll, NY: Orbis Books, 1998.

Westra, Laura, and Bill E. Lawson, eds. *Faces of Environmental Racism: Confronting Issues of Global Justice.* 2nd ed. New York: Rowman & Littlefield Publishers, 2001.

Websites

Coalition Against Environmental Racism
http://gladstone.uoregon.edu/~caer/home.html

Environmental Justice Resource Center (EJRC) at Clark Atlanta University
http://www.ejrc.cau.edu/

KUED-7, Public Television Companion Website for Skull Valley Documentary
http://www.kued.org/skullvalley/index_flash.html

Nuclear Energy Institute
http://www.nei.org/

Nuclear Waste Route Maps
http://www.mapscience.org/

President Clinton's Executive Order 12898 on Environmental Justice
http://www.epa.gov/civilrights/docs/eo12898.html

Private Fuel Storage, LLC
http://www.privatefuelstorage.com

Skull Valley Band of the Goshutes
http://skullvalleygoshutes.org

Videotapes

Skull Valley: Radioactive Waste and the American West
2001; 90 minutes
KUED-TV
101 Wasatch Drive
Salt Lake City, Utah 84112
(801) 581-3276 or (800) 477-KUED
http://www.kued.org

11

Chlorine Sunset?

Toxic Waste and the Precautionary Principle

Case

Amanda Felice had been hard at work on her senior thesis at the state university. Her major was environmental studies, a field she had selected in her sophomore year on the basis of her love of animals and passion for a clean environment. One reason she had gone to the university in the first place was its excellent reputation in environmental studies. Her program was well integrated, and her teachers had introduced her to a wide range of disciplines in the natural sciences, social sciences, and humanities. She now felt prepared to enter the interdisciplinary discussions she would encounter after graduation working for a local environmental organization concerned with clean water in the bay.

Her senior thesis on the chlorine chemical industry and its impact on the environment had been a real challenge so far. It required research into chlorine chemistry and the many chlorine-based chemicals the industry had released to the environment. She had also studied the history, economics, and politics of the industry. Last semester she had taken a course in environmental ethics.

Tonight's Earth Day program sponsored by the campus environmental organization gave her further opportunity to evaluate her direction with the thesis. In general, she agreed with Greenpeace that chlorine production should be phased out because so many chlorine-based products have caused harm to both humans and the natural environment. She knew the Greenpeace position from reading Joe Thornton's book, *Pandora's Poison*,[1] but still looked forward to hearing it articulated by a representative from a local environmental group. She would also hear the industry position from an executive at Davis Chemical Company, who would no doubt present the case for continued production. Her conclusion about the phase-out had implications for her senior thesis. She would have to be clearer about the industry perspective in order to make a judgment.

Robert L. Stivers prepared this case and commentary. The case is based on actual events. The names and places have been changed to protect the privacy of those involved.

ERIC HANSEN

Professor Eric Hansen from the university's Chemistry Department led the program off with a summary of chlorine chemistry and its commercial utility. He explained that chlorine is element seventeen in the periodic table and the eleventh most abundant element in nature. "It is found," he said, "mostly joined with sodium as salt, a stable bond in which it poses no threat to human health or the environment. Free chlorine disassociated from sodium is, however, a deadly gas and highly reactive because of its electron structure. It is attracted to elements like sodium because it needs one electron to complete its outer shell of electrons. Sodium is in turn attracted to chlorine because it has one electron to give up. Salt is thus a very stable molecule."

"Years ago," he continued, "chemists found that chlorine could be separated from sodium by passing an electrical current through salt water. The technique is called the chlor-alkali process, and is fundamental to all chlorine-based products. They also discovered that the free chlorine that results, while a deadly gas, could be used to disinfect water, bleach paper, and be easily combined with carbon-based organic molecules to form what are called organochlorines with useful properties.

"The other product of the chlor-alkali process is sodium hydroxide or caustic soda, also with useful properties. Indeed, caustic soda has been the more important in terms of profit for the chlorine chemical industry, although chlorine has attracted far more attention. I mention this," he added, "because it is important to see that caustic soda in a sense drives the production of chlorine. Industry cannot sell caustic soda unless it finds outlets for chlorine gas. And since chlorine gas is so deadly, and deadly because it is reactive with organic matter, industry does not want to ship or store it, but rather recombine it in a more stable and less deadly form as soon as possible.

"The useful properties of organochlorines (over 11,000 have been synthesized to date) are reactivity, persistence, water insolubility, and toxicity. Chlorine adds to the stability of these organic compounds by replacing hydrogen. The chlorine bond is stronger and increases resistance to degradation and further reactivity. Organochlorines generally do not dissolve in water, although many do so in fat. Organochlorines are frequently toxic to other organic matter, a property useful as a cleanser.

"Chemists have synthesized organochlorines to make use of one or more of these properties. Today organochlorines are used to protect crops, fight disease, clean clothes and machinery, and make medical equipment and drugs. The single biggest use is in PVC plastic, better known as vinyl, with multiple uses. Chlorine-based compounds are indeed versatile.

"The same properties that are so useful to industry, however, are also problematic," he went on to say. "Persistence means that they do not break down easily or rapidly in nature. Water insolubility and fat solubility mean they are not readily eliminated as waste by organisms but tend rather to accumulate in fatty tissue and pass on through the food chain in ever greater accumulations. They bioaccumulate, we say. Persistence and bioaccumulation can also work together to magnify the effects of certain organochlorines. Finally, toxicity is both short- and long-term. Elemental chlorine is a deadly gas. Used extensively in the trench warfare of World War I, it is acutely toxic. Chlorine-based compounds are not acutely toxic, but over the long term in sufficient doses can disrupt endocrine systems, cause cancer, impair reproductive systems and cognitive development, and suppress immune systems.

"Organochlorines are rare in nature, their presence almost all a result of the human release of synthesized compounds. They vary greatly in their damaging effects, although relatively little is known about how they work or the extent of damage. Some, like the so-called 'dirty dozen' persistent organic pollutants (POPS) and dioxins, are extremely damaging, the more exposure generally the more damage. The extent of the hazard represented by organochlorines and other chlorine-based compounds has not been definitively established, however. What we do know is that cancer rates are rising, that the rate of species extinction is high, and that habitat degradation is endemic. Nobody knows how much of this environmental damage can be attributed to chlorine.

"Before I close, I should also mention chlorofluorocarbons that deplete the earth's ozone layer. The chlorine industry has all but stopped their production, and the ozone layer is expected to recover, but it will take some time for this to happen. The release of these substances is an example of failure to take proper precautions."

LARRY BURTON

With this final remark Professor Hansen sat down and passed the microphone to Larry Burton, the leader of a local environmental group concerned with air and water pollution in the region. Larry thanked Professor Hansen for his summary and began to make his case for a phase-out of chlorine production.[2]

He started by citing the long train of environmental abuse created by chlorine-based products, especially organochlorines. He noted places like Love Canal in New York State, Times Beach in Missouri, and Cancer Alley on the lower Mississippi River. He reviewed the reactivity, the persistence, the bioaccumulation, and the toxicity of organochlorines. He talked briefly about pesticides, PCBs, and dioxins.

Larry then acknowledged that the chlorine industry had made some effort to clean up its production processes, to test new chemicals before release, and to curtail production of the dirty dozen and other obviously harmful organochlorines. He further acknowledged the industry's role in negotiating the POPS treaty to eliminate persistent pollutants. Finally, he saw progress in reducing the discharge of dioxins from incinerators and in general more effective management of the waste stream.

"In spite of these gains," he said, "we are still running a grand experiment on the health of humans, other species, and ecosystems. We continue to release chlorine in its many forms to the environment without knowing much about effects. What we do know about chlorine chemistry and past damage should put us on alert. Even though there is great variability in the capacity of these chemicals to cause damage, we have ample reason to suspect harm." Professor Hansen spoke about rising cancer rates, species extinction, and habitat degradation. "These are just the tip of the iceberg," he added.

"The efforts to manage this experiment rely on something that former Greenpeace associate Joe Thornton calls the 'risk paradigm.' The risk paradigm calls for managing individual pollutants using science-based technology. Studies of toxicity and of effects on human health (epidemiological studies) are used to assess health risks and damage to the environment. Safe levels of release are calculated by experimenting with laboratory animals and then extrapolating these findings to humans. If the risk is high, industry ceases production or does not produce the chemical in question in the first place. Otherwise it uses pollution control devices and improved waste control techniques to reduce whatever risk there may be. Whether risk is acceptable depends further on cost/benefit analysis where risk is weighed against the economic and social benefits of a product. If the benefits are high and the risk relatively low, industry proceeds with production."

At this point a hand shot up. "Has the risk paradigm worked?" asked a student. "It seems to me the record is rather mixed, at least if what you say is correct."

"The risk paradigm looks good on paper," Larry answered, "but it doesn't work very well and masks a lot of hazards. It has failed for several reasons. It focuses on localized health risks and misses the subtle and long-term effects on species and ecosystems. It considers only the risks that can be counted. It takes for granted the accuracy of scientists and technologists who measure and assess risk and extrapolate from laboratory animals to humans. It takes an atomistic and reductionistic view of cause and effect by focusing on individual chemicals and making simplifying assumptions about the chemicals studied. It assumes there are acceptable levels of risk that are measurable even at low doses. In fact low doses are seldom calculated and pose substantial hazards. It also assumes that biological systems have some capacity to assimilate toxic substances, an assumption that is difficult to confirm because these systems are extremely complex, the variables to factor in are so numerous, and the number of organochlorines so great. If biologists have learned anything in recent years, it is how little they know about complex ecosystems. Toxicologists and epidemiologists are nowhere near being able to predict or diagnose the long-term effects of low doses.

"They are also unsure about extrapolating from animals to humans. They have barely begun to assess the total pollution burden on health and the synergistic effects among chemicals. Finally, the risk paradigm assumes that regulation, industry good will, and pollution control will keep toxic damage to acceptable levels. These are also questionable assumptions; and even if accurate, they are not safe assumptions given our present state of scientific knowledge.

"The chemical industry parades the risk paradigm with all these flaws as 'sound science,' thereby creating the illusion that toxic pollution is under control and things are getting better. The industry sprinkles its risk assessments with precise numbers to suggest scientific objectivity and pads its cost/benefit analyses by understating the hazards and overstating the benefits. The risk paradigm is human-centered, or, as we say, anthropocentric, disconnected from nature, and atomistic. It is informed by notions of domination. In short, it is the ideological perspective of those who want to use the environment for profit. It is politics in the disguise of 'sound science.'

"Fortunately, there are alternatives," he insisted. "To start with, I suggest a paradigm shift, an alternative worldview. Following Thornton, I call it the 'ecological paradigm.' It is a perspective that is already well established in the environmental community and spreading rapidly. In contrast to the risk paradigm, it takes a biocentric, holistic, and integrated approach. It centers on ecosystems and their health and regards humans as parts of ecosystems. It focuses on long-term hazards and uses data from many disciplines. It uses sound scientific knowledge, but recognizes the limits of such knowledge.

"Part of the ecological paradigm is the treatment of organochlorines and other chlorine-based chemicals as a class of chemicals. Treating chlorine-based chemicals as a class stands in contrast to the one-by-one, chemical-by-chemical procedure in the risk paradigm. They are a class because they are produced by the same process and have many of the same harmful properties. This is not a radical approach. We already consider chlorofluorocarbons, PCBs, lead-containing substances, and even alcohol and tobacco as classes. Treating organochlorines as a class of substances avoids the high cost and impracticality of testing the over 11,000 organochlorines already synthesized. It puts the spotlight back on the industrial production of a single element, chlorine, as the constituent element in commercial uses. It points to the hazardous potential of all organochlorines because of persistence, bioaccumulation, and toxicity. Treating organochlorines as a class finally takes into account all that we do not know about how they damage organic systems."

With this statement another student raised her hand. "I have been hearing in class," she said, "about something called the precautionary principle. Can you tell us about it?"

"The precautionary principle," Larry explained, "has emerged recently in environmental thinking and has gained a lot of support. Basically, the precautionary principle is about prudence, the long neglected virtue that calls for caution and discretion. Chemicals that may cause damage should not be released to natural environments. While there are numerous definitions of the principle, I think the one by ethicist James Nash is good. His definition reads: 'In the absence of scientific surety, when scientific or other empirical evidence provides substantial reason for thinking that a process or product might cause unwarranted harm to human welfare or ecological integrity, whether that harm is reversible or irreversible, present or future, decision-makers shall exercise due care by acting appropriately to avoid or minimize such risk.'[3]

"In my interpretation of the principle three additional concepts give specificity: (1) reverse onus, (2) zero discharge, and (3) clean production. Reverse onus means that chlorine-related products, especially those containing organochlorines, are presumed guilty until proven innocent. The burden of proof rests on industry to show that organochlorines are safe. This shift reverses the present practice of placing the burden of proof on the public to provide evidence of damage before restrictions are placed.

"The second concept is zero discharge of persistent, bioaccumulative, and toxic substances. This concept has two important implications. First it prohibits all releases by demanding effective pollution control. Second, since pollution control technologies can never be totally effective, it means the phase-out of all persistent, bioaccumulative, and toxic substances, in this case all organochlorines.

"The third concept is clean production, which specifies how zero discharge can be accomplished. It is an approach that emphasizes upstream solutions instead of pollution control. It prevents the generation of pollutants at their source in the chlor-alkali process.

"What I am proposing is a chlorine sunset, a phasing out of organochlorines and other substances using chlorine. I know this will seem to those in the chlorine industry to be a radical policy, but consider the radical things industry is doing to human health and the environment. They are introducing chemicals into nature whose effects are irreversible. Who is the radical anyway? A chlorine sunset is the only way to protect people and the natural environment from toxic organochlorines. We do not have to accomplish this immediately, and it is reversible. As non-toxic alternatives become available, industry should make substitutions. Eventually all chlorine production should end, and with it our radical assault on the environment. Fortunately, cost-effective substitutes are available for most industrial uses of chlorine. Today the case for substitutes is even stronger. Chemical plants and other storage facilities for elemental chlorine are vulnerable to terrorist attacks. Large quantities of hazardous materials are shipped by rail and road and sit in storage tanks waiting to be used. Whole communities could be wiped out."

With that Larry sat down to loud applause. Amanda liked what she heard and joined in the applause. She was troubled, however, by the implications of Larry's paradigm for the chlorine industry and the global economy, especially for employment levels. To accomplish what Larry proposed would mean the end of a highly capitalized industry that employs thousands of workers, provides useful products, and contributes to economic development. Higher prices, assuming substitutes cost more, would put a crimp in the development plans of poorer countries. Larry was asking a lot, especially in an atmosphere of scientific uncertainty, but then past abuses had done a lot of damage to the environment.

LUCIA HERNANDEZ

Amanda hoped the next speaker, Lucia Hernandez, would address these concerns. Lucia was introduced as a corporate executive with Davis Chemical

Company and an associate with the Chlorine Chemical Council, an arm of the industry-wide Chemical Manufacturers Association. Lucia picked up the microphone.

"I am fully aware," she began, "that the chemical industry has in the past released harmful substances to the environment. This is a matter of record. Since becoming aware of the problems, the chlorine industry has taken giant strides to clean up its act. We have ceased the production of suspect chemicals, cleaned up manufacturing processes, dramatically improved the safe use and transport of our products, decreased our waste, undertaken substantial and often costly efforts to test our products, and cooperated with community and government agencies. We are well on our way to being a sustainable industry in the sense that we can maintain levels of production without causing undue harm to the environment. So I am not here tonight to be defensive or rebut critics of the industry who want to shut us down. I will stand on the positive initiatives we have taken and the contributions we make to economic and social life.

"The two previous speakers gave you some idea of the many useful commercial products of the chlorine industry. Chlorine is used in water purification, in prescription and over-the-counter medications, in the manufacture of cars, trucks, and computers, in home and office construction, in food processing and packaging, in plastics, and in the defense industry. The value added to the economy and overall society is tremendous, and I would be happy to share these benefits after the forum with anyone who would like to talk further. But let me instead speak to the environmental issues that are the primary concern of this Earth Day session.

"The foundation for our efforts to be good corporate citizens is the Responsible Care® initiative of the chemical industry started in the late 1980s. With this program each member company of the Chemical Manufacturers Association has committed itself to improve the industry's responsible management of chemicals. The program has several elements. It includes a set of ten Guiding Principles that make health, safety and environmental considerations our highest priorities. Each company signs on to these principles indicating its support.

"The ten principles are given greater specificity by five more detailed codes. First, the Pollution Prevention Code is designed to achieve a reduction in pollutants. It includes a Toxics Release Inventory where we record our emissions to the environment. Second, the Process Safety Code is aimed to prevent fires, explosions, and accidental releases. Third, the Distribution Code commits us to work with the carriers, distributors, contractors, and our own employees to reduce risk. Fourth, the Employee Health and Safety Code works to protect our employees and visitors. Fifth, the Product Stewardship Code makes environmental protection an integral part of designing, manufacturing, marketing, distributing, using, recycling, and disposing of products.

"In addition, the program brings together the chemical industry and local communities for cooperative emergency planning. The program also establishes a public advisory panel made up of knowledgeable leaders in the fields of health, safety, and environmental protection. The program calls for member self-evaluation. We require reports on how each company is implementing the codes. We have credible external performance measures to ensure progress. We have successfully encouraged member companies to assist each other and have measures in place, including disassociating a company from membership, to deal with those companies that do not perform well. All in all, Responsible Care® is one of the best programs of its kind, and we have evidence over the years to support our claims to environmental stewardship. We can demonstrate progress. Again, I would be glad to share more about the program and the evidence of success with you after the forum.

"The ethical basis for our Responsible Care® program is the norm of sustainable development. According to the Brundtland Commission in 1987: 'Sustainable development is globally recognized as meeting the needs of the present without compromising the ability of future generations to meet their own needs.' It consists of three major components: environment, economy, and society. The production of chemicals cannot be sustainable if it destroys its ecological foundation or harms human health. This is obvious.

"At the same time the present generation has a responsibility to pass on to future generations a productive and stable economy to meet basic needs. Productive capacity is determined among other things by the accumulation of capital, the provision of jobs, trade, and technological innovation, all things the chlorine chemical industry does well. We also produce socially useful products. Chlorine-based products are on the market because people want them and are satisfied by what we produce. So environmental concerns are important, but so are economic and social goods."

As Lucia paused, a student raised her hand. "My father," she said, "claims industry codes are so much smoke and mirrors designed to protect profits. When I mentioned sustainable development in a discussion at Christmas time, I though he would have a fit. He argued the concept is much too vague. What do you think?"

"I am glad you asked about that," Lucia answered. "In pursuing a course of sustainable development we have made an important discovery. In the 1960s and 1970s environmental improvement focused on pollution abatement, that is to say, end of pipe remediation. Environmental protection was looked on as a cost of production and a drain on profits.

"During the 1980s we shifted to a philosophy of pollution prevention. We found that prevention actually paid for itself by reducing wastes and fees for waste disposal. It also lowered our costs as we learned to recycle wastes and even to create new products by turning waste into a resource and by increasing efficiency as newer and cleaner technologies replaced those that were older and dirtier. Pollution prevention turned from a cost to a source of profit, reduced regulatory pressures, increased customer loyalty, improved financial performance, and pleased our shareholders. We firmly believe the norm of sustainable development that is the basis of our Responsible Care® program is a win-win for us, the environment, the economy, and society. Yes, we seek to be profitable. If we did not, we would go out of business and our workers would lose their jobs."

As Lucia paused, another student raised her hand and said: "The previous speaker, Mr. Burton, talked about the precautionary principle. What is your take on that?"

"We support this principle," she said, "although sometimes we find it vague, misleading, and given to extreme misinterpretations. We in the chlorine chemical industry believe that risks from our products are effectively managed by our Responsible Care® program and existing regulatory frameworks. We are practicing the precautionary principle.

"We recognize, however, there are those like Mr. Burton who think that risk assessment and risk management are inconsistent with the precautionary principle. Indeed, Mr. Burton leaves no room for any chlorine-based products because he dismisses the possibility that scientists and technologists can ever assess risk with acceptable precision. While he claims to use sound science, he only uses it to identify general hazards or intrinsic properties such as persistence and bioaccumulation. He ignores the great number of excellent studies done on specific chlorine-based products by respected toxicologists and epidemiologists. These studies conclude that our products are safe. When it comes to policy, Mr. Burton also ignores the great differences between organochlorines as to persistence, bioaccumulation, and toxicity. Mr. Burton's science seems to stop at the door of scientific principles. It should go on to study specifics. Absolute scientific certainty is rarely achievable, of course, but we are convinced that our products meet the test of safety; and where scientific evidence indicates otherwise, we are prepared to remove unsafe products from the market.

"What we in the chlorine industry advocate is a balanced approach to the precautionary principle. We agree with proponents of the principle that potential risks and uncertainty should be taken into account in risk assessment and management. We agree it is prudent to evaluate impacts of products and processes before they are introduced. We agree it is generally better to prevent adverse impacts than trying to mitigate such impacts after the fact. We agree risk management systems can always be improved.

"With these agreements in mind, here is how we interpret the precautionary principle in situations of risk and uncertainty. We believe:

1) That reasoned judgments can be made about thresholds of exposure, the capacity of systems to assimilate harmful substances, and acceptable levels of risk even when uncertainty remains.
2) That science-based risk assessment is the best tool to determine the seriousness of the hazard and the likelihood of adverse effects.
3) That regulators and industry should not insist on absolute scientific certainty as a precondition of controlling products or processes that may be harmful. By the same token, there should be credible scientific evidence that serious or irreversible harm is likely before restrictions are imposed.

4) That when uncertainties are large and the probabilities of harm remote restrictions are unwarranted.
5) That in situations of unacceptable harm, cost-effective risk management decisions should be selected.
6) That risk management decisions should be proportionate to the harm to be avoided.
7) That risk management decisions should be targeted to a specific chemical or application using best available scientific knowledge.
8) That in situations where substitution of one activity or product by another is considered, the following conditions be met:
    •   The substitute has a comparable function or effectiveness.
    •   Risk assessment and cost/benefit analysis are performed and compared for the original activity or product and the alternative proposed.
    •   The economic impact is proportionate to the environmental benefit.
    •   The substitute is not likely to cause an equally or more burdensome effect on health, safety, and the environment.
9) That decisions to restrict, manage, or substitute factor in economic and social considerations along with health, safety, and environmental impacts.
10) That efforts to reduce uncertainty and make decisions should depend on reasonable judgments about intended use, the potential of human or environmental exposure, the likelihood of harm, and the anticipated benefits of the activity or product.
11) That a credible threat of serious or irreversible harm must be established before the precautionary principle comes into play. Industry should not have to demonstrate the absence of adverse effects as a condition of introducing an activity or product. The absence of adverse effect is impossible to prove, and its use as a precondition would stifle industry and have negative economic consequences.

"To achieve the three major components of sustainable development—environment, economy, and society—we think our interpretation will serve better than outright proscription that focuses only on the environment. We think in addition that our Responsible Care® program satisfies the norm of sustainable development. Finally, we are well aware of our vulnerability to terrorist attack. We have beefed up security at our plants, improved storage facilities, and tried to get information about facilities and storage out of the public domain. Unfortunately, right-to-know groups and even Greenpeace are resisting efforts to limit information by putting it on their websites. This only helps the terrorists."

Lucia sat down to strong applause. Amanda liked the way Lucia turned suspicion of the chemical industry into a positive statement of accomplishments and service. She wondered, however, whether Lucia's characterization of the industry fit actual facts. Was it merely public relations, as one of the students who asked a question seemed to suggest, or was there real substance to the stated environmental concern of the industry? Also, did Lucia reflect the attitudes of managers and workers or just a few on the Chlorine Chemistry Council? She would have to investigate these claims further for her senior thesis.

JANET WHITE

The last speaker was Janet White from the Philosophy Department at the university. Janet was also the current head of the Environmental Studies Program. Amanda had a lot of respect for Janet and wondered how she would draw all this together.

Professor White rose and thanked Eric Hansen, Larry Burton, and Lucia Hernandez for their remarks. She confessed her befuddlement about how the two paradigms that Larry Burton described could be put together to achieve a coherent and effective policy. "The either/or of the situation," she said, "leads to a tug of war that will not clean up the environment. This either/or quality of environmental debates troubles me. Perhaps the best I can do in the time allotted is to present the differences and ask some hard questions.

"First of all I would like to rename Larry Burton's paradigms. Instead of paradigms, I would like to call them perspectives and give them the titles 'conservationist' and 'critical ecology.' Lucia Hernandez and the chlorine industry are conservationists who think in more anthropocentric fashion that nature should be used wisely for human good and that industry can keep risk to acceptable levels with scientific management. This is a time-honored perspective in the American environmental movement often associated with Gifford Pinchot in the early twentieth century.

"Larry comes from an emerging movement in American environmental thought that takes a biocentric approach and is critical of corporate efforts to remove environmental hazards by using scientific management. He is suspicious of management, of the capacity of scientists and technologists to trace the effects of over 11,000 organochlorines, and of finding technological fixes. His foremost interest is the protection of nature and human health.

"To some extent common ground exists. Both want to protect human health and the environment. Both value nature. Both appreciate 'sound science.' This common ground may be a starting point for dialogue, but their differences are profound and raise very important issues. Where, for example, should we stand on the spectrum between anthropocentrism and biocentrism? How much should economic and social good count in environmental decisions? Larry Burton would seem to count them far less than Lucia Hernandez, but then we must understand there will be no human economy or social good without healthy ecosystems. Put in slightly different terms: Are we willing to do a little or a lot of damage to nature to sustain our levels of economic growth and consumption?

"On another front Lucia claims scientists are in a position to determine acceptable levels of release for most toxins. At low levels of toxicity she says the products of the chlorine industry do not cause appreciable harm to the environment. Biological systems have a capacity to assimilate toxins. Larry contends in opposition that almost all organochlorines have some degree of persistence, bioaccumulation, and toxicity. Sound science points to harm, he says, so we should be suspicious of all chlorine-based products and take precautions unless there is definitive proof no harm exists. Since there can be no such definitive proof, chlorine should be phased out, its production eventually stopped at its source.

"This is a tough one to settle. Most established scientists seem to agree with Lucia, but a vocal minority disagrees. There is a high degree of uncertainty about the evidence, however. Non-scientists like myself do not have the tools to determine which side is correct. The waters are further muddied by the future nature of assessments. Both sides have the luxury of foretelling the future without fear of being proven wrong in the present. Verification will only come later on, if at all, and then the predictors will be long gone. So predictions easily follow current self-interest and disguise it. This points to the political nature of all claims to sound science. Science never determines acceptable levels. Humans do. Acceptability is an ethical and political determination. Indeed, both risk assessment and cost/benefit analysis, however helpful, are ultimately ethical and political, at least as currently practiced.

"Still other differences confound our deliberations. Should we consider chlorine-based chemicals as a class in Larry's holistic fashion? Or, alternatively, should we assess persistence, bioaccumulation, and toxicity on a chemical-by-chemical basis in Lucia's atomistic or individualistic approach? Larry's way is doable and reversible, but has rather drastic economic implications in the short run. Lucia's way is cumbersome and might create a lot of health and environmental harm in the long run.

"Who should have the burden of proof? Larry puts it on industry with his concept of reverse onus and would probably call for strict regulations to enforce it. That makes some sense. We test drugs before they go on the market and generally follow the 'polluter pays' principle in our legal framework to fix responsibility. Yet most of us benefit from the goods of chlorine-based products and their relatively low prices. The task of testing over 11,000 organochlorines would be costly, may be impossible, and would probably stifle innovation in the industry.

"Lucia was vague on where to place the burden. On the one hand she seemed to say industry regulated by environmental laws was already testing new chemicals before releasing them to the market. The Responsible Care® program is an indication that industry has accepted some part of the burden of proof. On the other hand in her interpretation of the precautionary principle she seemed to be troubled by governmental regulation and explicitly rejected the imperative that industry demonstrate no adverse effect before the precautionary principle comes into play. Her position is understandable. A strict application of reverse onus would be at best costly and at worst shut down her company.

"Larry also realizes these implications. One thing for sure, who does the determination of proof and what criteria are used will be hotly debated. Lawyers, politicians, and scientists will have plenty of work.

"Here I should also mention that the Responsible Care® program, however well it is doing, is still an industry initiative. While the industry has articulated admirable codes and principles, set up a public advisory board, and developed performance measures, no independent, outside accountability is in place. We have to take its word at face value. This is like students grading their own papers. Most of us would be more willing to accept this were there some system of independent auditing. We require financial audits. Environmental audits by outside auditors would seem appropriate as well.

"As for Lucia's interpretation of sustainability and precaution, she leaves the industry in full control of vague definitions and decisions about cost-benefit analysis. Sustainability needs to be more narrowly defined to ensure protection of the environment, not qualified by so many other considerations as to give industry license to avoid change. The determination of what constitutes precaution needs greater public input. As Lucia's interpretation now stands, it both reverses the meaning of precaution and is not very credible to people like myself.

"The matter of alternatives to organochlorines is another difficult issue. Larry calls for phase-out, not an immediate end to production. He thinks good substitutes exist for almost all uses. The industry differs, pointing to the trade-offs involved and the inadequacy of many substitutes. Lucia worded her interpretation of the precautionary principle on substitutes in such a way that industry could delay indefinitely.

"In conclusion, the debate between the chlorine industry and its most vocal critics is before us. The issues are many and their resolution critical to the future of ecological systems, human health, and levels of human consumption. As with most environmental debates, the two sides talk past each other because their perspectives and vital interests are so different. They seem to live in different worlds. Public awareness is weak at best. Those of us in the middle of this debate have a role to play in keeping pressure on industry and government to reduce the release of persistent, bioaccumulative, and toxic chemicals to the environment. This may seem to be siding with the critics, but without pressure the industry will probably relax.

"For the students in the audience, get yourselves informed first, then act. Don't let complexity and conflicting arguments dampen your spirits. Most important, don't lose your spirit and your sense of inner integrity. Those are the wellsprings of environmental action. Spirit and integrity empower the self especially when they are informed by a good vision of the future. As the Book of Proverbs in the Hebrew Scriptures puts it: 'Without vision the people perish.' For some your vision will come from your religious faith. That is a good source because it is grounded in community, but one whose concrete expression today must be better informed by holistic concerns for both justice and ecology."

With that Janet thanked the audience for attending. "Have a good Earth Week," she added.

AMANDA

As Amanda reflected on the forum the next day, she was not disappointed. The exhortation to get informed struck home. She had a good working knowledge of the issues and now felt renewed vigor for her project and future career. Perhaps this sense of renewal was the spirit Janet was talking about. She needed it. This senior thesis had a long way to go. So what should she conclude about the issues raised? Which of the perspectives should she adopt? Should she include a call for a phase-out in her thesis? Both sides had made reasonable cases. Now it was her turn to make some decisions.

Notes

1. Joe Thornton, *Pandora's Poison: Chlorine, Health, and a New Environmental Strategy* (Cambridge, MA: MIT Press, 2000).
2. Larry Burton's perspective is based on the work of Joe Thornton.
3. The 1998 Wingspread Declaration reads: "When an activity raises threats of harm to the environment or human health, precautionary measures should be taken even if some cause and effect relationships are not fully established scientifically." Article 15 of the Rio Declaration of 1992 reads: "In order to protect the environment, the precautionary approach shall be widely applied by states according to their capabilities. Where there are threats of serious or irreversible damage, lack of full scientific certainty shall not be used as a reason for postponing cost-effective measures to prevent environmental degradation. The Greenpeace definition reads: "Do not admit a substance until you have proof that it will do no harm to the environment."

Commentary

This is a difficult case. It calls for knowledge of chlorine chemistry, the chlorine industry, environmental politics in the United States, and skills in ethics.[1] It features the conflict between economic and environmental goods and more specifically between the "critical ecology" perspective of Larry Burton and the industry position of Lucia Hernandez that stands somewhere between the "developmentalist" and the "conservationist" perspectives described in Chapter One.[2]

The conflict between basic perspectives and the political and economic interests of the two parties makes the setting of public policy extremely difficult. Professor Janet White points to common ground, but it is probably too little for much dialogue. Larry Burton wants a sunset for chlorine-based chemicals and would prefer it sooner rather than later. His case is strengthened by the knowledge that a sunset could be reversed without ecological damage. He does not say who should impose the sunset. Presumably it would be a political decision imposed by government because the industry is highly unlikely to be the agent of its own demise. Whoever imposes the sunset, it could always be reversed without harming the environment.

Lucia Hernandez would have it much later, if at all. More important, she hedges the industry's interpretation of the precautionary principle and seems bent on industry retaining so much control of key processes, for example, risk assessment, cost/benefit analysis, the interpretation of general principles, and the auditing of toxic releases to the environment, that chlorine production and use could go on indefinitely. Not surprisingly, industry wants to be free of restrictions imposed by government or the public. It has a large investment to protect, employee welfare to consider, useful products to sell, and management prerogatives to maintain.

These conflicts of ideology and interest are made worse by scientific uncertainty. Larry Burton's case for sound science is based on past and continuing environmental damage and certain characteristics of chlorine-based chemicals, in particular persistence, bioaccumulation, and toxicity. His case appears to be based mostly on these theoretical characteristics of chlorine-based chemicals, but not entirely. The damage done by PCBs, dioxins, and chlorofluorocarbons, to name just a few, is well documented. Increasing cancer rates, species extinction, and loss of habitat add circumstantial evidence.

Lucia's claim for scientific support rests on the shoulders of toxicologists and epidemiologists whose studies indicate that chlorine chemicals are not alike and vary greatly in persistence, bioaccumulation, and toxicity. Their studies further conclude that many chlorine-based chemicals do not pose an "unacceptable" risk.[3] There is a lot they do not know, however, about the long-term effects of low doses, the total burden that releases of organochlorines place on ecosystems, or the synergistic effects on organisms. More troublesome, many of these chemicals have not been tested and may be causing irreversible environmental effects. A high degree of uncertainty remains after Larry and Lucia make their claims for sound science.

In the midst of this debate, however unprepared, citizens are called to decide between these two perspectives and their scientific claims. Middle ground exists, of course, but these two perspectives set the poles around which all other alternatives are oriented. If Larry Burton is correct, future generations may be healthier and better protected, but they will probably pay higher prices and lose the many benefits of chlorine-based products. If Lucia Hernandez is correct, future generations may enjoy these benefits without harm to ecosystems and human health. It is a tough and frustrating call.

Christians would do well to step back for a moment from the immediacy of this debate to be sure about their foundations. The center of the Christian faith is the relation of individuals and communities to God. Christians are theocentric, not bio- or anthropocentric. This relation to God provides the power of the Spirit that transforms and centers individuals and communities and calls them to take critical and constructive stands in ambiguous circumstances. Not deciding or avoiding responsibility are seldom acceptable.

The call, even imperative, to make tough decisions and to act on them does not tell Christians what they should decide to do. This is a matter of ethical choice based on situational relationships, knowledge of factual information, and ethical norms. This case offers a choice between two perspectives and a range of options on a spectrum between them.

For many, the easiest place to stand is in the middle, that is, to compromise. Indeed, compromise is often a virtue, extremism frequently a vice. Jesus is not a model of compromise, however. On critical issues, he took the way of the cross and did not compromise. Moreover, when it comes to environmental degradation, compromise can be deceptive. For example, if environmental degradation has already caused the decline of a species to a small fraction of its previous numbers, to compromise on what remains is a recipe for extinction. Or, if to compromise means the elimination of 50 percent of a toxic substance, the remaining 50 percent can still cause considerable damage. Compromise on toxic substances is especially dangerous and as a rule seldom acceptable.

Philosopher Holmes Rolston thinks of toxic substances as trumps.[4] According to Rolston, when ecosystems are used as toxic dumps, other uses are overridden and undermined. "The more permanent the poison, the more it counters large amounts of immediate goods." He concludes: "The primacy of the well being of organisms and the integrity of ecosystems, coupled with social and individual goods overriding individual preferences and market interests, makes a toxic threat a veto."

The problems remain, however: What constitutes a toxic substance? Are there acceptable levels of toxicity? Can toxicity be managed? Larry Burton claims all organochlorines are toxic to some degree. Lucia Hernandez and other industry supporters counterclaim that some organochlorines are "acceptably" toxic. Again, the sides are at loggerheads, and decision-makers are left with a high degree of scientific uncertainty, moral ambiguity, and frustration. Perhaps the best that can be said is that industry must be extremely cautious with toxics, governments extremely reluctant to grant release permits, and the public eternally vigilant. This conclusion leads to a consideration of the precautionary principle and the difficult issue of the burden of proof.

THE PRECAUTIONARY PRINCIPLE

All parties agree that prudence is a virtue when it comes to the production, transportation, use, and disposal of chlorine-based chemicals. The case offers a definition of the precautionary principle by James Nash and an endnote with three other definitions. In fact, more than twenty definitions are in current use. None is very precise, and, with the possible exception of Greenpeace, most are given to multiple interpretations. Note, for example, how far apart Larry Burton and Lucia Hernandez are in their interpretations. It would appear that the precautionary principle is another one of those general norms like sustainability that opposing groups use ideologically to support predetermined positions. Can the principle be salvaged? The answer is a provisional yes, the provisions being recognition of its limitations and insistence on a consistency of principle and performance.

First, the precautionary principle is potentially useful as a counterbalance to the power of transnational corporations (TNCs). The characters in the case do not mention an important contextual element in the case, the process of TNC-led globalization. In the past twenty years or so the balance of economic and political power has shifted to TNCs away from government, labor, and the general public. One of the ways TNCs have helped to shift the balance of power their way is by adopting the ethical principles of their critics and interpreting them in ways that preserve and even increase the prerogatives of corporate managers.[5]

In this case the industry presents itself as environmentally responsible by its reliance on risk assessment and cost/benefit analysis and by its adoption of precaution and sustainability as basic principles. These are real gains. Gone is the stonewalling that characterized early encounters between industry and its environmental critics. But what remains is the industry's determination to retain tight control of interpretation and accountability. To counter the power of TNCs, those who use these tools and basic principles must resist corporate self-serving interpretations and insist on wider accountability.

If industry is serious in its use of these tools and principles and not merely co-opting the language of its opponents, it will have to demonstrate it in substantive ways, such as accepting an increasing burden of proof, instituting independent environmental audits, and assuming cradle-to-grave oversight. The industry resists doing these three things, and in its own defense points to several problems.

If regulators put the onus on industry to "prove" a chemical is safe, they make a demand that cannot be met and pursue an unwise policy. Safety cannot be "proven" scientifically, and it is not wise to place the entire burden on industry. The work of independent scientists is critical, and if the economic and social goods of chlorine-based products are as important as many Americans think, then public assistance, particularly for research, development, and pollution control, is not out of the question.

Industry has a point. Accepting an increasing burden of proof does not necessarily imply full responsibility. Larry Burton's interpretation of reverse onus and the precautionary principle would shut the chlorine industry down in short order, indeed, shut most industries and research down because absence of harm can never be proven in any total way. Shutting the chlorine industry down may eventually be desirable or even necessary, but Burton surely knows that large, heavily capitalized chemical corporations will not agree to this. Reverse onus must rather be posed in a way that keeps pressure on the industry and encourages it to assume an increasing burden of cradle-to-grave responsibility for its products. In the not too distant future the public should expect the industry to produce only safe products that can be transported and disposed of without hazard. The safety standard should be high without being so absolutistic as to drive the industry to stonewall in self-defense.

Industry lawyers raise another problem. Independent environmental audits may seem appealing, they claim, but raise severe legal difficulties for producers of chemicals. Audits might reveal past practices that could entail multi-million dollar liabilities. Corporations are reluctant to expose themselves legally, given the adversarial nature of the legal system and the tendency of juries to make large awards. Outside audits could put firms in financial jeopardy and also expose proprietary information.

In rebuttal, critics point out that self-revelation of damage caused by past practices is usually better for companies than independent disclosure. Juries are particularly harsh on companies that withhold information or try to cover up. Critics also contend there are ways to limit liability and to protect proprietary information. Independent audits might also alert management to problems that remain concealed at lower levels of administration.

Assuming cradle-to-grave oversight raises a third problem. Such oversight is not as simple as industry critics maintain. Once chlorine leaves the point of manufacture, responsibility becomes diffuse. Railroads and trucking companies have responsibility for safe transport. Secondary manufacturers have responsibility for storage and for the products they manufacture using chlorine. Consumers have responsibility for the use and disposal of products they purchase. Waste management companies have responsibility for safe disposal at the end of the stream. With such a diffusion of responsibility it is no wonder chlorine manufacturers resist taking full responsibility from cradle to grave. They are prepared to work with transporters, secondary manufacturers, users, and waste managers, but feel that once the chlorine they produce passes into other hands, responsibility must be limited.

These three problems do not take the industry off the hook. The industry needs to take increasing responsibility, and insofar as it does so, is justified in using ethical principles in its own support. In any case, individuals and groups need to keep pressure on industry to accept further responsibility.

Second, the precautionary principle is useful because it embodies the virtue of prudence that is essential to the production and use of toxic substances. That it has not been prominent is clear from the past practice of the industry and the lax oversight of governments and the public. The characters in the case refer to a number of past abuses. The "use first and ask questions later" way of doing things is no longer acceptable. Chlorine is suspect for the very reason that prudence has not been practiced.

In the case Lucia Hernandez' interpretation of the precautionary principle comes within a hair of reversing it. Taken as a whole, her eleven points give wide latitude to the industry. In her last point she insists that harm must be established before the principle goes into effect, and industry should not have to demonstrate the absence of adverse effects before introducing a product or process. That interpretation gives industry permission to introduce new chemicals without precaution. Even the most liberal interpretation of the principle cannot allow such wide latitude.

Third, the precautionary principle assumes a scientific base, another element essential to any environmental strategy. Both Larry and Lucia appeal to sound science; and, as uncertain as the science is at this point, it is still important. There is a compelling need to identify and restrict the production and use of hazardous substances. That the precautionary principle includes a scientific component does not, however, insure objectivity, not with all the uncertainty and the ease with which scientific facts can be confused with political and ideological opinions. Recognizing the political nature of both scientific studies and the precautionary principle does not invalidate them, but should alert decision-makers and put them on guard.

The industry has for a long time thought the only science that counted as sound was that done by established toxicologists and epidemiologists. These scientists have done excellent but limited work. Larry Burton in the case criticizes their efforts as insufficient with regard to chlorine-based chemicals. He includes their work in what he calls the "risk paradigm." The criticisms he makes are generally correct and limit the validity of the reductionary approach of traditional science. They do not invalidate this work, however.

Larry is also correct about the need for another, more holistic approach, that considers the effects of chlorine chemicals on species and ecosystems. He calls it the "ecological paradigm." This approach is also valid. Humans and nature are more soundly served by pursuing both approaches simultaneously.

Fourth, most interpretations of the precautionary principle make room for calculations of proportionality. The more permanent the hazard, the greater the precaution; the lower the scientific certainty to trigger restrictions, the greater the imperative to find acceptable substitutes and the less cost considerations should be a factor. Even Larry Burton seems to accept some degree of proportionality, at least in principle. His principle of reverse onus opens the possibility that some chlorine-based chemicals could be proven to be without hazard.

Calculations of proportionality also raise the question of who should decide. In her interpretation of the precautionary principle where she assigns industry the primary role of decision-making about controversial issues and sound science, Lucia Hernandez also raises this question. Why industry wants free rein is easy enough to comprehend. Still, corporations are "social" institutions, however much they resist efforts by society to restrict and regulate. They have a large number of stakeholders including humans and non-humans whose health and safety are in jeopardy.

While corporations do need room to maneuver in competitive markets, *laissez-faire* is not sufficient, given the persistence, bioaccumulation, and toxicity of chlorine chemicals. Finding the right public-private balance to restriction and regulation will never be easy, but is an essential task of elected officials. And until the effects of chlorine-based chemicals are better understood, strong public oversight seems justified.

Fifth, since almost all organochlorines are suspect for reasons of persistence, bioaccumulation, and toxicity, some level of precaution is in order whenever these chemicals are produced. Substances not found in nature or found only in trace amounts should also be suspect because their absence suggests that they have made little or no contribution to evolutionary fitness. At minimum the precautionary principle places on industry the responsibility for testing new chlorine-based chemicals before placing them on the market. As for chemicals already on the market, the industry should take steps eventually to test each one.

Sixth, the precautionary principle allows for a commitment to full-cost pricing. In the present situation the environmental costs of many chlorine-based products are not known and cannot be known due to limited scientific understanding and the lack of incentives to find out what they are. As costs are identified, they should be counted and included in the price consumers pay.

Seventh and last, the threat of terrorist attack adds, if not a new element, at least a heightened concern for precaution. Here the main problem is the acute toxicity of elemental chlorine. Chemical manufacturers store it in tanks after production in the chlor-alkali process. They ship it by rail. It is stored on site where it awaits use, for example, at municipal water treatment plants. Indeed, one such plant is located on the Potomac River in Washington, DC, within gas cloud range of the Pentagon. Since the terrorist attack on the Pentagon, officials have been frantically redesigning facilities at the plant so chlorine can be stored as chlorine dioxide, a far less toxic form.

Precautions also include increased security for all storage sites and efforts to restrict public access to knowledge about storage.[6] Greenpeace and certain right-to-know groups are currently embroiled with the chemical industry and some public officials over access to previously published materials. Greenpeace insists on making information about chemical plants and storage available, reasoning that it is already in the public domain and accessible to terrorists whatever restrictions are imposed. The chemical industry and public officials object that this is aiding and abetting the enemy. Greenpeace further contends that security considerations add to its case for a sunset. In this they are certainly correct.

The precautionary principle should therefore be retained and used to keep pressure on the chemical industry. The purpose of the principle is eventually to bring industrial practices into line with the capacity of ecological systems to continue their evolutionary trajectory. The principle is an important tool in the service of sustainability.

THE ETHIC OF ECOLOGICAL JUSTICE

The norm of sustainability is also prominent in the case and like the precautionary principle is susceptible to a multiplicity of interpretations and misuses. Larry Burton does not define sustainability, but certainly implies that the release of organochlorines to the environment is not sustainable. Although he does not say much about the norm of economic sufficiency, he seems less concerned about it than the norm of sustainability.

Lucia Hernandez interprets the norm of sustainability more broadly than Larry. She uses the definition of the Brundtland Commission that includes economic sufficiency as a criterion. To environmental sustainability and economic sufficiency she adds social good by which she seems to mean things like safe drinking water and the durability of vinyl. This expansion of the principle allows her to advocate the use of chlorine-based chemicals even if environmental degradation results and serves her interest in continuing production. For Lucia, the economic and social goods of chlorine-based chemicals are compelling and give ample justification for taking some environmental and health risks. Thus interpreted, sustainability becomes the basic principle for the industry's Responsible Care Program®.

In the ethic of ecological justice presented in this volume the principles of sustainability and sufficiency are distinct norms. Both are important and cases where the two norms conflict force difficult choices. In this case they are in conflict as long as suitable substitutes for chlorine-based products are not available.

This twofold concern suggests a stance of using chlorine-based products where threat of harm or hazard is small or non-existent, and substitutes are inadequate or prohibitively expensive. When harm or hazards are substantial, production and use should cease. Where harm and hazards are uncertain or in the middle range, strong measures should be taken to find substitutes even if they are more expensive and reduce levels of overall consumption. This stance is considerably closer to Larry's position than Lucia's, but this is difficult to ascertain because her position could place heavy emphasis on environmental concern in some situations where it is weighed against economic and social good. The industry has, for example, participated and assisted in negotiations leading to the POPS treaty that bans twelve very toxic chemicals.

While the stance taken above allows for a range of options, it does not justify unlimited and expanding production and use of chlorine-based chemicals. Sustainability implies the protection of organisms and ecosystems. Sufficiency implies meeting the basic needs of plants and animals, including humans. The emphasis is on basic, not expanding and unlimited needs. Both norms call humans to reduce their use of chlorine-based chemicals.

The ethic of ecological justice also calls for solidarity with the poor. Solidarity as a norm further complicates the general stance taken above. In some poor countries, for example, DDT is being used to reduce populations of malaria-carrying mosquitoes, which, if unchecked, would cause a much greater number of human deaths. DDT is one of the so-called "dirty dozen" chemicals and hazardous to plants and animals. It is also effective in eliminating mosquitoes and relatively inexpensive, both attributes attractive to poor countries.

The norm of solidarity would seem to support limited use, but this presumes the status quo of rich and poor that consigns some nations to the periphery of the world economy where they remain with little hope for either economic or environmental security. Substitutes for DDT are available and rich countries have a weak record of assisting poor countries. Increased assistance could easily lead to the elimination of DDT. It is also reasonable to extend the meaning of solidarity to include plants and animals. The use of toxic chemicals degrades organisms and ecosystems creating a new class of poor.

THE EARTH CHARTER

This analysis so far has taken a realistic stance toward chlorine chemicals and the industry. By realistic is meant the balancing of political and economic power and the calculation of interests and goods. Room has been left for give and take and the possibility of avoiding the all or nothing of proscribing chlorine chemicals. The problem with such analysis is that it sometimes entails losing sight of goals in the effort to fine-tune calculations and engage in dialogue. The final speaker in the Earth Day program, philosophy professor Janet White, talks about visions of the future. Beginning in the 1970s a number of visionary models appeared that prominently featured environmental concerns.[7] Recently, as a result of inter-religious dialogue, another such vision appeared called *The Earth Charter*.[8] The charter attempts to overcome the limitations of realistic political analysis by keeping the goal of a sustainable future clearly in view.

Like the ethic of ecological justice, *The Earth Charter* has the twofold stress on human well-being and the well-being of species and ecosystems. The charter takes a holistic approach and tries to keep present need and future flourishing in tension. Relevant to this case, it offers the following guidelines:

- Protect and restore the integrity of earth's ecological systems, with special concern for biological diversity and the natural processes that sustain life.
- Adopt at all levels sustainable development plans and regulations that make environmental conservation and rehabilitation integral to all development initiatives.
- Manage the use of . . . resources . . . in ways that minimize . . . environmental damage.
- Prevent harm as the best method of environmental protection and, when knowledge is limited, apply a precautionary approach.
- Take action to avoid the possibility of serious or irreversible environmental harm, even when scientific knowledge is incomplete or inconclusive.
- Place the burden of proof on those who argue that a proposed activity will not cause significant harm, and make the responsible parties liable for environmental harm.
- Ensure that decision-making addresses the cumulative, long-term, indirect, long distance, and global consequences of human activities.
- Prevent pollution of any part of the environment and allow no build-up of radioactive, toxic, or other hazardous substances.
- Adopt patterns of production, consumption, and reproduction that safeguard Earth's regenerative capacities, human rights, and community well-being.
- Reduce, reuse, and recycle the materials used in production and consumption systems, and ensure that residual waste can be assimilated by ecological systems.
- Promote the development, adoption, and equitable transfer of environmentally sound technologies.

- Internalize the full environmental and social costs of goods and services in the selling price, and enable consumers to identify products that meet the highest social and environmental standards.
- Adopt lifestyles that emphasize the quality of life and material sufficiency in a finite world.
- Ensure that economic activities and institutions at all levels promote human development in an equitable and sustainable manner.
- Require multinational corporations and international financial organizations to act transparently in the public good, and hold them accountable for the consequences of their activities.

The vision articulated in *The Earth Charter* is idealistic. Critics will disparage it as utopian, and the industry will resist many of its provisions, frequently missing Janet White's point about the need for vision. Yes, *The Earth Charter* is idealistic, but such visions are needed to criticize present activity, to inspire new practices, institutions, and ideas, and to set direction.

The Earth Charter concludes:

> To realize these aspirations, we must decide to live with a sense of universal responsibility, identifying ourselves with the whole earth community as well as our local communities. We are at once citizens of different nations and of one world in which the local and global are linked. Everyone shares responsibility for the present and future well-being of the human family and the larger living world. The spirit of human solidarity and kinship with all life is strengthened when we live with reverence for the mystery of being, gratitude for the gift of life, and humility regarding the human place in nature.

The Earth Charter and the ethic of ecological justice are normative statements from religious traditions that put more pressure on the chlorine industry than it puts on itself. Appeals to voluntary responsibility are important, and the industry appears willing to go along to a point. Certainly voluntary acceptance of responsibility is better than laws and regulations that create adversarial situations and defensiveness. The history of environmental debates indicates, however, that established industries are normally reluctant to give up practices that involve large capitalization and substantial profits. Again this is understandable, but when it comes down to degrading the very systems that sustain those practices, this reluctance is counterproductive for industry and society. In the face of reluctance, the public must bring pressure to bear on industry and government.

The issue in this case is whether the degradation of nature caused by chlorine-related products warrants increased pressure and regulation. The authors of this book do not presume to answer this question for the reader, but they are certain that the pressure on industry and government must be continued and that overall the well-off in developed countries should be moving in a more biocentric, less consumptive direction.

Notes

1. Go to the websites of the Chlorine Chemistry Council and Greenpeace for further information.

2. See Chapter 1 for the discussion of these perspectives. The environmental concern expressed by Lucia Hernandez is conservationist in tone, but the business orientation of the industry and many of its leaders is probably developmentalist. To the degree that the developmentalist perspective drives the industry, the case may understate the conflict between economic and environmental goods.

3. These studies are available from the Chlorine Chemistry Council.

4. Holmes Rolston, III, *Environmental Ethics: Duties to and Values in the Natural World* (Philadelphia: Temple University Press, 1988), pp. 274ff.

5. This is not to imply that environmental groups have avoided self-serving interpretations. Environmental debates are often ideological and conflictual. Innocence is difficult to find.

6. "New Alarms Heat Up Debate on Publicizing Chemical Risks," *The Wall Street Journal*, 13 June 2002.

7. For example: "A Blueprint for Survival," in *The Ecologist*, vol. 2, no. 1 (Jan. 1972); Herman E. Daly, *Toward a Steady-State Economy* (New York: W.H. Freeman and Company, 1973); and the vision of the "Just, Participative, and Sustainable Society used in church and Society Discussions of the World Council of Churches," in Paul Abrecht, ed., *Faith, Science and the Future* (Geneva: World Council of Churches, 1978).

8. Earth Charter Commission. *The Earth Charter: Values and Principles for a Sustainable Future*, 2000. Available from the website of the Earth Council, http://www.earthcharter.org.

For Further Reading

Costner, P. *The Burning Question: Chlorine and Dioxin*. Washington, DC: Greenpeace, USA, 1997.

Euro Chlor. *The Natural Chemistry of Chlorine in the Environment: An Overview by a Panel of Independent Scientists*. Euro Chlor Publication, 1st Edition, February, 1995.

Fisher, L. J., et al. *Impacts of Chlorine Use on Environmental and Public Health*. Lansing: Michigan Environmental Science Board, http://www.michigan.gov/documents/cl-rpt 3827. 1994.

Freestone, D., and Hey, E., eds. *The Precautionary Principle and International Law*. Boston: Kluwer Law International, 1996.

Official Journal of the International Union of Pure and Applied Chemistry (IUPAC). *White Book on Chlorine*, Volume 68, No. 9, September 1996.

O'Riordan, T., and Cameron, J., eds. *Interpreting the Precautionary Principle*. London: Earthscan Publications, 1994.

Schmittinger, Peter. *Chlorine Principles and Industrial Practice*. Wiley-VCH, 2000.

The Texas Institute for the Advancement of Chemical Technology. *Insights-Chlorine in Perspective*, Volume 6, No. 1, 1995.

Thorton, Joe. *Pandora's Poison: Chlorine, Health, and a New Environmental Strategy*. Cambridge MA: MIT Press, 2000.

Websites

Chlorine Chemistry Council
http://c3.org/

Chlorine Free Products Association
http://www.chlorinefreeproducts.org/

Chlorine Online Information Resource
http://www.eurochlor.org/chlorine/generalinfo/industry.htm

Envirotruth.org: Chlorine
http://envirotruth.org/chlorine.cfm

Greenpeace Report: Chlorine and Dioxin
http://archive.greenpeace.org/~usa/reports/toxics/PVC/burning/rigotoc.html

12

Harvesting Controversy

Genetic Engineering and Food Security
in Sub-Saharan Africa

Case

I

"It's been quite a year," thought Tom Moline. On top of their normal efforts at hunger advocacy and education on campus, the twenty students in the Hunger Concerns group were spending the entire academic year conducting an extensive study of hunger in sub-Saharan Africa. Tom's girlfriend, Karen Lindstrom, had proposed the idea after she returned from a semester-abroad program in Tanzania last spring. With tears of joy and sorrow, she had described for the group the beauty and suffering of the people and land. Wracked by AIDS, drought, and political unrest, the nations in the region are also fighting a losing war against hunger and malnutrition. While modest gains have been made for the more than 800 million people in the world who are chronically malnourished, sub-Saharan Africa is the only region in the world where the number of hungry people is actually increasing. It was not hard for Karen to persuade the group to focus attention on this problem and so they decided to devote one of their two meetings per month to this study. In the fall, Karen and Tom led three meetings examining root causes of hunger in various forms of powerlessness wrought by poverty, war, and drought.

What Tom had not expected was the special attention the group would give to the potential which biotechnology poses for improving food security in the region. This came about for two reasons. One was the participation of Adam Paulsen in the group. Majoring in economics and management, Adam had spent last summer as an intern in the Technology Cooperation Division of Monsanto. Recognized, and often vilified, as a global leader in the field of agricultural biotechnology, Monsanto has also been quietly work-

---

James Martin-Schramm prepared this case and commentary. The case is based on actual events. Names and places have been changed to protect the privacy of those involved.

ing with agricultural researchers around the world to genetically modify crops that are important for subsistence farmers. For example, Monsanto researchers have collaborated with governmental and non-governmental research organizations to develop virus-resistant potatoes in Mexico, "golden mustard" rich in beta-carotene in India, and virus-resistant papaya in Southeast Asia.

In December, Adam gave a presentation to the group that focused on the role Monsanto has played in developing virus-resistant sweet potatoes for Kenya. Sweet potatoes are grown widely in Kenya and other developing nations because they are nutritious and can be stored beneath the ground until they need to be harvested. The problem, however, is that pests and diseases can reduce yields by up to 80 percent. Following extensive research and development that began in 1991, the Kenyan Agricultural Research Institute (KARI) began field tests of genetically modified sweet potatoes in 2001. Adam concluded his presentation by emphasizing what an important impact this genetically modified (GM) crop could have on food security for subsistence farmers. Even if losses were cut only in half, that would still represent a huge increase in food for people who are too poor to buy the food they need.

The second reason the group wound up learning more about the potential biotechnology poses for increasing food production in Kenya was because a new member joined the group. Josephine Omondi, a first-year international student, had read an announcement about Adam's presentation in the campus newsletter and knew right away that she had to attend. She was, after all, a daughter of one of the scientists engaged in biotechnology research at the KARI laboratories in Nairobi. Struggling with homesickness, Josephine was eager to be among people that cared about her country. She was also impressed with the accuracy of Adam's presentation and struck up an immediate friendship with him when they discovered they both knew Florence Wambugu, the Kenyan researcher who had initiated the sweet potato project and had worked in Monsanto's labs in St. Louis.

Naturally, Josephine had much to offer the group. A month after Adam's presentation, she provided a summary of other biotechnology projects in Kenya. In one case, tissue culture techniques are being employed to develop banana varieties free of viruses and other diseases that plague small and large-scale banana plantations. In another case, cloning techniques are being utilized to produce hardier and more productive chrysanthemum varieties, a plant that harbors a chemical, pyrethrum, which functions as a natural insecticide. Kenya grows nearly half the global supply of pyrethrum, which is converted elsewhere into environmentally-friendly mosquito repellents and insecticides.[1]

Josephine reserved the majority of her remarks, however, for two projects that involve the development of herbicide- and insect-resistant varieties of maize (corn). Every year stem-boring insects and a weed named Striga demolish up to 60 percent of Kenya's maize harvest.[2] Nearly 50 percent of the food Kenyans consume is maize, but maize production is falling. While the population of East Africa grew by 20 percent from 1989 to 1998, maize harvests actually declined during this period.[3] Josephine stressed that this is one of the main reasons the number of hungry people is increasing in her country. As a result, Kenyan researchers are working in partnership with the International Maize and Wheat Improvement Center (CIMMYT) to develop corn varieties that can resist Striga and combat stem-borers. With pride, Josephine told the group that both projects are showing signs of success. In January 2002, KARI scientists announced they had developed maize varieties from a mutant that is naturally resistant to a herbicide which is highly effective against Striga. In a cost-effective process, farmers would recover the small cost of seeds coated with the herbicide through yield increases of up to 400 percent.[4]

On the other front, Josephine announced that significant progress was also being made between CIMMYT and KARI in efforts to genetically engineer *"Bt"* varieties of Kenyan maize that would incorporate the gene that produces *Bacillus thuringiensis*, a natural insecticide that is used widely by organic farmers. Josephine concluded her remarks by saying how proud she was of her father and the fact that poor subsistence farmers in Kenya are starting to benefit from the fruits of biotechnology, long enjoyed only by farmers in wealthy nations.

A few days after Josephine's presentation, two members of the Hunger Concerns group asked if they could meet with Tom since he was serving as the group's coordinator. As an environmental studies major, Kelly Ernst is an ardent advocate of organic farming and a strident critic of industrial approaches to agriculture. As much as she respected Josephine, she expressed to Tom her deep concerns that Kenya was embarking on a path that was unwise ecologically and economically. She wanted to have a chance to tell the group about the ways organic farming methods can combat the challenges posed by stem-borers and Striga.

Similarly, Terra Fielding thought it was important that the Hunger Concerns group be made aware of the biosafety and human health risks associated with genetically modified (GM) crops. Like Terra, Tom was also a biology major, so he understood her concerns about the inadvertent creation of herbicide-resistant "superweeds" and the likelihood that insects would eventually develop resistance to *Bt* through prolonged exposure. He also understood Terra's concern that it would be nearly impossible to label GM crops produced in Kenya since most food goes directly from the field to the table. As a result, few Kenyans would be able to make an informed decision about whether or not to eat genetically engineered foods. Convinced that both sets of concerns were significant, Tom invited Kelly and Terra to give presentations in February and March.

The wheels came off during the meeting in April, however. At the end of a discussion Tom was facilitating about how the group might share with the rest of the college what they had learned about hunger in sub-Saharan Africa, Kelly Ernst brought a different matter to the attention of the group: a plea to join an international campaign by Greenpeace to ban GM crops. In the murmurs of assent and disapproval that followed, Kelly pressed ahead. She explained that she had learned about the campaign through her participation in the Environmental Concerns group on campus. They had decided to sign on to the campaign and were now actively encouraging other groups on campus to join the cause as well. Reiterating her respect for Josephine and the work of her father in Kenya, Kelly nevertheless stressed that Kenya could achieve its food security through organic farming techniques rather than the "magic bullet" of GM crops, which she argued pose huge risks to the well-being of the planet as well as the welfare of Kenyans.

Before Tom could open his mouth, Josephine offered a counter proposal. Angry yet composed, she said she fully expected the group to vote down Kelly's proposal, but that she would not be satisfied with that alone. Instead, she suggested that a fitting conclusion to their study this year would be for the group to submit an article for the college newspaper explaining the benefits that responsible use of agricultural biotechnology poses for achieving food security in sub-Saharan Africa, particularly in Kenya.

A veritable riot of discussion ensued among the twenty students. The group appeared to be evenly divided over the two proposals. Since the meeting had already run well past its normal ending time, Tom suggested that they think about both proposals and then come to the next meeting prepared to make a decision. Everybody seemed grateful for the chance to think about it for a while, especially Tom and Karen.

II

Three days later, an intense conversation was taking place at a corner table after dinner in the cafeteria.

"Come on, Adam. You're the one who told us people are hungry because they are too poor to buy the food they need," said Kelly. "I can tell you right now that there is plenty of food in the world; we just need to distribute it better. If we quit feeding 60 percent of our grain in this country to animals, there would be plenty of food for everyone."

"That may be true, Kelly, but we don't live in some ideal world where we can wave a magic wand and make food land on the tables of people in Africa. A decent food distribution infrastructure doesn't exist within most of the countries. Moreover, most people in sub-Saharan Africa are so poor they couldn't afford to buy our grain. And even if we just gave it away, all we would do is impoverish local farmers in Africa because there is no way they could compete with our free food. Until these countries get on their feet and can trade in the global marketplace, the best thing we can do for their economic development is to promote agricultural production in their countries. Genetically modified crops are just one part of a mix of strategies that Kenyans are adopting to increase food supplies. They have to be able to feed themselves."

"Yes, Africans need to feed themselves," said Kelly, "but I just don't think that they need to follow our high-tech approach to agriculture. Look at what industrial agriculture has done to our own country. We're still losing topsoil faster than we can replenish it. Pesticides and fertilizers are still fouling our streams and groundwater. Massive monocultures make crops only more susceptible to plant diseases and pests. At the same time, these monocultures are destroying biodiversity. Our industrial approach to agriculture is living off of biological capital that we are not replacing. Our system of agriculture is not sustainable. Why in God's name would we want to see others appropriate it?"

"But that's not what we're talking about," Adam replied. "The vast majority of farmers in the region are farming a one hectare plot of land that amounts to less than 2.5 acres. They're not buying tractors. They're not using fertilizer. They're not buying herbicides. They can't afford those things. Instead, women and children spend most of their days weeding between rows, picking bugs off of plants, or hauling precious water. The cheapest and most important technology they can afford is improved seed that can survive in poor soils and resist weeds and pests. You heard Josephine's report. Think of the positive impact that all of those projects are going to have for poor farmers in Kenya."

Kelly shook her head. "Come on, Adam. Farmers have been fighting with the weather, poor soils, and pests forever. How do you think we survived without modern farming methods? It can be done. We know how to protect soil fertility through crop rotations and letting ground rest for a fallow period. We also know how to intercrop in ways that cut down on plant diseases and pests. I can show you a great article in *WorldWatch* magazine that demonstrates how organic farmers in Kenya are defeating stem-borers and combating Striga. In many cases they have cut crop losses down to 5 percent. All without genetic engineering and all the dangers that come with it."

Finally Karen broke in. "But if that knowledge is so wide-spread, why are there so many hungry people in Kenya? I've been to the region. Most farmers I saw already practice some form of intercropping, but they can't afford to let their land rest for a fallow period because there are too many mouths to feed. They're caught in a vicious downward spiral. Until their yields improve, the soils will continue to become more degraded and less fertile."

Adam and Kelly both nodded their heads, but for different reasons. The conversation seemed to end where it began; with more disagreement than agreement.

III

Later that night, Tom was in the library talking with Terra about their entomology exam the next day. It didn't take long for Terra to make the connections between the material they were studying and her concerns about *Bt* crops in Kenya. "Tom, we both know what has happened with chemical insecticide applications. After a period of time, the few insects that have an ability to resist the insecticide survive and reproduce. Then you wind up with an insecticide that is no longer effective against pests that are resistant to it. *Bt* crops present an even more likely scenario for eventual resistance because the insecticide is not sprayed on the crop every now and then. Instead, *Bt* is manufactured in every cell of the plant and is constantly present, which means pests are constantly exposed. While this will have a devastating effect on those insects that don't have a natural resistance to *Bt*, eventually those that do will reproduce and a new class of *Bt*-resistant insects will return to munch away on the crop. This would be devastating for organic farmers because *Bt* is one of the few natural insecticides they can use and still claim to be organic."

"I hear you, Terra. But I know that *Bt* farmers in the U.S. are instructed by the seed distributors to plant *refuges* around their *Bt* crops so that some pests will not be exposed to *Bt* and will breed with the others that are exposed, thus compromising the genetic advantage that others may have."

"That's true, Tom, but it's my understanding that farmers are not planting big enough refuges. The stuff I've read suggests that if you're planting 100 acres in soybeans, 20 acres should be left in non-*Bt* soybeans. But it doesn't appear that farmers are doing that. And that's here in the States. How reasonable is it to expect a poor, uneducated farmer in East Africa to understand the need for a refuge and also to resist the temptation to plant all of the land in *Bt* corn in order to raise the yield?"

As fate would have it, Josephine happened to walk by just as Terra was posing her question to Tom. In response, she fired off several questions of her own. "Are you suggesting Kenyan farmers are less intelligent than U.S. farmers, Terra? Do you think we cannot teach our farmers how to use these new gifts in a wise way? Haven't farmers in this country learned from mistakes they have made? Is it not possible that we too can learn from any mistakes we make?"

"Josephine, those are good questions. It's just that we're talking about two very different agricultural situations. Here you have less than two million farmers feeding 280 million people. With a high literacy rate, a huge agricultural extension system, e-mail, and computers, it is relatively easy to provide farmers with the information they need. But you said during your presentation that 70 percent of Kenya's 30 million people are engaged in farming. Do you really think you can teach all of those people how to properly utilize *Bt* crops?"

"First of all, U.S. farmers do not provide all of the food in this country. Where do you think our morning coffee and bananas come from? Rich nations import food every day from developing nations, which have to raise cash crops in order to import other things they need in order to develop, or to pay debts to rich nations. You speak in sweeping generalizations. Obviously not every farmer in Kenya will start planting *Bt* corn tomorrow. Obviously my government will recognize the need to educate farmers about the misuse of *Bt* and equip them to do so. We care about the environment and have good policies in place to protect it. We are not fools, Terra. We are concerned about the biosafety of Kenya."

Trying to take some of the heat off of Terra, Tom asked a question he knew she wanted to ask. "What about the dangers to human health, Josephine? The Europeans are so concerned they have established a moratorium on all new patents of genetically engineered foods and have introduced GM labeling requirements. While we haven't done that here in the U.S., many are concerned about severe allergic reactions that could be caused by foods made from GM crops. Plus, we just don't know what will happen over the long term as these genes interact or mutate. Isn't it wise to be more cautious and go slowly?"

There was nothing slow about Josephine's reply. "Tom, we are concerned about the health and well-being of our people. But there is one thing that you people don't understand. We view risks related to agricultural biotechnology differently. It is reasonable to be concerned about the possible allergenicity of GM crops, and we test for these, but we are not faced primarily with concerns about allergic reactions in Kenya. We are faced with declining food supplies and growing numbers of hungry people. As Terra said, our situations are different. As a result, we view the possible risks and benefits differently. The people of Kenya should be able to decide these matters for themselves. We are tired of other people deciding what is best for us. The colonial era is over. You people need to get used to it."

With that, Josephine left as suddenly as she had arrived. Worn out and reflective, both Tom and Terra decided to return to studying for their exam the next day.

IV

On Friday night, Karen and Tom got together for their weekly date. They decided to have dinner at a local restaurant that had fairly private booths. After Karen's semester in Tanzania last spring, they had learned to cherish the time they spent together. Eventually they started talking about the decision the Hunger Concerns group would have to make next week. After Karen summarized her conversation with Kelly and Adam, Tom described the exchange he and Terra had with Josephine.

Karen said, "You know, I realize that these environmental and health issues are important, but I'm surprised that no one else seems willing to step back and ask whether anyone should be doing genetic engineering in the first place. Who are we to mess with God's creation? What makes us think we can improve on what God has made?"

"But, Karen," Tom replied, "human beings have been mixing genes ever since we figured out how to breed animals or graft branches onto apple trees. We didn't know we were engaged in genetic manipulation, but now we know more about the science of genetics, and that has led to these new technologies. One of the reasons we can support six billion people on this planet is because scientists during the Green Revolution used their God-given intelligence to develop hybrid stocks of rice, corn, and other cereal crops that boosted yields significantly. They achieved most of their success by crossbreeding plants, but that takes a long time and it is a fairly inexact process. Various biotechnologies including genetic engineering make it possible for us to reduce the time it takes to develop new varieties, and they also enable us to transfer only the genes we want into the host species. The first Green Revolution passed by Africa, but this second biotechnology revolution could pay huge dividends for countries in Africa."

"I understand all of that, Tom. I guess what worries me is that all of this high science will perpetuate the myth that we are masters of the universe with some God-given mandate to transform nature in our image. We have got to quit viewing nature as a machine that we can take apart and put back together. Nature is more than the sum of its parts. This mechanistic mindset has left us with all sorts of major ecological problems. The only reason hybrid seeds produced so much food during the Green Revolution is because we poured tons of fertilizer on them and kept them alive with irrigation water. And what was the result? We produced lots of grain but also huge amounts of water pollution and waterlogged soils. We have more imagination than foresight. And so we wind up developing another technological fix to get us out of the problem our last technological innovation produced. Instead, we need to figure out how to live in harmony with nature. Rather than be independent, we need to realize our ecological interdependence. We are made from the dust of the universe and to the dust of the earth we will return."

"Huh, I wonder if anyone would recognize you as a religion major, Karen? I agree that our scientific and technological abilities have outpaced our wisdom in their use, but does that mean we can't learn from our mistakes? Ultimately, aren't technologies just means that we put to the service of the ends we want to pursue? Why can't we use genetic engineering to end hunger? Why would God give us the brains to map and manipulate genomes if God didn't think we could use that knowledge to better care for creation? Scientists are already developing the next wave of products that will give us inexpensive ways to vaccinate people in developing nations from debilitating diseases with foods like bananas that carry the vaccine. We will also be able to make food more nutritious for those that get precious little. Aren't those good things, Karen?"

Karen, a bit defensive and edging toward the other side of the horseshoe-shaped booth, said, "Look, Tom, the way we live is just not sustainable. It scares me to see people in China, and Mexico, and Kenya all following us down the same unsustainable road. There has got to be a better way. Kelly is right. Human beings lived more sustainably in the past than we do now. We need to learn from indigenous peoples how to live in harmony with the earth. But instead, we seem to be tempting them to adopt our expensive and inappropriate technologies. It just doesn't seem right to encourage developing nations like Kenya to make huge investments in biotechnology when less expensive solutions might better address their needs. I really do have my doubts about the ability to teach farmers how to use these new seeds wisely. I've been there, Tom. Farmers trade seeds freely and will always follow a strategy that will produce the most food in the short-term because people are hungry now. Eventually, whatever gains are achieved by biotechnology will be lost as weeds and insects become resistant or the soils just give out entirely from overuse. But I am really struggling with this vote next week because I also know that we should not be making decisions for other people. They should be making decisions for themselves. Josephine is my friend. I don't want to insult her. But I really do think Kenya is heading down the wrong road."

"So how are you going to vote next week, Karen?"

"I don't know, Tom. Maybe I just won't show up. How are you going to vote?"

Notes

1. Florence Wambugu, *Modifying Africa: How Biotechnology Can Benefit the Poor and Hungry; A Case Study from Kenya* (Nairobi, Kenya, 2001), pp. 22–44.

2. J. DeVries and G. Toenniessen, *Securing the Harvest: Biotechnology, Breeding and Seed Systems for African Crops* (New York: CABI Publishing, 2001), p. 103.

3. Ibid., p. 101.

4. Susan Mabonga, "Centre finds new way to curb weed," *Biosafety News* (Nairobi), no. 28, January 2002, pp. 1, 3.

Commentary

This commentary offers background information on global food security, agricultural biotechnology, and genetically modified organisms before it turns to general concerns about genetically modified crops and specific ethical questions raised by the case.

FOOD SECURITY

The nations of the world made significant gains in social development during the latter half of the 20th century. Since 1960, life expectancy has risen by one third in developing nations, child mortality has been cut in half, the percentage of people who have access to clean water has more than doubled, and the total enrollment in primary schools has increased by nearly two-thirds. Similar progress has been made in achieving a greater measure of food security. Even though the world's population has more than doubled since 1960, food production grew at a slightly faster rate so that today per capita food availability is up 24 percent. More importantly, the proportion of people who suffer from food insecurity has been cut in half from 37 percent in 1969 to 18 percent in 1995.[1]

According to the International Food Policy Research Institute, the world currently produces enough food to meet the basic needs for each of the planet's six billion people. Nevertheless, more than 800 million people suffer from food insecurity. For various reasons, one out of every eight human beings on the planet cannot produce or purchase the food they need to lead healthy, productive lives. One out of every three preschool-age children in developing nations is either malnourished or severely underweight.[2] Of these, 14 million children become blind each year due to Vitamin A deficiency. Every day, 40,000 people die of illnesses related to their poor diets.[3]

Food security is particularly dire in sub-Saharan Africa. It is the only region in the world where hunger has been increasing rather than decreasing. Since 1970, the number of malnourished people has increased as the amount of food produced per person has declined.[4] According to the United Nations Development Programme, half of the 673 million people living in sub-Saharan Africa at the beginning of the 21st century are living in absolute poverty on less than $1 a day.[5] Not surprisingly, one third of the people are undernourished. In the eastern portion of this region, nearly half of the children suffer from stunted growth as a result of their inadequate diets, and that percentage is increasing.[6] In Kenya, 23 percent of children under the age of five suffer from malnutrition.[7]

Several factors contribute to food insecurity in sub-Saharan Africa. Drought, inadequate water supplies, and crop losses to pests and disease have devastating impacts on the amount of food that is available. Less obvious factors, however, often have a greater impact on food supply. Too frequently, governments in the region spend valuable resources on weapons, which are then used in civil or regional conflicts that displace people and reduce food production. In addition, many governments—hamstrung by international debt obligations—have pursued economic development strategies that bypass subsistence farmers and focus on the production of cash crops for export. As a result, a few countries produce significant amounts of food, but it is shipped to wealthier nations and is not available for local consumption. Storage and transportation limitations also result in inefficient distribution of surpluses when they are produced within nations in the region.[8]

Poverty is another significant factor. Globally, the gap between the rich and the poor is enormous. For example, the $1,010 average annual purchasing power of a Kenyan pales in comparison with the $31,910 available to a citizen of the United States.[9] Poor people in developing nations typically spend 50–80 percent of their incomes for food, in comparison to the 10–15 percent that people spend in the United States or the European Union.[10] Thus, while food may be available for purchase, fluctuating market conditions often drive prices up to unaffordable levels. In addition, poverty limits the amount of resources a farmer can purchase to "improve" his or her land and increase yields. Instead, soils are worked without rest in order to produce food for people who already have too little to eat.

One way to deal with diminished food supplies or high prices is through the ability to grow your own food. Over 70 percent of the people living in sub-Saharan Africa are subsistence farmers, but the amount of land available per person has been declining over the last thirty years. While the concentration of land in the hands of a few for export cropping plays an important role in this problem, the primary problem is population growth in the region. As population has grown, less arable land and food are available per person. In 1970, Asia, Latin America, and Africa all had similar population growth rates. Since then, Asia has cut its rate of growth by 25 percent, and Latin America has cut its rate by 20 percent.[11] In contrast, sub-Saharan Africa still has a very high population growth rate, a high fertility rate, and an age structure where 44 percent of its population is under the age of fifteen. As a result, the United Nations projects that the region's population will more than double by 2050, even after taking into account the devastating impact that AIDS will continue to have on many countries.[12]

Local food production will need to increase substantially in the next few decades in order to meet the 133 percent projected growth of the population in sub-Saharan Africa. Currently, food aid donations from donor countries represent only 1.1 percent of the food supply. The region produces 83 percent of its own food and imports the rest.[13] Given the limited financial resources of these nations, increasing imports is not a viable strategy for the future. Instead, greater efforts must be made to stimulate agricultural production within the region, particularly among subsistence farmers. Unlike Asia, however, increased production will not likely be achieved through the irrigation of fields and the application of fertilizer. Most farmers in the region are simply too poor to afford these expensive inputs. Instead, the main effort has been to improve the least expensive input: seeds.

A great deal of public and private research is focused on developing new crop varieties that are resistant to drought, pests, and disease and are also hardy enough to thrive in poor soils.[14] While the vast majority of this research utilizes traditional plant-breeding methods, nations like Kenya and South Africa are actively researching ways that the appropriate use of biotechnology can also increase agricultural yields. These nations, and a growing list of others, agree with a recent statement by the United Nations Food and Agriculture Organization:

> Biotechnology provides powerful tools for the sustainable development of agriculture, fisheries and forestry, as well as the food industry. When appropriately integrated with other technologies for the production of food, agricultural products and services, biotechnology can be of significant assistance in meeting the needs of an expanding and increasingly urbanized population in the next millennium. . . . It [genetic engineering] could lead to higher yields on marginal lands in countries that today cannot grow enough food to feed their people.[15]

AGRICULTURAL BIOTECHNOLOGY

The United Nations Convention on Biological Diversity (CBD) defines biotechnology as "any technological application that uses biological systems, living organisms, or derivatives thereof, to make or modify products or processes for specific use."[16] The modification of living organisms is not an entirely new development, however. Human beings have been grafting branches onto fruit trees and breeding animals for desired traits since the advent of agriculture 10,000 years ago. Recent advances in the fields of molecular biology and genetics, however, considerably magnify the power of human beings to understand and transform living organisms.

The cells of every living thing contain genes that determine the function and appearance of the organism. Each cell contains thousands of genes. Remarkably, there is very little difference in the estimated number of genes in plant cells (26,000) and human cells (30,000). Within each cell, clusters of these genes are grouped together in long chains called "chromosomes." Working in isolation or in combination, these genes and chromosomes determine the appearance, composition, and functions of an organism. The complete list of genes and chromosomes in a particular species is called the "genome."[17]

Like their predecessors, plant breeders and other agricultural scientists are making use of this rapidly growing body of knowledge to manipulate the genetic composition of crops and livestock, albeit with unprecedented powers. Since the case focuses only on genetically modified crops, this commentary will examine briefly the use in Africa of the five most common applications of biotechnology to plant breeding through the use of tissue culture, marker-assisted selection, genetic engineering, genomics, and bioinformatics.[18]

Tissue culture techniques enable researchers to develop whole plants from a single cell, or a small cluster of cells. After scientists isolate the cell of a plant that is disease-free or particularly hardy, they then use cloning techniques to produce large numbers of these plants *in vitro*, in a petri dish. When the plants reach sufficient maturity in the laboratory, they are transplanted into agricultural settings where farmers can enjoy the benefits of crops that are dardier or disease-free. In the case, Josephine describes accurately Kenyan successes in this area with regard to bananas and the plants that produce pyrethrum. This attempt to micro-propagate crops via tissue cultures constitutes approximately 52 percent of the activities in the 37 African countries engaged in various forms of biotechnology research.[19]

Marker-assisted selection techniques enable researchers to identify desirable genes in a plant's genome. The identification and tracking of these genes speed up the process of conventional cross-breeding and reduce the number of unwanted genes that are transferred. The effort to develop insect-resistant maize in Kenya uses this technology to identify local varieties of maize that have greater measures of natural resistance to insects and disease. South Africa, Zimbabwe, Nigeria, and Côte d'Ivoire are all building laboratories to conduct this form of research.[20]

Genetic engineering involves the direct transfer of genetic material between organisms. Whereas conventional crossbreeding transfers genetic material in a more indirect and less efficient manner through the traditional propagation of plants, genetic engineering enables researchers to transfer specific genes directly into the genome of a plant *in vitro*. Originally, scientists used "gene guns" to shoot genetic material into cells. Increasingly, researchers are using a naturally occurring plant pathogen, *Agrobacterium tumefaciens*, to transfer genes more successfully and selectively into cells. Eventually, Josephine's father intends to make use of this technology to "engineer" local varieties of maize that will include a gene from *Bacillus thuringiensis (Bt)*, a naturally occurring bacterium that interferes with the digestive systems of insects that chew or burrow into plants. Recent reports from South Africa indicate that smallholder farmers who have planted a *Bt* variety of cotton have experienced "great success."[21]

Genomics is the study of how all the genes in an organism work individually or together to express various traits. The interaction of multiple genes is highly complex and studies aimed at discerning these relationships require significant computing power. Bioinformatics moves this research a step further by taking this genomic information and exploring the ways it may be relevant to understanding the gene content and gene order of similar organisms. For example, researchers recently announced that they had successfully mapped the genomes of two different rice varieties.[22] This information will likely produce improvements in rice yields, but researchers drawing on the new discipline of bioinformatics will also explore similarities between rice and other cereal crops that have not yet been mapped. Nations like Kenya, however, have not yet engaged in these two forms of biotechnology research because of the high cost associated with the required computing capacity.

GENETICALLY MODIFIED ORGANISMS IN AGRICULTURE

The first genetically modified organisms were developed for industry and medicine, not agriculture. In 1972, a researcher working for General Electric engineered a microbe that fed upon spilled crude oil, transforming the oil into a more benign substance. When a patent was applied for the organism, the case made its way ultimately to the U.S. Supreme Court, which in 1980 ruled that a patent could be awarded for the modification of a living organism. One year earlier, scientists had managed to splice the gene that produces human growth hormone into a bacterium, thus creating a new way to produce this vital hormone.[23]

In 1994, Calgene introduced the Flavr-Savr tomato. It was the first commercially produced, genetically modified food product. Engineered to stay on the vine longer, develop more flavor, and last longer on grocery shelves, consumers rejected the product not primarily because it was genetically modified, but rather because it was too expensive and did not taste any better than ordinary tomatoes.[24]

By 1996, the first generation of genetically modified (GM) crops was approved for planting in six countries. These crops included varieties of corn, soybeans, cotton, and canola that had been engineered to resist pests or to tolerate some herbicides. Virus resistance was also incorporated into some tomato, potato, and tobacco varieties.

Farmers in the United States quickly embraced these genetically modified varieties because they reduced the cost of pesticide and herbicide applications, and in some cases also increased yields substantially. In 1996, 3.6 million acres were planted in GM crops. By 2000 that number had grown to

75 million acres and constituted 69 percent of the world's production of GM crops.[25] According to the U.S. Department of Agriculture's 2002 spring survey, 74 percent of the nation's soybeans, 71 percent of cotton, and 32 percent of the corn crop were planted in genetically engineered varieties, an increase of approximately 5 percent over 2001 levels.[26]

Among other developed nations, Canada produced 7 percent of the world's GM crops in 2000, though Australia, France, and Spain also had plantings.[27] In developing nations, crop area planted in GM varieties grew by over 50 percent between 1999 and 2000.[28] Argentina produced 23 percent of the global total in 2000, along with China, South Africa, Mexico, and Uruguay.[29]

In Kenya, no GM crops have been approved for commercial planting, though the Kenyan Agricultural Research Institute (KARI) received government permission in 2001 to field test genetically modified sweet potatoes that had been developed in cooperation with Monsanto.[30] In addition, funding from the Novartis Foundation for Sustainable Development is supporting research that KARI is conducting in partnership with the International Maize and Wheat and Improvement Center (CIMYYT) to develop disease- and insect-resistant varieties of maize, including *Bt* maize.[31] A similar funding relationship with the Rockefeller Foundation is supporting research to develop varieties of maize from a mutant type that is naturally resistant to a herbicide that is highly effective against Striga, a weed that devastates much of Kenya's maize crop each year.[32] Striga infests approximately 2040 million hectares of farmland in sub-Saharan Africa and reduces yields for an estimated 100 million farmers by 20–80 percent.[33]

GENERAL CONCERNS ABOUT GENETICALLY MODIFIED (GM) CROPS

The relatively sudden and significant growth of GM crops around the world has raised various social, economic, and environmental concerns. People in developed and developing countries are concerned about threats these crops may pose to human health and the environment. In addition, many fear that large agribusiness corporations will gain even greater financial control of agriculture and limit the options of small-scale farmers. Finally, some are also raising theological questions about the appropriateness of genetic engineering.

Food Safety and Human Health

Some critics of GM foods in the United States disagree with the government's stance that genetically engineered food products are "substantially equivalent" to foods derived from conventional plant breeding. Whereas traditional plant breeders attempt to achieve expression of genetic material within a species, genetic engineering enables researchers to introduce genetic material from other species, families, or even kingdoms. Because researchers can move genes from one life form into any other, critics are concerned about creating novel organisms that have no evolutionary history. Their concern is that we do not know what impact these new products will have on human health because they have never existed before.[34]

Proponents of genetically engineered foods argue that genetic modification is much more precise and less random than the methods employed in traditional plant breeding. Whereas most genetically engineered foods have involved the transfer of one or two genes into the host, traditional cross-breeding results in the transfer of thousands of genes. Proponents also note that GM crops have not been proven to harm human health since they were approved for use in 1996. Because the United States does not require the labeling of genetically engineered foods, most consumers are not aware that more than half of the products on most grocery store shelves are made, at least in part, from products derived from GM crops. To date, no serious human health problems have been attributed to GM crops.[35] Critics are not as sanguine about this brief track record and argue that it is not possible to know the health effects of GM crops because their related food products are not labeled.

The potential allergenicity of genetically modified foods is a concern that is shared by both critics and proponents of the technology. It is possible that new genetic material may carry with it substances that could trigger serious human allergic reactions. Proponents, however, are more confident than critics that these potential allergens can be identified in the testing process. As a case in point, they note that researchers working for Pioneer Seeds scuttled a project when they discovered that a genetically engineered variety of soybeans carried the gene that produces severe allergic reactions associated with Brazil nuts.[36] Critics, however, point to the StarLink corn controversy as evidence of how potentially dangerous products can easily slip into the human food supply. Federal officials had allowed StarLink corn to be used only as an animal feed because tests were inconclusive with regard to the dangers it posed for human consumption. In September 2000, however, StarLink corn was found first in a popular brand of taco shells and later in other consumer goods. These findings prompted several product recalls and cost Aventis, the producer of StarLink, over $1 billion.[37]

More recently the U.S. Department of Agriculture and the Food and Drug Administration levied a $250,000 fine against ProdiGene Inc. for allowing genetically engineered corn to contaminate approximately 500,000 bushels of soybeans. ProdiGene had genetically engineered the corn to produce a protein that serves as a pig vaccine. When the test crop failed, ProdiGene plowed under the GM corn and planted food grade soybeans. When ProdiGene harvested the soybeans, federal inspectors discovered that some of the genetically engineered corn had grown amidst the soybeans. Under federal law, genetically engineered substances that have not been approved for human consumption must be removed from the food chain. The $250,000 fine helped to reimburse the federal government for the cost of destroying the contaminated soybeans that were fortunately all contained in a storage facility in Nebraska. ProdiGene also was required to post a $1 million bond in order to pay for any similar problems in the future.[38]

Another food safety issue involves the use of marker genes that are resistant to certain antibiotics. The concern is that these marker genes, which are transferred in almost all successful genetic engineering projects, may stimulate the appearance of bacteria resistant to common antibiotics.[39] Proponents acknowledge that concerns exist and are working on ways to either remove the marker genes from the finished product, or to develop new and harmless markers. Proponents also acknowledge that it may be necessary to eliminate the first generation of antibiotic markers through regulation.[40]

Finally, critics also claim that genetic engineering may lower the nutritional quality of some foods. For example, one variety of GM soybeans has lower levels of isoflavones, which researchers think may protect women from some forms of cancer.[41] Proponents of genetically modified foods, meanwhile, are busy trumpeting the "second wave" of GM crops that actually increase the nutritional value of various foods. For example, Swiss researchers working in collaboration with the Rockefeller Foundation, have produced "Golden Rice," a genetically engineered rice that is rich in beta carotene and will help to combat Vitamin A deficiency in the developing world.

Biosafety and Environmental Harm

Moving from human health to environmental safety, many critics of GM crops believe that this use of agricultural biotechnology promotes an industrialized approach to agriculture that has produced significant ecological harm. Kelly summarizes these concerns well in the case. Crops that have been genetically engineered to be resistant to certain types of herbicide make it possible for farmers to continue to spray these chemicals on their fields. In addition, GM crops allow farmers to continue monocropping practices (planting huge tracts of land in one crop variety), which actually exacerbate pest and disease problems and diminish biodiversity. Just as widespread and excessive use of herbicides led to resistant insects, critics argue that insects eventually will become resistant to the second wave of herbicides in GM crops. They believe that farmers need to be turning to a more sustainable form of agriculture that utilizes fewer chemicals and incorporates strip and inter-cropping methodologies that diminish crop losses due to pests and disease.[42]

Proponents of GM crops are sympathetic to the monocropping critique and agree that farmers need to adopt more sustainable approaches to agriculture, but they argue that there is no reason why GM crops cannot be incorporated in other planting schemes. In addition, they suggest that biodiversity can be supported through GM crops that are developed from varieties that thrive in particular ecological niches. In contrast to the Green Revolution where hybrids were taken from one part of the world and planted in another, GM crops can be tailored to indigenous varieties that have other desirable properties. On the herbicide front, proponents argue that GM crops make it possible to use less toxic herbicides than before, thus lowering the risks to consumers. They also point to ecological benefits of the newest generation of herbicides which degrade quickly when exposed to sunlight and do not build up in groundwater.[43] Critics, however, dispute these claims and point to evidence that herbicides are toxic to non-target species, harm soil fertility, and also may have adverse effects on human health.[44]

Just as critics are convinced that insects will develop resistance to herbicides, so also are they certain that insects will develop resistance to *Bt* crops. Terra makes this point in the case. It is one thing to spray insecticides on crops at various times during the growing season; it is another thing for insects to be constantly exposed to *Bt* since it is expressed through every cell in the plant, every hour of the day. While the GM crop will have a devastating impact on most target insects, some will eventually survive with a resistance to *Bt*. Proponents acknowledge that this is a serious concern. As is the case with herbicides, however, there are different variants of *Bt* that may continue to be effective against partially resistant insects. In addition, proponents note that the U.S. Environmental Protection Agency now requires farmers planting *Bt* crops to plant refuges of non-*Bt* crops so that exposed insects can mate with others that have not been exposed, thus reducing the growth of *Bt*-resistant insects. These refuges should equal 20 percent of the cropped area. Critics argue that this percentage is too low and that regulations do not sufficiently stipulate where these refuges should be in relation to *Bt* crops.[45]

Critics are also concerned about the impact *Bt* could have on non-target species like helpful insects, birds, and bees. In May 1999, researchers at Cornell University published a study suggesting that *Bt* pollen was leading to increased mortality among monarch butterflies. This research ignited a firestorm of controversy that prompted further studies by critics and proponents of GM crops. One of the complicating factors is that an uncommon variety of *Bt* corn was used in both the laboratory and the field tests. Produced by Novartis, the pollen from this type was 40–50 times more potent than other *Bt* corn varieties, but it represented less than 2 percent of the *Bt* corn crop in 2000. When other factors were taken into account, proponents concluded that monarch butterflies have a much greater chance of being harmed through the application of conventional insecticides than they do through exposure to *Bt* corn pollen. Critics, however, point to other studies that indicate *Bt* can adversely harm beneficial insect predators and compromise soil fertility.[46]

Both critics and proponents are concerned about unintended gene flow between GM crops and related plants in the wild. In many cases it is possible for genes, including transplanted genes, to be spread through the normal cross-pollination of plants. Whether assisted by the wind or pollen-carrying insects, cross-fertilization could result in the creation of herbicide-resistant superweeds. Proponents of GM crops acknowledge that this could happen, but they note that the weed would be resistant to only one type of herbicide, not the many others that are available to farmers. As a result, they argue that herbicide-resistant superweeds could be controlled and eliminated over a period of time. Critics are also concerned, however, that undesired gene flow could "contaminate" the genetic integrity of organic crops or indigenous varieties. This would be devastating to organic farmers who trade on their guarantee to consumers that organic produce has not been genetically engineered. Proponents argue that this legitimate concern could be remedied with relatively simple regulations or guidelines governing the location of organic and genetically engineered crops. Similarly, they argue that care must be taken to avoid the spread of genes into unmodified varieties of the crop.[47]

Agribusiness and Economic Justice

Shifting to another arena of concern, many critics fear that GM crops will further expand the gap between the rich and the poor in both developed and developing countries. Clearly the first generation of GM crops has been profit-driven rather than need-based. Crops that are herbicide-tolerant and insect-resistant have been developed for and marketed to relatively wealthy, large-scale, industrial farmers.[48] To date, the benefits from these crops have largely accrued to these large producers and not to small subsistence farmers or even consumers. Proponents, however, argue that agricultural biotechnologies are scale-neutral. Because the technology is in the seed, expensive and time-consuming inputs are not required. As a result, small farmers can experience the same benefits as large farmers. In addition, proponents point to the emerging role public sector institutions are playing in bringing the benefits of agricultural biotechnology to developing countries. Partnerships like those described above between KARI, CIMMYT, and various governmental and non-governmental funding sources indicate that the next generation of GM crops should have more direct benefits for subsistence farmers and consumers in developing nations.

While these partnerships in the public sector are developing, there is no doubt that major biotech corporations like Monsanto have grown more powerful as a result of the consolidation that has taken place in the seed and chemical industries. For example, in 1998, Monsanto purchased DeKalb Genetics Corporation, the second largest seed corn company in the United States. One year later, Monsanto merged with Pharmacia & Upjohn, a major pharmaceutical conglomerate. A similar merger took place between Dow Chemical Corporation and Pioneer Seeds.[49] The result of this consolidation is the vertical integration of the seed and chemical industries. Today, a company like Monsanto not only sells chemical herbicides; it also sells seed for crops that have been genetically engineered to be resistant to the herbicide. In addition, Monsanto requires farmers to sign a contract that prohibits them from cleaning and storing a portion of their GM crop to use as seed for the following year. All of these factors lead critics to fear that the only ones who will benefit from GM crops are rich corporations and wealthy farmers who can afford to pay these fees. Critics in developing nations are particularly concerned about the prohibition against keeping a portion of this year's harvest as seed stock for the next. They see this as a means of making farmers in developing nations dependent upon expensive seed they need to purchase from powerful agribusiness corporations.[50]

Proponents acknowledge these concerns, but claim that there is nothing about them that is unique to GM crops. Every form of technology has a price, and that cost will always be easier to bear if one has a greater measure of wealth. They note, however, that farmers throughout the United States have seen the financial wisdom in planting GM crops and they see no reason why farmers in developing nations would not reach the same conclusion if the circumstances warrant. Proponents also note that subsistence farmers in developing nations will increasingly have access to free or inexpensive GM seed that has been produced through partnerships in the public sector. They also tend to shrug off the prohibition regarding seed storage because this practice has been largely abandoned in developed nations that grow primarily hybrid crop varieties. Harvested hybrid seed can be stored for later planting, but it is not as productive as the original seed that was purchased from a dealer. As farmers invest in mechanized agriculture, GM seed becomes just another cost variable that has to be considered in the business called agriculture. Critics, however, bemoan the loss of family farms that has followed the mechanization of agriculture.

The seed storage issue reflects broader concerns about the ownership of genetic material. For example, some developing nations have accused major biotech corporations of committing genetic "piracy." They claim that employees of these corporations have collected genetic material in these countries without permission and then have ferried them back to laboratories in the United States and Europe where they have been studied, genetically modified, and patented. In response to these and other concerns related to intellectual property rights, an international Convention on Biological Diversity was negotiated in 1992. The convention legally guarantees that all nations, including developing countries, have full legal control of "indigenous germplasm."[51] It also enables developing countries to seek remuneration for commercial products derived from the nation's genetic resources. Proponents of GM crops affirm the legal protections that the convention affords developing nations and note that the development of GM crops has flourished in the United States because of the strong legal framework that protects intellectual property rights. At the same time, proponents acknowledge that the payment of royalties related to these rights or patents can drive up the cost of GM crops and thus slow down the speed by which this technology can come to the assistance of subsistence farmers.[52]

Theological Concerns

In addition to the economic and legal issues related to patenting genetic information and owning novel forms of life, some are also raising theological questions about genetic engineering. One set of concerns revolves around the commodification of life. Critics suggest that it is not appropriate for human beings to assert ownership over living organisms and the processes of life that God has created. This concern has reached a fever pitch in recent years during debates surrounding cloning research and the therapeutic potential of human stem cells derived from embryonic tissue. For many, the sanctity of human life is at stake. Fears abound that parents will seek to "design" their children through genetic modification, or that embryonic tissue will be used as a "factory" to produce "spare parts."

While this debate has raged primarily in the field of medical research, some critics of GM crops offer similar arguments. In the case, Karen gives voice to one of these concerns when she suggests that we need to stop viewing nature as a machine that can be taken apart and reassembled in other ways. Ecofeminist philosophers and theologians argue that such a mechanistic mindset allows human beings to objectify and, therefore, dominate nature in the same way that women and slaves have been objectified and oppressed. Some proponents of genetic engineering acknowledge this danger, but argue that the science and techniques of agricultural biotechnology can *increase* respect for nature rather than *diminish* it. As human beings learn more about the genetic foundations of life, it becomes clearer how all forms of life are interconnected. For proponents of GM crops, agricultural biotechnology is just a neutral means that can be put to the service of either good or ill ends. Critics, however, warn that those with power always use technologies to protect their privilege and increase their control.

Another set of theological concerns revolves around the argument that genetic engineering is "unnatural" because it transfers genetic material across species boundaries in ways that do not occur in nature. Researchers are revealing, however, that "lower" organisms like bacteria do not have the same genetic stability as "higher" organisms that have evolved very slowly over time. In bacteria, change often occurs by the spontaneous transfer of genes from one bacterium to another of a different species.[53] Thus, species boundaries may not be as fixed as has been previously thought. Another example can be found in the Pacific yew tree that produces taxol, a chemical that is useful in fighting breast cancer. Recently, researchers discovered that a fungus that often grows on yew trees also produces the chemical. Apparently the fungus gained this ability through a natural transfer of genes across species and even genera boundaries from the tree to the fungus.[54]

Appeals to "natural" foods also run into problems when closer scrutiny is brought to bear on the history of modern crops. For example, the vast majority of the grain that is harvested in the world is the product of modern hybrids. These hybrid crops consist of varieties that could not crossbreed without human assistance. In fact, traditional plant breeders have used a variety of high-tech means to develop these hybrids, including exposure to low-level radiation and various chemicals in order to generate desired mutations. After the desired traits are achieved, cloning techniques have been utilized to develop the plant material and to bring the new product to markets. None of this could have occurred "naturally," if by that one means without human intervention, and yet the products of this work are growing in virtually every farm field. Given the long history of human intervention in nature via agriculture, it is hard to draw a clear line between what constitutes natural and unnatural food.[55]

This leads to a third, related area of theological concern: With what authority, and to what extent, should human beings intervene in the world that God has made? It is clear from Genesis 2 that Adam, the first human creature, is given the task of tending and keeping the Garden of Eden which God has created. In addition, Adam is allowed to name the animals that God has made. Does that mean that human beings should see their role primarily as passive stewards or caretakers of God's creation? In Genesis 1, human beings are created in the image of God (*imago dei*) and are told to subdue the earth and have dominion over it. Does this mean that human beings, like God, are also creators of life and have been given the intelligence to use this gift wisely in the exercise of human dominion?

Answers to these two questions hinge on what it means to be created in the image of God. Some argue that human beings are *substantially* like God in the sense that we possess qualities we ascribe to the divine, like the capacity for rational thought, moral action, or creative activity. These distinctive features confer a greater degree of sanctity to human life and set us apart from other creatures—if not above them. Others argue that creation in the image of God has less to do with being substantially different from other forms of life, and more to do with the *relationality* of God to creation. In contrast to substantialist views which often set human beings above other creatures, the relational conception of being created in the image of God seeks to set humanity in a proper relationship of service and devotion to other creatures and to God. Modeled after the patterns of relationship exemplified in Christ, human relationships to nature are to be characterized by sacrificial love and earthly service.[56]

It is not necessary to choose between one of these two conceptions of what it means to be created in the image of God, but it is important to see how they function in current debates surrounding genetic engineering. Proponents of genetic engineering draw on the substantialist conception when they describe the technology as simply an outgrowth of the capacities for intelligence and creativity with which God has endowed human beings. At the same time, critics draw upon the same substantialist tradition to protect the sanctity of human life from genetic manipulation. More attention, however, needs to be given to the relevance of the relational tradition to debates surrounding genetic engineering. Is it possible that human beings could wield this tool not as a means to garner wealth or wield power over others, but rather as a means to improve the lives of others? Is it possible to use genetic engineering to feed the hungry, heal the sick, and otherwise to redeem a broken world? Certainly many proponents of genetic engineering in the non-profit sector believe this very strongly.

Finally, another theological issue related to genetic engineering has to do with the ignorance of human beings as well as the power of sin and evil. Many critics of genetic engineering believe that all sorts of mischief and harm could result from the misuse of this new and powerful technology. In the medical arena, some forecast an inevitable slide down a slippery slope into a moral morass where human dignity is assaulted on all sides. In agriculture, many fear that human ignorance could produce catastrophic ecological problems as human beings design and release into the "wild" novel organisms that have no evolutionary history.

There is no doubt that human technological inventions have been used intentionally to perpetrate great evil in the world, particularly in the last century. It is also abundantly clear that human foresight has not anticipated enormous problems associated, for example, with the introduction of exotic species in foreign lands or the disposal of high-level nuclear waste. The question, however, is whether human beings can learn from these mistakes and organize their societies so that these dangers are lessened and problems are averted. Certainly most democratic societies have been able to regulate various technologies so that harm has been minimized and good has been produced. Is there reason to believe that the same cannot be done with regard to genetic engineering?

SPECIFIC ETHICAL QUESTIONS

Beyond this review of general concerns about GM crops and genetic engineering are specific ethical questions raised by the case. These questions are organized around the four ecojustice norms that have been discussed in this volume.

Sufficiency

At the heart of this case is the growing problem of hunger in sub-Saharan Africa. It is clear that many people in this region simply do not have enough to eat. In the case, however, Kelly suggests that the world produces enough food to provide everyone with an adequate diet. Is she right?

As noted earlier, studies by the International Food Policy and Research Institute indicate that the world does produce enough food to provide everyone in the world with a modest diet. Moreover, the Institute projects that global food production should keep pace with population growth between 2000 and 2020. So, technically, Kelly is right. Currently, there is enough food for everyone—so long as people would be satisfied by a simple vegetarian diet with very little meat consumption. The reality, however, is that meat consumption is on the rise around the world, particularly among people in developing nations that have subsisted primarily on vegetarian diets that often lack protein.[57] Thus, while it appears that a balanced vegetarian diet for all might be possible, and even desirable from a health standpoint, it is not a very realistic possibility. In addition, Adam raises a series of persuasive arguments that further challenge Kelly's claim that food just needs to be distributed better. At a time when donor nations supply only 1.1 percent of the food in sub-Saharan Africa, it is very unrealistic to think that existing distribution systems could be "ramped up" to provide the region with the food it needs.

Does that mean, however, that GM crops represent a "magic bullet" when it comes to increasing food supplies in the region? Will GM crops end hunger in sub-Saharan Africa? It is important to note that neither Adam nor Josephine make this claim in the case; Kelly does. Instead, Adam argues that GM crops should be part of a "mix" of agricultural strategies that will be employed to increase food production and reduce hunger in the region. When stem-borers and Striga destroy up to 80 percent of the annual maize harvest, herbicide- and insect-resistant varieties could significantly increase the food supply. One of the problems not mentioned in the case, however, is that maize production is also very taxing on soils. This could be remedied, to some extent, by rotating maize with nitrogen-fixing, leguminous crops.

In the end, the primary drain on soil fertility is the heavy pressure which population growth puts on agricultural production. Until population growth declines to levels similar to those in Asia or Latin America, food insecurity will persist in sub-Saharan Africa. One of the keys to achieving this goal is reducing the rate of infant and child mortality. When so many children die in childhood due to poor diets, parents continue to have several children with the hope that some will survive to care for them in their old age. When more children survive childhood, fertility rates decline. Thus, one of the keys to reducing population growth is increasing food security for children. Other keys include reducing maternal mortality, increasing access to a full range of reproductive health services including modern means of family planning, increasing educational and literacy levels, and removing various cultural and legal barriers that constrain the choices of women and girl children.

A third question raised by the sufficiency norm has to do with the dangers GM crops might pose to human health. Does Kenya have adequate policies and institutions in place to test GM crops and protect the health of its citizens? The short answer to this question is no. While the nation does have a rather substantial set of biosafety regulations, government officials have not developed similar public health regulations. One of the reasons for this is because Kenya is still in the research stage and does not yet have any GM crops growing in its fields. Thus, regulations have not yet been developed because there are no GM food products available for consumers. Nevertheless, even when products like GM sweet potatoes or maize do become available, it is likely that Kenya may still not develop highly restrictive public health regulations. This is because the Ministry of Health faces what it perceives to be much more immediate threats to public health from large-scale outbreaks of malaria, polio, and HIV-AIDS. The potential allergenicity of GM crops pales in comparison to the real devastation wrought by these diseases. In addition, it is likely that officials will continue to focus on more mundane problems that contaminate food products like inadequate refrigeration or the unsanitary storage and preparation of food.[58] In the end, people who are hungry tend to assess food safety risks differently from those who are well fed. Hassan Adamu, Minister of Agriculture in Nigeria, summarizes this position well in the following excerpt from an op-ed piece published in *The Washington Post:*

> We do not want to be denied this technology [agricultural biotechnology] because of a misguided notion that we do not understand the dangers and future consequences. We understand. . . . We will proceed carefully and thoughtfully, but we want to have the opportunity to save the lives of millions of people and change the course of history in many

nations. That is our right, and we should not be denied by those with a mistaken idea that they know best how everyone should live or that that they have the right to impose their values on us. The harsh reality is that, without the help of agricultural biotechnology, many will not live.[59]

Despite Adamu's passionate plea, other leaders in Africa are not as supportive of genetically modified crops. During the food emergency that brought over 30 million people in sub-Saharan Africa to the brink of starvation in 2002, President Levy Mwanawasa of Zambia rejected a shipment of genetically modified food aid furnished by the U.N. World Food Programme. Drawing on a report produced by a team of Zambian scientists, and appealing to the precautionary principle, Mwanawasa said, "We will rather starve than give something toxic [to our citizens]."[60] In addition to concerns about the impact that GM food may have on human health, Mwanawasa also expressed concern that the GM maize might contaminate Zambia's local maize production in the future. Given Josephine's ardent support for agricultural biotechnology in the case, it is important to note that not all Africans share her confidence about the benefits of GM crops.

Sustainability

If, however, Kenyans downplay the dangers posed to human beings by GM crops, how likely is it that the nation will develop policies and regulatory bodies to address biosafety and protect the environment?

In fact, Kenya does have serious biosafety policies on the books. Prompted by the work that Florence Wambugu did on GM sweet potatoes in collaboration with Monsanto in the early 1990s, these policies were developed with substantial financial assistance furnished by the government of the Netherlands, the World Bank, the U.S. Agency for International Development, and the United Nations Environment Programme. The *Regulations and Guidelines for Biosafety in Biotechnology in Kenya* establish laboratory standards and other containment safeguards for the handling of genetically modified organisms. In addition, the regulatory document applies more rigorous biosafety standards to GM crops than it does to crops that have not been genetically modified. In general, Kenya's extensive regulations reflect a very cautious approach to GM products.[61]

The problem, however, is that although Kenya has a strong biosafety policy on paper, the administrative means to implement and enforce the policy are weak. The National Biosafety Committee (NBC) was established in 1996 to govern the importation, testing, and commercial release of genetically modified organisms, but limited resources have hampered its effectiveness. In 2001, the NBC employed only one full-time staff person and had to borrow funds to do its work from Kenya's National Council for Science and Technology.[62] One of the consequences of this inadequate regulatory capacity has been a delay in conducting field tests on Wambugu's GM sweet potatoes. Clearly much progress needs to be achieved on this front before such tests take place on varieties of maize that have been genetically modified to be insect- or herbicide-resistant. It is important to note, however, that KARI and CIMMYT are both well aware of the biosafety dangers related to the development of these GM crops and are engaged in studies to determine, for example, the appropriate size and placement of refuges for *Bt* varieties of maize.[63] Because much of KARI's work is supported by grants from foreign donors, necessary biosafety research will be conducted and made available to the NBC. The problem is that the NBC currently lacks the resources to make timely decisions after it receives the data.

Another concern in the case has to do with the ecological consequences of industrial agriculture. Karen disagrees with Tom's glowing account of the Green Revolution. While it produced food to feed more than two billion people during the latter half of the 20th century, it did so only by exacting a heavy ecological toll.[64] It also had a major impact on the distribution of wealth and income in developing nations. As a result, Karen is concerned about Tom's view that GM crops could have a tremendous impact on increasing food supply in sub-Saharan Africa. Karen fears that GM crops in Kenya may open the floodgates to industrial agriculture and create more problems than it solves.

The question, however, is whether this is likely to happen. With the significant poverty and the small landholdings of the over 70 percent of Kenyans who are subsistence farmers, it is hard to see how the ecologically damaging practices of the Green Revolution could have a significant impact in the near future. The cost of fertilizers, herbicides, or irrigation puts these practices out of reach for most farmers in Kenya. If anything, most of the ecological degradation of Kenya's agricultural land is due to intensive cropping and stressed soils. Yield increases from GM crops might relieve some of this pressure, although much relief is not likely since food production needs to increase in order to meet demand.

This raises a third question related to the sustainability norm. Can organic farming methods achieve the same results as GM crops? Certainly Kelly believes that this is the case, and there is some research to support her view. On the Striga front, some farmers in East Africa have suppressed the weed by planting leguminous tree crops during the dry season from February to April. Since Striga is most voracious in fields that have been consistently planted in maize and thus have depleted soil, the nitrogen-fixing trees help to replenish the soil in their brief three months of life before they are pulled up prior to maize planting. Farmers report reducing Striga infestations by over 90 percent with this method of weed control. A bonus is that the uprooted, young trees provide a nutritious feed for those farmers who also have some livestock.[65]

A similar organic strategy has been employed in Kenya to combat stem-borers. In this "push-pull" approach, silver leaf desmodium and molasses grass are grown amidst the maize. These plants have properties that repel stem-borers toward the edges of the field where other plants like Napier grass and Sudan grass attract the bugs and then trap their larvae in sticky substances produced by the plants. When this method is employed, farmers have been able to reduce losses to stem-borers from 40 percent to less than 5 percent. In addition, silver leaf desmodium helps to combat Striga infestation, thus further raising yields.[66]

Results like these indicate that agroecological methods associated with organic farming may offer a less expensive and more sustainable approach to insect and pest control than those achieved through the expensive development of GM crops and the purchase of their seed. Agroecology utilizes ecological principles to design and manage sustainable and resource-conserving agricultural systems. It draws upon indigenous knowledge and resources to develop farming strategies that rely on biodiversity and the synergy among crops, animals, and soils.[67] More research in this area is definitely justified.

It is not clear, however, that agroecological farming techniques and GM crops need to be viewed as opposing or exclusive alternatives. Some researchers argue that these organic techniques are not as effective in different ecological niches in East Africa. Nor, in some areas, do farmers feel they have the luxury to fallow their fields during the dry season.[68] In these contexts, GM crops might be able to raise yields where they are desperately needed. It is also not likely that the seeds for these crops will be very expensive since they are being produced through research in the public and non-profit sectors. Still, it is certainly the case that more serious ecological problems could result from the use of GM crops in Kenya, and even though donors are currently footing the bill for most of the research, agricultural biotechnology requires a more substantial financial investment than agroecological approaches.

Participation

The source of funding for GM crop research in Kenya raises an important question related to the participation norm. Are biotechnology and GM crops being forced on the people of Kenya?

Given the history of colonialism in Africa, this question is not unreasonable, but in this case it would not appear warranted. Kenya's Agricultural Research Institute (KARI) began experimenting with tissue culture and micropropagation in the 1980s. A few years later, one of KARI's researchers, Florence Wambugu, was awarded a three-year post-doctoral fellowship by the U.S. Agency for International Development to study how sweet potatoes could be genetically modified to be resistant to feathery mottle virus. Even though this research was conducted in Monsanto's laboratory facilities, and the company provided substantial assistance to the project long after Wambugu's fellowship ended, it is clearly the case that this groundbreaking work in GM crop research was initiated by a Kenyan to benefit the people of her country.[69] In addition, the funding for GM crop research in Kenya has come almost entirely from public sector institutions rather than private corporate sources. Even the Novartis funds that support the insect-resistant maize project are being provided from a foundation for sustainable development that is legally and financially separate from the Novartis Corporation. Thus, it does not appear that transnational biotechnology corporations are manipulating Kenya, but it is true that the country's openness to biotechnology and GM crops may open doors to the sale of privately developed GM products in the future.

Josephine, however, might turn the colonialism argument around and apply it to Greenpeace's campaign to ban GM crops. Specifically, Greenpeace International urges people around the world to "write to your local and national politicians demanding that your government ban the growing of genetically engineered crops in your country."[70] Though Josephine does not pose the question, is this well-intentioned effort to protect the environment and the health of human beings a form of paternalism or neocolonialism? Does the Greenpeace campaign exert undue pressure on the people of Kenya and perhaps provoke a lack of confidence in Kenyan authorities, or does it merely urge Kenyans to use the democratic powers at their disposal to express their concerns? It is not clear how these questions should be answered, but the participation norm requires reflection about them.

The concern about paternalism also arises with regard to a set of questions about appropriate technology. Are GM crops an "appropriate" agricultural technology for the people of Kenya? Genetic engineering and other forms of agricultural biotechnology are very sophisticated and expensive. Is such a "high-tech" approach to agriculture "appropriate," given the status of a developing nation like Kenya? Is it realistic to expect that undereducated and impoverished subsistence farmers will have the capacities and the resources to properly manage GM crops, for example, through the appropriate use of refuges?

In the case, Josephine responds aggressively to concerns like these when she overhears Terra's conversation with Tom. She asserts that Kenya will do what it takes to educate farmers about the proper use of GM crops, and it is true that KARI is designing farmer-training strategies as a part of the insect-resistant maize project.[71] Compared to other countries in sub-Saharan Africa, Kenya has very high rates of adult literacy. In 2000, 89 percent of men and 76 percent of women were literate. At the same time, only 26 percent of boys and 22 percent of girls are enrolled in secondary education.[72] Thus, while literacy is high, the level of education is low. The hunger and poverty among many Kenyans, however, may be the most significant impediment to the responsible use of GM crops. In a situation where hunger is on the rise, how likely is it that subsistence farmers will plant 20 percent of their fields in non-*Bt* maize if they see that the *Bt* varieties are producing substantially higher yields?

This is a fair question. The norm of participation supports people making decisions that affect their lives, but in this case the immediate threat of hunger and malnutrition may limit the range of their choices. At the same time, GM crops have the potential to significantly reduce the amount of time that women and children spend weeding, picking bugs off of plants, and scaring birds away. Organic farming methods would require even larger investments of time. This is time children could use to attend more school or that women could use to increase their literacy or to engage in other activities that might increase family income and confer a slightly greater degree of security and independence. Aspects of the participation norm cut both ways.

Solidarity

Among other things, the ecojustice norm of solidarity is concerned about the equitable distribution of the burdens and benefits associated with GM crops. If problems emerge in Kenya, who will bear the costs? If GM crops are finally approved for planting, who will receive most of the benefits?

Thus far, critics argue that the benefits of GM crops in developed nations have accrued only to biotech corporations through higher sales and to large-scale farmers through lower production costs. Moreover, critics claim that the dangers GM crops pose to human health and biosafety are dumped on consumers who do not fully understand the risks associated with GM crops and the food products that are derived from them. It is not clear that the same could be said for the production of GM crops in Kenya where these crops are being developed through partnerships in the non-profit and public sectors. Researchers expect to make these products available at little cost to farmers, and few corporations will earn much money from the sale of these seeds. Thus, the benefits from GM crops should accrue to a larger percentage of people in Kenya because 70 percent of the population is engaged in subsistence agriculture. Like developed nations, however, food safety problems could affect all consumers and a case could be made that this would be more severe in a nation like Kenya where it would be very difficult to adequately label GM crop products that often move directly from the field to the dinner table.

Another aspect of solidarity involves supporting others in their struggles. Josephine does not explicitly appeal to this norm in the case, but some members of the Hunger Concerns group are probably wondering whether they should just support Josephine's proposal as a way to show respect to her and to the self-determination of the Kenyan people. There is much to commend this stance and, ultimately, it might be ethically preferable. One of the dangers, however, is that Josephine's colleagues may squelch their moral qualms and simply "pass the buck" ethically to the Kenyans. Karen seems close to making this decision, despite her serious social, ecological, and theological concerns about GM crops. Friendship requires support and respect, but it also thrives on honesty.

CONCLUSION

Tom and Karen face a difficult choice, as do the other members of the Hunger Concerns group. Next week they will have to decide if the group should join the Greenpeace campaign to ban GM crops or whether it wants to submit an article for the campus newspaper supporting the responsible use of GM crops to bolster food security in Kenya. While convenient, skipping the meeting would just dodge the ethical issues at stake. As students consider these alternatives and others, the goods associated with solidarity need to be put into dialogue with the harms to ecological sustainability and human health that could result from the development of GM crops in Kenya. Similarly, these potential harms also need to be weighed against the real harms that are the result of an insufficient food supply. The problem of hunger in sub-Saharan Africa is only getting worse, not better.

Notes

1. Klaus M. Leisinger et al., *Six Billion and Counting: Population and Food Security in the 21st Century* (Washington, DC: International Food Policy Research Institute, 2002), pp. 4–6. I am indebted to Todd Benson, an old friend and staff member at the International Food Policy Research Institute, for better understanding issues related to food security in sub-Saharan Africa.

2. Ibid., p. 57.

3. Per Pinstrup-Andersen and Ebbe Schiøler, *Seeds of Contention: World Hunger and the Global Controversy over GM Crops* (Baltimore: The Johns Hopkins University Press, 2001), p. 61.

4. Klaus M. Leisinger et al., *Six Billion and Counting*, p. 8.

5. Ibid., p. x. Globally, the World Bank estimates that 1.3 billion people are trying to survive on $1 a day. Another two billion people are trying to get by on only $2 a day. Half of the world's population is trying to live on $2 a day or less.

6. J. DeVries and G. Toenniessen, *Securing the Harvest: Biotechnology, Breeding and Seed Systems for African Crops* (New York: CABI Publishing, 2001), pp. 30–31.

7. The World Bank Group, "Kenya at a Glance," accessed on-line April 9, 2002: http://www.worldbank.org/data/countrydata/countrydata.html#DataProfiles.

8. J. DeVries and G. Toenniessen, *Securing the Harvest*, p. 29. See also Per Pinstrup-Andersen and Ebbe Schiøler, *Seeds of Contention*, pp. 59–67. I am indebted to Gary Toenniessen at the Rockefeller Foundation for his wise counsel as I began to research ethical implications of genetically modified crops in sub-Saharan Africa.

9. Population Reference Bureau, *2001 World Population Data Sheet*, book edition (Washington, DC: Population Reference Bureau, 2001), pp. 3–4. I am indebted to Dick Hoehn at Bread for the World Institute for helping me better understand the root causes of hunger in sub-Saharan Africa.

10. Per Pinstrup-Andersen and Ebbe Schiøler, *Seeds of Contention*, pp. 106–107.

11. Ibid.

12. Population Reference Bureau, *2001 World Population Data Sheet*, p. 2.

13. J. DeVries and G. Toenniessen, *Securing the Harvest*, p. 33.

14. Ibid., p. 7, 21.

15. Food and Agriculture Organization, *Statement on Biotechnology*, accessed on-line April 9, 2002: http://www.fao.org/biotech/stat.asp.

16. United Nations Environment Programme, Secretariat of the Convention on Biological Diversity, accessed on-line April 9, 2002: http://www.biodiv.org/convention/articles.asp?lg=0&a=cbd-02.

17. Per Pinstrup-Andersen and Ebbe Schiøler, *Seeds of Contention*, p. 33.

18. J. DeVries and G. Toenniessen, *Securing the Harvest*, pp. 59–66.

19. Ibid., p. 67.

20. International Maize and Wheat Improvement Center and The Kenya Agricultural Research Institute, *Annual Report 2000: Insect Resistant Maize for Africa*

(IRMA) Project, IRMA Project Document, no. 4, September 2001, pp. 1–12.

21. J. DeVries and G. Toenniessen, *Securing the Harvest*, p. 65.

22. Nicholas Wade, "Experts Say They Have Key to Rice Genes," *The New York Times*, accessed on-line April 5, 2002: http://www.nytimes.com/2002/04/05/science/05RICE.html.

23. Daniel Charles, *Lords of the Harvest: Biotech, Big Money, and the Future of Food* (Cambridge, MA: Perseus Publishing, 2001), p. 10.

24. Ibid., p. 139.

25. Per Pinstrup-Andersen and Marc J. Cohen, "Rich and Poor Country Perspectives on Biotechnology," in *The Future of Food: Biotechnology Markets and Policies in an International Setting*, P. Pardey, ed. (Washington, DC: International Food Policy Research Institute, 2001), pp. 34–35. See also, Bill Lambrecht, *Dinner at the New Gene Café: How Genetic Engineering Is Changing What We Eat, How We Live, and the Global Politics of Food* (New York: St., Martin's Press, 2001), p. 7.

26. Philip Brasher, "American Farmers Planting More Biotech Crops This Year Despite International Resistance," accessed on line March 29, 2002: http://www.pressanddakotan.com/stories/032902/ new_0329020005.shtml .

27. Robert L. Paarlberg, *The Politics of Precaution: Genetically Modified Crops in Developing Countries* (Baltimore: The Johns Hopkins University Press, 2001), p. 3.

28. Per Pinstrup-Andersen and Marc J. Cohen, "Rich and Poor Country Perspectives on Biotechnology," in *The Future of Food*, p. 34.

29. Robert L. Paarlberg, *The Politics of Precaution*, p. 3.

30. J. DeVries and G. Toenniessen, *Securing the Harvest*, p. 68. I am indebted to Jill Montgomery, director of Technology Cooperation at Monsanto, for better understanding how Monsanto has assisted biotechnology research and subsistence agriculture in Kenya.

31. International Maize and Wheat Improvement Center and The Kenya Agricultural Research Institute, *Annual Report 2000: Insect Resistant Maize for Africa (IRMA) Project*, pp. 1–12.

32. Susan Mabonga, "Centre finds new way to curb weed," *Biosafety News* (Nairobi), no. 28, January 2002, pp. 1, 3.

33. Debbie Weiss, "New Witchweed-fighting method developed by CIMMYT and Weismann Institute," *Today in AgBioView*, July 12, 2002, accessed on line July 12, 2002: http://www.agbioworld.org/.

34. Miguel A. Altieri, *Genetic Engineering in Agriculture: The Myths, Environmental Risks, and Alternatives* (Oakland, CA: Food First/Institute for Food and Development Policy, 2001), pp. 16–17. Concerns about the dangers GM crops could pose to human and ecological health lead many critics to invoke the "precautionary principle" in their arguments. For more information about this important concept, see sections of the case and commentary for the preceding case "Chlorine Sunset?"

35. Daniel Charles, *Lords of the Harvest*, pp. 303–304.

36. Bill Lambrecht, *Dinner at the New Gene Café*, pp. 46–47.

37. Per Pinstrup-Andersen and Ebbe Schiøler, *Seeds of Contention*, p. 90.

38. Environmental News Service, "ProdiGene Fined for Technology Blunders," accessed on-line December 10, 2002: http://ens-news.com/ens/dec2002/2002-12-09–09.asp#anchor1.

39. Miguel A. Altieri, *Genetic Engineering in Agriculture*, p. 19.

40. Per Pinstrup-Andersen and Ebbe Schiøler, *Seeds of Contention*, pp. 140–141.

41. Miguel A. Altieri, *Genetic Engineering in Agriculture*, p. 19.

42. Ibid., p. 20.

43. Per Pinstrup-Andersen and Ebbe Schiøler, *Seeds of Contention*, pp. 44–45.

44. Miguel A. Altieri, *Genetic Engineering in Agriculture*, pp. 22–23.

45. See Per Pinstrup-Andersen and Ebbe Schiøler, *Seeds of Contention*, pp. 45–46, and Miguel A. Altieri, *Genetic Engineering in Agriculture*, pp. 26–29.

46. See Per Pinstrup-Andersen and Ebbe Schiøler, *Seeds of Contention*, pp. 47–49, and Miguel A. Altieri, *Genetic Engineering in Agriculture*, pp. 29–31. See also Daniel Charles, *Lords of the Harvest*, pp. 247–248; Bill Lambrecht, *Dinner at the New Gene Café*, pp. 78–82; and Alan McHughen, *Pandora's Picnic Basket: The Potential and Hazards of Genetically Modified Foods* (New York: Oxford University Press, 2000), p. 190.

47. See Per Pinstrup-Andersen and Ebbe Schiøler, *Seeds of Contention*, pp. 49–50, and Miguel A. Altieri, *Genetic Engineering in Agriculture*, pp. 23–25. Controversy erupted in 2002 after the prestigious scientific journal *Nature* published a study by scientists claiming that gene flow had occurred between GM maize and indigenous varieties of maize in Mexico. Since Mexico is the birthplace of maize, this study ignited alarm and produced a backlash against GM crops. In the spring of 2002, however, *Nature* announced that it should not have published the study because the study's methodology was flawed. See Carol Kaesuk Yoon, "Journal Raises Doubts on Biotech Study," *The New York Times*, April 5, 2002, accessed on-line April 5, 2002: http://www.nytimes.com/2002/04/05/science/ 05CORN.html.

48. Miguel A. Altieri, *Genetic Engineering in Agriculture*, p. 4.

49. Bill Lambrecht, *Dinner at the New Gene Café*, pp. 113–123.

50. Opposition reached a fever pitch when the Delta and Pine Land Company announced that they had developed a "technology protection system" that would render seeds sterile. The company pointed out that this would end concerns about the creation of superweeds through undesired gene flow, but opponents dubbed the technology as "the terminator" and viewed it as a diabolical means to make farmers entirely dependent on seed companies for their most valuable input, seed. When Monsanto considered purchasing Delta and Pine Land in 1999, Monsanto bowed to public pressure and declared that it would not market the new seed technology if it acquired the company. In the end, it did not. See Bill Lambrecht, *Dinner at the New Gene Café*, pp. 113–123.

51. Robert L. Paarlberg, *The Politics of Precaution*, pp. 16–17.

52. Per Pinstrup-Andersen and Ebbe Schiøler, *Seeds of Contention*, pp. 123–126.

53. Ibid., pp. 33–34.

54. Richard Manning, *Food's Frontier: The Next Green Revolution* (New York: North Point Press, 2000), p. 195.

55. Ibid., 194. See also Per Pinstrup-Andersen and Ebbe Schiøler, *Seeds of Contention*, pp. 80–81.

56. See Douglas John Hall, *Imaging God: Dominion as Stewardship* (Grand Rapids: Eerdmans Publishing Company, 1986), pp. 89–116; and *The Steward: A Biblical Symbol Come of Age* (Grand Rapids: Eerdmans Publishing Company, 1990).

57. Per Pinstrup-Andersen and Ebbe Schiøler, *Seeds of Contention*, pp. 73–75.

58. Robert L. Paarlberg, *The Politics of Precaution*, pp. 58–59.

59. Hassan Adamu, "We'll feed our people as we see fit," *The Washington Post* (September 11, 2000), p. A23; cited by Per Pinstrup-Andersen and Marc J. Cohen, "Rich and Poor Country Perspectives on Biotechnology," in *The Future of Food*, p. 20.

60. James Lamont, "U.N. Withdraws Maize Food Aid From Zambia," *Financial Times* (Johannesburg), December 10, 2002. Reprinted in *Today in AgBioView*, accessed on-line December 11, 2002: http://www.agbioworld.org/.

61. Robert L. Paarlberg, *The Politics of Precaution*, pp. 50–54.

62. Ibid.

63. International Maize and Wheat Improvement Center and the Kenya Agricul-

tural Research Institute, *Annual Report 2000: Insect Resistant Maize for Africa (IRMA) Project*, pp. 15–16.

64. For a brief summary, see a section devoted to the rise of dysfunctional farming in Brian Halweil, "Farming in the Public Interest," in *State of the World 2002* (New York: W.W. Norton & Co., 2002), pp. 53–57.

65. Brian Halweil, "Biotech, African Corn, and the Vampire Weed," *WorldWatch* (September/October 2001), vol. 14, no. 5, pp. 28–29.

66. Ibid., p. 29.

67. Miguel A. Altieri, *Genetic Engineering in Agriculture*, pp. 35–47.

68. These observations are based on remarks made by researchers from sub-Saharan Africa, Europe, and the United States in response to a presentation by Brian Halweil at a conference I attended in Washington, DC, on March 6, 2002. The conference was sponsored by Bread for the World Institute and was titled *Agricultural Biotechnology: Can It Help Reduce Hunger in Africa?*

69. Florence Wambugu, *Modifying Africa: How Biotechnology Can Benefit the Poor and Hungry, A Case Study from Kenya* (Nairobi, Kenya, 2001), pp. 16–17; 45–54.

70. Greenpeace International. Follow "Act!" link at http://www.greenpeace.org/~geneng. Accessed on-line: April 19, 2002.

71. International Maize and Wheat Improvement Center and the Kenya Agricultural Research Institute, *Annual Report 2000: Insect Resistant Maize for Africa (IRMA) Project*, pp. 23–33.

72. Population Reference Bureau, "Country Fact Sheet: Kenya," accessed on-line April 19, 2002: http://www.prb.org/pdf/Kenya_Eng.pdf.

For Further Reading

Altieri, Miguel A. *Genetic Engineering in Agriculture: The Myths, Environmental Risks, and Alternatives*. Oakland, CA: Institute for Food and Development Policy, 2001.

Bailey, Britt, and Lappé, Marc, eds. *Engineering the Farm: Ethical and Social Aspects of Agricultural Biotechnology*. Washington, DC: Island Press, 2002.

Charles, Daniel. *Lords of the Harvest: Biotech, Big Money, and the Future of Food*. Cambridge, MA: Perseus Publishing, 2001.

Conway, Gordon. *The Doubly Green Revolution: Food for All in the 21st Century*. Ithaca, NY: Comstock Publishing Associates, 1997.

DeVries, J., and Toenniessen, G. *Securing the Harvest: Biotechnology, Breeding and Seed Systems for African Crops*. New York: CABI Publishing, 2001.

Halweil, Brian, "Farming in the Public Interest." In *State of the World 2002*. New York: W.W. Norton & Co., 2002, pp. 51–74.

———. "Biotech, African Corn, and the Vampire Weed." *WorldWatch*, vol. 14, no. 5, September/October 2001, pp. 26–31.

Lambrecht, Bill. *Dinner at the New Gene Café: How Genetic Engineering Is Changing What We Eat, How We Live, and the Global Politics of Food*. New York: St. Martin's Press, 2001.

Leisinger, Klaus M., Schmitt, Karin M., and Pandya-Lorch, Rajul. *Six Billion and Counting: Population and Food Security in the 21st Century*. Washington, DC: International Food Policy Research Institute, 2002.

Manning, Richard. *Food's Frontier: The Next Green Revolution*. New York: North Point Press, 2000.

McHughen, Alan. *Pandora's Picnic Basket: The Potential and Hazards of Genetically Modified Foods*. New York: Oxford University Press, 2000.

Paarlberg, Robert L. *The Politics of Precaution: Genetically Modified Crops in Developing Countries*. Baltimore: The Johns Hopkins University Press, 2001.

Pence, Gregory E. *Designer Food: Mutant Harvest or Breadbasket of the World?* Lanham, MD: Rowman & Littlefield, 2002.

Pinstrup-Andersen, Per, and Schiøler, Ebbe. *Seeds of Contention: World Hunger and the Global Controversy over GM Crops*. Baltimore: The Johns Hopkins University Press, 2001.

Pinstrup-Andersen, Per, and Cohen, Marc J. "Rich and Poor Country Perspectives on Biotechnology." In *The Future of Food: Biotechnology Markets and Policies in an International Setting*, edited by Philip G. Pardey. Washington, DC: International Food Policy Research Institute, 2001, pp. 17–47.

Shiva, Vandana. *Protect or Plunder? Understanding Intellectual Property Rights*. London: Zed Books, 2002.

———. *Stolen Harvest: The Hijacking of the Global Food Supply*. Cambridge, MA: South End Press, 1999.

Wambugu, Florence. *Modifying Africa: How Biotechnology Can Benefit the Poor and Hungry, A Case Study from Kenya*. Nairobi, Kenya, 2001.

Websites

Biotechnology Industry Organization
http://www.bio.org/

Greenpeace International
http://www.greenpeace.org/

International Food Policy Research Institute
http://www.ifpri.org/

Pew Institute on Biotechnology and Food
http://www.pewagbiotech.org/

Rockefeller Foundation
http://www.rockfound.org/

Third World Network
http://www.twnside.org.sg/

Union of Concerned Scientists
http://www.ucsusa.org/

United Nations Food and Agriculture Organization
http://www.fao.org/english/index.html

Videotapes

Harvest of Fear
2001; 120 minutes; $19.95
PBS Video
Item code: A5204
PBS Home Video
PO Box 751089
Charlotte, NC 28275
877-PBS-SHOP
www.shop.pbs.org/

Appendix: Resources for Teaching

This appendix contains various teaching resources for courses in environmental ethics. These resources include the description of an ecological autobiography assignment as well as several spectrum exercises that help students physically locate themselves in key debates about environmental ethics. In addition, the appendix contains instructions for examining power dynamics in cases, as well as guidelines for how students can write brief papers or make group presentations about the cases in this volume. These resources are addressed to students and their teachers; thus the style and tone are informal.

REFLECTION PAPER: ECOLOGICAL AUTOBIOGRAPHY

Personal experiences shape the way ethical issues are perceived, analyzed, and assessed. The purpose of this exercise is to reflect on the following question: "How has my relationship to the land and nature influenced the way that I approach environmental issues?" In a brief paper, structure your reflections around the following questions:

- What would you consider to be your most direct experience of nature? Has it been through work (like farming, logging, etc.) or through recreation (hiking, fishing, etc.)?
- How has your relationship to the land been influenced by the experience of your parents, grandparents, and ancestors? How did they acquire land, use it, and relate to nature?
- What have been some of the important historical, social, cultural, and economic factors that have shaped their experiences as well as your own? Were there major events that shaped their lives and changed their relationship to the land (e.g., the Great Depression, wars, social movements, etc.)?
- What insights do you gain from this exercise about ways you have been shaped to view the land and environmental issues?[1]

SPECTRUM EXERCISES: KEY DEBATES IN ENVIRONMENTAL ETHICS

The following set of spectrum exercises enable students to locate themselves physically in three key debates in environmental ethics.[2] The first spectrum exercise involves a dialogue between an anthropocentrist and a biocentrist over the value of other forms of life and the rights of nature. The second exercise focuses on the value of individual forms of life versus protecting the welfare of ecosystems as a whole. The third exercise involves a debate between a proponent of critical ecology and an advocate for ecological reform.

Students begin these exercises by standing in the middle of the room, equidistant from two readers who stand at opposite corners. As the dialogue unfolds between the readers, students are invited to locate themselves physically in the debate after each numbered paragraph is read. That is, they are encouraged to draw themselves closer to the perspective with which they more agree or to recoil from arguments with which they disagree. Often, students find themselves drawn back and forth as they recognize the strengths and weaknesses of either position. Sometimes they reject what they perceive to be false dichotomies and withdraw from both perspectives. When the dialogue ends, students are asked to explain why they are standing where they are in relation to the arguments that were presented. After this experiential introduction, students find it much easier to understand and critique key figures or positions in the field of environmental ethics as they are presented in lectures and readings.

Dialogue 1
Anthropocentrism vs. Biocentrism

BIOCENTRISM	ANTHROPOCENTRISM
1. When I look at the environmental mess we have gotten ourselves into, I think a big part of the problem is our attitudes toward other forms of life. We don't really appreciate or value the diversity of life forms. I've come to believe that all forms of life have equal value, and have an equal right to live and flourish. Until society believes that, we aren't going to be able to resolve the environmental crisis.	2. I agree with your concern for the environment, but I disagree with your views of other forms of life. There's a basic difference between human life and all other forms of life. It is obvious to me that a human life is more valuable than the life of a mosquito or some plant.
3. I knew you would say that! In your view, everything has to be subordinated to humanity. But I believe that *all* forms of life have intrinsic value, not just instrumental value. Mosquitoes may seem obnoxious to us, but they have a place in the scheme of things. And we should care about plants in the rainforest for their own sake, not merely because they might some day be useful to us.	4. Okay. I can agree that all forms of life have *some* value, but that doesn't mean that everything has *equal* value. Different forms of life have different levels of value, and it's clear that human beings have the highest value. Are you telling me that if your child had cancer and that plant in the rainforest held the cure, you wouldn't want someone to harvest it? In a world of many human needs, we have a right, even a duty, to intervene in nature to make life better for humanity.
5. That's the attitude that's at the root of our problems: Thinking that nature exists for our sake. Humans should only intervene in nature to satisfy our basic human needs—and we need to rethink what those really are. We have no right to destroy other forms of life just to satisfy our gluttonous appetite and desires. The human species is one species among all the others and part of an interdependent whole, and we are all of equal value.	6. We're back to where we started, and I still don't believe that all creatures and species are equal. Our rational and moral powers set us apart from all other species. We are the only creatures that can transcend instinct in order to choose whether to do good or evil to another creature. For this reason there is a qualitative difference between the value of human life and all other forms of life. After all, we alone are made in the image of God.

7. I agree with you that human beings have some outstanding abilities that are superior to those of other animals. But other animals also have abilities far superior to ours, such as flying, or the hearing abilities of whales. Isn't it convenient and a bit self-serving that we choose the qualities we do best and construct a hierarchy of values that places us at the top? It's just this tendency towards hierarchical thinking that gets us into problems in the first place!

8. I agree that hierarchical thinking has led to serious problems in Western civilization, but we can't throw the baby out with the bath water. We need to avoid rigid dualisms but we also need to continue making valid and key distinctions. Not all forms of life are of equal value; some are more important than others. It is our God-given responsibility to discern and act on these differences in our calling to be good stewards of creation.

Dialogue 2
Ecological Holism vs. Concern for Individual Life Forms

ECOLOGICAL HOLISM

1. Do you remember the heroic efforts that were made a few years ago to save two whales that were trapped under the ice in Canada? I can appreciate the concern that was demonstrated, but in terms of environmental ethics, I think it was misplaced. We should be more concerned about maintaining the health of the ocean ecosystems that whales depend on, instead of becoming fixated on the plight of those two individual whales.

3. I appreciate your moral sensitivity, but I think that it is a little misguided. We have limited resources available, and we need to focus them on preserving the health of entire ecosystems, rather than on particular animals within them. I think that whenever creatures or species act in ways that undermine the health and integrity of an ecosystem, they can and should be limited—and in some cases eliminated—for the greater ecological good. That includes human beings. There are far too many of us, and our numbers are destroying the ecological well-being of the planet.

INDIVIDUAL CONCERN

2. You're right that we should be concerned about the health of the ecosystems that support all forms of life, but I disagree with you that protecting those eco-systems is more important than the individual lives of those creatures that live within them. The thought that we should not have tried to save those whales is morally repugnant. Each individual animal is a sentient being with rights that should be respected.

4. There's a term for your position and it's called "environmental fascism." We must never try to protect the common good by abandoning individual rights. I think that the best way to protect the integrity of ecological systems is precisely by protecting the environmental rights of all creatures. Sacrificing the lives and rights of individual creatures for the sake of the whole is never morally acceptable—whether those creatures are human or other animals.

5. I'm sorry, but I disagree. The survival of the planet's ecosystems is more important than what happens to individual creatures that live within them. The overall well-being of nature and its ecosystems as a whole is more important than the individual rights of creatures, and we must act accordingly.

6. Your position is exceedingly dangerous. In effect you have declared yourself God, deciding who lives and who dies. If we don't keep a clear focus on the moral value of *each* individual creature, we become morally desensitized to all life and start down that slippery slope of trying to calculate who is worthy to survive and who is not. We have no business doing that!

7. I admit that my position may sound strange at first, but when you think about it, it's humans who have set ourselves up as God with respect to the ecosystem. Always putting emphasis on individual rights is just a way to maintain domination over the ecosystem rather than finding our appropriate place in it.

8. It is outrageous to suggest that a legitimate emphasis on rights can result in the domination of others. The whole concept of rights evolved precisely to protect those who were threatened with domination by others. What we need to do is figure out what to do when rights conflict. This is a task that involves responsibility, not domination.

Dialogue 3
Critical Ecology vs. Ecological Reform

CRITICAL ECOLOGY

ECOLOGICAL REFORM

1. Let's face it, the world is a mess! It seems the more we try to solve things, the more we mess things up. What we need is a completely different understanding of our relationship to and place in the natural world. We will not be able to transform our ecological problems until we transform ourselves, and our societies.

2. Yes, we do need to be more careful and intelligent about our relationship to nature, but we don't need some profound change in our worldview or philosophy to see what is wrong and take action. We can correct our ecologically harmful behavior by using better technologies, by updating our economic theories, and by passing laws with incentives to reduce environmental degradation.

3. Don't get me wrong, I'm not saying that we shouldn't take action where we can, but even those actions will inevitably be flawed until we change some of our basic assumptions about our relationship to the world. For example, we need to get rid of our false notions that neatly separate mind from body, subject from object, and human nature from the rest of nature. We need to cast off our myth of independence and accept our true interdependence with all other forms of life.

4. It is true that our narrow anthropocentric perspective has caused enormous harm. We are deeply indebted to people like you who stress the interdependence of all forms of life. I think we are beginning to understand how we as human beings are dependent on other forms of life and how we need to take care of them in order for all of us to live. We need to be better stewards of the earth.

5. Excuse me, but your stewardship model assumes precisely the paternalistic attitude that we need to reject and avoid. It flows out of a patriarchal and hierarchical mindset—that always has someone or something on top of somebody or something else—"managing" and controlling things for the good of those "underneath." Historically, that has meant men in charge of women, one race in charge of another, owners in charge of workers. I think that this attitude is the underlying root of not only the ecocrisis, but also of racism, sexism, and class exploitation. Until we demolish this foundation of patriarchy, all our efforts will only exacerbate the ecocrisis.

6. Whoa! That was a fast jump from stewardship to patriarchy! We have to be realistic about what we can change. We don't have a lot of time for deep philosophical introspection and creating a whole new culture. Unless we act quickly and wisely in the next 10–20 years, the ecological systems that support life on earth may collapse. We don't have the luxury to spend much time reflecting on *why* we are in this mess; we need to direct our energies toward *how* we can get out of it. For better or worse, given the enormity of the problems that face us, this means working *within* the system we already have in place, and using the technology and political power already available to us.

7. Everyone agrees that we have to act now, immediately, but working within the system is no answer because the system itself *is* the problem! It's what has caused our current problems. We might be able to limit some of the damage in the short term by working within the system, but the only effective long-term solution will require a total transformation of both the system and the culture that supports it.

8. You want to think our way into a new way of acting, but I think we need to *act* our way into a new way of thinking. Utopian thinking will get us nowhere. Reform of the system is possible. Just look at the significant accomplishments of environmental legislation in the U.S. over the last 30 years. Witness the success of the Montreal Protocol to limit the emission of chlorofluorocarbons. Transformation of human beings and social systems takes place one step at a time.

POWER DYNAMICS EXERCISE

Ethical reflection presumes that those engaged in moral deliberation have the power they need to put their values into action. This exercise helps individuals and groups identify and understand the role that power dynamics play in ethical situations.[3]

For individuals engaged in moral deliberation, it is helpful to identify the main characters or forces of power in a case and then develop a diagram or picture that sketches the power dynamics between them. Poster boards, crayons, and other drawing materials can be used in creative ways to complete this exercise.

Groups engaged in moral reflection about a case may want to use various props and draw upon fellow classmates to create a human sculpture that probes the distribution of power in the case. In classroom settings, these sculptures tap into the creativity of students and allow them to step into a case physically in order to identify with certain characters or institutions in the case.

When shared with others, these diagrams and sculptures help identify forces that empower or disempower key players or stakeholders. They can also expose whose voices are heard or not heard within the case. Sometimes they help identify key stakeholders or forces that are invisible in the case as it is presented.

When creating a diagram or sculpture, consider that power can be manifested in many ways. For example, individuals and institutions can wield power politically, economically, socially, or religiously. The following questions may help expose some of the power dynamics in a case:

- How is economic power distributed among characters in the case?
- To what extent do class, race, or gender play a role in the power dynamics?
- Who has the power to make decisions?
- Do laws protect or adversely affect certain people or institutions?
- Are religious or cultural values powerful or disempowered?

Finally, in a book focused on environmental ethics, it is also important to recall the power of nature and the consequences of violating ecological limits.

GUIDELINES FOR CASE BRIEFS

Chapter Three in this volume offers a three-stage method to address the moral problems posed by the cases in this volume. The following guidelines can be used to structure moral deliberation about these cases in written assignments. These guidelines should be revised or supplemented to accommodate diverse learning situations.

The case-study method is a participatory method of learning. It involves the study and discussion of a life-situation for the purpose of discovering general insights. There is no *one* right answer and both the students and the instructor bear responsibility for sharing their insights and points of view in class. Careful preparation is in order not just to insure a good grade, but more importantly to learn and help others to learn. The following notes are some basic suggestions on how to study cases and write case briefs. You will soon develop your own style of working through these cases.

A.   *Preparation*
    1.   Immerse yourself in the case and get to know the details.
- Read the case at least twice;
- Write out the cast of characters;
- Develop a chronology of events;
- Identify the primary ethical problem(s) and possible solutions;
- Consult the case commentary, lectures, readings, and friends for relevant norms;
- Think critically about the various alternatives offered by the case and the positions of key characters in the case;
- Remember: there is no *one* right answer, but you do need to give reasons for your decision in the end.

B. *Writing the Case Brief*
1. The length of the brief is to be 5–6 typed, double-spaced pages.
2. Several skills are crucial in writing a case brief:
   - Ability to be concise and to summarize well;
   - Capacity to identify the ethical problems, the decisions to be made in the case, and the ethical resources relevant to the problems;
   - Openness to innovation. You can use a variety of formats beyond the standard paper. For example, some students have written briefs in the form of journal entries, letters to friends, hypothetical dialogues, and in one case even as a chronicle of the activities of "Super-Ethicist." Don't be afraid to be creative.
3. Consider one of the following approaches:
   - Exploratory: Carefully explore conflicting or contrasting Christian positions on the issue. Put an emphasis on being "objective." Think with an open mind, then decide.
   - Persuasive: After you have carefully thought through the alternatives, pick one position and develop it in depth. Do not dismiss other perspectives, but concentrate on making your position as persuasive as possible.
4. Utilize the following questions to structure your ethical reflection about the case:

Stage 1: Analysis

Personal Factors
- How does your personal experience shape the way you view this case?
- Do you have something at stake?

Power Dynamics
- Who are the key players or stakeholders?
- How is power distributed between them?
- What forces disable or empower them?
- Whose voices are heard or not heard?

Factual Information
- Are there historical roots to the problem?
- What are the key facts?
- Are these facts in dispute?
- Are stakeholders using different theories to interpret key facts?

Complicating Factors
- Are there things that make it hard to grasp the context of the case? Is important information unavailable or very complex?

Relationships
- Are there relational or character issues that complicate the choices facing key players or stakeholders?

Ethical Issue(s)
- What do you perceive to be the primary moral problem or ethical issue?
- Are there secondary or additional moral problems that need to be resolved?

Alternatives and Consequences
- What realistic alternatives exist to address the primary ethical issue?
- What are the likely consequences of each alternative?
- Who will reap the benefits and bear the costs of each alternative?

Stage 2: Assessment

Ethical Vision and Moral Imagination
- Ideally, how would you like to see the ethical problem(s) resolved?
- What aspects of the Christian tradition shape your moral vision and imagination about this case?

Moral Norms
- How is your moral vision expressed in specific norms?
- How are the *eco-justice* norms relevant? (Sustainability, Sufficiency, Participation, Solidarity)
- Are these moral norms in conflict with each other or other moral, legal, economic, or religious norms?

Moral Theory
- What role does moral theory (deontology, teleology, virtue ethics) play in shaping the views of key players or stakeholders in the case?
- What role does moral theory play in shaping your assessment of this case?

Ethical Assessment
- What conclusions do you reach as you assess the various alternatives and consequences in relation to the moral norms you have identified and the moral theory you feel is most relevant or appropriate?

Stage 3: Action

Justification
- Which alternative is morally preferable and how will you justify it in relation to the moral norms you identified and the alternatives you rejected?

Viability
- Do the key players or stakeholders have the power they need to put the decision into action?

Strategy
- What strategies will be necessary to implement the alternative you have selected?

Reflection
- How do you feel now that you have reached a decision about how this case should be resolved ethically?

C. *Grading of Case Briefs*
    1. Case briefs will be evaluated on the degree to which they:
        - incorporate insights gleaned from the commentary, lectures, assigned readings, and class discussion;
        - fully develop the steps of analysis, assessment, and decision;
        - are written in a concise and coherent manner.

GUIDELINES FOR GROUP CASE PRESENTATIONS

The following guidelines can be used by groups to structure moral deliberation about cases in this volume. These guidelines should be revised or supplemented to accommodate diverse learning situations.

Each student is randomly assigned to a group and a case. Students who would like to switch to a different group must find someone in a different group willing to switch with them.

Each group will facilitate ethical reflection about the assigned case over a two-day period in class. The first class session will be devoted to analyzing the case. During the second class session, the group will assess the alternatives they have identified and then take a position with regard to how the primary moral problem should be resolved ethically. (See *Guidelines for Case Briefs* above.) These presentations should last no more than 30 minutes each day, leaving 20 minutes for discussion by the rest of the class. To the degree that it is possible, the goal is for the group to reach consensus about the appropriate course of moral action. If consensus is not possible, a minority report will be permitted, but in no case may the presentation on the second day last longer than 40 minutes.

All members of the group are expected to participate fully in the various aspects of this project (meetings, research, presentations). While responsibilities will be divided among the members, care should be taken to ensure that the information presented is coherent and reflects the consensus of the group.

Groups are welcome to be creative. You may wish to use skits, talk-show formats, role-plays, audio-visual resources, etc., in your presentations. A word of caution, however. Creative formats often work well for analyzing a case, but not for assessing it ethically. The goal is to do ethics as a group; it is not to entertain each other—though there's nothing wrong with having some fun!

After the group has concluded its presentation, each student in the group must turn in a 1–2 page, typed, double-spaced reflection paper on the *next class day*. The purpose of this brief paper is to have you reflect on what it was like to do moral deliberation as a group. *Do not* simply reiterate what your group said in its presentation. Rather, focus on what it was like to do this project as a group and what you learned. These papers are not given letter grades, but they must be turned in to receive credit for the group project.

You will also have an opportunity to evaluate your own performance as an individual along with the performance of the other members of your group through an evaluation sheet. Please attach this form to your reflection paper. This information, along with peer evaluation comments and the instructor's observations, will be utilized to determine individual grades for each student in the group. Normally each member of the group receives the same grade.

Notes

1. This assignment was developed by Daniel T. Spencer and is used with his permission.

2. These exercises were developed originally by James B. Martin-Schramm and have been revised in collaboration with Daniel T. Spencer.

3. This exercise is adapted from "The Three-Storey Building: An Exercise in Social Analysis," in Center for Global Education, *Crossing Borders, Challenging Boundaries: A Guide to the Pedagogy & Philosophy of the Center for Global Education* (Minneapolis, MN: Center for Global Education, Augsburg College, 1988), 11:9–10.

Index

Also in the Ecology and Justice Series